T5-DIA-652

THE PIANO IN NINETEENTH-CENTURY
BRITISH CULTURE

The Piano in Nineteenth-Century British Culture

Instruments, Performers and Repertoire

Edited by
THERESE ELLSWORTH and SUSAN WOLLENBERG

Foreword by Nicholas Temperley

31208 04 6605756
Scherman Music Library
The New School
150 West 85th St.
New York, NY 10024

ASHGATE

ML
678.4
E45
2007

© Therese Ellsworth and Susan Wollenberg 2007

All rights reserved. No part of this publication may be reproduced, stored in a retrieval system or transmitted in any form or by any means, electronic, mechanical, photocopying, recording or otherwise without the prior permission of the publisher.

Therese Ellsworth and Susan Wollenberg have asserted their moral right under the Copyright, Designs and Patents Act, 1988, to be identified as the editors of this work.

Published by
Ashgate Publishing Limited
Gower House
Croft Road
Aldershot
Hampshire GU11 3HR
England

Ashgate Publishing Company
Suite 420
101 Cherry Street
Burlington, VT 05401-4405
USA

Ashgate website: http://www.ashgate.com

British Library Cataloguing in Publication Data
The piano in nineteenth-century British culture: instruments, performers and repertoire. – (Music in nineteenth-century British culture)
   1. Piano music – Great Britain – History and criticism 2. Music – Social aspects – Great Britain – History – 19th century 3. Piano – Great Britain – History – 19th century 4. Piano music – Great Britain – Analysis, appreciation 5. Piano music – 19th century
   I. Ellsworth, Therese Marie II. Wollenberg, Susan
   786.2'0941'09034

Library of Congress Cataloging-in-Publication Data
Ellsworth, Therese Marie.
   The piano in nineteenth-century British culture: instruments, performers and repertoire / edited by Therese Ellsworth and Susan Wollenberg.
       p. cm. – (Music in nineteenth-century Britain)
   Includes bibliographical references and index.
   ISBN 978-0-7546-6143-6 (alk. paper)
1. Piano–Great Britain–History–19th century. 2. Piano music–Great Britain–19th century–History and criticism. 3. Pianists–Great Britain. I. Wollenberg, Susan. II. Title.
   ML678.4.E45 2007
   786.20941'09034–dc22

2007000577

ISBN 978-0-7546-6143-6

Printed and bound in Great Britain by MPG Books Ltd, Bodmin, Cornwall.

Bach musicological font developed by (c) Yo Tomita.

Contents

List of Figures

List of Tables

List of Music Examples

Notes on Contributors

Michael Allis is Senior Lecturer in Music at the University of Leeds. His publications include articles on narrative in the music of Elgar, Handel reception in Britain, and Stanford's piano music. He has published an extended source-study on Hubert Parry, *Parry's Creative Process* (2003) and editions of Parry's piano and chamber music. Recent work includes a chapter on musical settings of Tennyson in *The Figure of Music in Nineteenth-Century Poetry*, ed. Phyllis Weliver (2005), and studies of Walter Bache and British Liszt reception.

Dorothy de Val is Associate Professor of Music and Associate Dean of the Faculty of Fine Arts at York University, Toronto. A pianist and musicologist, she has concentrated on music in Britain from the late eighteenth century onwards. Her published work deals with the pianist–composer Clementi and later developments in pianos and pianism. She has also published on the first folk music revival in Britain and is currently working on a biography of the folk music pioneer Lucy Broadwood.

Therese Ellsworth is an independent scholar living in Washington, DC. Her doctoral dissertation, 'The Piano Concerto in London Concert Life between 1801 and 1850' has led to further research, paper presentations and publications on nineteenth-century London concert life and women pianists in particular. She taught at universities in the US before settling for eight years in Brussels (1998–2006). She is currently working on a book about women pianists in nineteenth-century London.

Peter Horton is Deputy Librarian (Reference and Research) in the Royal College of Music Library, London. He read Music at Magdalen College, Oxford. His research since then has concentrated on music in nineteenth- and early twentieth-century Britain. He edited the complete anthems of Samuel Sebastian Wesley for *Musica Britannica* and published *Samuel Sebastian Wesley: A Life* (2004). He has also written on T.A. Walmisley, Battison Haynes and Hugh Blair, and is now planning a life and works study of William Sterndale Bennett.

Roy Johnston is an independent scholar living in Belfast. He was awarded a doctorate from Queen's University, Belfast for his dissertation on 'Concerts in the musical life of Belfast to 1874'. His publications include 'Bunting's *Messiah*' (2003) and essays on eighteenth- and nineteenth-century music in Ireland, most recently in *Music in Nineteenth-Century Ireland*, edited by Jan Smaczny and Michael Murphy (forthcoming). He is a contributor to the new *Dictionary of Irish Biography* (also forthcoming).

Janet Ritterman has published on the development of the conservatoire, on instrumental pedagogy, and on aspects of nineteenth-century European concert life, in particular the contribution of pianists, and has spoken at many national and international conferences. Director of the Royal College of Music, London (1993–2005), she has specialized in the education and training of gifted performers and has worked professionally as pianist and accompanist. In 2002 she was appointed DBE for services to music.

Rohan Stewart-MacDonald is Director of Studies in Music at New Hall and Fitzwilliam College, Cambridge, and also Director of Music at New Hall. He specializes in British music of the eighteenth and nineteenth centuries, with a particular emphasis on the works of Muzio Clementi. His most recent publication in this field is a book on Clementi's keyboard sonatas, *New Perspectives on the Keyboard Sonatas of Muzio Clementi* (2006). He is also deputy lay clerk in the choir of Ely Cathedral.

R. Larry Todd is Arts & Sciences Professor of Music at Duke University, and the author of *Mendelssohn: A Life in Music*, named best biography of 2003 by the Association of American Publishers. He has written extensively about nineteenth-century music and is currently preparing a new biography of Fanny Hensel.

Yo Tomita is a Professor in the School of Music at Queen's University, Belfast and a specialist in the keyboard works of J.S. Bach. His most recent articles are published in *The English Bach Awakening: Knowledge of J.S. Bach and his Music in England 1750–1830*, ed. Michael Kassler (2004). He is currently working on a two-volume monograph *The Genesis and Early History of Bach's Well-Tempered Clavier, Book II: A Composer and his Editions, c. 1738–1850* for Ashgate.

William Weber is Professor of History at California State University, Long Beach. He has published *Music and the Middle Class: The Social Structure of Concert Life in London, Paris and Vienna between 1830 and 1848* (1975/2004) and *The Rise of Musical Classics in Eighteenth-Century England: A Study in Canon, Ritual and Ideology* (2002). He is also editor of *The Musician as Entrepreneur, 1700–1914* (2004) and co-editor (with David Large) of *Wagnerism in European Culture and Politics* (1984).

Susan Wollenberg is Reader in Music at the University of Oxford and Fellow and Tutor of Lady Margaret Hall. She has published widely on a variety of subjects, including Schubert and C.P.E. Bach, and has longstanding interests in the study of women composers, in keyboard music studies, and in the social history of English music. She is the author of *Music at Oxford in the Eighteenth and Nineteenth Centuries* (2001) and co-editor, with Simon McVeigh, of *Concert Life in Eighteenth-Century Britain* (2004).

Foreword

Nicholas Temperley

Today the piano is the most ordinary of musical instruments. We can play or hear it with as little sense of novelty as when we drive a car or ride in one. It is true that it remains at the core of musical experience for many and is still one of the most popular instruments in existence, especially if we include its electronic derivatives. And it is true, also, that some of the most famous musicians in the world are pianists. Certainly a piano, like a car, can still on occasion raise excitement to white heat.

But the novelty wore off about a century and a half ago, when the Steinway became accepted as the perfect model, when the piano's place in cultural life was thoroughly established, and when its classical repertoire settled into permanence. Minor additions, changes and experiments have been made since that time, both in the instrument and its uses, and of course in its repertoire. But they have not altered the fundamental character of the piano or the music it primarily represents. Why innovation slowed down in the mid-nineteenth century is still not fully understood, but this volume offers several hints.

With the piano and its music so immutably set in our lives, it is not easy to recapture the excitement and romance that the instrument embodied when it first became widely used after about 1770. The piano was perceived by all but the oldest and most conservative musicians as a vast improvement on its predecessors. Its greater brilliance and expressive powers left the harpsichord in the shadows, seemingly bound for extinction, to be rescued only by antiquarians of our own time with a new aesthetic of historical propriety. As Charles Burney put it at the turn of the century, 'the harsh scratching of the quills of a harpsichord can now no longer be borne'.[1]

Musicians, professional and amateur, almost fell over each other in their intense desire to explore and exploit the piano's potential for both brilliance and subtlety of expression. Despite its limited sustaining powers, it was often treated as if it were a singing instrument, and was said to be 'accompanied' by stringed instruments in the designations of violin sonatas, piano trios and the like – the exact reverse of the normal treatment of the harpsichord in the Baroque period. Rival manufacturers looked for innovations to enhance its powers; retailers touted their instruments' qualities in novel marketing techniques; virtuosi outdid each other's spectacular feats; young women (*and* their husbands[2]) tried to tie their rising status to that of the piano.

---

1   Abraham Rees, ed., *The Cyclopaedia; or, Universal Dictionary of Arts, Sciences, and Literature* (London: Longman, Hurst, 1819), vol. 17, s.v. 'Harpsichord'. Burney is known to have written this article in or soon after 1800.

2   'Joddrell, who has no more ear than a post, went and married her [a piano-playing niece of Mrs. Stanhope], because he had a mind to set up for a connoisseur in music; and

The only comparable phenomenon that comes to mind is the creative energy generated by the violin family in the seventeenth century. In much the same way, the violin's unprecedented powers of expression and virtuosity gradually left the viol behind. It was the Italians, beyond all doubt, who developed the violin itself and the music most appropriate to it; the rest of Europe sought out Italian instruments, players, teachers and violin music. The piano had more diverse progenitors. But the part played by Britain in the process has been sadly underestimated in the past. This book goes a long way towards setting that record straight.

Britain's prominent role in the earlier history of the piano was largely due to economics – but not entirely. It is true, of course, that the main reason for Britain's leadership of the boom in piano manufacture and sheet music publishing was that it was the only country that had the wealth and technological advances to make them possible.[3] And many of the composers, pianists and entrepreneurs taking part in the boom were foreigners. Colonies of Continental musicians were attracted to London, Edinburgh and some provincial cities, swollen by émigrés from the French Revolution; others came in droves for short musical tours, principally to take advantage of the abundant patronage of the wealthy classes.[4]

These facts are undeniable. But they have been interpreted by a long procession of historians with xenophile agendas to suggest that the musical boom was superficial and reflected no genuine musicality on the part of the British public. They forget that people, however rich, are not generally inclined to spend their money on something they don't like or don't understand, nor to raise their social standing by acquiring something unless it is highly valued and prized by society.

In an extreme case, coming near the end of the xenophile 'procession' of scholars and critics, A.V. Beedell has claimed that in the late eighteenth century 'English music was actually about to confront its nadir … The Church had long since ceased either to encourage or inspire, domestic music had yet to be reinvented'– in this last short sentence she sweeps aside much of the work of the late Stanley Sadie among others; 'folk music in England had slipped out of sight and out of mind, and the great European forms – the opera (or at least opera without spoken dialogue), the symphony, instrumental music, and the *Lied* – seemed totally alien to English propensities.'[5] Note that Beedell in her flight of fancy has chosen to omit any reference

---

Mrs. Stanhope flattered him that he was one.' Maria Edgeworth, *Belinda* (London: J. Johnson, 1801), chapter two.

3   See C. Ehrlich, *The Piano: A History* (London, J.M. Dent & Sons, 1976), pp. 15–20. In contrast Italy, still in this period the primary source of singers and vocal music, held a position of prestige in the European musical world that was not shared by Britain. Yet Italy entirely lacked a vigorous music publishing industry, presumably because of the scarcity of capital there and the absence of a free market.

4   London was 'the world's shining citadel of publicly performing pianism', according to Arthur Loesser: *Men, Women and Pianos* (New York: Simon and Schuster, 1955), p. 242.

5   A.V. Beedell, *The Decline of the English Musician 1788–1888* (Oxford: Clarendon Press, 1992), pp. 40–41. As for 'folk music', had Beedell looked at some of the hundreds of surviving English operas of the time, instead of dismissing them out of hand because they failed to use a type of music (recitative) that was indeed alien to English language and culture, she would have found popular songs in abundance, including the sources of several that would

to the London Pianoforte School, unless she means it to be covered by the phrase 'instrumental music'. If piano music was 'totally alien to English propensities', why did the English buy it up in huge quantities, supporting several dozen publishers of sheet music, both light and serious, with and without other instruments, for domestic use? On the serious side, the English reception of such works as Bach's *Well-Tempered Clavier* and Clementi's *Gradus ad Parnassum*, discussed here in the essays of Yo Tomita and Rohan Stewart-MacDonald, was at least as strong as in other countries, even though it may everywhere have been confined to a relatively small elite.

No: the rage for the piano, pianists and piano music in Britain, which lasted through much of the nineteenth century, is a fact that cannot be explained away. It tells us, quite simply, that many British people liked to play and hear piano music. The intensity of feeling which some women, in particular, invested in their piano playing is brought out in many novels and poems. Certainly, much piano music was superficial, a mere diversion or a background to dancing and social activities. But the increasing number of journals carrying reviews biased towards the classical canon proves that one strand of the affluent public took its studies seriously. This was demonstrated even more plainly by the rise of classical chamber concerts in Victorian times, as chronicled in detail here by Janet Ritterman and William Weber. Ritterman and Weber also show that the singling out of the piano for solo recitals was a practice led and pioneered in Britain.

The growth of the piano trade itself, already well understood with regard to Great Britain from the work of Cyril Ehrlich and others, is now documented by Roy Johnston for Belfast, showing that many would go to some lengths to ensure that the piano took its due place in lives chiefly dedicated to the practicalities of commerce or administration. Again, just as citizens of Belfast bought beds so that they could lie on them, we must also assume that they bought (or transported) pianos because they wanted to play or hear them. For each type of furniture there was no doubt an unexpressed hope that it might also afford excitement and emotional satisfaction for both men and women.

The importance of women in the history of the piano can hardly be exaggerated. Keyboard instruments had been their special province in the home since Elizabethan times, and in the nineteenth century many a famous composer relied for the greater part of his income on teaching the piano to young ladies.[6] This association must have made it easier for female pianists (together with singers) to emerge into the professional world than for women who played other instruments. But we should not underestimate the difficulties and prejudices they still had to overcome, against both their sex and their nationality. Arabella Goddard and Fanny Davies, whose

---

later be labelled as 'folksongs'. See also E.D. Mackerness, *A Social History of English Music* (London: Routledge & Kegan Paul, 1964), chapter four. The lied, as we now understand it in English usage, did not exist anywhere at the time, but English songs were in quite as healthy a state as German ones, as we can see (to take one example) by comparing Haydn's specimens in the two languages.

6   As Therese Ellsworth cites in her chapter (p. 150 below), more and more piano teachers were also female: nearly half of them by 1891.

careers are chronicled in these pages, required both personal determination and the strong support of others to break through the ivory ceiling. They probably needed not just to equal but to surpass their male counterparts in brilliance of execution before they could win their places in the top layer of public esteem. On the other side of the matter, Susan Wollenberg tells of three privileged male pianists, better known for other accomplishments, whose common background in Oxford favoured their pianistic success. They were hardly professionals in the fullest sense, but their stories show that the philistinism of which upper-class Victorian males have been rightly accused was by no means universal.

What did these legions of pianists play? We have been learning more and more on that subject in recent decades through the study of reception history and musical life. For amateurs at home, musical publications are the chief guide; for professionals in public, programmes and reviews provide the answer. It seems clear that through most of the century there were two strands of serious piano programming, one conservative, the other radical. The 'ancients' and 'moderns' had already declared their positions in the early 1800s. Ritterman and Weber discuss the formation of the classical canon, and Peter Horton expands on William Sterndale Bennett's part in the process. It emerges from Therese Ellsworth's and Dorothy de Val's essays that Goddard and Davies were also important interpreters of this repertoire. Of course, it was largely made up of German music, and both women, like Bennett, received much of their training and influence from German teachers, Davies forming a vital link with Robert and Clara Schumann and Johannes Brahms. Yet both also championed British music. Goddard, we learn, kept before the public several masterpieces from composers of the London Pianoforte School, while Davies explored early English keyboard music.

But we should not overlook the fact that each generation embraced a few progressives, who were determined to acquaint the music-loving public with difficult modern works. Both John Cramer and Cipriani Potter performed concertos by Mozart and Beethoven when these works were virtually unknown in London; later, Bennett performed relatively unfamiliar chamber works with piano by those same masters and by Spohr and Mendelssohn, while Charles Hallé was an indefatigable promoter of Beethoven's sonatas. The next generation, as Michael Allis now documents, saw Walter Bache's noble championship of the German avant-garde, especially the works of Liszt; he was supported by a small group of fellow radicals. Davies, too, in her later career gave full attention to modern composers. In all these cases there was a faithful if not extensive audience which presumably approved of the music it heard, and the wider public was ultimately won over.

As for the production of new piano music, this was an area in which British-born composers admittedly failed to match those from several other countries, above all Germany. That fact has unduly influenced judgements about the 'musicality' of the British. I hope I have said enough to show that the historical evidence of our musicality rests on very different foundations. (If I haven't, read this book.)

For reasons that have often been discussed, but are still not fully understood, the British have tended to favour foreign music over their own for several centuries, and this attitude continues to affect judgements of the worth of native-produced compositions. No such prejudices are to be found in this book. Larry Todd, while rightly emphasizing the profound influence that Mendelssohn exerted over Bennett, gives due respect to Bennett's creative imagination and even, in some cases, points out ideas that flowed from Bennett to Mendelssohn. Peter Horton offers a fresh, balanced analysis of Bennett's compositions, showing links in both directions with a wide variety of other composers.

It is interesting that Clementi has been tacitly recognized as a 'British' composer by the inclusion of Stewart-MacDonald's analytical account in this book. In biographical terms Clementi was at least as British as Handel or Benedict, more so than Onslow or Delius. Yet what mattered in the end was his intimate relationship with the British public. He undoubtedly aimed his music far beyond the English Channel, as can be shown by his publication plans; but the same is true of Beethoven and Chopin, most of whose piano music was published, by the composers' design, in London at about the same time that it appeared in Vienna or Paris.

In a period when most professionally composed music was pan-European in its appeal, the nationality by birth of a composer is important only to nationalists. This volume rightly concentrates on the culture of the piano in Britain, whether expressed in composition, performance or appreciation.

Acknowledgements

The core of this book formed a themed session at the Fifth International Biennial Conference on Music in Nineteenth-Century Britain, held at the University of Nottingham in July 2005. We wish to record our warm thanks to the conference organizer, Philip Olleson, for his support of that session, and to Bennett Zon for encouraging us originally to develop the idea of this book. Robyn Carpenter gave skilful research assistance during its preparation, and Will Goring provided expert technical help. We are grateful to them both, and to Peter Ward Jones for his unfailingly helpful advice on bibliographical and archival matters. We also wish to express our gratitude to Heidi May and her colleagues at Ashgate Publishing, who constantly smoothed the way to the book's production.

Abbreviations

BL	British Library, London
CPH/RCM	Centre for Performance History, Royal College of Music, London
DNB	*Oxford Dictionary of National Biography*
MMR	*Monthly Musical Record*
MSt	*Musical Standard*
MT	*Musical Times*
MW	*Musical World*
PRO	Public Records Office, London
RAM	The Royal Academy of Music, London
RCM	The Royal College of Music, London
Times	The [London] *Times*

General Editor's Series Preface

Music in nineteenth-century Britain has been studied as a topic of musicology for over two hundred years. It was explored widely in the nineteenth century itself, and in the twentieth century grew into research with strong methodological and theoretical import. Today, the topic has burgeoned into a broad, yet incisive, cultural study with critical potential for scholars in a wide range of disciplines. Indeed, it is largely because of its interdisciplinary qualities that music in nineteenth-century Britain has become such a prominent part of the modern musicological landscape.

This series aims to explore the wealth of music and musical culture of Britain in the nineteenth century and surrounding years. It does this by covering an extensive array of music-related topics and situating them within the most up-to-date interpretative frameworks. All books provide relevant contextual background and detailed source investigations, as well as considerable bibliographical material of use for further study. Areas included in the series reflect its widely interdisciplinary aims and, although principally designed for musicologists, the series is also intended to be accessible to scholars working outside of music, in areas such as history, literature, science, philosophy, poetry and performing arts. Topics include criticism and aesthetics; musical genres; music and the church; music education; composers and performers; analysis; concert venues, promoters and organisations; the reception of foreign music in Britain; instrumental repertoire, manufacture and pedagogy; music hall and dance; gender studies; and music in literature, poetry and letters.

Although the nineteenth century has often been viewed as a fallow period in British musical culture, it is clear from the vast extent of current scholarship that this view is entirely erroneous. Far from being a 'land without music', nineteenth-century Britain abounded with musical activity. All society was affected by it, and everyone in that society recognised its importance in some way or other. It remains for us today to trace the significance of music and musical culture in that period, and to bring it alive for scholars to study and interpret. This is the principal aim of the Music in Nineteenth-Century Britain series – to advance scholarship in the area and expand our understanding of its importance in the wider cultural context of the time.

Bennett Zon
Durham University, UK

Chapter 1

Introduction

Therese Ellsworth and Susan Wollenberg

This book presents the fruits of recent research into the piano's role in nineteenth-century British culture. The project arose from our awareness of the new work currently being done in a field – that of nineteenth-century British music scholarship – altogether notable for its development over recent decades. At the forefront of this development has been Nicholas Temperley. We are delighted and gratified that he has provided the Foreword to the volume.

The present book is not conceived as a survey of the piano in nineteenth-century Britain but rather as a critical introduction to the topic, highlighting historical developments and revealing new perspectives on the subject. Chapters explore key issues concerning the instrument itself, the repertoire heard by audiences in Britain, the performers, both British and foreign, who played that repertoire, and developments in concert structure that produced the piano recital. In Chapter 2, for example, Roy Johnston draws on his unrivalled knowledge of the history of music in Belfast, and related source-material, to develop his account of piano manufacturing in that city. In Chapters 3 and 4, Yo Tomita and Rohan Stewart-MacDonald bring their expertise in Bach and Clementi studies respectively to bear on the reception of two seminal keyboard collections – J.S. Bach's *Well-Tempered Clavier* and Clementi's *Gradus ad Parnassum*. Throughout these and other chapters, a variety of individual figures emerges strongly from the narrative, whether these are the makers who peopled the piano manufacturing industry, in competition with one other, or the composers and performers who displayed their prowess on the concert platform, often networking among themselves and among the wider circle of musicians in a spirit of cooperation. It is fitting that at the centre of the book are two contributions (Chapters 5 and 6) by R. Larry Todd and Peter Horton, singling out for our attention the piano compositions of the most significant pianist–composer of the mid-Victorian era, William Sterndale Bennett. Investigations into the careers of three other native pianists – Arabella Goddard (Chapter 7, by Therese Ellsworth), Walter Bache (Chapter 9, by Michael Allis) and Fanny Davies (Chapter 10, by Dorothy de Val) – contribute to our understanding of the different ways in which a professional concert career as a pianist might develop in nineteenth-century Britain, while Chapter 8, the results of a fruitful search for the origins of the piano recital in England presented by William Weber and Janet Ritterman, and Chapter 11, Susan Wollenberg's study of three Oxford pianistic careers, provide new detail on the contexts in which such careers might flourish.

The various chapters range across the sweep of the nineteenth century and beyond. The reception of Bach's *Well-Tempered Clavier* begins with the appearance of printed editions in London after 1801 (gathering momentum in the 1820s and 1830s); Clementi's *Gradus ad Parnassum* brings us to 1817–25. At the other end of the century are five individuals who form the subjects of three of the chapters and who all lived well into the twentieth century. Arabella Goddard died in 1922, although her professional career had ended in the 1880s. By contrast, Fanny Davies (d. 1934) continued her professional engagements far into the next century; nevertheless, her training as well as her most important work occurred within the 'long' nineteenth century. Donald Francis Tovey, Paul Victor Mendelssohn Benecke and Ernest Walker – all of whom lived well into the twentieth century – studied at Oxford during the 1880s and 1890s, and it was in this period that the formative phase of their musical careers was shaped.

From 1801 until 1922, the term 'British' referred to the United Kingdom of Great Britain and Ireland. Pockets of British culture existed well beyond these boundaries in the nineteenth century, extending to territories, protectorates or colonies that gradually became part of the British Empire. Description of the worldwide tour of Arabella Goddard in the 1870s provides a glimpse of expatriate culture as well as the hazards of travel and issues of concert arrangements in places far from the capital of the Empire. London functioned as the economic, political and cultural hub of Britain (while at the same time having claim to status as the commercial capital of the world) and, as a result, continued to be its centre of musical life. Recent scholarly enterprise has highlighted musical life in provincial locations outside London, and while the events that occurred in those peripheries might reflect the strong impact of London concert life, the process could be two-way.

Above all the capital is significant for a study of piano music in that it served as one of the principal centres, along with Paris and Vienna, that nurtured the rise of that remarkable nineteenth-century phenomenon, the international piano virtuoso. In addition, the city contained flourishing music publishing businesses and the headquarters of many of the leading British piano-manufacturing companies. It was famously at the Crystal Palace in London, where the Great Exhibition of 1851 took place, that pianos by some 38 British manufacturers were displayed. This event highlights the combination of art or craft with commercial enterprise that nourished the growth of British culture in the nineteenth century.

Current scholarship on piano music in nineteenth-century Britain owes a very particular debt to Professor Temperley. His dissertation 'Instrumental Music in England 1800–1850' (University of Cambridge, 1959) opened the door to the wealth of musical activity that occurred during a period previously thought to contain little of interest. Of special importance is his *London Pianoforte School*, a series of facsimile editions of the music with introductory essays.[1] The generation that has passed since its publication has seen a flourishing of research into pianists, their repertoire and the structures of concert life that helped support them. Temperley set the boundaries for the London Pianoforte School at 1766 to 1860 and demonstrated the many significant developments in piano music that originated with or received important stimulus from the composers, foreign-born and indigenous, who worked in London

---

1   Nicholas Temperley (ed.), *The London Pianoforte School* (20 vols, New York: Garland Publishing, 1984–7).

during that period. Among these are the use of the sustaining pedal, emergence of new genres such as the nocturne, the study and the characteristic rondo, and the expansion of idiomatic piano textures.[2]

Temperley has also pointed out a divide that occurred within London piano music during the 1820s and 1830s when a more conservative branch appeared, represented most prominently by Cipriani Potter (1792–1871). A pupil of Joseph Wölfl, with whom he studied Bach's *Well-Tempered Clavier* during the first decade of the century, Potter was appointed the first piano teacher at the Royal Academy of Music (RAM) and in 1832 became Principal of that institution, remaining in the post until 1859. As a consequence he influenced at least a generation of students. He advocated a classical 'legitimate' style of performing, which he passed on to such RAM graduates as George Alexander Macfarren and William Sterndale Bennett, a style that contrasted with the virtuosic manner favoured by, for example, Julius Benedict.

As a *Times* critic observed at mid-century, foreign influence was crucial to developments in nineteenth-century Britain. He noted that 'English music ... would seem to be looking up; and the foreigners who annually flock to London have begun to discover that there are both players and composers in this country with whom it would be somewhat difficult for the majority of them to compete'. Moreover, he noted, 'thanks to the influence and frequent presence' of foreign musicians such as Weber, Mendelssohn and Spohr, 'commercial England is unconsciously becoming the most musical country in Europe'.[3] With these remarks, the writer identified issues that can be applied in particular to piano music and performance: the acknowledgement of the importance of foreign musicians, high standards of performance among soloists (both native-born and émigrés) and the contribution of increased wealth brought about by commerce. These ideas extended beyond London as virtuosi expanded their tours to provincial cities throughout the United Kingdom and Ireland, in some cases settling there as did, for example, Charles Hallé in Manchester.

Mendelssohn, who visited Britain ten times between 1829 and 1847, was welcomed as a composer and equally as a pianist. The critic George Hogarth considered that he ranked 'among the greatest masters of the day' as both organist and pianist.[4] The impact he exerted on the musical culture of Victorian England is well documented. Yet the influence of foreigners (whether visitors, temporary residents or permanent settlers) on piano music began generations before the *Times* article appeared. Their

---

2   David Rowland has contributed important publications charting the development of piano technique in tandem with the instrument's evolution: see particularly his *History of Pianoforte Pedalling* (Cambridge: Cambridge University Press, 1993) and *The Cambridge Companion to the Piano* (Cambridge: Cambridge University Press, 1998). Other core texts on the instrument and its repertoire include Cyril Ehrlich, *The Piano: A History*, rev. edn (Oxford: Clarendon Press, 1990) and R. Larry Todd, *Nineteenth-Century Piano Music*, rev. edn (New York and London: Routledge, 2004).

3   *Times*, 14 May 1853. The remarks are contained in a review of a concert by Arabella Goddard and most probably written by J.W. Davison who, from 1846, occupied the post of chief writer on music for that newspaper.

4   G. Hogarth, *Musical History, Biography, and Criticism* (London: John W. Parker, 1835), p. 151.

contribution to developments in repertoire and performance may be traced back as far as J.C. Bach (1735–82). Many others followed, among them Joseph Haydn, Hummel, J.B. Cramer, A.F.C. Kollmann, Dussek, Wölfl, Kalkbrenner and Ries. The pianist Wilhelm Kuhe, who settled in London in 1847 at age 24, declared that the most prominent musicians in London during the 1840s were Louise Dulcken, Ignaz Moscheles and Julius Benedict, all émigrés like himself, and all of them pianists.[5] The economic dislocations caused by political events on the Continent in 1848 brought many refugees to Britain, including musicians such as Hallé. At the same time, 'successive waves of influence emanated from London to the Continent'.[6]

Among many Continental links, the German influence was particularly strong in Britain.[7] The connections between British and German culture extended of course to the British monarchy itself, which descended from the House of Hanover. Within the present volume we learn of the reception of printed editions of German music, specifically Bach's *Well-Tempered Clavier* (Chapter 3). Mendelssohn's influence on Sterndale Bennett is considered, along with possible influences conveyed from Bennett to Mendelssohn, in Chapter 5; Bennett's travels to Germany and friendship with Schumann and Ferdinand David exercised a great impact on his development. Furthermore, Bennett's music was reviewed in the German press and printed by German publishers. A number of soloists trained in Germany, for example Fanny Davies (as a pupil of Clara Schumann) and Walter Bache (who studied at the Leipzig Conservatory). Others studied with teachers of German heritage, as witness Arabella Goddard's lessons with Thalberg. In addition, pianists from Britain such as Goddard included German cities and the prestigious Gewandhaus concert series on their tours. Special attention is paid by William Weber and Janet Ritterman to Clara Schumann, Charles Hallé and Hans von Bülow in their discussion of the development of the piano recital (Chapter 8). We learn that British premieres of music by Brahms, among others, took place at Oxford. And among the pianists considered in the chapter on Oxford is Paul Victor Mendelssohn Benecke, grandson of Felix Mendelssohn.

One of the most far-reaching areas in the development of British pianism was in the field of musical education (the educational system as a whole being subject to expansion in nineteenth-century Britain). The training of pianists changed during the nineteenth century from exclusively private tutelage to the new opportunities afforded by the opening of conservatoires. The RAM, founded in 1822, figures in these chapters as the training ground for William Sterndale Bennett and as a source of employment for Bennett and others cited here, including Cipriani Potter and G.A. Macfarren. In May 1883 the Royal College of Music (RCM) opened its doors; that institution provided brief employment for Goddard before her retirement. On the university scene, Bennett was appointed Professor of Music at Cambridge in 1856. Piano pedagogy developed alongside other trends. With the introduction of the *Well-*

5   Wilhelm Kuhe, *My Musical Recollections* (London: R. Bentley & Son, 1896), p. 76.
6   Nicholas Temperley, 'London and the Piano, 1760–1860', *Musical Times*, 129 (1988), p. 289.
7   Rosemary Ashton's *Little Germany: Exile and Asylum in Victorian England* (Oxford: Oxford University Press, 1986) sets the scene for an exploration of the influx of German cultural representatives into Britain at this period.

Tempered Clavier into Britain, that work fulfilled the function of a teaching tool. So too did the genre of the study, exemplified by Clementi's *Gradus ad Parnassum*, a work which, as Rohan Stewart-MacDonald reminds us, continued to be drawn on for the syllabuses of the Associated Board well into the twentieth century.

A fundamental division can be seen growing during the nineteenth century between virtuosic playing and classical interpretation; this emerged as the number of pianist–interpreters outpaced the composer–pianists. Fantasias and virtuosic display pieces confronted the question of the ethics of transcriptions and arrangements, a subject addressed by Walter Bache in particular. In addition, a developing canon of piano works formed a core against which 'early music' by J.S. Bach, Handel, Couperin, Rameau and Scarlatti and 'revivals' of such late eighteenth- and early nineteenth-century piano composers resident in London as Dussek, Hummel and Wölfl were highlighted. Performance-practice concerns led to increased interest in harpsichord performance; Fanny Davies played the clavichord and harpsichord, as did Donald Tovey from his undergraduate years onwards. Pianists functioned as advocates for contemporary piano repertoire, as with Fanny Davies's performances of music by Fauré, Saint-Saëns, Debussy and Elgar, and Ernest Walker's of late Brahms, Rachmaninoff and Scriabin, among others.

As mentioned, certain genres received particular impetus from composers and pianists of the London Pianoforte School. The development of the nocturne is seen in the music of John Field, even though those pieces were little performed publicly in Britain. The studies of J.B. Cramer and Clementi found important use as teaching (rather than concert) pieces. The 'Song without Words' flourished; W.S. Bennett is believed to have achieved the first performance of Mendelssohn's *Lieder ohne Worte* in London in 1838, music destined to become phenomenally popular in Britain. Of particular significance is the growth of interest in the piano sonata, especially as it came to represent 'serious' repertoire for the solo artist. The Beethoven sonatas received frequent performances by pianists establishing their 'classical' credentials.[8] Alexandre Billet, Charles Hallé and Arabella Goddard were key figures in presenting these works to London audiences during the 1850s and 1860s. Among sonatas composed by British musicians, Bennett's Sonata in F minor, op. 13 receives close scrutiny in the chapters by R. Larry Todd and Peter Horton as fertile ground for detailed study of a mid-century work of that genre as well as for its programmatic aspects.

Recent research has brought to light the many changes that occurred in concert life during that period. The sheer number of events increased considerably; William Weber, for example, has determined that the annual total during the concert season jumped 305 per cent, from 125 to 381 concerts, between 1826 and 1845.[9]

---

8   On Caroline Reinagle's promotion of these works in her treatise of 1855 (*A Few Words on Piano Playing*), which was serialized in the *Musical Times* in 1862, see Susan Wollenberg, 'Pianos and Pianists in Nineteenth-Century Oxford', *Nineteenth-Century Music Review*, 2/1 (2005): 115–37.

9   William Weber, *Music and the Middle Class: The Social Structure of Concert Life in London, Paris, and Vienna between 1830 and 1848*, 2nd edn (Aldershot: Ashgate, 2004), p. 159.

Equally important was the specialization of concerts, a development that led to the decrease in 'miscellaneous' presentations of vocal and instrumental solo, chamber and orchestral works and to the spread of chamber music events and solo recitals. New series evolved to provide increased opportunities for pianists to perform. The Philharmonic Society, founded in 1813, officially admitted piano concertos to their programmes in 1819 and from then on featured piano soloists more than any other for works that involved a solo instrument and orchestra. The Monday Popular Series, founded in 1859 as a forum for chamber music, emphasized the piano above any other instrument. Between 1859 and 1892 over 40 per cent of its repertoire called for solo piano music while 24 per cent comprised a chamber ensemble that included a piano.

Concert promotion incurred fundamental changes during this era. Whereas in the early decades of the century an event might be sold by the accumulation of prominent musicians on the programme or the diversity of programme offerings, later on concerts were promoted with the spotlight being shone on the works performed and on the artist's particular interpretation.[10] The connection was strengthened between virtuoso soloists and printed music in an attempt to reach the large domestic music-making market. During the latter part of the century, soloists found advantages in engaging a concert agent to ensure their interests, while musical criticism and the advent of analytical programme notes encouraged more informed audiences.

In addition, modern research into nineteenth-century musical life has illuminated the realities for musicians of making a living. This effort has benefited particularly from the work done by social and economic historians.[11] The scholarly legacy of Cyril Ehrlich continues to exert its influence, providing, like Temperley, inspiration for much of the research now emerging, and certainly for much that is featured in this volume. In the chapters that follow we encounter pianists who supplemented their income through teaching either privately or in conservatoires, as well as those who expanded their professional activities to include piano selling, music printing, composing and conducting. (The economic necessity of combining several of these activities simultaneously could interfere with productivity, particularly in relation to composing.) Some performers turned to writing on music and earned a reputation more for music criticism and history than pianism, for example J.W. Davison, Donald Tovey and Ernest Walker.

Gendered expectations, for both men and women, affected a musician's ability to forge a viable career. Such issues are taken up in the chapters on W.S. Bennett as composer and pianist, as well as in those on Goddard and Davies. As late as the 1860s, according to the English pianist–composer Francesco Berger, 'musicians were still looked down upon, and a man who admitted that he lived by Music was considered little better than an imbecile or a pauper. No "gentleman born" devoted

---

10 See Jim Samson (ed.), 'The musical work and nineteenth-century history', in *The Cambridge History of Nineteenth-Century Music* (Cambridge: Cambridge University Press, 2002), pp. 1–28.

11 See especially Cyril Ehrlich, *The Music Profession in Britain since the Eighteenth Century* (Oxford: Clarendon Press, 1985); and Deborah Rohr, *The Careers of British Musicians 1750–1850: A Profession of Artisans* (Cambridge: Cambridge University Press, 2001).

himself to it'.[12] The uneasy social perceptions of music as a career emerge in the chapter on Oxford, especially in relation to Tovey, with Joseph Joachim functioning as an 'ambassador' in Britain for the profession's respectability.

Touring also had gender implications. This could be an exceptionally strenuous activity of a kind normally disapproved of for women. The difficulties associated with extended concert tours are illustrated in the case of Arabella Goddard. These ventures were especially problematic when they involved bringing one's own instrument (to head off disaster with inferior instruments at concert venues). Nevertheless, as advances occurred in rail and sea travel, musicians found it easier to reach an increasing number of concert locations, including those ones far distant. For resident musicians as well as Continental artists, these developments expanded opportunities for travel to a wider range of provincial cities within Britain and continental Europe. Travel between America and Europe also expanded, leading European soloists to seek their fortune in the United States much as Continental musicians did in Britain beginning in the mid-eighteenth century. Some virtuosi ventured to Asia, Australia and New Zealand, stopping chiefly at outposts of the British Empire. In the chapter on Belfast we learn that Kalkbrenner, Thalberg, Liszt and Goddard all gave concerts in that city. Liszt and Chopin between them toured provincial towns throughout England as well as Scotland and Ireland.

Any researcher investigating nineteenth-century pianists longs to hear how particular artists actually performed. How reliable are descriptions in critical reviews and contemporary accounts? The reception of repertoire is easier to examine historically than is the reception of performances; reactions to printed repertoire can be examined with the score in hand, whereas valuations of pianists' performances rely heavily on the background and biases of the writer. Walter Bache's frustrations with the press are documented in Michael Allis's chapter. Yet reception history can tell us a great deal about what were the important concerns of the day: in the case of the piano at the time, these included the question of 'legitimate' versus 'virtuoso' players, and 'classical' versus 'virtuosic' repertoire. And it can reveal those elements that were considered as constituting a genuine or at least justifiable interpretation of a work. Recordings, which today function as such a key ingredient in making a reputation as a pianist, were in their infancy during the period covered by this book. Few such relics of piano soloists have come down to us from the nineteenth century;[13] Fanny Davies, however, belonged to a generation recent enough to have left recordings.

Many common threads link the chapters that follow here: the Anglo-German connection, the two contrasting styles of pianism, the advocacy of both old and new repertoire, and the building of pianistic careers in the context of expanded concert structures and touring opportunities – and, of course, the instrument itself that was

---

12 Francesco Berger, *Reminiscences, Impressions and Anecdotes* (London: Sampson Low, Marston & Co., 1913), p. 167.

13 Timothy Day has suggested that the earliest recordings of classical music most probably featured the pianist Josef Hofmann in 1887. Timothy Day, *A Century of Recorded Music: Listening to Musical History* (New Haven, CT, and London: Yale University Press, 2000), p. 1.

at the centre of all this activity, an instrument that was destined to retain its hold on British culture through to the present day.

Until now, these strands in the history of nineteenth-century British pianism received attention primarily in histories of British music or in books on piano music in general, such as Henry Davey's *History of English Music*, which appeared in 1895 (2nd edn, 1921); Ernest Walker's *A History of Music in England* (1907);[14] Eric Blom's *Music in England* (1942, rev. edn 1947); and more recently Percy Young's *A History of British Music* (1967). None of these had scope to offer more than a limited consideration of the topic, and it was not until Nicholas Temperley's *The Romantic Age, 1800–1914* (1981)[15] that a more detailed and comprehensive approach was taken. That volume divides its coverage of piano music into two chapters spanning the 'long' nineteenth century: 1800–70 (by Nicholas Temperley) and 1870–1914 (by John Parry).

Seminal work on the history and development of the piano was already undertaken in nineteenth-century Britain, however. The English musicologist and antiquarian Edward Rimbault (1816–76), for example, produced *The Pianoforte, its Origin, Progress, and Construction* (London, 1860), providing a detailed explanation of piano structure as well as an historical survey of instruments that preceded the piano (concluding in the year of the Great Exhibition, 1851). One chapter is devoted specifically to the piano in England. Similarly, Alfred J. Hipkins (1826–1903), who spent his professional career at the Broadwood piano company and was well known amongst figures discussed in the present volume, wrote *A Description and History of the Pianoforte and of the Older Keyboard Stringed Instruments* (1896; 2nd edn, 1898; 3rd edn, 1929; 3rd edn repr. with an introduction by Edwin M. Ripin, 1975). For four shillings the reader could purchase this concise compendium, with its detailed plates and illustrations; the subject is partitioned into pre- and post-iron-frame construction, with 1820 forming the dividing point. Ripin, in the introduction to the reprint edition, summarizes the general view of this classic work, still considered an accurate and valuable contribution to the field: '[it is] one of the most extraordinary books about musical instruments ever written and a model for the lucid exposition of a complex and technical subject'.[16] Other works on the piano drew from Continental scholarship. Oscar Bie's *A History of the Pianoforte and Pianoforte Players* (trans. and rev. from the German by E.E. Kellett and E.W. Naylor, London, 1899; repr., 1966) devotes one of its nine chapters to 'Old England'; unlike the previously mentioned books, this addresses equally aspects of performers, composers and instruments.

---

14 Walker's *History of Music in England* was revised and enlarged in a third edition for Oxford University Press by Jack Westrup in 1952; John Caldwell's two-volume *Oxford History of English Music* (published 1991, 1999) has now replaced it.

15 See Nicholas Temperley, 'Piano Music: 1800–1870' in *The Romantic Age, 1800–1914*, Blackwell (formerly Athlone) History of Music in Britain, 5 (London: Athlone Press, 1981; Oxford: Basil Blackwell, 1988).

16 Alfred J. Hipkins, *A Description and History of the Pianoforte and of the Older Keyboard Stringed Instruments*, in *Novello, Ewer and Co.'s Music Primers and Educational Series, no. 52*, 3rd edn, repr. (Detroit: Information Coordinators, 1975), p. ix.

Other works have expanded research into the history of the piano to incorporate social and economic contexts, such as Rosamund Harding's still useful *The Piano-forte: Its History Traced to the Great Exhibition of 1851* (Cambridge, 1933; 2nd edn, 1978), Arthur Loesser's *Men, Women and Pianos: A Social History* (New York, 1954; repr. 1990), and more recently Edwin Good's *Giraffes, Black Dragons and Other Pianos: A Technological History from Cristofori to the Modern Concert Grand* (Stanford University Press, 1982; rev. edn, 2001). Cyril Ehrlich approaches the subject from a manufacturing and economic historian's perspective in *The Piano: A History* (London, 1976; rev. edn, 1990), including among its eleven chapters four on British topics: the Victorian piano, the British market from 1880 to 1914, and the English industry (first from 1870 to 1914 and then during the First World War). A further contribution to the field is a study by David Wainwright of the most celebrated of Britain's nineteenth-century piano manufacturers, Broadwood (*Broadwood, by Appointment: A History*, London, 1982).

Another significant type of literature on the piano is the method book written expressly for the instrument. Among the earliest examples are two important volumes published in London: Jan Dussek's *Instructions on the Art of Playing the Piano-Forte or Harpsichord* (1796) and Muzio Clementi's *Introduction to the Art of Playing on the Piano Forte* (1801; 11th edn, 1826). A generation later, *A Complete Theoretical and Practical Course of Instruction on the Art of Playing the Pianoforte* by J.N. Hummel appeared on the London market (trans. from an 1828 German edition and published in London, 1829). These works, in particular Clementi's, explained the new skills – technical and interpretative – required to perform early nineteenth-century piano repertoire. The number of instructional books on the market grew, especially during the later 1800s and early 1900s. Ernst Pauer (1826–1905), an émigré pianist who held positions at the RAM and RCM, produced *The Art of Pianoforte Playing* (London, 1877). A later example from Britain is *The Leschetizky Method* by Marie Prentner, a pupil and assistant of Leschetizky (London, 1903).

Complementary to method books are genre studies, amongst them the pioneering work of the English pianist and writer on music J.S. Shedlock (1843–1919), whose *The Pianoforte Sonata: Its Origin and Development* (London, 1895; repr., 1964) was printed in translation into German within two years of its British publication. One chapter treats the sonata in England, the only chapter to address a specific location, discussing the piano sonatas of such prominent figures as John Field, Cipriani Potter, G.A. Macfarren, William Sterndale Bennett and C.H.H. Parry. Shedlock, who was particularly renowned for his Beethoven scholarship, also produced *Beethoven's Pianoforte Sonatas: The Origins and Respective Values of Various Readings* (London, 1918). The multi-volume study of the sonata by William S. Newman has considerably expanded and updated Shedlock's work. In *The Sonata in the Classic Era* (Chapel Hill, 1963; 3rd edn, 1983), Newman provides an extensive discussion of the genre and a geographical survey of composers and their music. Great Britain is covered from the mid-eighteenth century through to Clementi and his contemporaries. Newman brings his investigation forward in *The Sonata since Beethoven* (New York, 1969; 3rd edn, 1983), which considers the composers of J.B. Cramer's generation through to C.V. Stanford and his contemporaries. A more recent and selective survey of the genre can be found in *The British Piano Sonata, 1870–1945* by Lisa Hardy

(Woodbridge, 2001). A study of another genre, the piano concerto, in Britain can be found in Therese Ellsworth's 'The Piano Concerto in London Concert Life between 1801 and 1850' (PhD diss., University of Cincinnati, 1991).

Nineteenth-century periodicals, general reference books and musical biographies provide an extremely informative source on performers and composers. Journals such as the *Quarterly Musical Magazine and Review* (*QMMR*) (1818–28) and the *Harmonicon* (1823–33) carried biographical sketches of pianist–composers including Clementi (*QMMR*, 2 (1820), pp. 308–16); Kalkbrenner (*QMMR*, 6 (1824), pp. 499–513); Ries (*Harmonicon*, 2 (1824), pp. 33–4); and Moscheles (*Harmonicon*, 2 (1824), pp. 103–104); while Pauer's *A Dictionary of Pianists and Composers for the Pianoforte* (London, 1896) dealt with these figures encyclopaedically. C.E. Hallé and M. Hallé's *Life and Letters of Sir Charles Hallé, being an Autobiography, 1819–1860, with Correspondence and Diaries* (London, 1896), Michael Kennedy, ed., *The Autobiography of Charles Hallé* (1972; repr., 1981), and Charlotte Moscheles's edition of her husband's diaries and correspondence, published as *The Life of Moscheles* (London, 1873; later as *Recent Music and Musicians* in 1873 and repr., 1970), contribute an abundance of information about musicians and concert life of the times.[17] Moscheles's association with the most important musicians of his day makes this *Life* a valuable work, although the reader should be aware that the original source material has been edited by the subject's wife and freely translated by Coleridge. Other important biographies include Constance Bache's *Brother Musicians: Reminiscences of Edward and Walter Bache* (London, 1901) and J.R. Sterndale Bennett's *The Life of William Sterndale Bennett* (Cambridge, 1907), and brief biographical sketches can be found in James Brown and Stephen Stratton, *British Musical Biography* (Birmingham, 1897; repr., 1971). The authors assert that they were motivated by 'the desire to present the true position of the British Empire in the world of music'[18] by detailing the work not only of musicians well known in major urban centres but also those from the provinces and colonies of the Empire.

Finally, an essential reference source for the piano, its performers and its repertoire in nineteenth-century Britain compiled during that period is *A Dictionary of Music and Musicians* by George Grove (1st edn, London, 1879–89). Its biographies and worklists feature authors who were distinguished musicians in their own right – for example Edward Dannreuther, who wrote the article on Clementi – and who were often contemporaries or even associates of the subject. 'Pianoforte Music' and 'Pianoforte Playing' were penned by Ernst Pauer. The latter article treats composers from C.P.E. Bach to those born in the 1850s, including Moritz Moszkowski and Natalia Janotha. Alfred Hipkins chronicled changes in the instrument for the entry 'Pianoforte'; this article includes technical illustrations, pictures and chronological

---

17 A.D. Coleridge translated and adapted into English the original publication by C. Moscheles. For this English version, Coleridge enlisted the help of the composer's son, Felix Moscheles, who provided additional material.

18 James Duff Brown and Stephen S. Stratton, *British Musical Biography: A Dictionary of Musical Artists, Authors and Composers Born in Britain and Its Colonies*, repr. (New York: Da Capo Press, 1971), p. i.

lists of developments. C.H.H. Parry contributed a comprehensive survey of the sonata.

Grove, in his Preface to the first edition of his *Dictionary,* expressed his sense of the century's musical developments and the resulting needs:

> A growing demand has arisen in this country and the United States for information on all matters directly and indirectly connected with Music, owing to the great spread of concerts, musical publications, private practice, and interest in the subject, and to the immense improvement in the general position of music which has taken place since the commencement of the present century.[19]

This book, in examining the nineteenth-century cultivation of the piano in Britain that formed such a strong element in the developments noted by Grove, also responds to our sense of the 'growing demand' in our own time for information about musical life in nineteenth-century Britain, with the aim of contributing to a fuller historical understanding of that 'great spread' of musical culture observed by Grove.

---

19 Dated London: 1 April 1879, and reprinted in Stanley Sadie and John Tyrrell, eds, *The New Grove Dictionary of Music and Musicians* (29 vols, London: Macmillan, 2001), vol. 1, p. xxxv.

Chapter 2

'That Domestic and Long-suffering Instrument': The Piano Boom in Nineteenth-Century Belfast

Roy Johnston

The Piano as Commodity

There drift through the pages of the late eighteenth-century Belfast newspapers sporadic advertisements for the sale of pianos. The seller who consistently advertised over a period of years, and had the market in its early days almost entirely to himself, was William Ware, who arrived in the town in 1776 to become organist of the new parish church of St Anne's. Most other domestic instruments could be housed, displayed and demonstrated in modest premises; maintenance was largely a matter of strings and reeds, which in a good many cases could be bought, fitted and tuned by the purchaser of the instrument. The piano was a quite different commodity. Delicate as it might be in many parts of its mechanism, it occupied a bulk and weight that posed many problems in getting it to the purchaser. Even if the 'manufactory' was in the same town, transport involved careful carriage in a cart over imperfectly surfaced roads and streets. Where the manufactory was in Dublin the difficulty was magnified; such was the state of the roads between Belfast and Dublin that it took the stage coach, established in 1752, three days to make the 80-mile journey.[1] Transport to Belfast from London also involved a sea journey.

Approaching Belfast the ship could come no closer than the Pool of Garmoyle, a place of deep water into which the river Lagan meandered, dropping to a depth of two feet in mid-stream at low tide. When the tide was right, smaller craft, called lighters, plied the three miles between the Pool of Garmoyle and the Belfast quays.[2] A piano had to be loaded from the ship on to a lighter and from the lighter on to the quay. The tasks of un-crating, of checking that the case, frames and mechanisms were in order, and of tuning were not to be undertaken on the quayside or in the open street. Anyone contemplating the sale of pianos on a systematic scale must first supply himself with adequate covered space, preferably in his own establishment. Ware's house was big enough to accommodate Mrs Ware's boarding school 'for the

---

1   *Belfast News-Letter* (*BN-L*), 13 August 1752.
2   Robin Sweetnam, 'The Development of the Port', in J.C. Beckett *et al.*, *Belfast: The Making of the City 1800-1914* (Belfast: Appletree Press, 1983), p. 58.

reception of young ladies', in which her husband taught music.[3] Ware advertised in his own right, but also made a practice of including his own business in his wife's advertisements for her school:

> Mrs. Ware informs her friends and the public, that she opens school (after the Christmas holidays) on Monday 24th of Jan. 1785.

> Mr. Ware has for sale a very fine toned HARPSICHORD, with a Swell, made by Schudi, London, which on trial will be found superior in tone, and more compleatly finished than any yet made in this kingdom; he has also a PIANO FORTE, which he got lately from London to dispose of.[4]

There was obviously space in the house for keyboard instruments. Ware kept his prospective competitors at bay in other ways: 'Mr. Ware solicits orders for musical instruments and can supply them at short notice from London or Dublin on more reasonable terms than formerly. All instruments chosen by him are kept in tune (in town gratis) for 12 months.'[5]

Ware, however, was a man of the eighteenth century. When he died in 1826 at the age of 68 the piano boom was in sight, and Ware's working methods would not have been adequate to take advantage of it. He had always worked alone and shown no inclination to become an employer. What he bequeathed to the piano-sellers of the boom era was the need to know and be known by the makers, to have adequate space to house stock, work on it and display it, and to provide expert tuning and repair. What he could not bequeath was his near-monopoly of the trade. The Belfast to which he came was a little town of 14,000 inhabitants, in which for 30 years he would be the only church organist. When he died there were other churches with organs and the population had risen more than threefold to 45,000, with Belfast a late starter in the Industrial Revolution.

Early in the new century general merchants already established in Belfast began advertising instruments as well as music. Not for some years did they offer pianos; these were still an unwieldy commodity in the transport conditions of the time. Then in 1819 Samuel Munn, 'British and foreign perfumery, patent medicines, toys', added music and musical instruments to his stock-in-trade in his 'piano and music warehouse'.[6] A year later he was selling pianos with 'tuning and repairing',[7] then offering three Clementis and three Broadwoods, more than Ware had ever offered at one time.[8] No fly-by-night, he kept up this high-pressure advertising for several years, moving several times to more commodious premises. The amount of piano music he had on sale gives a further indication of the burgeoning domestic market. The makers of his pianos included not only Clementi and Broadwood but also Tomkison and Wornum. By 1822 he had brought over a man from Clementi's as a full-time

3   *BN-L*, 19 September 1780.
4   *Belfast Mercury* (*BM*), 14 January 1785.
5   *BN-L*, 9 December 1800.
6   *BN-L*, 22 June 1819.
7   *BN-L*, 28 July 1820.
8   *BN-L*, 20 October 1820.

tuner and repairer.[9] The piano demand was now strong enough and the established suppliers tenacious enough for strangers to be unwelcome. Felix O'Neill, offering grand pianos made by a Dublin maker, Lyon of Nassau Street, set up in 1822.[10] He too had brought over a tuner and repairer from Clementi's. His pianos could be tuned 'in 1 hour 50 minutes and immediately after played on for several hours without derangement'. Later in the year, however, in the face of the aggressive advertising of Munn and others, he ended an advertisement with the words 'No attention to animosity!!'; this proved to be his last advertisement.[11]

Under Munn's pressure other merchants left the music scene. But not all did so: the piano trade passed into the hands of professional musicians who learnt to be businessmen. Munn, with two years of flamboyant trading behind him, placed two advertisements for squares and cabinet pianos in autumn 1821.[12] Between the two insertions there appeared an advertisement offering a variety of musical instruments, including four pianos, and stating 'pianos tuned, hired out or exchanged'.[13] This was the first piano advertisement of William Robert Hart. Well known in Belfast as a church organist and general musician, he was the first professional since Ware to enter the market consistently. A later Munn advertisement was placed in the same column of the newspaper as that of another competitor, John Willis.[14] Willis, who was Ware's successor at St Anne's and was to become a major force in Belfast musical life for many years, was making his piano-selling debut with the offer of three Broadwood squares, and the news that he had moved house 'for the better accommodation of his pupils' to an address 'where the pianos may be seen'. In 1825 he was assuring customers that 'persons wishing any particular piece of music can have it the third day after order'; an interesting promise in the days before turnpike roads, the railways and the straightening of the Lagan.[15]

Meanwhile Vincenzo Guerini had arrived in Belfast in 1806, via Dublin, from Naples, where he had played the violin in one of the opera houses. He would, he said, teach the Italian language, piano and singing 'with the advantage of accompanying on the violin'; he would also 'instruct such gentlemen as may be desirous of obtaining a knowledge on the instrument last mentioned' (the violin was still not generally deemed a lady's instrument).[16] When the Anacreontic Society was formed in 1814, Guerini became the leader of its band. In 1823 he began selling pianos:

V. Guerini is just landing from on board the *Iris* and expects daily from London on the *Emerald* several cabinet and square pianos which he has selected himself. Mr. Guerini has corresponded with an eminent professional gentleman from London … he can get any piano his friends may wish to order.[17]

---

9   *BN-L*, 26 November 1822.

10 *BN-L*, 2 April 1822.

11 *The Irishman (IR)*, 25 October 1822.

12 *BN-L*, 21 September, 23 October 1821.

13 *BN-L*, 2 October 1821.

14 *BN-L*, 3 January 1823.

15 *BN-L*, 20 April 1825.

16 *BN-L*, 8 August 1806.

17 *IR*, 29 August 1823.

In 1826 Guerini and John Willis went into partnership, offering a large variety of instruments, music and accessories.[18] Pianos would be 'carefully sent to all parts of the kingdom – old ones taken in exchange'. They had engaged a person for repairs and tuning who would be 'constantly in attendance'. The imminent appearance of a partnership of two professional musicians in competition with him was too much for Munn. His final advertisement was in the *Belfast Commercial Chronicle* of 11 March 1826 and made no mention of pianos.

If a general merchant wished to sell pianos he would need musical knowledge to compete with the now-adept professionals, but it could be done. Frederick Fletcher, who had a lace warehouse, entered the music market while Munn was still in business.[19] Primarily a merchant, he was also a musician, who taught flute and clarinet as well as piano,[20] and occasionally composed songs and dance music; at the opening of the Music Hall in 1840 he played the bassoon in the Anacreontic band. When the amateur brass band came into vogue, Fletcher stocked trombones and 'brass military instruments direct from Vienna'.[21] No piano business, however, matches that of the Hart family in longevity. William Robert Hart was succeeded by his son Joseph, who tuned his own pianos until the arrival in 1858 of a tuner from Collard and Collard called William Grant Churchill.[22] His son Edward Bunting Hart (Joseph Hart had succeeded Bunting as organist of St George's parish church) took Churchill into partnership, and the firm of Hart and Churchill remained in business in Belfast until recent years. Since William Robert Hart first appears as a musician in 1792, the family could reasonably claim to have been involved with the piano in Belfast for almost two centuries.

The Makers

The partnership between Guerini and Willis proved short-lived and was dissolved after two years. While Willis continued in business in the same premises, Guerini developed his trade in a new direction. Assuring customers that he was still regularly supplied with London-made pianos, he declared that he had commenced making upright pianos himself, a few of which were ready for delivery; he would exchange any instrument of his own manufacture 'within six months from delivery if not approved of'.[23] By the spring of 1830 he was offering 'a large assortment of cabinet, cottage and square pianos of his own manufacture'.[24] He had a foreman who was constantly at the manufactory.[25] In the following year William Reid, identifying himself as 'late foreman to Mr Guerini', declared that he was now repairing and tuning on his own account.[26] The reason for Reid's departure became clear not long

---

18 *BN-L*, 5 September 1826.
19 *BN-L*, 27 September 1825.
20 *BN-L*, 2 November 1827.
21 *BN-L*, 2 October, 6 November 1835.
22 *BN-L*, 18 September 1858.
23 *BN-L*, 30 September 1828.
24 *The Guardian and Christian Advocate* (*GCA*), 11 May 1830.
25 *Northern Whig* (*NW*), 13 May 1830.
26 *GCA*, 5 August 1831.

afterwards, when Guerini told the Anacreontic Society that he wished to resign on account of ill health. The Society thanked him warmly for his services, made him a handsome presentation of silver plate[27] and kept him on in his position as leader of the band. By the winter of 1836–7, however, Guerini had to discontinue his piano-making business and sell off his stock.[28] Some two years later he had to resign entirely from the Anacreontic Society, 'being obliged for ill health (which frequently disables him from pursuing his profession) to quit this country'.[29] Many members of the Dublin Anacreontic Society travelled up to his farewell concert on 23 April 1839, at which there was standing room only.

A late source, the reminiscences of a retired musician in an 1890s journal, is patronising and condescending to Guerini, and depicts him as living in penury with newspapers for blankets; the whiff of xenophobia is not entirely absent.[30] The picture is certainly contradicted by the advertisement in May 1839, on his leaving the country, of the sale of his household furniture:

At the House of Mr. GUERRINI, in Ballymacarrett,
on TUESDAY next, the 21ˢᵗ May instant,
at ELEVEN o'clock,

THE HOUSEHOLD FURNITURE, of which
the greater part is nearly new, comprising large Mahogany
pillar Dining Tables; Parlour and Drawing-Room
Chairs; Sofas; Chimney Glass; Carpets; Fenders and
Fire-Irons; Four-post and other Bedsteads; Feather Beds
and Bedding; Chests of Drawers; Secretaries; Dressing
Tables and Glasses; an Eight-day Clock; Glass and Delf;
Kitchen Utensils; a large Filtering Stone, &c., &c.
AND AT THREE O'CLOCK,
A number of Cabinet and other PIANO-FORTES; several
Valuable Foreign VIOLINS; a SPRING CARAVAN, for carrying
Pianos; a quantity of Mahogany VENEERS; an Inside
JAUNTING-CAR; a Cow in Calf, &c. [31]

Of Guerini's piano-making, all that is evident in the advertisement is a few pianos, the spring caravan and some veneers. The rest had presumably been sold off over the previous few years. Some of it, perhaps all, no doubt went to William Reid, who ran his own business as a piano maker from 1832 to 1838, when he announced that he was 'resigning manufacture' to devote his attention to tuning and repairing.[32]

---

27 Anacreontic Society Minutes (ASM), held in the Linenhall Library, Belfast (LL), meeting of 21 February 1832.

28 *NW*, 2 March 1837.

29 *NW*, 6 April 1839.

30 *The Pen*, a weekly journal published in Belfast, the third of a series of six (unsigned) articles on 'Musical Life in Belfast', issue of 6 February 1897.

31 *NW*, 16 May 1839.

32 *NW*, 19 May 1838.

Another piano maker, John McCullough (the surname is variously spelt), made his appearance in the Belfast newspapers a few months after Guerini's departure. He had, he declared, 'on sale by private bargain' two six-octave grand square pianos 'constructed on the most approved principle and embracing all the modern improvements'.[33] These were on view in Devlin's Great Rooms in Donegall Place. McCullough's 'manufactory' was in the town of Newtownards, some nine miles away in County Down. He made a triumphant announcement four years later to the effect that the Royal Dublin Society Exhibition Committee had awarded him the Society's large silver medal for superior workmanship; he made pianos, he said, for 'little more than half the price paid for the same style of London work'.[34] By 1845 he had moved to Belfast and by 1849 had taken new warerooms in the fashionable Donegall Square North.[35] After he died in 1851 his widow tried to keep the business going,[36] but within a few months it was up for auction:

> The stock-in-trade of Rosewood, Mahogany, Sycamore, Beech, Oak,
> Zebrawood and Veneers, at the Piano Manufactory, Arthur Place,
> of the late John McCullagh, 1st May at 11 a.m.,
> also other woods, a turning lathe; a spring covered van; benches,
> hand screws, clamps etc. Stove and piping, gas fittings.
> At 3 p.m. Pianos, semi-cabinet, cottage piccolo and squares, also a seraphine... [37]

The premises comprised a dwelling-house, warerooms and large workshops. Some eight months later the McCullough pianos in his showroom in Donegall Square North were sold off.[38]

There may have been other piano makers in Belfast over the years; Guerini and McCullough are the only ones who have left sufficient information about themselves in the sources to enable some sort of picture of their activity to come into focus. It is appropriate here to consider what 'maker' may have meant in the context of this provincial town. Cyril Ehrlich has shown that in London in 1851, of the larger manufacturers who undertook every operation from raw material to finished product, by far the greatest firm was Broadwood's, admired for, inter alia, its large labour force embodying high-level skills 'not likely to be supplanted by any automatic machinery'.[39] Annual production at Broadwood's during the 1850s was about 2,500, a total approached by no other firm. In England Collard came second with 1,500, followed by 'perhaps eight firms' whose annual output ranged from 300 to 500

33 *NW*, 9 January 1840.
34 *NW*, 13 July 1844.
35 *NW*, 9 August 1849.
36 *BN-L*, 3 November 1851.
37 *BM*, 29 April 1852. Zebrawood is 'any of several kinds of ornamentally striped wood used by cabinet-makers' (*Oxford English Dictionary*). The seraphine was a keyboard reed instrument which appeared in London in 1833, and by 1852 had been superseded by the harmonium. It had bellows and swell but, in the opinion of A.J. Hipkins, who no doubt had played it, a 'harsh and raspy tone' ('A.J.H.', article 'Seraphine', George Grove, *Dictionary of Music and Musicians* (4 vols, London, 1879–89), vol. iii, pp. 466–7).
38 *NW*, 21 December 1852.
39 Cyril Ehrlich, *The Piano: A History*, rev. edn (Oxford: Clarendon Press, 1990), p. 35.

instruments.[40] That left some 190 makers in Britain in the provincial towns, their output 20–30 pianos a year, perhaps fewer. It is obviously in this last category that any Belfast piano maker would belong. The small output would be related not only to the demand (which was seasonal, centred on Christmas and the spring weddings) but also to the small size of the work force such a maker could afford to employ.

The absence of metals and metal-working tools in both Belfast firms is to be expected: machinery played hardly any part in the piano industry of 1851.[41] Ehrlich lists the range of operations carried out by Broadwood's in the making of their pianos;[42] the craftsmen included the key maker, the hammer and damper makers, the notch-maker, the hammer-leatherer, the beam maker, the various 'music-smiths' contributing metal parts to what was still fundamentally a wooden frame, and the spun-string maker. There is a total absence of these materials in Guerini's and McCullough's advertisements. Guerini had stopped making pianos for some years before his departure from Belfast and the absence is no surprise, but the McCullough firm had only just gone out of business; some tools and materials may of course have been lost or disposed of, or were the property of individual craftsmen. One is forced to consider, nonetheless, what the local maker could hope to do on his own, and what he could not. Many if not all of these 16 or so of Ehrlich's 30 categories may well have been beyond him (although the possibility of a placement or an apprenticeship in Broadwood's or Collard's cannot be ruled out). There was some likelihood on the other hand that local cabinet-making skills and experience could supply some or most of the remaining categories – the sawyer, the bent-side maker, the case-maker, the brace-maker, and the bottom-maker. It is also possible that an expert work force guided by an experienced boss or supervisor might have supplied the functions of the marker-off, the stringer, the finisher who assembled and fixed the action, bringing the whole mechanism into playing order, and the rougher-up who gave the first tuning, followed by the tuner, the regulator of action and regulator of tones; it is not beyond belief that William Reid and Adam Craig, Guerini's and McCullough's tuners respectively, on their own or with helpers, could have seen the instrument into use by the exercise of these skills. A different light, however, is thrown on the situation by Ehrlich's statement that 'a pattern of manufacture can be discerned in which the piano maker is already able to buy partly-processed materials and components'.[43] It may well have been the possibility of buying in such components that attracted Guerini and McCullough to piano making in the first place.

With important elements bought in, and others within the competence of the local work force, there remains an essential component not yet covered. Complete actions were not offered for sale until 1855.[44] Where then did Guerini and McCullough acquire the actions of their pianos? Even had they been able to construct the action themselves, their pianos would surely not have borne comparison with the professional output of Broadwood and Collard. A hypothesis suggests itself, based

40 Ibid., p. 37.
41 Ibid., p. 18.
42 Ibid., p. 36.
43 Ibid., p. 35.
44 Ibid., p. 35.

on the fact that there was by now in the local environment a proliferation of pianos. Guerini's and McCullough's tuners would have encountered a good many. A tuner doing his rounds would be in a position to identify and acquire for his firm the occasional instrument no longer required, or in dire need of structural repair, but with a good intact action; and which could be acquired from its owner, brought into the 'manufactory' and incorporated in a 'new' piano. Cabinet-making skills would be applied to the construction of a new case to the design of the day, with the currently fashionable woods and veneers, and using the bought-in elements. The tuner, having been responsible for the acquisition of the action, would now be responsible for combining the action with the new case and the extraneous elements, into an instrument to which the firm could attach its name. Such, in this hypothesis, would have been the processes which enabled Guerini and McCullough to make and market – and in the latter's case, submit successfully to competitive scrutiny – a modest annual output of their own pianos. It would plainly be, however, an undertaking of great effort for minimal profit. One can understand why a tuner such as Reid or Craig should decide that tuning and repairing would offer a sufficient career in themselves.

As Ehrlich and others have shown, the great revolution in piano design and manufacture took place in the second half of the century; the Steinway family opened their workshop in New York in 1853.[45] In Ehrlich's list of piano makers after 1851 there is only one Irish entry, 'Macintosh, G. (Dublin). *fl.* 1881'.[46] In Belfast Guerini and McCullough remained exotic figures. Those professional musicians who sold pianos, such as Dalton and Hart, did not venture into manufacture but gave great attention to their tuning and repairing services. It was worth the while of a London-trained tuner to come to a provincial town such as Belfast to make his living either on his own or with a single piano merchant. In the year after McCullough died, having with his small annual output achieved a fashionable address for his showroom in Donegall Square North, William Coffey, one of the new breed of merchants with musical knowledge, who had established himself just round the corner in Donegall Place, was advertising that he had nearly 50 new and secondhand pianos for sale or hire and was employing a full-time Collard and Collard tuner.[47]

When Jenny Lind visited Belfast in 1859, Coffey supplied the piano and offered it for sale shortly afterwards as 'used by Mrs. Lind-Goldschmidt during her stay in Belfast and which Herr Goldschmidt pronounced as the best semi-grand of Broadwood's he ever performed on'.[48] A local piano maker could not live with this quality of competition. Guerini, had his health allowed it, had a better chance of competing with the merchants of the 1830s. By the time McCullough died in 1851 the vast improvements in communication favoured the merchants and gave him very little chance; the era of 'cheap pianos for the million' was only a generation away. The railways now enabled goods, however crated and bulky, to be transported in great numbers to the English towns and the English ports. A spectacular marine enterprise

---

45 Ibid., pp. 47–8.
46 Ibid., p. 207.
47 *NW,* 20 November 1852.
48 *BN-L,* 21 January 1859.

at Belfast had reached its completion in 1849. The Belfast harbour commissioners had put in train the straightening and deepening of the Lagan, a mighty enterprise which enabled ships of considerable draught to dock at the reorganized Belfast quays, and left the Pool of Garmoyle a memory.[49]

The Virtuosi

With the popularity of the piano went a great appetite for music to play on it. The advertisements of Coffey and the other merchants included sheet music, with promises of regular supply and quick delivery from Dublin and London; the desire for novelty ensured that it was an enduring and expanding market. Teachers throve. To learn a piece for one's teacher was one thing, however; to see and hear it on the platform quite another. It was the virtuoso pianist on tour who would give the drawing-room pianists some idea of how the notes on the printed score were to be played, and of the standards of insight and performance which the composer had had in mind. Frédéric Kalkbrenner was the first pianist of international reputation to visit Belfast. He did so in 1824, when the roads and the seaways were not much improved from the previous century and the railways in Ireland did not yet exist. Kalkbrenner had been invited by the Belfast Anacreontic Society, and he was able to play with their orchestra, composed largely of amateurs but led by Guerini and with some professional visitors. There were close links with the Dublin Anacreontic Society; of the Dublin members who came north for the occasion, three – Alday, violinist and composer; Perceval, cellist; and the singer Larkin – took part in the concert. The 'principal nobility and gentry of the neighbourhood' arrived early to ensure good seats. The concert began with Alday's Symphony in C, the second half with a symphony by Haydn. The eminent visitor was thus honourably welcomed and showcased. Kalkbrenner accompanied Alday's violin solo and with the orchestra played in an introduction and variations on a popular Scots song, 'My lodging is on the cold ground'. In the second half he gave an 'extemporaneous performance'. The usual form which this took was an appeal to the audience for melodies and the selection by the soloist of one of them on which he would extemporise a fantasia; Liszt was still doing this in his tour of Ireland 16 years later. The concert concluded with Kalkbrenner and the orchestra in 'new variations on "God save the King"'. He played, then, no music but his own, and of that he chose neither piano concerto nor sonata, but his variation pieces. It was appropriate for the Belfast visit; the melodies would be familiar to all, the variations giving him the chance to display his 'brilliancy, imagination and science'.[50] To choose pieces involving the orchestra was, as will be seen, unusual and a courteous compliment to his hosts.

Sigismond Thalberg arrived 13 years later, his famous contest with Liszt fresh in the public mind. It was proudly announced by Charles Dalton, another local organist who also sold pianos, that Thalberg would play on a 'new horizontal grand piano by Collard and Collard' supplied by him.[51] He played in the theatre,

49 Sweetnam, 'The Development of the Port', pp. 58–63.
50 *NW*, 16 September 1824.
51 *NW*, 26 December 1837.

between main piece and after-piece, with songs and glees by members of the theatre company; 'parties desirous of being near Mr. Thalberg during his performance' could have seats on the stage.[52] A few days later he gave a matinée, entirely on his own, an early example of the solo recital.[53] His evening concert had consisted of fantasias and variations on known airs, but he included in his matinée a 'new grand capriccioso'.[54] When he returned the following year, he gave two concerts,[55] sharing the programme with Michael Balfe and Mrs Balfe, appearing as baritone and soprano singers. Thalberg's fantasias and variations were on themes from *Don Giovanni*, Rossini's *La donna del lago* and Meyerbeer's *Les Huguenots*, and ended with his now celebrated fantasia on the prayer in Rossini's *Moïse*; but he also included his own 'andante in D flat, followed by selections from new studies'. After Thalberg's first visit, Belfast did not have long to wait for his adversary and the greatest of this trio of early touring virtuosi. Franz Liszt arrived in the town at half-past four in the afternoon of Friday 15 January 1841. It was the final concert of the Irish section of a tour which had originally expected to be confined to the south of England. The young and inexperienced organizer, Lewis Lavenu, encountering less remunerative audiences than he had anticipated, extended the tour to northern England, then to Ireland and Scotland. After arriving in Dublin in December 1840 to a good welcome at the centenary concert of the Dublin Anacreontic Society, Lavenu then had the party traverse the south and west of Ireland in the winter weather of December and January in the frantic search for full houses, until they finally came to Belfast en route to Scotland (Belfast's placing on this route between Dublin and Scotland was to be beneficial to the development of its musical life). Liszt was not on his own, as Kalkbrenner and Thalberg had been, but in a party which also included two women singers, Miss Bassano and Miss Steele, a flautist, Joseph Richardson, and a baritone, John Orlando Parry. Parry, who had written comic songs including the popular 'Wanted, a Governess', kept a diary.[56] It is a personal diary; he places himself in the centre of the stage. The Anacreontic Society had looked forward to meeting the company: 'Should Mr. Liszt, Mr. Parry and other professional gentlemen come to Belfast, an opportunity should be taken to invite them to the Society'.[57]

By the time the party reached Belfast they were greatly fatigued by the travelling, the length of the tour and the rigours of the winter. After a short rest, however, they went to the Anacreontic Society's new Music Hall in May Street and gave their concert (see Fig. 2.1).

52 *NW*, 30 December 1837.

53 Further on the development of the solo recital see Janet Ritterman and William Weber, 'Origins of the Piano Recital in England, 1830–1870', Chapter 8 below.

54 *BN-L*, 5 January 1838.

55 *NW*, 10 October 1839.

56 John Orlando Parry, 'Diaries of Liszt's Tours of Britain', MS, Library of Wales, Aberystwyth, call number nlw.17717A.

57 ASM, meeting of 4 January 1841.

CONCERT.

MONSIEUR LISZT

HAS the honour to announce to the Nobility and Gentry of Belfast, that he will give a

GRAND EVENING CONCERT,

IN THE MUSIC-HALL,

On *FRIDAY, January* 15, 1841.

PROGRAMME.

PART I.

TRIO—" Soave sia il vento," Miss STEELE,
Miss BASSANO, and Mr. J. PARRY,......... *Mozart.*
ARIA—" Non piu de fiori," Miss STEELE,... *Mozart.*
SOLO—Flute, Mr. RICHARDSON.
RECITATIVE—" My prayers
are heard,"...................
ARIA—" Tears such as tender }Mr. PARRY. *Handel.*
Fathers shed,".................
ARIA—" L'Amor suo," Miss BASSANO,.... *Donizetti.*
OVERTURE—Piano-forte, "Guillaume Tell,"
M. LISZT, ... *Rossini.*
TRIO—Buffo Italiano; or, " Recollections of an Italian
Opera," performed extemporaneously, by Mr. J. PARRY.

PART II.

DUETTO—"Quanto Amore," Miss BASSANO
and Mr. J. PARRY, ... *Donizetti.*
SONG—Miss STEELE, " The Wanderer,"
accompanied on the Piano-forte by M.
LISZT.
DUET—" The Sisters," Miss STEELE and
Miss BASSANO, ... *Wade.*
ANDANTE—Finale from "Lucia de Lammer-
moor" and " Galop Chromatique," Piano-
forte, M. LISZT, ... *Liszt.*
BALLAD—" I've left a sweet home," Miss
BASSANO.
FANTASIA—Flute, Mr. RICHARDSON.
Mr. J. PARRY will Sing his celebrated song,
" Wanted, a Governess,"..................... *Parry.*
TRIO—" 'Tis a very merry thing," Miss
STEELE, Miss BASSANO, and Mr. J.
PARRY, ... *Wade.*

Conductor,...........Mr. LAVENU.

To commence at EIGHT o'clock.
Tickets of Admission, 5s each, to be had of Mr. FLET-
CHER; also, of R. W. DYKE, at his Music Warehouse,
25, Castle-Place, where every information, relative to the
Concert, may be obtained.
In consequence of other important engagements, the
above will be the only Concert which M. LISZT can
have the honour of giving in Belfast.   105

Figure 2.1   The Programme of Liszt's Concert, as advertised in the *Northern Whig*, 9 January 1841

Parry, by his own account, was the hit of the evening:

> There were seven encores! – I never sang to an audience fonder of fun! 'twas capital. Every word, every note almost they laughed at, and at the Grand Flute Solo in 'A Wife wanted' they gave me a round of applause. I sang 'Trio' – encored – and 'The Governess', encored loudly. Liszt, Joey [Richardson] (twice) and Miss Steele were also loudly encored![58]

Liszt by this time had a formidable list of compositions for solo piano to his credit, but the only ones he played, in a miscellaneous concert such as this, were the 'Grand galop chromatique' of 1838 and two of his opera-based fantasias. Utterly exhausted, and to the disappointment of the Anacreontic members, the party went straight to their hotel after the concert and to bed. The following day, Saturday, walking about the town, Parry was delighted in Dyke's music shop to find 'Wanted, a Governess' on sale. In the early evening the party left for the seaside town of Donaghadee some 18 miles away on the County Down coast. From there a paddle-steamer ferry ran to Portpatrick in Scotland, a distance of 21 miles. They boarded it on the following afternoon, Sunday 17 January.

There is a discrepancy between the excited expectation evident in the preliminary reports of the Liszt concert and the newspaper coverage of the actual event.[59] The audience no doubt reacted as warmly as Parry reports it did, but the Music Hall was less than half full. The *Northern Whig* blamed the weather (it was a period of snow and hard frost),[60] but it was disingenuous to give the impression that this was the only cause. Another factor provides the only example in Belfast musical life of music and politics coming near to clashing. Daniel O'Connell, outstanding orator and born leader, famed as 'The Liberator' for his success in the cause of Catholic emancipation some years earlier, had turned to agitation for the repeal of the legislative union of Britain and Ireland and was stumping the country. He had been invited to speak in Belfast by the Loyal National Repeal Association.[61] Those responsible for public order, however, knew that in no part of Ireland could he expect so hostile a reception, and at the time of the Liszt concert his arrival in the town was awaited with apprehension. A regiment of infantry and an artillery company with field guns had been embarked at Dublin for the sea journey to Belfast, bringing, with the garrison already in Belfast, the total of troops expecting O'Connell to upwards of 1,200 infantry with 200 artillery and cavalry.[62] O'Connell arrived on Saturday 16th, the day the Liszt party left; they were unaware of each other, and Parry makes no mention of O'Connell in his diary. In the circumstances, the wonder must be not that so few had attended the Liszt concert on the previous evening, but that it attracted so many. The Anacreontic Society feared for their new building, and with justification. O'Connell kept a low profile at first; he 'literally stole into our town as a thief in

---

58 Parry, 'Diaries of Liszt's Tours of Britain', entry of 15 January 1841.

59 *NW*; *Belfast Commercial Chronicle*, 16 January 1841.

60 Weather records for January 1841, held in MS in LL.

61 Jonathan Bardon, *A History of Ulster* (Belfast: Blackstaff Press, 1992), p. 255.

62 *NW*, 16 January 1841 (in the same column as the review of the concert, and immediately below it).

the night'[63] and did not leave the safety of his hotel to attend Mass the following morning.[64] But he made a dramatic speech on the following Tuesday and evoked 'yells, hisses, groans, cheers and exclamations of all descriptions'.[65] St Patrick's Orphan Society had been granted the use of the Music Hall on that evening for a soirée, which O'Connell attended, while a stone-throwing battle raged outside and a mob ranged the town breaking windows.[66] The Liszt party by that time had arrived in Scotland.

As virtuoso pianists, Kalkbrenner, Thalberg and Liszt formed a mighty and unique vanguard. Their successors would continue to visit Belfast, but they would come in a different context. When the Liszt concert took place the Music Hall was less than a year old. The Anacreontic Society opened it with a large capital debt and a laudable determination not to spend money rashly. But with concert audiences, supply created demand. In no time at all, audiences at first glad to welcome soloists from the musical life of Dublin were clamouring for the best from London and Europe. The Anacreontic tried to satisfy the demand and to exercise economy; they had to struggle to meet either goal. At this point a new phenomenon made its appearance. The desire of concertgoers to hear the best was not confined to Belfast, and a generation of London promoters, of whom Willert Beale is probably the best known, arose with the solution. Provincial audiences and concert providers recognized the advantages in having a London-based promoter include their towns on the touring schedule of not one but a group of first-rate artists with whom they would have found it difficult to communicate in advance and whose fees, on individually negotiated contracts, they would have had difficulty in meeting. The artists themselves, aware of the need to bring themselves, their skills and their compositions before the widest possible audience, saw the advantage of entering into a contractual obligation which, if it meant a diminution, in some centres, of the fee they could have obtained on their own, balanced this against the annoyances and uncertainties of touring from some of which the impresario was shielding them. The individual artist, of course, however distinguished, had to submit to membership of a party not of supporting artists but of his or her peers. Of its nature, such a party gave miscellaneous concerts. As Weber has suggested, the miscellaneous concert had its virtues:

> A concert programme usually offered a variety of musical genres – chiefly opera, song, and instrumental works – and would alternate between vocal and instrumental selections … The word 'miscellaneous' therefore not only had a positive connotation, but it also implied a coherent set of practices that gave shape and balance to the concert experience.[67]

---

63 *The Repealer Repulsed*, contemporary pamphlet (unsigned) held in LL, p. 27.
64 Bardon, *A History of Ulster*, p. 255.
65 *The Repealer Repulsed*, p. 38.
66 Bardon, *A History of Ulster*, p. 256.
67 William Weber, 'Miscellany vs. Homogeneity: concert programmes at the Royal Academy of Music and the Royal College of Music in the 1880s', in Christina Bashford and Leanne Langley, eds, *Music and British Culture, 1785–1914: Essays in Honour of Cyril Ehrlich* (Oxford: Oxford University Press, 2000), p. 301.

BELFAST

ANACREONTIC SOCIETY.

FORTY-FIRST SEASON.

FIRST CONCERT

Music Hall, Monday, 19th November, 1855.

ARTISTES ENGAGED.

Vocalists.

MADAME CLARA NOVELLO.   MISS MESSENT.
HERR REICHARDT.   MR. LAND.

Instrumentalists.

Violin—SIGNOR SIVORI.   Solo Pianoforte.
Violoncello—SIGNOR PIATTI.   ARTHUR NAPOLEON.

Conductor,...............MR. LAND.

Conductor to the Society,...............................MR. ALDRIDGE.

PROGRAMME.

Part First.

OVERTURE—" Euryanthe," (First time)	*Weber.*
FOUR-PART SONG—" The Letter."	*Hatton.*
TRIO in A Flat (2nd)—Violin, Violoncello, & Pianoforte...SIGNOR SIVORI, SIGNOR PIATTI, and ARTHUR NAPOLEON.	*Mayseder.*
DUET—" List, dearest, list."................ (*Keolanthe*) ....,MISS MESSENT and HERR REICHARDT.............	*Balfe.*
ARIA—" Batti, batti."......(*Don Giovanni*)....MADAME CLARA NOVELLO......Violoncello Obligato, SIGNOR PIATTI...	*Mozart.*
VIOLIN SOLO—" Recitatif, Prière de Moise, et théme varié executé sur une seule corde (la 4ᵐᵉ)."...SIG. SIVORI	*Paganini.*
ARIA—" In terra solo."................(*Don Sebastian*)...........................HERR REICHARDT......	*Donizetti.*
CAVATINA—" Io l'udia." ....MISS MESSENT............................	*Donizetti.*
VIOLONCELLO SOLO—" Barcarolle de Marino Faliero,' "....................SIGNOR PIATTI	*A. Piatti.*
DUETTO—" Forse te mai."...... ..(*Violetta*)........... MADAME CLARA NOVELLO and HERR REICHARDT	*Mercadante.*
OVERTURE—" Midsummer Night's Dream." (First time)	*Mendelssohn.*

Part Second.

OVERTURE—" Fra Diavolo."	*Auber.*
QUARTETT—" Where's the gain, of restless care."	*L. de Call.*
TERZETTO—" Angiol di pace."......(*Beatrice di Tenda*).....MADAME CLARA NOVELLO, MISS MESSENT, and } HERR REICHARDT.	*Bellini.*
PIANOFORTE SOLO—" La Cracovienne."..........................ARTHUR NAPOLEON................................	*Wallace.*
ENGLISH SONG—" Oh ! could my spirit fly to thee." ....HERR REICHARDT	*Land.*
NATIONAL SONG..MADAME CLARA NOVELLO	
VIOLIN SOLO—" Le Carnaval de Cuba."...... ....SIGNOR SIVORI............................	*Sivori.*
FOUR-PART SONG—" Down in yon green vale."..	*Geo. B. Allen*
NEW IRISH SONG ....MR. LAND...............	*S. Lover.*
FINALE—" To Music's Cheerful measure.". ....MADAME CLARA NOVELLO, MISS MESSENT, & HERR REICHARDT...	*E. J. Loder.*

Figure 2.2   Programme of the Belfast Anacreontic Society Concert of 19
November 1855

It would be supplanted eventually by the homogeneous concert familiar to present-day concertgoers, the characteristics of which would include 'a narrower Austro-German repertoire with a smaller list of great composers ..., the isolation of vocal from instrumental music; fewer, larger works in shorter programmes; and an ideological distinction between "serious" and "popular" music'.[68] The Anacreontic concert of Monday 19 November 1855 shows the Beale-type party, and the miscellaneous concert, at their fullest extension (see Fig. 2.2).

Clara Novello, the soprano, was English, and Alexander Reichardt, tenor, Hungarian. They, with the Italians Sivori and Piatti, were at their peak as soloists. Arthur Napoleon was a 12-year-old prodigy, born in Oporto, who would opt in his early forties for a music business career in Rio de Janeiro. The present-day concertgoer can only envy an audience which heard Clara Novello sing 'Batti, batti' with Piatti's cello obbligato. Miss Messent appears to have been a regular supporting artist; at a performance of *Lucia di Lammermoor* in London in 1848, when the prima donna failed to appear, a Miss Miran, contralto, 'bravely went through the first act, book in hand, and meanwhile Miss Messent, who was a soprano and who knew the music, had been sent for and appeared in the second and third acts'.[69] Edward Land, a well-known London musician, composer of songs, pianist and accompanist, sang a song, but his important role was evidently that of 'conductor'. Since Arthur Napoleon as the star pianist would hardly be expected to play accompaniments, it seems likely that Land sat at the piano, played accompaniments for the soloists and conducted the ensembles.

The London-based impresario, having in mind those towns on the circuit which lacked locally based concert artists and ensembles of their own, made up a party which could provide the programme of an entire concert. Land was not the only conductor, however. The Anacreontic Society had an orchestra, which by this date featured overtures and symphonies in its repertoire, including works by Haydn and Beethoven, and expected to play in both halves at the Society's concerts. Henry Aldridge is described as 'conductor to the Society'. On its merger in 1836 with the Belfast Catch and Glee Club, the Anacreontic acquired a 'vocal band', a small band of male amateurs who sang the glee repertory. Aldridge, then, had the orchestra play three overtures: *Euryanthe* and *Midsummer Night's Dream* in the first half and *Fra Diavolo* in the second. Of the vocal ensembles, it may reasonably be assumed that those sung by the visitors have their names on the programme. If the others are by the Anacreontic vocal band, and it seems likely, they include Hatton's 'The letter' and 'Where's the gain of restless care' by L. de Call. Of 'Down in yon green vale' there is no doubt: its composer, George Benjamin Allen, well known in Belfast musical life and soon to become conductor of its major choral society, was probably in the audience. As a total programme, it made for a long evening, especially with encores. The miscellaneous format militated against extended pieces from the visitors. An outstanding exception was the playing by Ernst Pauer in 1858 of the 'Waldstein'

---

68 Weber, 'Miscellany vs. Homogeneity: concert programmes at the Royal Academy of Music and the Royal College of Music in the 1880s', p. 300.

69 Charles E. Pearce, *Sims Reeves: Fifty Years of Music in England* (London: Stanley Paul & Co., 1924), p. 103.

sonata. This emboldened the young Arabella Goddard, on her first visit to Belfast later in the same season, to play the 'Pathétique'.[70] Neither, however, on succeeding visits played a Beethoven sonata. In terms of actual performing, the separation of the local contribution from that of the visitors is total. No doubt it suited both groups for it to be so. For the largely amateur Anacreontic orchestra, to be involved in playing with the visitors would have set up the need to rehearse music which might not have been in their repertoire and which indeed might not have been used on the night. For the visitors it was a matter of standards of performance; artists of this calibre had their reputations at stake. Participation with, and accompaniment by, local forces might be less risky in some provincial towns than others, but it was not something to encourage as a custom.

The Vanishing Concerto

In a concert programme where the miscellaneous character demanded brevity of individual items and where a divide existed between the local performers and the visitors, a major casualty was the concerto. Most concerts in the eighteenth century had included concertos; the charity concert of March 1778 had three.[71] Edward Bunting regularly played a piano concerto in his concerts in the early nineteenth century. However, the miscellaneous concert tightened its grip. In 1840, when May was leader of the Anacreontic orchestra, he played the first movement of a Hummel piano concerto; in the following year his successor, Murray, had Charles Dalton play a piano concerto by Herz. Thereafter, in the seasons leading up to the opening of the Ulster Hall more than twenty years later, there were no piano concertos (although fantasias by Thalberg on *Moïse* and *Lucia* and the Weber 'Konzertstück' were described as concertos). The violin concerto fared only a little better, although in some excellent hands. Collins played a Bellini concerto (or was it a fantasia on a Bellini opera?) in 1843, Sivori a concerto of his own in 1844. Karl Rosi and Henry Cooper played Spohr's 'Dramatic' concerto in 1856 and 1857 respectively. The Mendelssohn E minor violin concerto had four performances; in full by Wieniawski in 1859, and of two movements only by Kerbusch (1859), Joachim (1859) and Becker (1861). Kerbusch played two movements of his own concerto in 1862.

While the miscellaneous concert was no doubt the main reason for the dearth of concertos, was there another reason? Had so great a discrepancy evolved between metropolitan and provincial orchestral playing standards that soloists were not prepared to risk their reputations by playing with local accompaniment? If so, one might have expected concertos from Jullien, who visited Belfast first in 1842, and then annually from 1850 to 1859, with his professional orchestra and touring virtuosi; yet only in his farewell concert in 1859 did he have Wieniawski play the Mendelssohn. This is the only example in these years of a professional orchestra playing a concerto with a major soloist.

---

70 Further on Goddard's concert career, see Therese Ellsworth, 'Victorian Pianists as Concert Artists: The Case of Arabella Goddard (1836–1922)', Chapter 7 below.

71 *BN-L*, 27 February–3 March 1778.

The concerto was usually described in the newspapers as 'solo', and it is rare to find mention of orchestral accompaniment in either advertisement or review. Concertos were not infrequently played with piano or small ensemble accompaniment. When Pauer played the 'Waldstein' sonata in 1858 a reviewer, who was not, to judge from the body of his review, an unmusical person but obviously one with limited experience of the concerto repertoire, mistook it for a concerto and declared that it lost by being unaccompanied. However, he went part of the way to redeeming himself with a useful comment: 'Of course there is always the difficulty that strangers do not decide until a late hour what they will play or sing, and rehearsals are generally out of the question'.[72]

It would seem reasonable to suppose that the orchestra accompanied in a concert when the soloist was not a visitor – May and Kerbusch when each was both conductor and soloist, Murray conducting with the local soloist Charles Dalton – since soloist and orchestra would have had the chance to rehearse together. Even this supposition is weakened by the fact that usually in the reviews the soloist is praised, on his or her own, and the orchestra is specifically praised for symphony and overture, but not in connection with the concerto. The only concerto for which accompaniment of any kind can be certain is in 1862, when Spohr's 'Dramatic' violin concerto is reported as being played by Kerbusch 'with piano accompaniment'.

The opening of the Ulster Hall in 1862 brought Belfast a capacious new concert auditorium and a musician of outstanding ability, Edmund Thomas Chipp, to play its organ and conduct the town's two principal musical societies. Chipp was able to impose his will in important areas. He conducted only two concertos, but one of them is of significance for the purposes of this survey: this was a performance in March 1864 of the Mendelssohn G minor Piano Concerto. Mrs Robinson, the soloist, was locally based, and Chipp had obviously taken the opportunity to rehearse soloist and orchestra together, to the benefit of both.[73] It was a pity that Chipp's sojourn in Belfast was to last for only three years, and that both orchestral and choral music went into a decline after he left (although there were other reasons). This performance of the Mendelssohn G minor was to remain for many years the only piano concerto, and for that matter the only one by a composer of canonic status, to have been played in the Ulster Hall.

It was an important requirement of Chipp's appointment as organist of the Ulster Hall that he should give solo recitals on the organ; it was one which he honoured, giving 57 recitals in his first season. The same obligation applied to his successor, Alfred Cellier. Concertos and concerto movements were played in these organ-based

---

72 *BN-L*, 23 April 1858.

73 The point was still of both provincial and metropolitan significance nearly 30 years later, when George Bernard Shaw wrote of a performance in London in 1891: ' ... even the artistic satisfaction must have been qualified by the impossibility of getting a good performance of a concerto out of a scratch orchestra, however well manned, with a casual conductor, however eminent. Only those orchestras which, like the Crystal Palace, the Richter, the Henschel, and the Manchester, are organized by a permanent conductor as going concerns, can achieve really good work in this department. All that could be said was that Stavenhagen was as well served as the circumstances permitted.' *Music in London 1890–94* (3 vols, London: Constable and Company, 1932), vol. i, p. 113.

concerts. They were nearly all solo performances on the organ, the organist playing the solo and taking advantage of the versatility of the organ in making his arrangement of the orchestral parts. Some of these recitals merit special notice. Chipp included Handel's Organ Concerto, op. 4 no. 2 in B♭, and later added op. 4 no. 5 in F. Cellier added, from the same opus, nos. 4 in F and 6 in B♭. Chipp also at one organ recital had Karl Liebich, who was locally based and available for rehearsal, play de Bériot's first violin concerto to Chipp's organ accompaniment. Cellier regularly introduced other singers and players at his recitals, and he and Mrs Robinson gave three performances together; the advertisement in one case specifically stated 'orchestral parts by Mr Cellier on the organ'. All three performances were noteworthy as regards repertoire. One item was the rondo finale of Beethoven's 'Emperor' concerto. The other two items were movements from Sterndale Bennett piano concertos: the Romance from no. 3 and the Barcarolle from no. 4. On the departure of Cellier from Belfast after five seasons, the Ulster Hall Company did not appoint a resident organist; thereafter, with visiting organists and visiting soloists, circumstances did not favour rehearsal of a concerto. The blight that descended on the local concert world lasted throughout the remainder of the 1860s, but it was followed by a revival. In 1874 the two major musical societies of the time – the Classical Harmonists, which was a choral society, and the Belfast Musical Society, which was instrumentally based – amalgamated to form the Philharmonic Society. Belfast entered the European concert mainstream with a single society with its own orchestra and chorus and access to a large modern concert hall.

The Belfast concertgoer, however, if starved of concertos, had been nourishingly fed in other musical areas. The soloists in the miscellaneous concerts may not have played extended compositions but they demonstrated superlative execution and musicianship. A healthy culture of concerts in small auditoria given by Chipp, Kerbusch, Mrs Robinson and others brought in the chamber music repertoire. The touring opera companies had now reached a pitch of excellence and reliability which attracted large audiences. The arrival of the Philharmonic Society, however, did nothing for the dearth of piano concertos. By then the dominant form of concert, ousting the miscellaneous concert in esteem, was the oratorio, with a large amateur chorus. Accompanying the Belfast Philharmonic oratorio performances was the prime duty of its orchestra, which was composed of amateur players with professional stiffening assembled for *Messiah* and the two or three other oratorio concerts of the season. When the orchestra came together, as it occasionally did, to play a non-oratorio concert, it played symphonies, overtures and miscellaneous items, but not concertos. The virtuosi visited, but audiences were content to hear them perform as soloists.

It was a durable musical diet. Audiences remained content with it even after the advent of gramophone recording. Edward Godfrey Brown, who had studied conducting and came to Belfast to conduct the Philharmonic Society in 1912, laboured mightily, but with slow progress, to found a Belfast symphony orchestra. But in fact taste was changing and in time a swing away from oratorio toward the orchestral repertoire set in in the provinces. It was left to Sir John Reith's BBC to make the breakthrough by equipping each of its 'regions' with a professional orchestra. That allocated to the Northern Ireland region in 1926 consisted of 17 players, but Godfrey

Brown, who had been appointed the station's director of music, could augment at will from national as well as local sources. He was encouraged also, in the interest of good public relations with the new medium, to take his orchestra out and put on public concerts. Brown seized both opportunities with a will, and in the flood of orchestral music of the 1920s and 1930s the piano concerto at last took its place, over the air and on the platform.

Chapter 3

'Most ingenious, most learned, and yet practicable work': The English Reception of Bach's *Well-Tempered Clavier* in the First Half of the Nineteenth Century seen through the Editions Published in London

Yo Tomita

In Germany Bach held unparalleled esteem and fame as a virtuoso organist and composer of keyboard works; but it was many decades before his showcase compositions such as the *Well-Tempered Clavier* penetrated into the core repertoire of keyboard music in other countries. In England, it took nearly half a century after Bach's death – a timing which roughly coincided with the publication of the first complete printed editions of the *Well-Tempered Clavier* issued by three competing publishers in mainland Europe in 1801, namely Simrock,[1] Nägeli,[2] and Hoffmeister & Kühnel[3] – to begin the process of catching up.

There were reasons for such a delay in England, which can be explained partly by unenthusiastic reactions to Bach's works expressed there, and partly as non-reaction due to the scarcity of information itself. The most symbolic is the case of Charles

---

1 Nicolaus Simrock of Bonn and his brother Henri in Paris published the *Well-Tempered Clavier* (*WTC*) II (plate number 138) between April and June 1801 as 'I Partie', followed by the *WTC* I (plate number 166). See *Allgemeine Musikalische Zeitung*, 3 (1800–1801): Intelligenz-Blatt, Nr.V, and Nägeli's letter to Breitkopf (dated 6 June 1801) reproduced in Edgar Refardt, 'Briefe Hans Georg Nägelis an Breitkopf & Härtel', *Zeitschrift für Musik*, 13/7 (1930–31): 384–400, here at p. 397.

2 Hans Georg Nägeli must have published his *WTC* I volume by August 1801, and *WTC* II by January 1802, if we trust his statements in his letters to Breitkopf that the engraving of the first volume was ready by 16 May, and the second by 9 September 1801. See Refardt, 'Briefe Hans Georg Nägelis an Breitkopf & Härtel': 397–8.

3 Franz Anton Hoffmeister of Leipzig and Ambrosius Kühnel of Vienna formed a partnership in December 1800, and jointly issued *Œuvres complettes de Jean Sebastien Bach* (1801–1804) in 16 instalments, covering most of Bach's keyboard works. The *WTC* I portion was fully published by 30 April 1802, and *WTC* II by June 1803. See Karen Lehmann, *Die Anfänge einer Bach-Gesamtausgabe 1801–1865* (Hildesheim: G. Olms, 2004), pp. 125–46.

Burney, arguably the most prominent and influential music critic of his time.[4] While he is often credited with introducing the name of J.S. Bach to his English readers, he was clearly reluctant to promote Bach's keyboard works. In his book commonly known as the 'German Tour', he describes how Carl Philipp Emanuel Bach introduced the work to him when visiting Burney at his Hamburg residence in October 1772:

> Mr Bach shewed me two manuscript books of his father's composition, written on purpose for him when he was a boy, containing pieces with a fugue, in all the twenty-four keys, extremely difficult, and generally in five parts, at which he laboured for the first years of his life, without remission.[5]

The erroneous description of the work – if these 'two manuscript books' indeed refer to parts 1 and 2 of the *Well-Tempered Clavier* – is striking. Where did these inaccuracies originate? It is almost unimaginable for Carl Philipp Emanuel to tell Burney that the majority of the fugues are in five parts when showing the music to him. It is far more likely that it was Burney who misunderstood or misinterpreted what was being said to him. It is surprising, to say the least, that Burney in fact received a manuscript copy of the work from Carl Philipp Emanuel as a gift.[6] Thus, if he so desired, he could have revised the passage in question. Burney's inaction can perhaps be best explained by his lack of interest in Bach's fugues.[7]

---

4   For a detailed discussion of Burney's changing attitudes to Bach's keyboard works, see Yo Tomita, 'The Dawn of the English Bach Awakening manifested in Sources of the "48"', in Michael Kassler (ed.), *The English Bach Awakening: Knowledge of J.S. Bach and His Music in England 1750–1830* (Aldershot: Ashgate, 2004), pp. 35–167, especially pp. 49–64.

5   Charles Burney, *The Present State of Music in Germany, the Netherlands, and United Provinces, or, the Journal of a tour through those countries, undertaken to collect materials for a General History of Music* (London: T. Becket & Co., 1773), vol. 2, p. 272.

6   It is unclear whether Burney received both volumes of *WTC* or just the first volume, and whether it was on the day when he left Hamburg in 1772 or on later occasions. In the second edition of *The Present State of Music in Germany*, vol. 2 (London: T. Becket, 1775), p. 273, he adds the following footnote: 'Since that time Mr. Bach has obliged me with several of his own and his father's most curious compositions.' In his letter to Benjamin Jacob dated 17 September 1808, Samuel Wesley reports that 'this rare Present … happens to contain only the 24 first Preludes & Fugues'. See Michael Kassler and Philip Olleson, *Samuel Wesley (1766–1837): A Source Book* (Aldershot: Ashgate, 2001), p. 241 and *The Letters of Samuel Wesley: Professional and Social Correspondence, 1797–1837*, ed. Philip Olleson (Oxford: Oxford University Press, 2001), pp. 74–8. This manuscript must be the volume offered for sale at White's auction on 12 August 1814 in lot 626 'Preludes and Fugues (24) and Fugues and Pieces – Organ and Harpsichord Studies, in score, MS'. Its current whereabouts are not known. However, Crotch later hints that Burney also possessed the *WTC* II volume around 1790. In his copy of the Wesley/Horn edition (RCM H622), Crotch writes 'Dr Burney shewed me this about 1790 & it made a deep impression on me. It is the finest of all I think!' in the bottom margin of the E major fugue of part 2. If this is correct, then it is possible that Burney possessed the *WTC* II volume until *c*.1790, but then gave it away perhaps thinking that he had a duplicate (that is, two identical copies).

7   A vivid account of Burney's delight in discovering the positive qualities of the work in 1808 can be learnt from the same Wesley letter described in n. 6 above.

As the years passed, Burney's antipathy to Bach's fugal style gradually stiffened. This is most clearly reflected in the comments he made in 1789:

> The very terms of *Canon* and *Fugue* imply restraint and labour. Handel was perhaps the only great Fughuist, exempt from pedantry. He seldom treated barren or crude subjects; his themes being almost always natural and pleasing. Sebastian Bach, on the contrary, like Michael Angelo in painting, disdained facility so much, that his genius never stooped to the easy and graceful. I never have seen a fugue by this learned and powerful author upon a *motivo*, that is natural and *chantant*; or even an easy and obvious passage, that is not loaded with crude and difficult accompaniments.[8]

Perhaps this statement was only meant to praise Handel, a Royal composer and the favourite of the king, George III, and therefore it may not have been Burney's intention to tarnish Bach's reputation as the composer of fugues. Still, this was the unfortunate consequence of Burney's careless judgement when few people knew about Bach and his works in England.

A.F.C. Kollmann: The First Apostle of Bach in England

So far as I have been able to find, it was A.F.C. Kollmann, a German immigrant, who took the first positive step to publicize the *Well-Tempered Clavier* in England, in his treatise *An Essay on Practical Musical Composition* of 1799. Kollmann knew Burney, as well as his views on Bach's fugues.[9] Having dealt carefully with the thorny issue of the fugal styles of Bach and Handel earlier in this book,[10] he introduces the *Well-Tempered Clavier* to his English audience towards the end of the book in the following manner:

> The three particulars mentioned above in § 18 [organ sounds and their continuance with equal strength], 19 [the temperament of the scale], and 20 [the construction of its fingerboard, which is applicable in every key], have been attended to in *Sebastian Bach*'s work, entitled *Wohl temperirtes, Clavier*, (well tempered Harpsichord, or Keyed Instrument in general,) consisting of twice twenty[-]four Preludes and Fugues, or two in every major and minor Key. Every Prelude and Fugue may be considered as a Sonata of two Movements, each of which can be used as a piece by itself. *This most ingenious, most learned, and yet practicable work, is so highly esteemed by all who can judge of it, that as it is grown scarce, I intend to offer it to the public analyzed.* The first Prelude and Fugue of it, see at Plate LII, & *seq.*[11]

---

8   Charles Burney, *A General History of Music, from the Earliest Ages to the Present Period* (4 vols, London: Printed for the author, 1789), vol. 3, p. 110.

9   Kollmann dedicated his earlier work, *An Essay on Musical Harmony* (London, 1796), to Burney. On this occasion, however, Kollmann did not quote Bach's 'learned' fugues from the *WTC* but the F minor prelude from part 2.

10   A.F.C. Kollmann, *An Essay on Practical Musical Composition* (London: Printed for the author, 1799), p. 27 and p. 55. See Tomita, 'The Dawn of the English Bach Awakening manifested in Sources of the "48"', p. 113, for further discussion of this point.

11   Kollmann, *An Essay on Practical Musical Composition*, pp. 97–8 (my italics). This edition was apparently prepared from a manuscript copy of the work now held at the St

The penultimate sentence, in italics in the quotation above, was a concise but carefully worded rebuttal of the view of Bach's works commonly held in England at the time. By 'ingenious', Kollmann hints that Bach's compositions are intellectual in conception, showing the evidence of inventiveness and originality, whereas with 'learned' he appreciates in a positive light Bach's compositional skills as well as knowledge of various styles and techniques; and finally with 'practicable', he seems to be claiming that Bach's fugues can be used effectively in both teaching and performance, which he commends to the public unreservedly. While the topic of this debate is remarkably similar to the Scheibe–Birnbaum dispute of 1737–8,[12] the setting is very different: a senior but naïve and careless accuser versus a junior but both careful and knowledgeable defender, which, unlike the Scheibe–Birnbaum case, apparently sparked no further dispute. To add weight of conviction to his argument, Kollmann proposes to publish the *Well-Tempered Clavier* in an analysed form, so that his readers can judge how the ingenuities and the learned style of composition may be fully appreciated. As we shall see, these three aspects of the *Well-Tempered Clavier* that Kollmann identified – the ingenious, learned yet practicable – were explored by his followers almost immediately.

Meanwhile, the news of Kollmann's pre-publication announcement of his edition of the *Well-Tempered Clavier* spread quickly in Germany, spurred by Johann Nicolaus Forkel, who reported it in the *Allgemeine Musikalische Zeitung* of 2 October 1799.[13] There are some grounds for speculation that Kollmann's gesture caused a stir in Germany, effectively increasing the sense of obligation and urgency in publishing German editions of the *Well-Tempered Clavier*, which in turn caused Kollmann to give up publishing his own edition, as he explained later that the printed copies from the Continent quickly reached English soil in large quantity.[14] Yet Kollmann's effort to sow the seeds of interest in the *Well-Tempered Clavier* in England had its effect on English musicians who read his book, and we can recognize today the fulfilment of his role as the first apostle of Bach in England. Among his followers was Samuel Wesley, whose first encounter with the music of Bach, according to Wesley's daughter Eliza, was through the publications of Kollmann and Diettenhofer; this presumably refers to Kollmann's treatise cited above and Diettenhofer's edition of miscellaneous fugues published in 1802 (discussed below).[15] Wesley's significant contributions to the promotion of Bach's works in England have been discussed in depth in recent years by both Michael Kassler and Philip Olleson, who successfully identified numerous references in which Wesley discusses Bach and his music.[16]

Andrews University Library, shelfmark MS M24.B2.

12 See *The New Bach Reader: A Life of Johann Sebastian Bach in Letters and Documents*, ed. Hans T. David and Arthur Mendel, rev. and enlarged by Christoph Wolff (New York: W.W. Norton & Company, 1998), pp. 337–53.

13 *Allgemeine Musikalische Zeitung*, 7/1 (2 October 1799): 6–7, repeated in 2/5 (30 October 1799): 104; see also *Quarterly Musical Register*, 1 (1812): 29.

14 *Quarterly Musical Register*, 1 (1812): 30.

15 See C.W. Pearce, 'Wesley and Horn editions of Bach' [letter to the editor], *Musical Times*, 67 (1926): 544.

16 Kassler and Olleson, *Samuel Wesley (1766–1837): A Source Book*, especially p. 78f.; Philip Olleson, 'Samuel Wesley and the English Bach Awakening', *The English Bach*

Another Bach convert owing his knowledge to Kollmann was James William Windsor, whose name is found as one of 103 subscribers to Kollmann's 1799 *Essay on Practical Musical Composition* as 'Mr J. Windsor, Organist of St. Margaret's Chapel, Bath'. Two years after its publication, Windsor copied the entire work very neatly and carefully, and inscribed 'J. W. Windsor | Nov[r] 30 | 1801 | Bath' on the inside front cover of the manuscript.[17] Textually, this is a very curious source, for Windsor's manuscript was copied from the manuscript that is not related closely to any known surviving copies of the work.[18] Since the paper was made in England,[19] it must have been copied from the manuscript possibly of German origin that is now lost. More important, however, are the other circumstantial aspects of the source that seem to reveal a fair reflection of the English reception of Bach the composer, and his work, to which I shall now turn.

A Case Study: J.W. Windsor's Awakening to Bach

James William Windsor was born in London in 1776 and died in 1853 in Bath, where his reputation seems to have been established as an able pianist before the age of twenty.[20] He was nicknamed 'The Harmonious Blacksmith', apparently because of his frequent performances of the air and variations from Handel's suite in E major.[21] From the fact that he subscribed to Kollmann's 1799 treatise, he must have been a keen student of music as well as a practitioner. He was also listed as a subscriber to Wesley and Horn's edition of the *Well-Tempered Clavier* published in 1810, and, as I have demonstrated elsewhere,[22] he most probably communicated with Samuel Wesley about textual matters concerning his edition in a sensible and

---

Awakening, pp. 251–313.

17 The manuscript is now held at the Royal College of Music, London, shelfmark MS 743.

18 Its textual origin can be traced to some extent to J.C. Altnickol's copy of 1755, held in the Staatsbibliothek zu Berlin Preußischer Kulturbesitz, shelfmark Mus. ms. Bach P 402.

19 Contrary to what I reported earlier in 'The Dawn of the English Bach Awakening manifested in Sources of the "48"', p. 125, my more recent study of the manuscript reveals that the paper was not made by Whatman, but is a mixture of several laid papers by John Taylor (watermark 'ITAYLOR'), Edmeads & Pine (watermark 'EDMEADS & PINE' and stylised 'E & P' in script form), and possibly William Elgar (watermark 'W E'). Other marks identified include part of strasburg shields, fleur-de-lis, and year of manufacture '1794', '1796' and '1798'. The flyleaf is wove paper, bearing the watermark 'WS', initial of either William Slade or William Sharp. According to Alfred H. Shorter, *Paper Mills and Paper Makers in England, 1495–1800* (Hilversum: Paper Publications Society, 1957), p. 349, the date of these marks falls in 1786 and 1789 respectively.

20 For a fuller biographical account, see Tomita, 'The Dawn of the English Bach Awakening manifested in Sources of the "48"', pp. 122ff.

21 Kenneth James, 'Concert Life in Eighteenth-Century Bath' (PhD diss., University of London, 1987), p. 649.

22 Yo Tomita, 'Pursuit of Perfection: Revisions of the Wesley/Horn "48"', in *The English Bach Awakening*, pp. 341–77, here at pp. 272–3.

modest manner.[23] In a letter dated 1824 he was described as 'the very accomplished Professor of the Piano-Forte'.[24]

When Windsor made his own copy of the *Well-Tempered Clavier* in 1801, he was 25 years old. His interest in the work must have been related to his professional career as a pianist, for it appears that he did not know much about Bach, as one learns from the following note (see also Fig. 3.1) that he wrote on the flyleaf of the manuscript:

Sebastian Bach was contemporary with Handel

John Sebastian Bach was born, March 21–1685, at Eisenach in Upper Saxony — Died, July 30 – 1750. In the 66th year of his age.

George Frederic Handel was born, Feb:ʸ 24 – 1684 at Halle in Lower Saxony — Died, April 13 – 1759. In the 76th year of his age.

The young Practitioner when sitting down to the study of this masterly work should recollect the <u>Instruments</u> in vogue at the time it was written, namely, the Organ and Harpsichord, only the Piano Forte not then being invented! Consequently the Effects producible from the last named Instrument are not to be expected in the performance of these admirable compositions. Nothing more being required than an equable tone on the P_F_ and a clear and clean execution on the part of the Performer. In order to the right understanding of the complicated and elaborate style of Fugue writing to the Auditor.

The manner in which Bach is put alongside Handel in this historical context seems to confirm that Windsor's interest in Bach's music stemmed from his interest in Handel's music, which he must have known very well. One cannot help but notice, however, that the biographical details of both composers are somewhat erroneous.[25]

23 See Kassler and Olleson, *Samuel Wesley (1766–1837): A Source Book*, p. 328.

24 Philip H. Highfill, Jr, Kalman A. Burnim and Edward A. Langhans, 'Windsor, William' in *A Biographical Dictionary of Actors, Actresses, Musicians, Dancers, Managers & Other Stage Personnel in London, 1660–1800* (16 vols, Carbondale: Southern Illinois University Press, 1973–1993), vol. 16, pp. 182–3. Windsor's letter is in the Sainsbury & Co. manuscripts at Glasgow University Library.

25 Handel was born on 23 February 1685 and died on 14 April 1759. The erroneous year of Handel's birth as 1684 originated in John Mainwaring, *Memoirs of the Life of the Late George Frederick Handel* (London: R. & J. Dodsley, 1760); I do not know where Windsor found the date '[Feb.] 24'. The wrong date of Handel's death, '13 [April]', derives from Burney. See Percy A. Scholes, *The Great Dr Burney: His Life, his Travels, his Works, his Family and his Friends* (2 vols, London: Oxford University Press, 1948), vol. 2, pp. 74–5. The date of Bach's death was 28 July 1750; 30 July was the day Bach was buried (Werner Neumann and Hans-Joachim Schulze (eds), *Fremdschriftliche und gedruckte Dokumente zur Lebensgeschichte Johann Sebastian Bachs, 1685–1750. Bach Dokumente* II (Kassel: Bärenreiter, 1969), nos. 609 and 611). The obituary published in 1754 gives the date of his death as 28 July, while Forkel (1802) gives the date erroneously as 30 July, which may have been the ultimate source of information for Windsor.

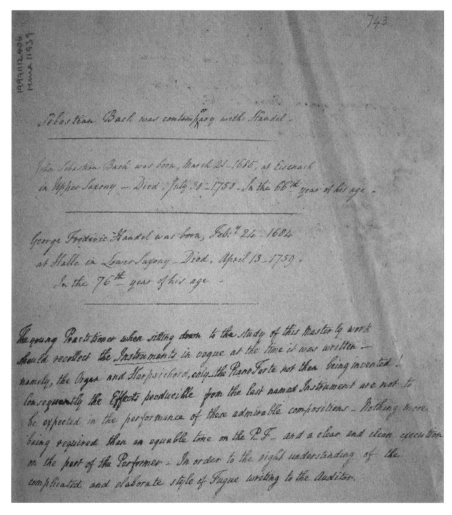

Figure 3.1 J.W. Windsor's Memoranda written on page 1 of the flyleaf in his copy of the *Well-Tempered Clavier*

As for the date of Bach's death, the accurate information – 28 July 1750 – was not readily available to the early English biographers of Bach at the time, namely Hawkins,[26] Heck[27] and Burney.[28] As late as November 1808 Crotch had asked Samuel Wesley for this information, but the latter was unable to answer at the time.[29]

Immediately below this memorandum, a longer, expanded note was inscribed, in a different style of handwriting and a darker shade of ink, which is clearly a later addition. On the reverse side of the flyleaf, the sources for these notes were recorded:

> For remarks on Sebastian Bach's Style[,] see the Preface to D[r] Crotch's "Specimens of Various Styles of Music["] in Three volumes, London, Birchall. Vol: 1. [*sic*] and D[r] Crotch's Lectures on Music.

> Also "Life of John Sebastian Bach: with a Critical View of his Compositions["]. By J. N. Forkel. Author of the Complete History of Music, &c, &c, London, Boosey & C° 1820.

From the references mentioned – William Crotch's *Specimens of Various Styles of Music* (London, 1807–1809), 'Dr Crotch's Lectures on Music', which presumably refers to *Substance of Several Courses of Lectures on Music* (London, 1831) and Forkel's *Life of John Sebastian Bach: With a Critical View of his Compositions* (London, 1820) – it is clear that this page was written after 1820, possibly by Windsor in his forties or even fifties. The correspondence of contents between the first two sentences on the first page of this flyleaf and the cited literature on the second page confirms that the first sentence was taken from Crotch's *Specimens*, published in 1809,[30] and the second – containing the erroneous information about the date of Bach's death as 30 July – from Forkel.[31] The way this memorandum is formulated is interesting, for it seems to offer some clues for understanding how both Crotch and Windsor collected information about Bach. Clearly, Crotch was unable to obtain Bach's dates of birth and death by the time of this publication (as no one, including Wesley, seems to have been able to help), and while Windsor had access to the English translation of Forkel's biography he started his memorandum with Crotch's opening sentence about Bach's biographical note, suggesting not only how much

---

26 John Hawkins, *A General History of the Science and Practice of Music* (5 vols, London: T. Payne and Son, 1776), vol. 5, pp. 254–8.

27 John Casper Heck, *The Musical Library and Universal Magazine of Harmony* (London, *c*.1780), pp. 15–19.

28 Burney, *The Present State of Music in Germany*, p. 80. Burney's article on Bach in Rees's *Cyclopaedia* (London, 1804) still incorrectly had 1754 as the year of Bach's death.

29 This can be learnt from Samuel Wesley's reply of 25 November 1808 (see Olleson (ed.), *The Letters of Samuel Wesley*, pp. 89–91; Kassler and Olleson, *Samuel Wesley (1766–1837): A Source Book*, pp. 246–7) to Crotch's letter (not preserved).

30 William Crotch, *Specimens of Various Styles of Music* (3 vols, London: R. Birchall, 1807–1809), vol. 3, p. i.

31 J.N. Forkel, *Life of John Sebastian Bach*, trans. B. Stephenson (London: T. Boosey & Co., 1820), p. 7 and pp. 17–18; See also *The New Bach Reader: A Life of Johann Sebastian Bach in Letters and Documents*, ed. Hans T. David and Arthur Mendel, rev. and enlarged by Christoph Wolff (New York: W.W. Norton & Company, 1998), p. 425 and p. 430.

Figure 3.2   J.W. Windsor's Memorandum written on the last page of his copy of the *Well-Tempered Clavier*

respect he had for Crotch at the time as a scholar, but also how little was known about Bach in England then. As for the remainder of the text on the first page of the flyleaf, I have so far been unable to find its source: it could well have originated with Windsor,[32] especially since the authoritative tone of his writing conforms well to the image of a mature professor of piano.

What is more striking, however, is a further memorandum written at the end of the volume, in the remaining space after the final fugue of part 2, and reproduced in Fig. 3.2. As transcribed below, it is a full citation of Crotch's commentary on the style of Bach's fugues given in the preface of the *Specimens of Various Styles of Music*, volume 3:

> Sebastian Bach was contemporary with Handel. His most celebrated productions are organ fugues, very difficult of execution; profoundly learned, and highly ingenious. The prevailing style of these compositions is the Sublime; sometimes a mixture of the Sublime & Ornamental; but the Beautiful also occasionally appears as will be fully seen in the *ninth fugue of this second set*.[33] The student should be careful not to form a hasty judgment of his character as the riches of his learning are not scatter[e]d superficially, but lie too deeply buried to be immediately perceived. In the management of a strict fugue he stands unrivalled, and he seems to be the most scientific of all composers.
>
> Extract from the Preface to the 3rd Vol: of Dr Crotch's Specimens of Music.

Since there is nothing else to suggest that Windsor disagreed with Crotch's view, one must assume that Windsor, a keen student of music, considered Crotch's aesthetic judgement helpful to an understanding and appreciation of Bach's fugal style.

Crotch was a very influential scholar who appreciated Bach's fundamental attitudes to composition. As Bennett Zon observes, Crotch held to his belief that 'the composer must not write down to please his audience, but must remain true to his inspiration, despite the consequences', which helped Bach to achieve such a refined taste.[34] It seems significant that here Crotch refers to the three positive qualities of Bach's fugues that Kollmann described earlier, namely, 'most ingenious, most learned and yet practicable' in reverse order: 'very difficult of execution', 'profoundly learned' and 'highly ingenious'.[35] Even though Crotch emphasises the degree of practicability as a formidable barrier, the shift in attitudes towards musical appreciation since the day of Burney is significant, and must be seen as one vital step forward to accommodating

---

32 In *Substance of Several Courses of Lectures on Music* (London: Longman, Rees, Orme, Brown & Green, 1831), p. 115, for example, Crotch posits that the *Well-Tempered Clavier* was written for Clavichord, and not Harpsichord or Organ (as Windsor claims here).

33 The words marked in italics (my emphasis) were presumably substituted by Windsor for 'specimens given in this volume'.

34 Bennett Zon, *Music and Metaphor in Nineteenth-Century British Musicology* (Aldershot: Ashgate, 2000), pp. 25–6.

35 Crotch's knowledge of Kollmann's 1799 publication is not disputed. Howard Irving argues, for example, that Crotch quietly attacks Kollmann's unreasonable discussion of Haydn's harmonic language in one of his lectures (Norfolk Record Office, MS 11231/6). See Howard Irving, *Ancients and Moderns: William Crotch and the Development of Classical Music* (Aldershot: Ashgate, 1999), p. 190.

Bach's fugues as an object of musical study. One ought to remember, however, that this extract was entered here in Windsor's copy at least seven years after the copy was made. During these years, he perhaps found no other information that was worthwhile adding to his precious copy, a possibility that is equally revealing.

Meanwhile, Windsor's sustained interest in Bach's music led him to subscribe to the Wesley/Horn edition of the *Well-Tempered Clavier*.[36] Our observation of Windsor's manuscript so far has revealed a number of issues that can be considered important when trying to understand how the *Well-Tempered Clavier* became better known in England. In the remainder of this chapter, I shall look at how and in what form the work was disseminated and how the public interacted with it, primarily through a survey of the editions printed in London, so that the case of Windsor may be put into a broader historical context. For the following discussion, readers are asked to refer to Tables 3.1–3.5 and Figs 3.3–3.6, where the editions of the *Well-Tempered Clavier* produced in England between 1800 and 1850 are described briefly and grouped according to the modes of reception.[37]

Complete Editions

Perhaps the most visible aspect of the *Well-Tempered Clavier* that can be considered distinct or unique is the fact that Bach explored in this work all the 24 keys. In order for the work to gain 'canonic' status in the nineteenth century, it was important that it be available in a complete printed edition. This course of events took place on the Continent, where the work had already been well known, and when the edition appeared it was quickly imported into London. As we shall see, all the early English editions were based on one of three continental editions – namely, Simrock, Nägeli, and Hoffmeister & Kühnel – which were all laid out in oblong format without any editorial additions such as performance directions and fingering, the features that were transformed by the time Carl Czerny published his edition with C.F. Peters in 1837. A list of editions discussed in this section is given in Table 3.1, and Fig. 3.3 shows how these editions are textually related. It will also be demonstrated that while the English editions were usually on the receiving end of information, there

---

36 Windsor's decision to subscribe to the Wesley/Horn edition may well be influenced by the acknowledgement Crotch gives to Wesley in a footnote of the quoted paragraph, which reads: 'The public will be happy to hear that the life and several works of this great composer will shortly be published by Mr. Horn and Mr. Samuel Wesley; to the latter, I am much indebted for the use of his valuable and correct manuscript copy of the above work.' I believe the copy of the Wesley/Horn edition now held at the William F. Maag Library of the Youngstown State University, Ohio (shelfmark M38.B32) was once owned by Windsor, because it also contains the near-identical passages from Crotch's 1809 book except for some changes to the isolated phrase referred to in n. 33, which reads 'ninth fugue of the second set. (The 33rd).' inscribed by the hand that matches closely with that in the RCM MS 743. For further discussion on this copy, see Tomita, 'Pursuit of Perfection: Revisions of the Wesley/Horn "48"', p. 346.

37 The chronological information of 1800–1830 in Tables 3.1, 3.3–3.5 and Fig. 3.3 is taken from 'Chronology of the English Bach Awakening' in *The English Bach Awakening: Knowledge of J.S. Bach and his Music in England 1750–1830*, ed. Michael Kassler (Aldershot: Ashgate, 2004), pp. 12–32.

Table 3.1   Complete Editions of the *Well-Tempered Clavier*

Date	Publisher	Editor(s)	Notes
6.1802	Broderip & Wilkinson	anon.	Book I ('1. Partie') containing nos.1–12 of part 2 only. Musical text is based on the Simrock edition. The Riemenschneider copy (Kenney 2462) bears watermark '1801' and 'R G' [or 'G R'].
11.1808			Book II ('II. Partie') containing the remainder of part 2 starting with a duplicate of fugue no.12 (but freshly engraved); they also sell the reprint of Book I. The copies examined bear watermarks '1807' and '1808'.
c.1810	T. Preston	anon.	Preston buys the engraved plates of Broderip & Wilkinson and reprints the edition of part 2 in two books. The copies examined bear watermarks '1809', '1811' and '1813'.
4.1811	L. Lavenu	anon.	Issued in two books containing all the 48 preludes and fugues; musical text is based on the Nägeli edition. The BL copy (R.M.15.g.13) bears the watermark '1807'. The publisher's address was given as '26 New Bond Street'.
(1816) (1824)			It appears to have been reissued, as the Riemenschneider copy (Kenney 2467) bears later watermark '1816'. Another copy bears watermark '1821' with the publisher's address '24. Edward Street', clearly a later reissue. My copy bears watermark of a clover with 'J C' and '1829' below.
9.1810	R. Birchall	S. Wesley & C.F. Horn	Book I (nos.1–12 of part 1). No watermark. This issue lists 144 names of subscribers.
5.1811			Book II (nos.13–24 of part 1). No watermark. Around this time, a slightly revised Book I was issued with 152 names of subscribers.
12.1811			Book III (nos.1–12 of part 2). Watermark '1811' and 'S'
7.1813			Book IV (nos.12–24 of part 2). Watermark '1812'

Date	Publisher	Editor	Notes
(c.1819)			Birchall reissues the Wesley/Horn edition of the '48' with minor amendments to both title-page and musical text. Watermarks '1817' and [1819] in the copies examined.
(c.1824)			A minor correction was made to the title-page, changing the publisher's address from '133' to '140 New Bond Street'. Watermarks '1824' and '1827'
1818–19	T. Boosey & Co.	[J.N. Forkel]	Boosey imports copies of the C.F. Peters' edition of parts 1 and 2 of the '48' and sell this with only the title-page altered.
c.1834	C. Lonsdale	S. Wesley & C.F. Horn	Lonsdale succeeded the business of Birchall, and sold the Wesley/Horn edition with newly designed title-page.
(c.1845)			Lonsdale reissued the same with a slightly modified title-page.
c.1837	Coventry & Hollier	anon.	Succeeds the Preston firm, and sells the edition of part 2 using the Broderip & Wilkinson plates. Fg.f is not duplicated this time, however. The Riemenschneider copy (Kenney 2464) gives no watermark
1838	R. Cocks & Co.	C. Czerny	Based on the C.F. Peters 1837 with the publisher's address '20 Princes Street, Hanover Square' (University of Edinburgh, Reid Music Library, Accession number D2193)
(1845)			A revised edition (by an unnamed editor) with a different publisher's address, '6 New Burlington Street', appeared after 1845 (Kenney 2397)
(1848)			Another reissue with 'revised by John Bishop of Cheltenham' by 'Robert Cocks & Co. New Burlington Street' appeared after 1848 (Kenney 2408)
1839	[L.H. Lavenu]	C. Potter	It uses L. Lavenu's old plates, and adds some performance directions, fingerings and analytical icons similar to the Wesley/Horn up to Fg.d of part 1. No copy of 1839 is located. The Riemenschneider copy (Kenney 2436) is a reprint of 1845.
(1845)	Addison & Hodson		
c.1850	Chappell & Co.	C. Hallé	Publisher's address is given as '50 New Bond Street'. Sold as piece but based on Czerny[R].

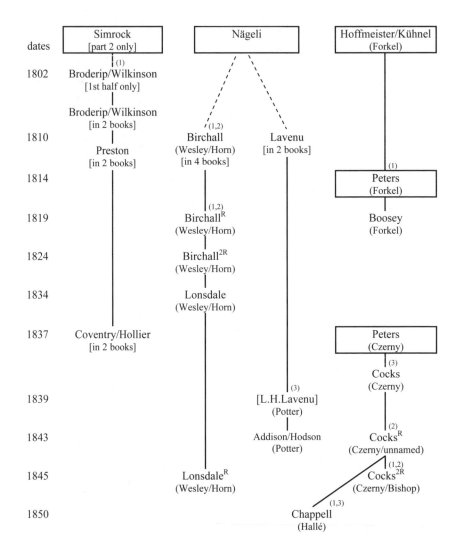

Figure 3.3   Diagram showing the Genealogy of the English Editions of the ***Well-Tempered Clavier*** **in relation to the Imported Editions shown in the box**

was at least one occasion when they introduced new features affecting the German editions.

It is difficult to estimate how many copies were imported and sold initially in London. Although we learn from Kollmann's recollection in 1812 that 'numerous copies of the three first editions were imported in England',[38] Wesley's observation that by April 1808 they 'are now become exceedingly scarce in England, & almost unattainable' seems to indicate that the *Well-Tempered Clavier* was not in great demand at that time.[39] From my own survey of the London auctions of musical libraries in the nineteenth century, the London market for imported copies of the *Well-Tempered Clavier* appears to have been dominated by the Nägeli edition.[40] The surviving Wesley documents give the same picture; there I find no hint of either the Simrock or Hoffmeister editions that Wesley knew.[41]

The first English edition of the *Well-Tempered Clavier*, which contained the first half of part 2 only, was issued by Broderip & Wilkinson in June 1802.[42] As shown in Fig. 3.4, the title-page as well as music engraving was clearly modelled on the Simrock edition, including the dedication to the Paris Conservatoire, and, as was common with the other Continental editions of the work, the presentation of music was in oblong format and without any editorial additions such as performance directions.[43] This London edition does not appear to have sold well, however. Besides the fact that the first imprint of this edition survives with a single specimen, that it took six years for the publisher to issue Book II containing the second half of part 2 of the *Well-Tempered Clavier* can mean only one thing: poor business performance. They never

---

38 *Quarterly Musical Register*, 1 (1812): 30. Kollmann was referring to the Simrock, Nägeli and Hoffmeister editions.

39 Letters from Wesley to Burney dated 14 April 1808, reproduced in Olleson (ed.), *The Letters of Samuel Wesley*, pp. 59–61; Kassler and Olleson, *Samuel Wesley (1766–1837): A Source Book*, pp. 233–4. See also Samuel J. Rogal, 'For the love of Bach: the Charles Burney–Samuel Wesley correspondence', *Bach*, 23/1 (1992): 35. The scarcity of the copies of *WTC* can also be explained from the sudden increase of sales as a direct result of Wesley's promotional activities around that time. However, there is no proof, as far as I am aware, that either theory is more credible than the other.

40 In the auction sale catalogues that I examined of English musical libraries auctioned between 1800 and 1855, 17 contained the editions of the *WTC*. Of these, the Nägeli edition appeared five times and the Hoffmeister/Kühnel once only. The Simrock edition did not appear at all.

41 See Tomita, 'The Dawn of the English Bach Awakening manifested in Sources of the "48"', pp. 146–51.

42 The date of publication is ascertained by its advertisement in the *Times* (14 June 1802) as 'NEW PIANO FORTE MUSIC – Just printed' and the watermark of the edition held at the Riemenschneider Bach Institute (Kenney 2462): '1801' and 'G R' [or 'R G']. See M. Kassler, 'Broderip, Wilkinson and the first English edition of the "48"', *Musical Times*, 147 (2006): 67–76.

43 I am not aware of any archival record showing business dealings between the two publishers, and thus it is unclear if Broderip & Wilkinson received authorization from Simrock to sell their edition in England in this manner. Simrock's *WTC* II volume was the first to appear in print, ahead of the *WTC* I volumes by Nägeli or Hoffmeister & Kühnel. See also nn. 1, 2, and 3 above.

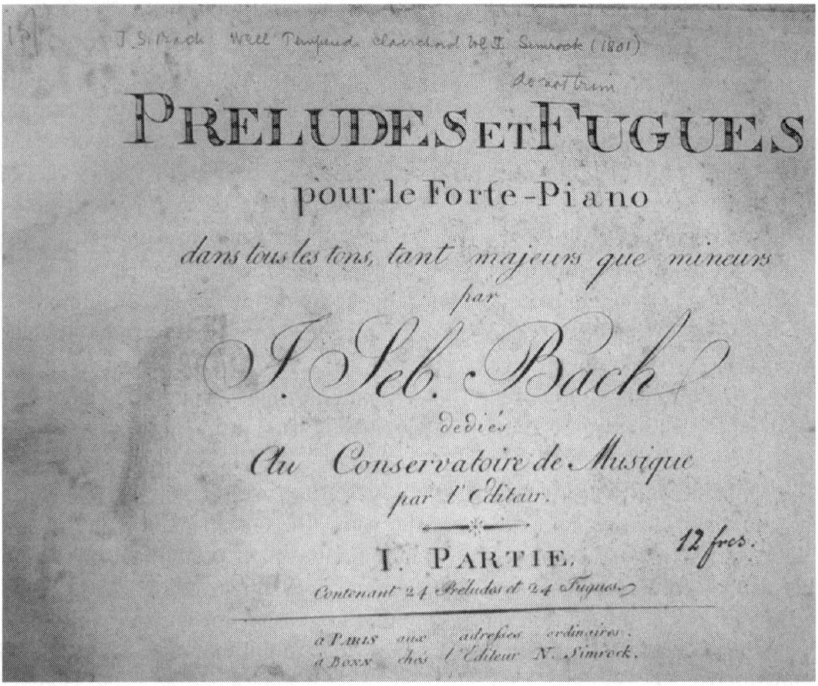

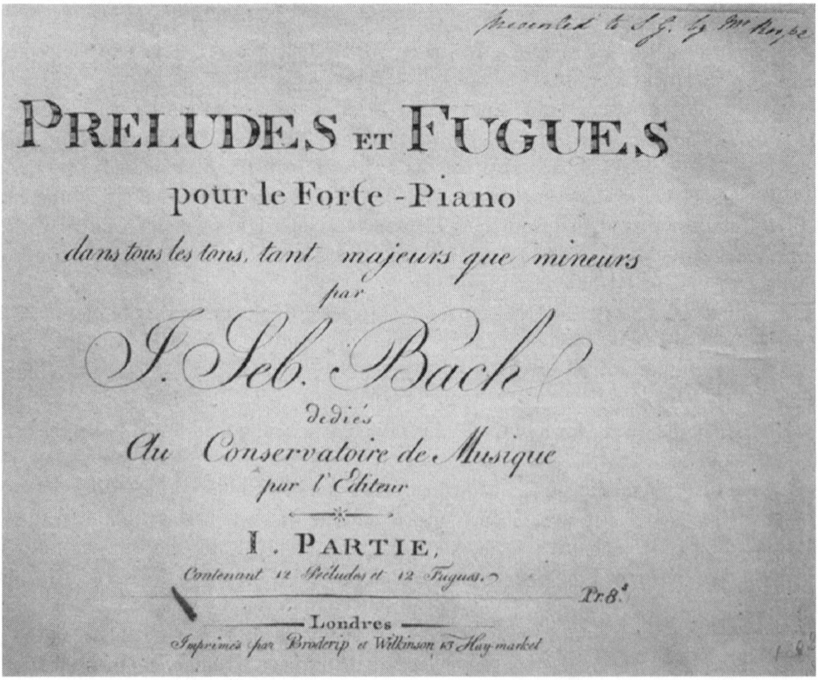

Figure 3.4   Title-pages of the Simrock (above) and Broderip/Wilkinson
              (below) Editions

came round to publishing part 1. Still, Crotch apparently owned a 'Book I' copy of this edition when he contacted Wesley for his advice on textual matters in late 1808 in conjunction with his work on the third volume of the *Specimens of Various Styles of Music*, in which he printed the E major fugue from part 2.[44] From their communication, we learn Wesley's view that the textual quality of the Broderip & Wilkinson edition was appalling. The firm Broderip & Wilkinson changed their name to Wilkinson & Co. in January 1808,[45] and later that year they issued the second half of part 2 of the *Well-Tempered Clavier*.[46] The business was then in turmoil, and in the 25 August 1809 issue of the *Times* they advertised the sale of their stock at half price. Their business was eventually taken over by Thomas Preston in January 1811,[47] and again by Coventry & Hollier in 1837, who respectively reprinted this ill-fated edition.

From the surviving letters, we know that Wesley and Horn started working on their edition by October 1808 using the Nägeli edition as their model, the text they considered most reliable. But unlike their forerunner, they rigorously examined the text. The phrase 'new and correct edition' engraved on the title-page (see Fig. 3.5, upper image) reflects their pride and enthusiasm for this publication project. In effect, they fulfilled Kollmann's dream of publishing the edition with analysis, setting a new model for publishing fugues.[48] This became the trademark of the English approach to annotating fugues; the idea was replicated by Cipriani Potter (1838f.) and even in Germany by Jean André (1846).[49] There is another innovative feature for which Wesley and Horn can claim to have set a new standard of publishing Bach's *Well-Tempered Clavier*: their instructive 'introduction', where they explained how to practise the pieces and stressed the importance of an analytical approach to the study of fugues.[50] The Wesley/Horn edition was reissued many times up to 1845.[51] The frequent appearance of this edition in the auction sales of musical libraries also

---

44 For the Wesley letter, see Olleson (ed.), *The Letters of Samuel Wesley*, pp. 89–91. See also n. 36 above and Tomita, 'The Dawn of the English Bach Awakening manifested in Sources of the "48"', pp. 141f.

45 See *Music Entries at Stationers' Hall, 1710–1818*, ed. Michael Kassler (Aldershot: Ashgate, 2004), p. xx. Broderip & Wilkinson's last entry at Stationers' Hall was made on 1 January 1808; Wilkinson & Co.'s first entry was on 1 February 1808.

46 The date of publication is deduced from the reference to this edition in Samuel Wesley's letter to William Crotch of 25 November 1808 (see Olleson (ed.), *The Letters of Samuel Wesley*, pp. 89–91) and the watermark '1807' and '1808' in the extant copies of this edition.

47 *Musical Publications selected from the Catalogue published by Broderip and Wilkinson, lately purchased, and now printed and sold by Preston ... No. 97, Strand, and Exeter 'Change, London* (copy at BL Hirsch IV 1113 (10)). This advertisement lists on p. 4, under the heading 'Voluntaries', 'Bach's (Sebastian) 1st Set Fugues [£] 0 8 0' and '— 2d Ditto [£] 0 8 0'.

48 Examples of this are given in Tomita, 'Samuel Wesley as Analyst of Bach's Fugues', in *The English Bach Awakening*, p. 402, n. 36.

49 For further details of these editions, see ibid., p. 380.

50 For further discussion of this topic, see ibid., pp. 379ff.

51 See further Tomita, 'Pursuit of Perfection: Stages of Revision of the Wesley/Horn "48"', in *The English Bach Awakening*, pp. 341–77.

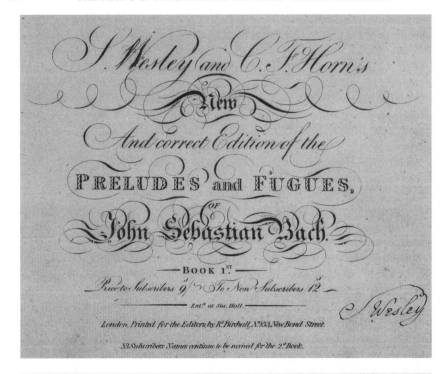

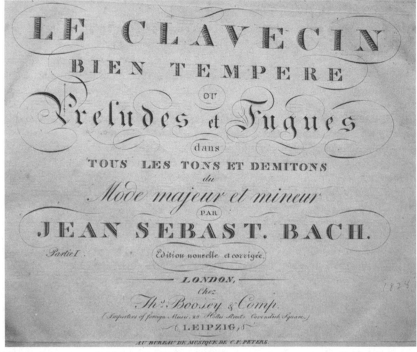

Figure 3.5   Title-pages of the Birchall (above) and Boosey (below) Editions

testifies that the Wesley/Horn edition was the most popular choice in England for much of the first half of the nineteenth century.

Published around the same time as the Wesley/Horn edition was the Lavenu edition. It was a straightforward re-engraving of the Nägeli edition, and thus the musical presentation is just as plain as the Broderip/Wilkinson. Judging from a fairly good number of copies that survive with their watermarks ranging from 1807 to 1829, it is strange, to say the least, that there is no mention of this edition in Wesley's surviving letters. In 1839, Lavenu's plates were reused in Potter's edition mentioned above, as Fig. 3.6 shows.[52] The remaining edition brought from the Continent is Hoffmeister & Kühnel,[53] which was edited by Forkel. His edition of the *Well-Tempered Clavier* was part of a bigger publication project of Bach's complete keyboard works, and while it was presumably imported into England it was not until around 1819 that Thomas Boosey was appointed as their official agent in London to promote this edition (see Fig. 3.5, lower image).[54] Crotch apparently owned an edition published in Leipzig as well, but it is unclear whether it was the one imported by Boosey or one of the earlier variants of this edition.[55] There are also other contemporary editions such as that issued by Breitkopf in around 1819 (which is virtually a revised edition of Simrock); but they do not appear to have been circulated very much in London.

The real change of scene was brought about by Hoffmeister & Kühnel's successor, C.F. Peters, with their second attempt in 1837 to publish Bach's complete keyboard works (which they called *Œuvres complets*), this time with Carl Czerny as their editor. It is the first Continental edition to include a one-page preface in two languages, German and French, in which the editor stresses how carefully the text was prepared, how one should practise, and what extra information the editor supplied for the benefit of the performer as regards the tempo and style, and how the performer should interpret the music. While these issues might be somewhat familiar if one knew the Wesley/Horn edition, Czerny offered two new features: fingering and performance directions – not only dynamics, phrasing and articulation marks but also

---

52 According to Charles Humphries and William C. Smith, *Music Publishing in the British Isles from the Beginning until the Middle of the Nineteenth Century* (Oxford: Basil Blackwell, 1970), p. 206, Potter's publishers, Addison and Hodson, took over the business of Louis Henry Lavenu (presumably the son of Lewis Lavenu (which had succeeded in *c.*1839 the business of Mori and Lavenu, *c.*1828–39), in 1844. This implies that Potter's first edition was issued in 1839 by L.H. Lavenu. No copy of this edition is known to have survived.

53 The partnership of Hoffmeister & Kühnel was split up on 2 January 1805, and the latter took on the business as 'Bureau de Musique, A. Kühnel' from 6 March 1806. After Kühnel's death in 1813, Carl Friedrich Peters bought the business under the name 'Bureau de Musique von C.F. Peters'. See *The Forkel-Hoffmeister & Kühnel Correspondence: A Document of the Early 19th-Century Bach Revival*, ed. George Stauffer (New York: C.F. Peters, 1990), p. xi and Karen Lehmann, *Die Anfänge einer Bach-Gesamtausgabe 1801–1865*, p. 66.

54 The earliest advertisement I have found so far is the *Times*, 3 August 1819, which reads 'New Classical Music for Pianoforte, Violin, Violoncello, just published by T. Boosey and Co. importers of foreign music, 28, Holles-street, Oxford-street, John Sebastian Bach's 48 Preludes and Fugues, a beautiful and exceeding correct edition, price 25s'.

55 See Tomita, 'The Dawn of the English Bach Awakening manifested in Sources of the "48"', p. 143, esp. n. 341.

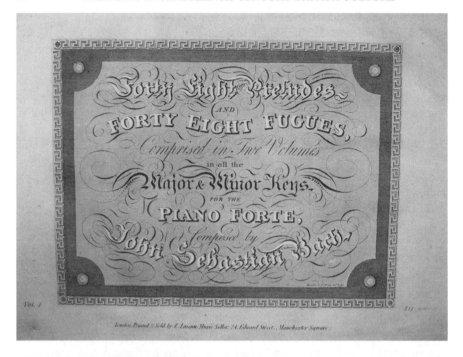

Figure 3.6   Title-pages of the Lavenu (above) and Addison & Hodson (below) Editions

tempo, indicated in words as well as with Maelzel's metronome markings. Czerny's edition was quickly imported to England by T. Boosey & Co., R. Cocks & Co., and J. Ewer & Co.[56] The review published in the *Musical World* was rather harsh, however. It writes in Wesley's favour, as follows:

> In some instances he [Czerny] differs from the mode of performance adopted by Wesley, and, we think, to a disadvantage. … Wesley possessed a kindred spirit with the German giant … M. Czerny's reading, in these instances, does not meet either with our sympathy or approval. … We perceive M. Czerny has adopted the text of Mr. Wesley, and in some instances also his mistakes.[57]

While it is not entirely clear what is meant by Wesley's 'mode of performance', the reviewer seems to be saying that he disagrees with much of Czerny's performance directions. Regarding the last accusation on adopting Wesley's text, it is difficult to prove, as much of the readings in Wesley's text originated from the Nägeli edition, and it is unclear whether or not the reviewer consulted a wide range of editions in arriving at this critical view. There is, however, one isolated instance in Czerny's edition where Wesley's analytical icon appears to have been copied by mistake, as shown in Fig. 3.7, which is otherwise inexplicable.[58]

Figure 3.7   Bar 12 of the Fugue in C major from Part 1 of the *Well-Tempered Clavier* as it appears in the Wesley/Horn (left) and Czerny (right) Editions

Despite this criticism, Robert Cocks appears to have been unscathed. Within a few weeks of this review, he announced he would shortly publish 'Bach's (J. S.) 48

---

56 *LE CLAVECIN BIEN TEMPÉRÉ … Edition nouvelle … par CHARLES CZERNY. … LEIPZIG, au Bureau de Musique de C.F. Peters*; the plate numbers are 2635 (part 1) and 2636 (part 2). It was advertised in the wrapper of the *Musical World* (15 December 1837) as 'Bach's (J.S.) 48 Preludes and 48 Fugues, a new Edition, fingered by Czerny, and the Metronome marked to each subject, 2 vols … 27s.' listed under 'Organ Music'. I am grateful to Michael Kassler for this information.

57 *Musical World*, 8/97, New Series 1/3 (1838): 39.

58 This caret has never been removed from Czerny's editions. It is still included in the revised edition by F.A. Roitzsch (plate number is still 2635); a revised edition by Adolf Ruthardt (plate number 7694 and its English edition issued by Augener, plate number 14850); and a revised edition dated 1906 by Philipp Wolfrum (plate number 7916), the edition that is still on sale in music shops today. To my knowledge, the edition prepared by Charles Hallé (see below) is the only one based exclusively on Czerny's edition (although not naming Czerny anywhere) but removes the symbol in question.

Preludes and 48 Fugues, fingered by Czerny for the English student'.[59] Cocks's new engraved edition, with English fingerings (for example, '+' designating the thumb), appeared in May 1838.[60] Cocks's enthusiasm for this project is most clearly seen in the extended 'Address' that was specially prepared for this English edition. He opens his argument as follows:

> THE Musical World possesses no more splendid monument of the highest perfection of the Musical Art than the Works of J. S. BACH, the admirable and unequalled co[n]temporary of HANDEL. And as it required several centuries before we could comprehend and appreciate the beauties of a SHAKESPEARE, so SEB. BACH still stands a gigantic image before us, rather wondered at than understood – rather known and esteemed by name, than by his works.

> All the compositions of this immortal Master are written in that strict, classical, and imperishable style, which alone remains elevated above every change of fashion, and every variation of taste, – which, like the eternal truths of mathematical science, is subjected to no caprice; and which even *He*, himself, only brought to the highest degree of perfection, by knowing how to unite all the secrets of the most abstract and subtle harmonic combinations with true beauty and sublimity; and who became thereby the Teacher and Lawgiver to all future times.

One cannot help but notice that although Czerny's name is printed as the author, the text has such strong resonance with Crotch's above-quoted paragraph on Bach – especially with Bach being placed alongside Handel in historical context, and the reference to Bach's styles with two of Crotch's favourite keywords, 'beauty' and 'sublimity' – that one can sense there was an involvement of an English writer who used Crotch's writings as reference. This suggests that Crotch's view was still considered relevant nearly thirty years after its original publication.[61] The marketing of this edition was equally vigorous. In the *Times*, Cocks frequently advertised his edition among other items using the captions shown in Table 3.2.

Contrary to its claims on the title-page that 'This Edition is carefully revised, corrected', the quality of Cocks's musical text was poor, initially, in two specific areas: ties (missing in large number) and inconsistencies with regard to the placement of fingerings (above or below the notes, which determines which hand the notes are meant to be played with), suggesting the great haste in which the edition was produced. These mistakes were not picked up quickly, for it appears that the later imprint bearing the publisher's new address '6, New Burlington Street', where Cocks moved in 1845, still retains the majority of them. In fact, this imprint is a revised edition, sometimes replacing Czerny's readings with those found in the Wesley/Horn

---

59 The advertisements were published on 8 [*recte* 9] February 1838 in the *Musical World*, 8/100, New Series 1/6 (1838): 96, and again in the next number (16 February 1838): 111.

60 Plates number 3233 (part 1) and number 3234 (part 2). This edition was advertised as 'Just published' in the *Times*, 26 May 1838, under 'Organ Music'.

61 This is no surprise, as Crotch's *Specimens of Various Styles of Music*, first published in 1807–1809, was continually available throughout the first half of the nineteenth century. For information regarding the revised editions, see Table 3.4. Crotch's authority as scholar was seriously questioned, possibly for the first time, by Rimbault in 1842. See Jonathan Rennert, *William Crotch (1775–1847): Composer, Artist, Teacher* (Lavenham: Dalton, 1975), p. 76.

Table 3.2   Advertisements placed by Robert Cocks in the *Times* that included his Edition of the *Well-Tempered Clavier* (1838)

Title	Date(s)
'Organ Music'	26 May 1838; 14 December 1839; 22 May 1844; 12 February 1848; 9 September 1848; 20 November 1849; 18 February 1850
'Works on the Theory of Music'	25 February 1839
'New Works on Musical Education'	25 February 1839
'Classical Music, for the Pianoforte'	27 August 1839
'Standard Musical Works for New Year's Gifts'	30 December 1839
'Royal Music Institution. Standard Musical Works'	15 July 1845
'New Pianoforte Music'	22 August 1846
'Classical Music for Presents'	24 February 1848

edition. It was after 1848 that John Bishop produced the first official revised edition for Cocks (Czerny[2R]). With it the English edition reached an acceptable quality. It is worth noting that the majority of readings taken from the Wesley/Horn edition at the previous imprint (Czerny[R]) reverted to Czerny's original as well.

Charles Hallé's edition published around 1850[62] appears to have been based solely on the first revised version of the English Czerny edition (Czerny[R]), inheriting not only the majority of performance directions and textual errors, but also the variants of the Wesley/Horn edition incorporated by the unnamed editor. The layout of the score also closely follows its model, although this edition was sold by piece, containing a single prelude-fugue pair with the title-page. So far as I can tell, the only notable difference from his model is in the Maelzel's metronome markings: in three-quarters of the movements, Hallé gives different tempo markings from Czerny, in all cases slower. Among these movements, the average tempo is 85 per cent of that specified by Czerny. The greatest tempo change was from minim = 80 to 54 (prelude 24 of part 2), which is 68 per cent of the original speed. That there is no mention of Czerny's name in this edition is striking. Considering the fact that the John Bishop edition reverted to the majority of revisions carried out by his predecessor to Czerny's original, and the fact that Charles Hallé does not mention the name of Czerny in his edition, it is tempting to suppose that the unnamed reviser of the Czerny edition may have been Hallé. What seems significant, from a broader context, is the dominance of Czerny's text in the English market by the 1850s, which effectively signalled the end of the Wesley/Horn era.

---

62   The date is given in *Catalog of the Emilie and Karl Riemenschneider Memorial Bach Library*, ed. Sylvia W. Kenney (New York: Columbia University Press, 1960), p. 259. The copy in the British Library (h.25) is described in their online catalogue as '1866, 67'.

Figure 3.8   The first page of the C major fugue from Part 2 of the *Well-Tempered Clavier* in A.F.C. Kollmann's *Essay on Practical Musical Composition*, London, 1799

Theoretical Treatises

The two English publications listed in Table 3.3 came from the two separate traditions of theoretical treatises and keyboard instructions fashioned in the eighteenth century. Bach's works were often cited in the writings of Mattheson, Marpurg and Kirnberger in Germany, but it was rare that the pieces from the *Well-Tempered Clavier* were reproduced fully.[63] These English examples were thus considered exceptional.[64] Obviously, the printing of these examples was justified in England where the work was not as widely circulated in manuscript copies as it was in Germany. This hybrid type of theory book with fully reproduced movements from the *Well-Tempered Clavier* disappeared as soon as complete editions of the work began to appear.

Kollmann's edition of the C major prelude and fugue from part 2 (not 'part 1' as he erroneously referred to it) was prepared from the manuscript which he obtained from Germany.[65] His printing of this pair of movements was meant to show the forthcoming edition he promised, 'being analysed'. But as shown in Fig. 3.8, it does not contain any analysis; it in fact has serious textual errors in the prelude.[66] Furthermore, it is worth noting that while Kollmann's manuscript is in oblong format, which was rare at the time, Kollmann printed his edition in portrait form, in line with many editions for harpsichord and pianoforte.

William Shield's edition of the D minor prelude follows the format and presentational style of Kollmann, as shown in Figs 3.9–3.10. However, most revealing are the comments: the composer is introduced without clear reference to his name, Bach being described as 'The Father of a wonderful family of Harmonists', who 'produced many such masterly modulations as the following to delight and instruct his sons', as if it were taboo to utter his name in public. On the top margin of the second page of the prelude, he comments on Bach's harmonic excursions from bar 14 onwards as follows: 'The Extraneous Modulations in this Page will perhaps be too harsh for the common Ear, yet enrapture the educated admirers of Mozart'. And at the bottom of the page, he adds comments on the cadenza-like passagework of bars 24–5: 'The above is regularly measured with bars, as it is not a Prelude to show

---

63 The only example of its kind is found in F.W. Marpurg, *Abhandlung von der Fuge* (Berlin, 1753–4), Tab. XLII–XLIII in which 2-Fg.d is given in open score for his analysis. The abbreviation 'Fg.' is used to indicate 'Fugue', and 'Pr.' is used to indicate 'Prelude'. The number preceding these abbreviated references indicates the part of the *WTC*: lower case letters are used for minor, and upper case for major, keys.

64 In addition to the treatises listed in Table 3.3, the following London publications contain extracts from the *Well-Tempered Clavier*: A.F.C. Kollmann, *Essay on Musical Harmony* (London, 1796), 2-Pr.f in plates 8 and 17; John Wall Callcott, *A Musical Grammar*, 1-Fg.C, p. 283.

65 Kollmann most probably obtained this volume – the manuscript now held at the St Andrews University Library, shelfmark ms M24.B2 – from Breitkopf. The error most probably originated from his source, Breitkopf, who published his edition of the *WTC* in this way. Further on Kollmann's source, see Tomita, 'The Dawn of the English Bach Awakening manifested in Sources of the "48"', pp. 118f.

66 See Tomita, 'The Dawn of the English Bach Awakening manifested in Sources of the "48"', p. 117.

Figure 3.9   **First page of the D minor prelude from Part 1 of the *Well-Tempered Clavier* in William Shield's *Introduction to Harmony*, London, 1800**

Figure 3.10   Second page of the D minor prelude from Part 1 of the *Well-Tempered Clavier* in William Shield's *Introduction to Harmony*, London, 1800

Table 3.3   **Pieces from Bach's *Well-Tempered Clavier* included in theoretical treatises**

Date	Title-page (author in bold)	Piece from the '48' (*WTC*)	Notes
1799 (1812)	Essay on Practical Musical Composition … by **Augustus Frederic Christopher Kollmann**, … London: Printed for the Author (Friary, St. James's Palace,) …	2-PrFg.C	Printed on plates 52–55 as first publication of this pair of movements anywhere. The second edition was issued in 1812 with some corrections to the musical text of the prelude.
1800 (*c*.1814)	An Introduction to Harmony by **William Shield** … London. Printed for the Author & Sold by G. G. & J. Robinson, Pater-Noster Row	1-Pr.d	Printed on pp. 114–15 as the first publication of this movement anywhere. The 'New Edition (being the Second)' was issued with no change to the musical text.

the powers of a Performer, but to prepare the auditor for the piece that is to follow.' For Shield, Bach was an 'ingenious' harmonist.

Assembled and Arranged for Public Consumption

Those musicians in London who were fortunate enough to be able to try out playing some of the fugues from the *Well-Tempered Clavier* found that they were 'gratified' with the effect, and were convinced that Bach's music should be promoted to the public for enjoyment in whatever form. The first two items listed in Table 3.4 belong to this category.

In his preface, entitled 'Advertisement', Diettenhofer explains that these fugues 'have been tried at the *Savoy Church, Strand*, before several Organists and eminent Musicians attending the Performance, who were highly gratified, and recommended their Publication'.[67] It is also worth noting that Diettenhofer describes Bach as 'the most learned Composer of his Time'. His source may have been the Simrock

---

67 This edition was studied from the three copies held at the British Library, London. The 'Advertisement', a single sheet printed separately by 'S. Gosnell, Little Queen Street, Holborn', is inserted between two blank open-pages of the book, that is, verso-side of the title-page and recto-side of the first page of music paginated as 'p. 2'; this sheet is only found in the second edition of *c*.1810 [watermarks '1807' (or '1808') and '1809']. Yet because the watermark of this 'Advertisement' is '1801', it is likely that it was printed for the first edition of *c*.1802 [watermark '1801'], but that the sheet was lost from this copy. The third edition, also marked as 'Second Edition Revised & Corrected' but using wove paper that does not bear any watermark, no longer has the blank pages. Presumably it was at this point that the decision not to include the 'Advertisement' was taken.

edition published in 1801–1802 (or possibly Broderip & Wilkinson), but unlike these editions he adds occasional analytical comments where the subjects and other noteworthy contrapuntal devices such as contrary motion and canon appear. The timing of Diettenhofer's publication is interesting, as it suggests he was in the same circle as Kollmann who declared his intention to publish an analysed edition of the *Well-Tempered Clavier* only several years earlier. This publication was noticed by several key figures in an early stage of the English Bach Awakening, including Samuel Wesley[68] and John Wall Callcott.[69] For his work of revision, Diettenhofer does not appear to have consulted other published editions, but proceeded from his musical instinct alone. In addition to the correction of obvious errors, the following pitch corrections in the C major fugue of part 1 are noteworthy:

1. bar 19, Tenor, last quaver note $f\sharp'$ (or f') was ambiguous in his earlier imprint: Diettenhofer added a natural sign to make the pitch unambiguous;
2. bar 23, Bass, first semiquaver note f was revised to g.

In both cases, the motivation for the revision seems to have been to reduce the intricacy of Bach's harmony.

A similar reasoning was given by Charles Frederick Horn in his edition. In the preface, dated 1 May 1807, Horn writes:

> Some time ago, I arranged them for a private party, as Quartettos; and as many of my friends were much gratified with the effect they produced, I was prevailed upon to publish them by subscription. Since that time, many lovers of Harmony wished to accompany them on the Piano-forte: instead of a simple *Violoncello* part, I therefore added a *Basso-Continuo*, or Thorough-Bass, which may serve a variety of purposes.

Horn's source was initially his own manuscript copy, which he proofread with the Nägeli edition.[70] His text, however, is substantially changed from his models. Besides the alterations required for stringed instruments (to avoid going below the lowest notes that can be played), Horn occasionally introduced different textural treatments and further chromatic shades, which reveal much about Horn's attitudes and character as both an experienced and enthusiastic editor.

Listed as the third item in Table 3.4 is the third volume of Crotch's anthology published in 1809. It appears to have had a much wider and lasting impact on the positive appreciation of Bach's fugues. In addition to the case study of Windsor seen above, we may also count William Russell (1777–1813) and Charles Stokes (1784–1839) among those who learned Bach's E major fugue, in all probability, through

---

68 See C.W. Pearce, 'Wesley and Horn editions of Bach' [letter to the editor], *Musical Times*, 67 (1926): 544.

69 In *A Musical Grammar* (London, 1806), Callcott acknowledges Diettenhofer's publication as source of the opening fugue and discusses (pp. 283–4) the structure of the fugue.

70 See Tomita, 'The Dawn of the English Bach Awakening manifested in Sources of the "48"', pp. 97ff.

Table 3.4   Pieces from Bach's _Well-Tempered Clavier_ assembled and arranged in a Miscellaneous Collection

Date	Title page (author in bold)	Pieces from the '48'	Notes
1802	Set of Ten Miscellaneous Fugues ... for the Organ or the Piano Forte ... and Four, with the Voluntary, by the late Celebrated John Sebastian Bach, Organist, Composer, & Conductor of the Music at the Cathedral at Leipzig in Germany. Chiefly intended for the Use of Organists; ... Third Set... by **Joseph Diettenhofer** ... London, Printed by & for Goulding, D'Almaine, Potter & Co, 2C, Soho Square, & 7, Westmorland Street, Dublin.	1-Fg.C, 1-Fg.c♯, 1-PrFg.b	Printed on pp. 19–25. The _WTC_ pieces were preceded by three fugues by Handel, three fugues by Diettenhofer, and the final fugue from Bach's _Art of Fugue_ with Diettenhofer's own conclusion.
(c.1810) (c.1815)			The 'Second Edition Revised & Corrected' was issued by the same publisher in _c_.1810 [BL, h.2732.l.(1.)], and again (with no further changes to Bach's fugues) in _c_.1815 [BL, R.M.11.f.6.(1.)] with different publisher's address: 'London, Printed by Goulding, D'Almaine, Potter & Co, 2C, Soho Square, & 7, Westmorland Street, Dublin.'
1807	A Sett of Twelve Fugues, Composed for the Organ by Sebastian Bach, Arranged as Quartettos ... by **C. F. Horn.** ... Printed & Sold for the Author, 13 Queen's Buildings, Knightsbridge.	2-Fg.D, 2-Fg.E♭, 2-Fg.d♯, 2-Fg.E, 2-Fg.g, 2-Fg.A♭, 2-Fg.b♭, 2-Fg.B, 1-Fg.c♯, 1-Fg.C	This edition consists of a set of parts. The _WTC_ pieces were preceded by BWV 898/2 and 538/2.
1809	Specimens of Various Styles of Music Referred to in a Course of Lectures read at Oxford and London. and Adapted to Keyed Instruments by **Wm Crotch** ... London, Printed and sold for the Author by R. Birchall, N°. 133 New Bond Street.	2-Fg.E	The Bach fugue heads this volume as 'N°.1' with the subtitle 'Fugue 9th. of the 2nd.' Set in the Zurich Edition [space] Sebastian Bach.', and found on pp. 2–3.
(c.1821) (c.1845)			'A new edition with corrections & additions' was printed by the Royal Harmonic Institution in _c_.1821 and again in _c_.1845 by Cramer, Beale & Co., 201, Regent Street & 67, Conduit Street. The musical text of Fg.E was not revised.
1820	The Beauties of Mozart, Handel, Pleyel, Beethoven and Other Celebrated Composers adapted ... by **an eminent Professor**. London, Printed by Samuel Leigh in the Strand.	1-Pr.C, 2-Pr.G, 1-Pr.D, 1-Pr.G (trsp. to A), 1-Pr.C♯ (trsp. to E), 1-Pr.F♯ (trsp. to F), 1-Pr.B♭, 1-Pr.E, 1-Pr.A♭	All nine preludes were crudely truncated to fit into a single page. Queen's University Belfast Library owns 'A new and improved edition' issued by the same publisher. The texts of Bach's pieces are lightly corrected.

Date	Title page (author in bold)	Pieces from the '48'	Notes
1823	Introduzione, Largo and Fuga from the Works of J^{no} Seb^n Bach. Adapted expressly for Two Violins, Viola, Violoncello & Contra Basso. By **J. B. Cramer** … London, published for the Adapter by the Royal Harmonic Institution. (Argyll Rooms,) 246, Regent Street.	1-Fg.D, 2-Fg.D	Plate number is 1208. The pieces of the '48' were the outer movements, sandwiching BWV 572/2. The edition consists of five parts only, without score. Performance indications (slurs and staccatos) are lightly added.
1823–4	Organ Voluntaries. Consisting of Preludes & Fugues, Selected from the Works of John Sebastian Bach. (with such alterations additions and accommodations, as have been deemed necessary for their general use in Churches,) by George Drummond, …	1-PrFg.C, 1-PrFg. D, 1-PrFg.C♯ (trsp. to C), 1-PrFg. c♯ (trsp. to c)	According to Andrew McCrea,[a] it was published by the Royal Harmonic Institution and bears plate number 1398. The editor acknowledges the model of his edition printing on the left top. Pr.C is marked thus: 'Altered from the 1st Prelude and Fugue of the 1st. Set Wesley & Horn's Edition.' Each movement is given both Pendulum and Maelzel's Metronome marks.
1827–8	Handel's Cuckoo and Nightingale Concerto, with a new Pastorale (composed by B. Jacob) and a Fugue by John Sebastian Bach, arranged for the Organ or Piano Forte … by **B. Jacob**. … London, Published by Clementi & Co. 26, Cheapside.	2-Fg.F	Time-signature was given as 6/8 (rather than 6/16), and metronome mark as crotchet=100. 'T' and '(2)' are given in the score indicating the subject and the second part of the subject respectively. Change of registration was given frequently.
1845	The Celebrated 48 Preludes and Fugues … Arranged as Duets for Four Hands on the Piano Forte or Organ, by **Henri Bertini**. … London Sacred Music Warehouse. J. Alfred Novello … 69, Dean Street, Soho.	entire collection	Plate number 1145. The BL copy [h.722.z.(2.)] is the only known copy, which consists of Book I only (lacking II–IV), but it appears to be the imported and rebadged edition issued by Schott in Mainz, c.1841 [p/n 6481]. It does not include introductory remarks by the editor. The music is edited with performance directions including tempi, mood in Italian, dynamics, pedals and articulation marks.

[a] Andrew McCrea, 'Professional Annotations: William Crotch's Study of the "48"', *BIOS Journal*, 28 (2004): 58–64.

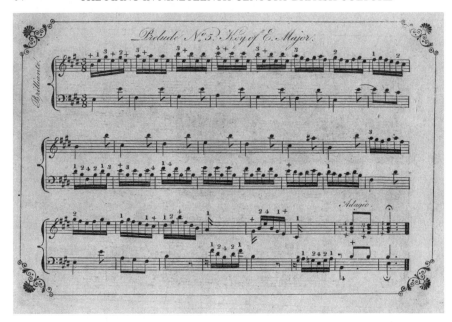

Figure 3.11   Prelude in C♯ major transposed to E major and shortened as appears in *The Beauties of Mozart, Handel, Pleyel, Beethoven and Other Celebrated Composers* (London, c.1820)

this publication.[71] Crotch's source was a manuscript copy specially made for him by Wesley,[72] as a result of their correspondence on the textual problems in the 'London copy' in Crotch's possession (Broderip & Wilkinson).[73]

From the 1820s, the public attitude towards Bach softened, indicating that the *Well-Tempered Clavier* had successfully entered the popular repertoire. The fourth item listed in Table 3.4 is a book of hymn tunes, but it starts with nine preludes from the *Well-Tempered Clavier*, all shortened and deliberately made less difficult. In the prefatory remarks, the unnamed editor writes that 'The Preludes have been selected from the celebrated Work of Sebastian Bach, but are now rendered less difficult of execution, therefore more generally acceptable than the extremely profound work from which they have been extracted'. Even though the structural logic and drama

---

71 Russell wrote an Organ Concerto (dated 7–18 March 1810) in which Bach's fugue subject was used in the final movement. His autograph manuscript is now held at the Bodleian Library, shelfmark MS.Mus.c99, ff.75–100. Stokes wrote this fugue in E♭ major and arranged it for voices to the words 'Ostende nobis benignitatem tuam'. This manuscript is held at the British Library, shelfmark Add Ms 65473 (Novello coll., v 42), f.6ʳ–8ᵛ. Textually, it is much closer to the Wesley/Horn edition, and it is very likely that Stokes used this edition for his work. But this does not eliminate the possibility that Stokes first became acquainted with this fugue in Crotch's edition.

72 See nn. 36 and 44.

73 See Tomita, 'The Dawn of the English Bach Awakening manifested in Sources of the "48"', pp. 147ff.

of Bach's harmony is ruined, the idea is maintained that a pianist with only limited technical facility can get sufficient satisfaction from being able to play the pieces. Shown in Fig. 3.11 is one entitled 'Prelude No. 5. Key of E Major', originally the prelude in C♯ major from part 1. It basically shows the approaches that the unnamed editor took to all the Bach preludes in this publication. His model apparently was one of Forkel's editions, presumably the Boosey edition that had recently appeared on the market, which prints the early versions of some preludes in part 1. For example, the prelude in C♯ major is 68 bars long as opposed to 104 bars in the later version. To make this short version even shorter, the editor skipped from bars 16 to 59 in his model. In this instance, no further work was needed to join the two originally unrelated segments, but there are other movements where the editor had to add a small bridge to connect them.

The piano duet version of the *Well-Tempered Clavier* edited by Henri Bertini that Novello published in 1845, essentially the Schott edition of *c.*1841 with a modified title-page, follows this trend of 'Bach appreciation'.

Piano Tutors

Clementi began to include Bach's music in his published piano tutors from 1801,[74] but he published nothing from the *Well-Tempered Clavier* until about 1821, when he included 'two masterly fugues' from part 2. He was always interested in producing well-balanced piano tutors that had the stylistic diversity he considered important for pedagogical reasons, and he chose lively fugues, designating the tempo mark 'Allegro'. It is worth noting that these were technically advanced fugues, and appeared in print around the same time as shortened and mangled versions of the preludes published by Samuel Leigh in 1820. It may be worth noting that in Paris, a similar tutor that includes the lively fugues from the *Well-Tempered Clavier* was published in 1805; it took eight years for an English publisher to catch up (see the first item in Table 3.5). One feature common to all these editions is the supply of fingering and tempo indications by their respective editors. Although they stop short of Czerny's expression and articulation marks in terms of both thoroughness and boldness of their application, one can recognize a clear advance from the approach that was taken by Wesley and Horn in their edition with analysis: Bach's fugues have descended from academic study to performance studies. Czerny's edition that appeared almost 15 years later is thus seen as the remoulding of Bach's image as the composer of piano music.

Conclusion

From this brief survey of editions printed in London between 1800 and 1850, a blurred and pale picture seems to have emerged. In it one can perhaps see how quickly Bach's *Well-Tempered Clavier* established its receptive life there and captured its audience from various social groups. Two reports published in *The Gentleman's Magazine* in 1813 seem particularly relevant here: the one contains a

---

74 Ibid., pp. 78ff.

Table 3.5   Pieces from Bach's *Well-Tempered Clavier* as part of studies included in 'Keyboard Tutors'

Date	Publication	Pieces from the 48	Notes
1813	Six Fugues for the Pianoforte or Organ, selected from ... Handel, Mozart, and Seb. Bach by Jean Jousse	1-Fg.C, 2-Fg.c♯	Published by T. Preston. No copies have been located, but according to a review in *The Gentleman's Magazine* v 84/2 (Dec. 1814), its contents were taken entirely from Jean Louis Adam, *Méthode de piano du conservatoire*..., Paris, year XIII [=1805]
1821	Second Part of Clementi's Introduction to the Art of Playing on the Piano Forte ... An Appendix Containing ... Two masterly Fugues of Sebastian Bach ... Op.43. London, Published by Clementi, Collard, Davis & Collard. 26, Cheapside.	2-Fg.C, 2-Fg.c♯	Fg.C was transcribed from Bach's autograph MS (BL, Add.MS 35021) in Clementi's possession at the time. Both fugues are marked 'Allegro' and fingered.
1829	A Complete Theoretical and Practical Course of Instructions on the Art of Playing the Piano Forte ... written ... by J.N. Hummel ... London, T. Boosey & Co, ..., 28, Holles Street, Oxford Street.	1-Fg.c♯	Fg.c♯ is found on pp. 298–301, entitled 'Fuga. 1.', with the heading 'in the strict style'. It does not give tempo marks, but adds fingerings as well as clear instructions for which hands are to be used.

general comment on 'ladies' who would refer to Bach's fugues as 'ugly old-fashioned stuff',[75] and the other describes Caroline Kerby, a young girl of 13 years of age who can 'execute with ease and accuracy' Bach's fugues, presumably those from the *Well-Tempered Clavier*.[76] While such inconsistencies can be seen as a fair reflection of London's diverse society then, they can also be considered to represent a general trend that shows the *Well-Tempered Clavier* beginning to enter the 'canon' of piano repertoire in England. There is evidence to suggest that not only Bach's fugues but also fugue as a genre itself became fashionable, as many fugues were published around this time by the London publishers.[77] Samuel Leigh's decision to publish the short and simplified preludes from the *Well-Tempered Clavier* thus appears symbolic, indicating that the *Well-Tempered Clavier* had been accepted widely as core repertoire.

In order to see the finer details of this picture in more vivid colours, it is essential to widen the investigative horizons, looking at London and its citizens not only from the perspective of a cosmopolitan trade centre, but also against the historical tides and events such as war with France, which presumably affected not only trades but also people's notion of national identity. As Jeremy Dibble points out, nationalist developments in Britain in the nineteenth century are complex and less easily definable than those of other European countries,[78] and hence it is difficult to delineate how a specific genre of music came to capture the imagination of the general public in England. A fuller conclusion to this paper can only be reached when we understand the complex social, cultural and economic situation to which the musicians and music lovers in London were subject.

---

75 Review of S. Wesley and C.F. Horn's 'New and Correct Edition of the Preludes and Fugues of John Sebastian Bach. Book 1, 2, 3, and 4' in *The Gentleman's Magazine*, 83, New Series 6 (January 1813): 60.

76 Review of Caroline Kerby, 'An Introduction, March, and Rondo, for the Pianoforte' in *The Gentleman's Magazine*, 83, New Series 6 (May 1813): 461.

77 Among the British Library collections, the authors of fugues printed by London publishers between 1810 and 1820 include such names as Thomas Adams, J.S. Bach, Ludwig van Beethoven, Muzio Clementi, Benjamin Cooke, George Drummond, Johann Ernst Eberlin, Timothy Essex, George Guest, G.F. Handel, John Jeremiah Jones, A.F.C. Kollmann and Johann Bernhard Logier, a list that is significantly more varied than in the next decade.

78 Jeremy Dibble, 'National Developments in Britain and Ireland: a Matter of Style and Morality', in Peter Andraschke and Edelgard Spaude (eds), *Welttheater: Die Künste im 19. Jahrhundert* (Freiburg im Breisgau: Rombach, 1992), pp. 58–65.

Chapter 4

The Faces of Parnassus: Towards a New Reception of Muzio Clementi's *Gradus ad Parnassum*

Rohan Stewart-MacDonald

The Modern Reputation of the *Gradus ad Parnassum* and its Historical Roots

Dorothy de Val recently described Muzio Clementi's *Gradus ad Parnassum* as the 'crowning point in [the composer's] career as pianist, pedagogue and composer' that 'stands as a monument both to Clementi's compositional art in particular and to the developments of the London school in piano writing in general'.[1] This description echoes the initially enthusiastic reception of the *Gradus ad Parnassum* when it first appeared between 1817 and 1825. In 1827 a reviewer for the *Repository of the Arts* compared the work with the 'Preludes and Exercises' of Bach and anticipated that:

> more than any of his other labours, [the *Gradus ad Parnassum*] will hand [Clementi's] name down to the children of our grand-children […] [and] will form a guide to the students of every country, in the present as well as in future ages; like Bach's works it will stand as a record of the attainments in pianoforte playing, and, indeed, of the harmonic knowledge possessed by the living generation.[2]

The reviewer's comments have not proved totally prophetic in that detailed knowledge of the *Gradus*'s contents has become unusual. This was confirmed by a small survey I undertook involving a group of undergraduate music students at Cambridge University and at the Open University. Many of the students had received several years of formal keyboard training and several were first-study pianists. About half of the students had never heard of the *Gradus*, and of those who had, many owed their encounters with it to Debussy's famous parody of it in the first piece of his *Children's Corner* Suite, 'Doctor Gradus ad Parnassum'. Several believed that the work contained nothing but short technical exercises, and few had any concept of the work's multi-volume scale. No one, moreover, seemed aware of its internal diversity or that, in addition to short-to-medium-length exercises aimed at particular

1   Dorothy de Val, 'The Ascent of Parnassus: Piano Music for the Home', in Roberto Illiano, Luca Sala and Massimiliano Sala, eds, *Muzio Clementi: Studies and Prospects*, *Opera omnia*, vol. 61 (Bologna: Ut Orpheus Edizioni, 2002), pp. 51–66, here at 59.
2   *The Repository of Arts*, *&c*, 3rd Series, vol. ix (1827), pp. 53–4. Quoted in Leon Plantinga, *Clementi: His Life and Music* (London: Oxford University Press, 1977), p. 270.

aspects of keyboard technique, it also contains a range of sonata-type movements, fugues, fugatos, canons and character pieces whose pedagogical functions are rather less clear-cut.

The widespread view of the work as consisting of nothing but short technical exercises has its roots in the highly selective assimilation of only small parts of it into nineteenth-century keyboard teaching traditions. Chopin is widely known to have used Clementi's *Preludes and Exercises* and also parts of the *Gradus* to prepare students for studying his own works, usually in conjunction with scales, exercises by other composers and also works by J.S. Bach. Karol Mikuli states that '[i]n conjunction with scales ... Chopin made his pupils study Clementi's *Preludes and Exercises*, a work whose usefulness he valued very highly'.[3] Mikuli goes on to mention that Chopin then 'prescribed a selection from Cramer's *Etudes*, Clementi's *Gradus ad Parnassum*, Moscheles's *Stylstudien zur höheren Vollendung* ... and J.S. Bach's Suites and individual Fugues from *Das Wohltemperierte Klavier*'.[4] Chopin is reported to have 'held that Clementi's *Gradus ad Parnassum*, Bach's pianoforte Fugues and Hummel's compositions were the key to pianoforte-playing'.[5] Liszt also made use of parts of the *Gradus* in lessons. August Göllerich recounts one lesson on Tuesday 3 June 1884 that began with Liszt demonstrating the first two studies from the *Gradus*.[6]

There is no evidence that either Chopin or Liszt made comprehensive use of the full range – or even of substantial parts – of the *Gradus* in their teaching. Instead, they appear only to have used small parts of it in conjunction with material from other sources. This highly selective usage of the *Gradus* was perpetuated by the compressed single-volume edition prepared by Carl Tausig in 1865 and published by Trautwein in Berlin. This contained only 29 of the more 'mechanical' studies and most probably reflected the by then established view of the work as a source of purely 'digital' instruction. The importance of Tausig's edition in perpetuating this distorted view of the *Gradus* cannot be underestimated. As late as the 1960s, compressed editions of the *Gradus* were still available from Durand, Schirmer and Ricordi, and Tausig's edition was being strongly recommended in a reprint of a standard history as late as 1969.[7]

It is some time since even small parts of the *Gradus ad Parnassum* have had a central place in keyboard training programmes. The work's importance as a didactic source seems to have declined quite sharply in the first half of the twentieth century – certainly by comparison with the same composer's Sonatinas, op. 36 and also Johann Baptist Cramer's studies, which have retained a fairly central place in keyboard

---

3   Jean-Jacques Eigeldinger, *Chopin: Pianist and Teacher, as Seen by his Pupils*, trans. Naomi Shohet with Krysia Osostowicz and Roy Howat, ed. Roy Howat (Cambridge: Cambridge University Press, 1986), p. 59.

4   Ibid., p. 60.

5   Ibid.

6   August Göllerich, *The Piano Master Classes of Franz Liszt, 1884–1886: Diary Notes of August Göllerich*, trans., ed. and enlarged by Richard Louis Zimdars (Bloomington and Indianapolis: Indiana University Press, 1996), p. 21.

7   See C.F. Weitzmann, *A History of Pianoforte-Playing and Pianoforte-Literature* (New York: Da Capo, 1969), p. 69.

training up to the present. This situation is reflected in the relative representation of the *Gradus*, the Sonatinas and Cramer's studies in the syllabuses for piano performing examinations set by the Associated Board of the Royal Schools of Music during the years for which information was available – namely 1918 to 2004 (see Table 4.1).[8] As Table 4.1 shows, movements from the *Gradus* were set for Advanced-level examinations with some frequency between 1919 and 1931, specifically in 1919, 1921, 1923, 1925, 1928, 1929, 1930 and 1931. There then follows a gap of some 17 years until 1948, when No. 9 was set for Grade VII, and then again in 1949. This latter year, however, is the last year in which any part of the *Gradus* was set for a piano performing examination run by the Associated Board. Between 1918 and 1949, individual movements from the Sonatinas, op. 36 were frequently selected for the lower grades, as were studies by Cramer for the intermediate and higher ones. This situation continued beyond 1949, when the *Gradus* disappeared. Studies by Cramer become steadily less frequent, particularly from the beginning of the 1960s, but Clementi's Sonatinas continue to appear, with the first movement of op. 36 no. 6 being set for Grade VI as recently as 2003. The other major recent development in the representation of Clementi's works has been the more frequent inclusion of his larger sonatas in the requirements for the higher grades, particularly from the 1980s onwards.

Given that Clementi's Sonatinas and not the *Gradus* have been consistently included in keyboard examinations – a sphere encountered by so many people of varying musical ability and aspirations – it is unsurprising that the most direct association with Clementi in people's minds is that of the Sonatinas rather than the *Gradus ad Parnassum*.

The *Gradus ad Parnassum*: Biographical Context and Compositional Process

The modern-day scholarly view of the *Gradus* as the 'crowning point' in Clementi's career[9] in many ways seems justified. The three volumes were published respectively in 1817, 1819 and 1826: a single volume containing the complete work appeared in 1829. The completion and publication of the *Gradus* coincided with the apex of Clementi's career, when his international reputation was fortified by frequent and largely successful performances of his symphonies in Britain and abroad,[10] stimulated by such factors as his involvement with the London Philharmonic Society from its establishment in 1813.[11] Clementi's participation in the running of the Society, including his direction of half of the concerts in the first season, meant that there was a platform on which his orchestral works could be performed with frequency, using a

---

8   The Associated Board of the Royal Schools of Music was established in 1889.

9   Dorothy de Val, 'The Ascent of Parnassus: Piano Music for the Home', pp. 51–66.

10   See Massimiliano Sala, 'Muzio Clementi's Symphonies. Contributions Towards a New Edition', in *Muzio Clementi: Studies and Prospects*, pp. 229–45.

11   See Simon McVeigh, 'Clementi, Viotti and the London Philharmonic Society', in *Muzio Clementi: Studies and Prospects*, pp. 67–80.

Table 4.1 Works by Clementi and J.B. Cramer in Associated Board Syllabuses (piano performing): 1918–2004
[Numbered studies by Cramer are from his *Studio per il Piano Forte*]

Year	Clementi: *Gradus*	Grade/level	Clementi: other	Grade/level	Cramer: *Studio*	Grade/Level
1918			Sonatina, op. 36 no. 2/I	Elementary		
1919	No. 28 in B major	Advanced	Sonatina, op. 36 no. 4/I	Elementary	No. 17 in F major	Higher
1920			Sonatina, op. 36 no. 3/I	Elementary	No. 65 in E minor	Higher
1921	No. 2 in F major	Advanced	Sonatina, op. 36 no. 3/III	Elementary	No. 46 in A minor No. 9 in G major	Higher Intermediate
1922					No. 4 in C minor No. 78 in G major	Higher Advanced
1923	No. 76 in E major	Advanced			No. 59 in C minor	Advanced
1924			Sonatina, op. 36 no. 4/I Sonatina, op. 36 no. 6/I	Elementary Lower		
1925	No. 8 in D major	Advanced	Sonatina, op. 36 no. 1/I	Primary	No. 16 in F minor	Intermediate
1926					No. 3 in A minor No. 5 in F♯ minor	
1927					No. 41 in B♭ major	Intermediate
1928	No. 5 in B♭ major	Advanced	Sonatina, op. 36 no. 4/II	Elementary		
1929	No. 12 in C major	Advanced			No. 23 in E minor No. 22 in G major	Intermediate Advanced
1930	No. 9 in A major	Advanced			No. 10 in C major	Intermediate

Year	Clementi: *Gradus*	Grade/ level	Clementi: other	Grade/ level	Cramer: *Studio*	Grade/ Level
1931	No. 2 in F major	Advanced	Sonatina, op. 36 no. 3/II	Primary	No. 1 in C major No. 22 in F♯ minor No. 78 in G major	Higher Intermediate Advanced
1932						
1933					No. 65 in E minor	Grade V
1934					No. 14 in D minor	Grade V
1935						
1936			Sonatina, op. 36 no. 3/I	Elementary		
1937			Sonatina, op. 36 no. 6/I	Grade IV		
1938					No. 41 in E minor No. 47 in A major	Grade VI Grade VII
1939					No. 23 in E minor No. 22 in G major	Grade VI Grade VII
1940			Sonatina, op. 36 no. 6/III Sonata in D major, op. 26, No. 3/Rondo	Grade IV Grade V		
1941			Sonatina, op. 36 no. 3/II	Grade I		
1942			[as above]	[as above]		
1943			[as above]	[as above]		
1944			[as above]	[as above]		
1945			Sonata in D major, op. 26 no. 3/II	Grade V		

Year	Clementi: *Gradus*	Grade/level	Clementi: other	Grade/level	Cramer: *Studio*	Grade/Level
1946			[as above]	[as above]		
1947			Sonatina, op. 36 no. 6/I	Grade III	No. 1 in C major	Grade V
1948	No. 9 in A major	Grade VII			No. 14 in D minor	Grade V
					No. 16 in F minor	Grade VI
1949	No. 9 in A major	Grade VII			[as above]	[as above]
1950			Sonatina, op. 36 no. 1/I	Grade I	No. 22 in F♯ minor	Grade VII
			Sonatina, op. 36 no. 2	Grade II		
1951						
1952					No. [?] in E♭ minor	Grade VII
1953						
1954			Sonatina, op. 36 no. 6/I	Grade VI		
1955						
1956					No. 1 in C major	Grade VI
					No. 22 in F♯ minor	Grade VII
1957			Sonata in B♭ major, op. 47 no. 2/I	Grade VII		
1958						
1959						
1960			Sonatina, op. 36 no. 4/I	Grade IV	No. [?] in E major	Grade VI
					No. [?] in A major	Grade VII
1961						

Year	Clementi: *Gradus*	Grade/level	Clementi: other	Grade/level	Cramer: *Studio*	Grade/Level
1962			Sonata, op. 33 no. 1/I	**Grade VII**		
1963						
1964						
1965			Sonatina, op. 36 no. 4	**Grade II**		
			Sonatina, op. 36 no. 4	**Grade IV**		
1966						
1967					No. [?] in F♯ minor	**Grade VII**
1968						
1969			Sonata, op. 26 3/II	**Grade V**		
1970			Sonatina, op. 36 no. 6/I	**Grade VI**		
1971			Sonatina, op. 36 no. 1/I	**Grade II**		
1972						
1973						
1974						
1975						
1976						
1977						
1978						
1979			Sonatina, op. 36 no. 4/I	**Grade IV**		
1980			Sonatina, op. 36 no. 3/III	**Grade V**		

Year	Clementi: *Gradus*	Grade/level	Clementi: other	Grade/level	Cramer: *Studio*	Grade/Level
1981			Sonata in B♭ major, op. 47, no. I–III	**Grade VIII**		
1982						
1983						
1984			Sonata in F major, op. 4 no. 6/I	**Grade V**		
1985					No. 33 in D major	**Grade VII**
1986						
1987			'Arietta' in C from *Introduction*…	**Grade I**		
			Sonata in F♯ minor, op. 25 no. 5/II	**Grade VI**		
1988						
1989			Sonata in E♭ major, op. 4 no. 2/I	**Grade VI**		
1990						
1991			'Arietta' in F from *Introduction*…	**Grade II**		
			'Waltz' from *Twelve Waltzes*…	**Grade IV**		
1992						

Year	Clementi: *Gradus*	Grade/level	Clementi: other	Grade/level	Cramer: *Studio*	Grade/Level
1993			Sonatina, op. 36 no. 3/II	**Grade II**		
			Sonata in B♭ major, op. 24 no. 2/I–III	**Grade VIII**		
1994					No. 2 in E minor	**Grade VI**
1995			Sonata, op. 25 no. 6/II	**Grade V**		
			Sonata in F♯ minor, op. 25 no. 5/II	**Grade VI**		
1996			Sonata, op. 25 no. 6/I–III	**Grade VIII**		
1997			Sonata in D major, op. 40 no. 3/I	**Grade VIII**		
1998			Sonatina, op. 36 no. 4/II	**Grade IV**	No. 33 in D major	**Grade VII**
			Sonata in D major, op. 40 no. 3/I	**Grade VIII**		
1999			'Arietta' in C from *Introduction…*	**Grade I**		
2000			[as above]	[as above]		
2001						
2002						
2003			Sonatina, op. 36 no. 6/I	**Grade VI**		
2004			[as above]	[as above]		

large and good-quality orchestra.[12] The frequent and largely successful performances of Clementi's symphonies in various locations in London and also in France and Germany did much to secure and develop his international standing.[13]

Running parallel with the increased importance that orchestral composition was assuming for Clementi in these years was a diminished emphasis on the keyboard sonata. The last sets of piano sonatas to appear were opp. 40 and 50. Although the latter were not published until 1821, Leon Plantinga has suggested that the op. 50 set of sonatas in A major, D minor and G minor is likely to have been composed as early as 1804–1805 and withheld from publication until the 1820s.[14] Clementi's transfer of his energies away from piano sonatas and towards projects such as the *Gradus* is evidence of his responsiveness to changing market conditions, specifically those that reduced the popularity of the solo sonata and increased the demand for both popular and didactic piano music. These demands emanated from the rise in social status of the newly rich, a process that took longer to gather momentum on the Continent than in England.[15] Clementi's acute awareness of market conditions is most clearly reflected in the catalogues he published during this period, dominated as they are by popular airs, military marches, orchestral transcriptions and also keyboard studies.[16] The growth in the demand for didactic keyboard music led to the emergence of a large repertoire of keyboard studies by a wide range of composers, both British-based and Continental. Cramer's *Studio per il Piano Forte*, op. 39, dating from 1804,

---

12 See ibid., and also Massimiliano Sala, 'Muzio Clementi's Symphonies. Contributions Towards a New Edition', p. 230 and n. 5.

13 For a concise summary of the international performances of Clementi's symphonies see Clive Bennett, 'Clementi as Symphonist', *Musical Times*, 120 (1979): 207–10. For a list of the documented performances of Clementi's orchestral works in England and abroad, see the Preface to Manuel De Col and Massimiliano Sala's edition of Clementi's Symphony no. 1 in C major, WO 32 (Bologna: Ut Orpheus Edizioni, 2003) (*Opera omnia*, vol. 56), p. viii.

14 Plantinga introduced this hypothesis in 1977 and elaborated it in his contributions to *Muzio Clementi: Studies and Prospects*, vol. [56], and to the Rome conference suggesting that op. 50 may have originally been intended as the second half of op. 40, another set of three piano sonatas in G major, B minor and D major, first published in 1802. He noted that 'Book 1' appears on the title page of the first edition of op. 40, as if to anticipate a 'Book 2' that never emerged as such but may have been what eventually became op. 50 – probably the 'three new sonatas' mentioned in Clementi's letters of 1804–1805. Plantinga's new evidence is a recently discovered letter, dated 20 December 1809, and addressed to Härtel of Leipzig. In this letter, Clementi offers Härtel three new sonatas for publication 'in my better style' [*tre sonate, nella mia miglior maniera*]. Plantinga considers that Clementi's 'better style' must refer to his 'modern' idiom, or the 'late' style found in the works post-dating 1800, and concludes that the 'Op. 40, Book 2' offered to Härtel were the three sonatas eventually published as op. 50. See Plantinga, *Clementi*, pp. 116–17 and 'Clementi: The Metamorphosis of a Musician', in *Muzio Clementi: Studies and Prospects* pp. xxi–xxvii.

15 See Nicholas Temperley, 'Piano Music: 1800–1870', in *The Romantic Age, 1800–1914*, ed. Nicholas Temperley, Blackwell (formerly Athlone) History of Music in Britain, 5 (London: Athlone Press, 1981; Oxford: Basil Blackwell, 1988), pp. 402–403.

16 Massimiliano Sala, 'Muzio Clementi's Symphonies. Contributions Towards a New Edition', p. 233.

Table 4.2   British and Continental Didactic Piano Works between 1804 and 1833

Composer	Title	Year
J.B. Cramer	St*udio per il Piano Forte*	1804
D.G. Steibelt	*Etude pour le pianoforte contenant 50 exercices* de différents genres	1805
J.B. Cramer	*Etude pour le piano forte*	1810
J. Field	*Exercice modulé dans tous les tons* majeur et mineurs	1816
M. Clementi	**Gradus ad Parnassum, vol. I**	**1817**
J.H. Müller	*Préludes et exercices*	*c.*1817
M. Clementi	**Gradus ad Parnassum, vol. II**	**1818**
L. Berger	*Etüden*	1819
F. Kalkbrenner	*24 études*	1820
M. Szymanowska	*20 exercices et préludes*	1820
C. Potter	*24 études*	1826
I. Moscheles	*Studien zur höheren Vollendung bereits ausgebildeter Klavierspieler*	1826
M. Clementi	**Gradus ad Parnassum, vol. III**	**1826**
C. Czerny	*Schule der Geläufigkeit*	1830
H. Bertini	*25 études caractéristiques*	1832
R. Schumann	*6 études d'après les caprices de Paganini*	1832
F. Chopin	*12 grandes études*	1833

is one of the earliest and most enduring examples from this repertoire; Chopin's celebrated *Etudes*, op. 10, are among the latest and most prestigious (see Table 4.2).

The perception of the *Gradus* as a direct product of Clementi's responsiveness to changing market conditions in the first years of the nineteenth century is obscured by the non-publication of the first volume until 1817. Nonetheless, there is evidence indicating that the project was conceived as early as 1801 – namely a letter to Paul Härtel dating from 1818 in which Clementi mentions his intention, in about 1801, of assembling a series of keyboard exercises and calling them 'Studio'.[17] If Plantinga's dating of op. 50 to 1804–1805 is to be accepted, this would mean that

---

17 See Max Unger, *Muzio Clementis Leben* (New York: Da Capo, 1971), p. 213. Summarizing in detail the contents of Clementi's letter to Härtel of 12 April 1818, Unger writes: 'Ungefähr im Jahre 1801 habe [Clementi] dem Harfenbauer in London, der ihn um ein bedeutendes Studienwerk für seine Pariser Nichten gebeten hatte, erzählt, dass er sich schon lang mit einer Sammlung von Übungen zur Bildung fertiger Klavierspieler getragen habe, und diese habe er "Studio" nennen wollen'.

the beginnings of the *Gradus* coincided roughly with the composition of the last two sets of piano sonatas. This reinforces the likelihood that at a particular point in Clementi's career, predictions of changing market conditions led to a direct transfer of emphasis from one compositional medium to another. Clementi's awareness of market conditions was an inevitable consequence of the beginnings of the career as a publisher and manufacturer on which he had embarked in the mid-1790s: by 1800, Clementi had become senior partner in Clementi and Co., the direct successors to Longman and Broderip, one of the largest and most significant music publishing and instrument-making businesses in Europe at this time.[18] Significantly, 1801 also saw the publication of two other didactic – and very successful – works by Clementi, namely his *Introduction to the Art of Playing on the Piano Forte* and his *Selection of Practical Harmony*, a compilation of voluntaries, fugues and canons.[19] The *Gradus* can be seen as a further direct outcome of Clementi's change from composer–performer to composer–entrepreneur during the 1790s.

The assembly of the *Gradus* was prolonged and complex, and is difficult to reconstruct with any precision. What is certain is that it involved a mixture of new composition and the insertion of a good deal of material from other sources, usually after thorough revision. The *Gradus* contains eleven fugal movements, seven of which had already been published many years earlier in Oeuvre 1 and opp. 5 and 6. The versions introduced into the *Gradus* were thoroughly revised, mainly through truncation and the eradication of resemblances to fugues by J.S. Bach.[20]

Compared with the contemporary didactic piano works listed in Table 4.2, the *Gradus* is much larger in scale and more diverse in content. However much the original stimulus for the *Gradus* may have been Clementi's desire to exploit a buoyant market for didactic keyboard music, there can be little doubt that the work eventually became an arena for compositional experimentation of as sophisticated, if not more sophisticated, a type as the keyboard sonata had increasingly done up to that point, and as the symphony was to do in the decade that followed. This led to a complicated sharing of priorities among the *Gradus*, the Sonatas opp. 40 and 50 and the last four surviving symphonies. Points of stylistic intersection between the *Gradus* and Clementi's other later works can be explicit, but their full significance tends to be obscured by the 'didactic' classification of the *Gradus* and the popular perception of the work as nothing but a collection of short technical exercises.

---

18 For a detailed account of the early stage of Clementi's business career, see David Rowland, 'Clementi's Early Business Career: New Documents', in Richard Bösel and Masimiliano Sala, eds, *Muzio Clementi: Cosmopolita della Musica: Atti del convegno internazionale in occasione del 250° anniversario della nascita (1752–2002), Roma, 4–6 dicembre, 2002*, Quaderni Clementiani, 1 (Bologna: Ut Orpheus Edizioni, 2004), pp. 49–60.

19 The *Introduction* was registered at Sationers Hall on 26 October 1801. Vol. 1 of the *Selection of Practical Harmony* was advertised in the *Morning Post* on 20 November 1801, vol. 2 on 15 February 1802 and vol. 3 was published soon afterwards. See Rowland, 'Clementi's Early Business Career: New Documents', p. 57, n. 23 and n. 24.

20 Leon Plantinga, *Clementi*, p. 273. The revised fugues are: Exx. 13, 25, 40, 45, 57, 69 and 74.

The Interior of the *Gradus* and Parallels with other parts of Clementi's output

The size and diversity of the *Gradus ad Parnassum* makes it hard to come to terms with, either as a composite artistic production or as a purely pedagogical work with a clearly defined didactic purpose. Its assimilation into the teaching canon in the nineteenth century necessitated radical compression and it has never attracted concert performances. The *Gradus* therefore suffers by comparison both with sets of studies whose pedagogical functions were more streamlined, and also with those, like Chopin's *Etudes*, that have been fully assimilated into the performing canon. Temperley subdivides the exercises in the *Gradus* into five categories:

(1) Examples of contrapuntal learning (fugues and canons);
(2) Movements of sonata type;
(3) Introductory movements;
(4) Studies for technical development;
(5) Character pieces or studies of pianoforte expression.[21]

Temperley's nuanced perception of the work to some extent reflects established distinctions between three types of didactic keyboard composition: the 'exercise', in which a 'didactic objective […] is assigned primary attention'; the 'etude', in which 'musical and didactic functions properly stand in a complementary and indivisible association'; and 'concert studies', whereby the 'didactic element is mostly incidental to the primary characteristic substance'.[22] The relationship between the *Gradus* and these three categories is far from straightforward, nonetheless. Although the category of 'studies for technical development'[23] is fairly distinct, the others are not, and there are a great number of exercises that are impossible to classify in this manner. The model is more directly applicable to the études of Cramer or Chopin, which display greater internal uniformity of purpose, or where a 'delicate equilibrium between expressive style and technical content' is more consistently maintained.[24] Given that an artistic and technical equilibrium tends to be regarded as the ideal condition of the study or étude, the ambivalent and marginal status of the *Gradus* outside the immediate sphere of Clementi scholarship is unsurprising. Compared with the studies of Chopin, which display a 'consistently high degree of integration and fusion of musical content, form, style, and technical exploitation of the instrument',[25] the *Gradus* unfolds as a landscape that appears vast, fragmented and bewildering.

---

21 Nicholas Temperley, editorial introduction to *The London Pianoforte School, 1766–1860: Clementi, Dussek, Cogan, Cramer, Field, Pinto, Sterndale Bennett, and other Masters of the Pianoforte* (New York: Garland, 1985), vol. 5, p. xv.

22 Simon Finlow, 'The Twenty-Seven Etudes and their Antecedents', in Jim Samson, ed., *The Cambridge Companion to Chopin* (Cambridge: Cambridge University Press, 1992), p. 53.

23 Ibid.

24 Ibid., p. 63.

25 Robert Collet, 'Studies, Preludes and Impromptus', in Alan Walker, ed., *Frédéric Chopin: Profiles of the Man and the Musician* (London: Barrie and Rockliff, 1966), p. 114.

The remainder of this discussion will trace certain central compositional objectives that link some of these facets with one another and also with other works by Clementi, in order to articulate more clearly its true significance in the composer's career and in the era in which it was written. The scale of the work necessitates a highly selective approach in this context. I will be focusing on sonata-type movements that incorporate archaic contrapuntal styles, in order to explore the relationship between strict counterpoint and heightened developmental processes that are also exemplified by the later piano sonatas and surviving symphonies, WO 32–5.

The *Gradus* and Strict Counterpoint

To what extent is the *Gradus* predominantly a demonstration of contrapuntal technique? Temperley suggests that Clementi had J.S. Bach's *Das wohltemperierte Klavier* in mind when composing the *Gradus*[26] and points out a resemblance between Ex. 90 and the B major fugue from the first volume of Bach's work.[27] Many of the exercises in the *Gradus* make sustained use of a particular contrapuntal form. The number of contrapuntal movements is greatest in volume 3 (see Table 4.3), and Clementi's view of this part of the work, expressed in a letter to his publisher Paul Härtel on 4 July 1826, is perhaps significant: 'I think it superior to the first and second volumes, and hope it will be found so by the learned critics of our country.'[28] One of the central purposes, particularly of the third volume of the *Gradus*, was undoubtedly to explore the propensities of different types or degrees of contrapuntal elaboration. Often this involves infusing strict counterpoint into predominantly non-learned contexts – a preoccupation seen frequently in the later keyboard sonatas and surviving symphonies. Temperley notes the sustained preoccupation with invertible counterpoint that permeates many of the non-contrapuntal movements.[29] Canonic procedures are similarly ubiquitous – an important link with the later keyboard sonatas and symphonies. The development section of Ex. 4 from volume 1, for instance, contains several bouts of canon. In Ex. 58 from volume 3, a two-part canon at the octave is sustained for the entire development section, much as in the finales of the Piano Sonatas in A major, op. 50 no. 1 and G minor, op. 50 no. 3, 'Didone abbandonata'.

Clementi's preoccupation with archaic styles and with infusing strict counterpoint into predominantly non-contrapuntal contexts can be traced at least as far back as the early 1780s and the production of opp. 5 and 6. Plantinga has linked the contrapuntal predilections in opp. 5 and 6 with Clementi's engagement with the music of J.S. Bach around this time.[30] The ramifications of Clementi's interest in archaic styles developed and diversified during the 1790s and especially after 1800, finding outlets in the later piano sonatas, the symphonies and also, of course, the *Gradus*.

---

26 Nicholas Temperley, editorial introduction to *The London Pianoforte School*, p. xv.
27 Ibid., p. xvii.
28 Quoted in Plantinga, *Clementi*, p. 244.
29 Temperley, editorial introduction to *The London Pianoforte School*, p. xx.
30 Leon Plantinga, 'Clementi, Virtuosity, and the "German Manner"', *Journal of the American Musicological Society*, 25/3 (1972): 318–29.

Table 4.3 **Distribution of Contrapuntal Movements in the three volumes of the *Gradus ad Parnassum***

Volume I

Number	Volume	Movement type
1		
2		
3		
4		
5		
6		
7		
8		
9		
10	I	Canon (two-part)
11		
12		
13	I	Fugue (four-part)
14		
15		
16		
17		
18	I	Introduction-Fugato
19		
20		
21		
22		
23		
24		
25	I	Introduction-Fugue (four-part)
26	I	Canon (two-part)
27		

Volume II

28		
29		
30		
31		
32		

Number	Volume	Movement type
33	II	Canon (four-part)
34		
35		
36		
37		
38		
39		
40	II	Fugue (four-part)
41		
42		
43	II	Fugue (four-part)
44		
45	II	Introduction-Fugue (four-part)
46		
47		
48		
49		
50		
51		

Volume III

Number	Volume	Movement type
52		
53		
54	III	Fugue (double)
55		
56		
57	III	Fugue (four-part)
58		
59		
60		
61		
62		
63	III	Canon (two-part)
64		
65		
66		
67	III	Canon (two-part)

Number	Volume	Movement type
68		
69	III	Fugue (four-part)
70		
71		
72		
73	III	Canon (two-part: contrary motion)
74	III	Fugue (double)
75	III	Canon (two-part)
76		
77		
78		
79		
80		
81		
82		
83		
84	III	Ternary: canonic central section
85		
86		
87		
88		
89		
90	III	Fugato
91		
92		
93		
94		
95		
96		
97		
98		
99		
100		

Another manifestation of these preoccupations is *Practical Harmony*, a selection of contrapuntal movements by a range of composers, which was published at around the time that the *Gradus* was initially conceived.[31]

The constitution of volume 3 of the *Gradus*, coupled with Clementi's attitude towards it as revealed in the letter to Härtel, reflects the degree to which the composer's preoccupation with strict counterpoint gained momentum during the first three decades of the nineteenth century. Contrapuntal, and particularly canonic, procedures figure frequently in the four surviving symphonies, dating from after about 1810. In the second movement of the 'Great National' Symphony no. 3 in G major, WO 33, Clementi subjects the British national anthem to exhaustive contrapuntal treatment; but one of the most impressive instances of Clementi instilling strict counterpoint into predominantly non-'learned' contexts and using it as a catalyst for intensive motivic processing is the two-part canon that emerges about halfway through the second movement of the Symphony no. 1 in C major, WO 32. Very much as in the longer canonic passages in opp. 40 and 50, this canon brings together the movement's main and subordinate themes, revealing links between them that previously were too subtle to be noticeable.[32]

The notion that Clementi's preoccupation with archaic styles gradually gathered momentum in the second half of his career is strongly suggested by the contrapuntal nature of many of his very late works, including various unpublished and unfinished ones. His last publication, dated 1830, is the *Canon ad Diapason* for solo piano, a movement that is canonic throughout. There is also an unpublished canon for two violins and viola, and an incomplete canonic movement in C♯ minor for piano, of which only 45 bars survive. There is moreover some evidence that Clementi had become interested in the music of Palestrina at around the time of the publication of the third volume of the *Gradus*, namely a passage in a work on Palestrina by Giuseppe Baini that appeared in 1828, alluding to visits that Clementi made to Baini that Plantinga dates to 1827. Baini writes the following:

> I myself can testify that the works of [Palestrina] are held in the very highest esteem by Muzio Clementi […]. During his latest stay in Rome […] he visited me nearly every evening so that I could show him the most beautiful examples from the works of [Palestrina]. And when he saw them he was delighted, and he copied a section here or there into his notebook, confessing to me that however much music he had seen in his life, in the works of [Palestrina] he discovered new lands, new heavens, new mines of inspiration; and that he could scarcely have imagined that such learning could have existed more than two-and-a-half centuries ago.[33]

---

31 For a more detailed account of *Practical Harmony*, see Andrea Coen, 'Le fonti della *Practical Harmony* di Muzio Clementi: primi riscontri e acquisizioni', in *Muzio Clementi: Studies and Prospects*, pp. 101–124.

32 For a discussion of the motivic processing in the canonic passages of the Sonatas opp. 40 and 50 see R.H. Stewart-MacDonald, 'Canonic Passages in the Later Piano Sonatas of Muzio Clementi: Their Structural and Expressive Roles', *Ad Parnassum. A Journal of Eighteenth- and Nineteenth-Century Instrumental Music*, 1 (2003): 51–108.

33 Giuseppe Baini, *Memorie storico-critiche della vita e delle opere di Giovanni Pierluigi da Palestrina* (2 vols, Rome: della Società tipografica, 1828). Quoted in Plantinga, *Clementi*,

It thus seems reasonable to imagine that, in the course of his career, Clementi's engagement with 'learned' styles travelled full circle, from his early musical education centred on sixteenth-century vocal models through to the stimulating influence of J.S. Bach and the Baroque, then returning to Palestrina later on.

The *Gradus* also, of course, offers direct evidence of Clementi's archaic preoccupations, as reflected in his borrowing of the title from J.J. Fux's 1725 treatise. Although his initial decision had been to call the work '*Studio* for the Piano Forte', Cramer's use of this name for his own set of keyboard studies (published in May 1804) made it necessary for Clementi to select an alternative that, in fact, conveys rather more about the work's aims and priorities than the original title would have done.[34]

Expansion of the Developmental Function I: Merged Developments and Recapitulations

Like the later piano sonatas and symphonies, the *Gradus ad Parnassum* provided an important arena for Clementi's experimentation with form and with thematic processing. Often, this led to an expansion of the developmental parts of the structure. One relatively specialized means through which Clementi accomplishes this in the keyboard sonatas and in parts of the *Gradus* is through the strategic merging of developments and recapitulations.[35] The avoidance of a 'double return' of the opening theme and the tonic key prolongs the tonal instabilities of the central part of the structure for longer, as seen in the first movement of the Sonata in F minor, op. 13 no. 6, dating from 1785.[36] Here, the return of the tonic is delayed until the onset of the 'codetta' reprise in bars 101ff. (see Fig. 4.1). Preceding this is a structurally indeterminate area in which explicit contact is made with early parts of the exposition, but not in the tonic. A dominant pedal on G is prolonged in bars 64–7 followed, from bar 69, with an explicit thematic reference to the opening. The key at this point is C minor. A dominant pedal on C is reached in bars 79–82 but is followed (after a bar-long silence) by a reference to the version of the opening theme that emerged in the second half of the exposition.[37] The dominant that is prolonged in bars 93–100 then re-launches the tonic. By this method, a clear distinction between 'development' and 'recapitulation' is avoided, the tonic return is delayed until later in the structure and certain recapitulatory events assume a 'developmental' aspect.

---

p. 246. Plantinga carefully weighs up the evidence concerning the likely dating of Clementi's visit to Baini.

34 The evidence for this emerges in the letter of 1818 from Clementi to Paul Härtel quoted above: see n. 17. See also Alan Tyson, 'A Feud between Clementi and Cramer', *Music & Letters*, 54 (1973): 281–8.

35 Such merging is never carried out in the surviving symphonies, although op. 18 no. 1 in B♭ major does have a 'subdominant' recapitulation.

36 A similarly elliptical approach to the recapitulation can be found in the first movement of Clementi's Sonata in F♯ minor, op. 25 no. 5.

37 This exposition is of the 'monothematic' variety, as seen with some frequency in Clementi.

Figure 4.1   Muzio Clementi, Sonata in F minor, op. 13 no. 6, first movement.
Sonates pour Piano de Clementi, **ed. Henry Litolff, vol. III (Braunschweig–New York, 1868)**

Figure 4.1 *concluded*

Clementi carries out a similar process in Ex. 38 in F major from volume 2 of the *Gradus*. The development is arrested by a 'false' recapitulation of part of the first thematic group in E♭ major, the (unprepared key) of the flattened seventh: see bars 83ff. in Fig. 4.4. Unlike some of his other 'off-tonic' recapitulations, where he returns to the tonic quite quickly for a 'true' recapitulation, Clementi here staves off harmonic stability for some time until the (tonic) recapitulation of the second group.[38] The expansion of the development section is sensed quite acutely because the false recapitulation re-establishes some anticipation of recapitulatory processes that are unexpectedly delayed.

Cases like Ex. 38 and its equivalents in the sonatas might seem to belong to their own subset of works in which Clementi makes play over the division between development and recapitulation.[39] Equally, though, his practices in this area can be related to his broader interest in the developmental function – an issue of some significance. The historical implications of Percy Young's assertion that 'Clementi amplified the sonata by raising the status of the "development" section' are considerable and worthy of fuller exploration than is possible here.[40]

---

38 See, for instance, the first movements of the Sonata in B♭ major, op. 25 no. 3 and the Sonata in D major ('La Chasse', op. 16); and the finale of op. 10 no. 2 in D major.

39 This topic is investigated in greater depth in the second chapter of my book *New Perspectives on the Keyboard Sonatas of Muzio Clementi* (Bologna: Ut Orpheus Edizioni, 2006).

40 Percy M. Young, *A History of British Music* (London: Ernest Benn Limited, 1967), p. 409.

Expansion of the Developmental Function II: The Phenomenon of the 'Central Episode'

As already mentioned, contrapuntal activity of a fairly elaborate kind often directly stimulates motivic processing in Clementi's developmental passages. This is seen quite explicitly in various parts of the *Gradus*, in sonata-type movements as well as the fugues, and establishes important links between the work's different facets. In the development sections of some of Clementi's larger-scale movements in the piano sonatas and also in the *Gradus*, the contrapuntal processing of motivic elements converges with distant key relationships and certain syntactical characteristics to form a phenomenon I will call the 'central episode'. A 'central episode' is a passage of heightened developmental activity, often incorporating distant keys, strong chromaticism and intense contrapuntal processing of motifs extracted from one or other of the main themes. Such episodes lie at the approximate centre of the development sections in which they occur. They continue normal developmental processes, but distinguish themselves from their surroundings by heightening one or several aspects of the developmental activity already established. Often they are set apart by a break in the syntax, which can occur on one or both sides. The purpose of a central episode appears to be to extend or demarcate the most intense, processive 'core' of a development.[41]

One of Clementi's most explicit central episodes occurs in the first movement of the Sonata in B minor, op. 40 no. 2, in bars 152–86 (see Fig. 4.2b). This episode is clearly set apart on both sides by the remission of quaver activity and also by the retreat into higher registers. At the heart of this central episode lies a two-part canon in the distant key of E♭ minor (see bars 165ff.). The motivic source of this canonic passage is not immediately evident, but its main melodic substance is derived from the exposition's second theme (see Figure 4.2a). In its original statement in bars 77ff., this melodic idea contains two elements: an ascending scale in crotchets (bars 77 and 79, beats 2–4) and a descending third (bars 78 and 80). In the canon, Clementi reverses the order of these two motivic elements whereby, in bars 165 and 166 for instance, the descending third appears twice successively (bars 165, beat 4–166, beats 1–3) followed by the scalar descent (bar 166, beats 3–4 and bar 167, beats 1–2). The composer thus produces a derivation whose subtlety – indeed tenuousness – is proclaimed by the distance of key, topic and expressive mode at this point in the section. A clear distinction can be drawn between the type of motivic processing seen within this central episode and the more explicit thematic referencing that occurs in the surrounding body of the development. Whereas at the start of the section the entire first theme is quoted twice successively, in the central episode fragments from both main themes are more extensively reinterpreted as well as being recontextualized harmonically and topically. The impression is almost of a shift from casual, conversational quotation to a fantasizing process in

---

41 This term is borrowed from William Caplin, *Classical Form: A Theory of Formal Functions for the Music of Haydn, Mozart and Beethoven* (New York and Oxford: Oxford University Press, 1998), pp. 142–7.

which memory fragments are introjected and distorted through various forms of condensation and displacement.[42]

(a)

(b)

Figure 4.2   Muzio Clementi, Sonata in B minor, op. 40 no. 2, first movement.
Sonaten für das Pianoforte von Muzio Clementi: Neue sorgfältig revidirte Ausgabe, Dritter Band **(Leipzig: Breitkopf & Härtel, 1881)**

---

42 'Condensation' and 'displacement' were two terms used by Sigmund Freud to quantify the processes by which daytime thoughts and memory traces were reinterpreted and distorted in the dreaming state. See Sigmund Freud, *The Interpretation of Dreams*, trans. Joyce Crick (Oxford: Oxford University Press, 1999), pp. 212–36.

The development section of Ex. 61 from volume 3 of the *Gradus* contains a long central episode similar in certain respects to the one in op. 40 no. 2. It stretches from bar 125 to bar 165 and is set off on either side by a clear cadence (compare bars 123–4 with bars 162–4 in Fig. 4.3b). From bar 125 there is a marked reduction of quaver motion, which is reinstated from bar 149. Bars 125ff. are 'episodic' in being harmonically parenthetical. Bar 125 interrupts a cadence into G minor under preparation since bar 115, a harmonic goal that is delayed until bar 157; the rest of the section then articulates D minor as the final destination of the section (see bars 160–64). The harmonic interior of the central episode is unstable, dominated by chromatic sequences: this provides a winding continuum within which contrapuntally assisted motivic processing is carried out.

The entire episode exhaustively examines a motif consisting of an upward-moving crotchet and two quavers that originates early on in the exposition and which can ultimately be related to the opening (see bars 17–18 in Fig. 4.3a, and compare the melody in bars 18–19 with the melody in bars 1–2). Towards the beginning of the central episode Clementi combines two versions of his motif. The alto part in bars 125 and 127 refers explicitly to the version given in bars 17 and 18, the tenor and bass having a rhythmically 'magnified' version of the ascending part of the motif. This produces a freely imitative effect that also involves augmentation. From bar 137 the composer inverts the motif in the right hand, slightly modifying its shape in bars 144–5. Starting in bar 148, elements extracted from the motif are distributed throughout the texture so that the outer parts state the rhythmically

Figure 4.3(a)   Muzio Clementi, Ex. 61 from *Gradus ad Parnassum. Gradus ad Parnassum, ou l'art de jouer le Pianoforte, démontré par des Exercices dans le style sévère et dans le style élégant … par Muzio Clementi*, vol. II (Leipzig–Berlin, 1868)

Figure 4.3(b) **Muzio Clementi, Ex. 61 from** *Gradus ad Parnassum. Gradus ad Parnassum, ou l'art de jouer le Pianoforte, démontré par des Exercices dans le style sévère et dans le style élégant … par Muzio Clementi,* **vol. II (Leipzig–Berlin, 1868)**

elongated version of the scalar part of the motif (prevalent since bar 126) in contrary motion, whilst the alto has a truncated version of the inverted form of the motif first introduced in bar 137. By this point the processing and reinterpretation of the basic motif has reached an advanced stage. As if to recall the original point of reference, in bars 155–6, Clementi slips in a furtive but fairly direct recollection of bars 1–2 in augmentation in the treble part: thus the composer quotes the original source of the motif under examination at the very point when the derivations have reached their most distant and abstruse permutations and, significantly, when the harmony reaches its destination of G minor, effectively suspended from bar 125.

In this central episode, then, the composer does not use counterpoint in the explicit manner of his Sonata, op. 40 no. 2, but contrapuntal techniques such as imitation, inversion and augmentation are directly implicated; and, as in op. 40 no. 2, there is a clear shift of focus from a more casual citation of thematic elements to more intensive processes of reinterpretation and recombination.

Expansion of the Structural Foreground in Clementi's Later Works

The central episode in the development section of Ex. 61 represents a point of intersection for many of the fundamental compositional concerns of the *Gradus ad Parnassum* shared by such works as the Sonatas opp. 40 and 50: these are forms of thematic processing intensified by contrapuntal procedures, underpinned by complex, chromatic harmony, contributing to an expansion of the structural proportions. It is possible to contextualize these factors more broadly, in fact, within Clementi's frequent expansion of the structural foreground and establishment of tension between the processes set up within it and middleground coherence. This is a trait seen quite frequently in the composer's later works, and is reflected most directly in the digressive and parenthetical units that frequently emerge in the later piano sonatas, symphonies and parts of the *Gradus* – something that, in the *Gradus*, Clementi takes to extremes unprecedented in his work.

Ex. 38 has already been cited as an example where Clementi expands the developmental space by delaying the return of the tonic. The composer's strategy is in fact more pointed than this would suggest. The brief false reprise of the first group in E♭ major in bars 83ff. merges, from bar 88, into a transitional passage that approaches the dominant (see Fig. 4.4). The dominant is then prolonged in bars 96–7 in the manner of a retransition. Up to bar 98 the composer maintains the expectation of a tonic reprise of the opening, as if retrospectively to 'correct' the false reprise that occurred shortly before. The sudden shift of harmonic direction in bar 98 when the augmented sixth of bar 97 is resolved to B major, rather than being treated as a dominant seventh resolving to the tonic, confounds such expectations; and what follows, in bars 98ff., is experienced as a long digression that lengthens the proportions of the development, in the face of the expected return of the tonic. The events of bars 98ff. establish great tension, not only because they are structurally redundant, but also because of their harmonic audacity. Undoubtedly the most poignant harmonic progression occurs in bars 105–106 when a B♭ seventh in second inversion shifts suddenly to a C♭ major 6–4 (see Fig. 4.4). Various rationales can be

Figure 4.4   Muzio Clementi, Ex. 38 from *Gradus ad Parnassum. Gradus ad Parnassum, ou l'art de jouer le Pianoforte, démontré par des Exercices dans le style sévère et dans le style élégant … par Muzio Clementi*, vol. II (Leipzig–Berlin, 1868)

continued overleaf

Figure 4.4   *concluded*

put forward for this progression: for instance, that the primary relationship between the G minor root in bar 105 and the C♭ major 6–4 of bar 106 is to be understood on the basis of the contrary-motion chromatic movement in the outer parts (D–E♭; G–G♭).[43] It can also be linked with the chromatic motion from D to E♭ that launched the false reprise in bars 82–3 and an enharmonically reinterpreted version of the A♯–B that produced the change of harmonic direction in bars 97–8, as if to echo and retrospectively to 'contain' the two structurally most significant harmonic shifts from earlier in the development section – an interpretation that assigns some structural importance to the passage.

Foreground expansion is taken to epic extremes in Ex. 39 from volume 2, a character piece entitled 'Scena patetica'. This is structured as a slow introduction followed by a main body, consisting of an antecedent unit (bars 23–34), a consequent one (bars 35–40) and a closing tailpiece (bars 41ff.). After a tonic pedal has been prolonged in bars 49ff., the structure is essentially complete. The final resolution is sidestepped halfway through bar 53, however. What follows is a giant parenthesis, extending all the way from bar 53 to bar 120 where the tonic is finally resumed. This parenthesis is a *tour de force* of foreground elaboration that falls into several stages. The first part processes figuration from the first two bars of the piece. Making its way to E♭ major in bar 58, the episode moves through a lengthy cycle of fifths sequence, passing through the enharmonic boundary at bars 65–6. C major is established as a secondary dominant from bar 73, and from this point onwards the orientations are cadential. Bar 84 prolongs the C major that was established in bar 73, the dominant is prolonged from bar 85 and a 'subdominant reprise' follows in bars 90ff. The dominant prolongation is sustained from bar 85 until the resolution in bar 120.

Comparisons could easily be made between Clementi's approaches to both structure and rhetoric in the 'Scena patetica' and what occurs in the second movement of the Sonata in G minor, op. 50 no. 3, subtitled 'Didone abbandonata'. Structuring this movement as an incomplete unit that begins in the dominant and ends by resolving directly into the finale, the movement articulates such keys as E♭ and A♭ major quite strongly towards the centre. In this way Clementi again establishes tension between middleground progressions and foreground elaboration. The difference is that the process is taken much further in the 'Scena patetica'. The dispositional and idiomatic similarities between the two pieces remain striking, as indeed is the subject matter implied by each subtitle: this might suggest that such foreground elaboration, or rather the manipulation of the relationship between structural levels taken to such extremes, was something Clementi reserved for situations requiring heightened, almost melodramatic expression. That this process is taken to such an extreme in the 'Scena patetica' and also Ex. 38 illustrates one respect in which the *Gradus ad Parnassum* contains the ultimate expansion of some of Clementi's central compositional concerns.

---

43 This interpretation of the chord progression was put forward by Elizabeth French during a detailed discussion of this passage at Cambridge University in March 2005. I am indebted to her for her useful insights.

Towards a New Perception of the *Gradus ad Parnassum*

The object of this discussion of the *Gradus ad Parnassum* might seem to have been the construction of a more 'integrated' vision of the work by showing how some of its facets are linked by certain central compositional objectives and how these, in turn, permeate other areas of the composer's output. One could easily expand the discussion by comparing the motivic and contrapuntal processes at work in the fugues with what occurs in the development sections of the sonata-type movements. Even then, only a small proportion of the work would be encompassed. Particularly hard to reconcile with an 'integrated' vision of the work are the introduction-type movements. Many of these do indeed function as slow introductions to longer movements, but others seem more autonomous and obscure in their purpose. These 'miscellaneous' aspects of the *Gradus* force one to confront its diverse, fragmentary nature. Indeed, the global aesthetic of the *Gradus* may be strategically diverse, and its 'fragmentary' aspect may ultimately be embraced as an attribute. One might even compare the work with an entity like Horace Walpole's Strawberry Hill as another creation whose aesthetic is strategically 'chaotic', bewildering yet appealing. Beginning in 1750, over a period of 16 years, Walpole's 22-room country house was renovated at great expense. The aim was to create a visual replica of a Gothic fantasy, not unlike what emerges from Walpole's novel of 1764, *The Castle of Otranto*. The most obvious feature of Strawberry Hill is its diversity and what Walpole characterized in his written *Description* as 'an assemblage of curious trifles' from geographical locations including the Mediterranean, the Near and Far East and North America. Archaic architecture is imitated and honoured, and Walpole's *Description* alludes to 'memory places' that evoke the past.[44] Suggesting parallels between the *Gradus* and Strawberry Hill is useful in as much as it illustrates the possibility of embracing eclecticism and large-scale diversity as aesthetically viable. The obvious difference between the two is that, whereas the objective of Strawberry Hill is, or can be seen to be, entertainment,[45] that of the *Gradus* is ultimately didactic. Nonetheless, as with Strawberry Hill, the end product of the *Gradus* is emblematic of Clementi's laborious – but also whimsical – way of working in the second half of his career which, increasingly, led to the production of works that resisted 'completeness' and unfolded as 'works in progress'. This applies most literally to the four surviving later symphonies, which Clementi altered from performance to performance and continually put off publishing; the non-survival of parts means that they are still effectively going through processes of reworking that can never come to a definitive end. In the *Gradus*, the 'incompleteness' is not literal, but as one moves through the work – and particularly between those areas informed by similar compositional objectives approached in different ways – one can almost directly sense Clementi revising, recasting and trying out different possibilities. One of the most intriguing and perhaps alienating aspects of the *Gradus* is the extent to which the compositional approach is encoded in the end product, much as it is in

---

44 Dianne S. Ames, 'Strawberry Hill: Architecture of the "as if"', *Studies in Eighteenth-Century Culture*, 8 (1979): 354.

45 Ibid., p. 355.

a more literal sense in the symphonic manuscripts, covered as they are in mazes of cancellations and reworkings.[46]

Embracing the *Gradus*'s diversity as a logical extension of Clementi's manner of working in the second half of his career acknowledges its uniqueness and reinforces the irrelevance of making comparative value-judgements of that work and contemporary sets of keyboard studies: the objectives underlying the *Gradus* were simply different. Accordingly, it also becomes harder to see the *Gradus* as the straightforward culmination of Clementi's career, or as some kind of 'magnum opus'. As a project, it ran parallel with Clementi's activities after 1800, emerging almost as a series of kaleidoscopic reflections or expansions of his changing compositional preoccupations and objectives between about 1800 and 1827 as shown in the other material he produced during that time.

So what exactly were the artistic and pedagogical purposes of the *Gradus* ad Parnassum as envisaged by the composer? There is a clear danger of seeing the work merely as some kind of receptacle for discarded parts of Clementi's output, as Temperley tends to do, or of predilections taken to such extremes that they could not be accommodated elsewhere. In this discussion, I have made links between the *Gradus* and other parts of Clementi's output, notably the symphonies and the Sonatas opp. 40 and 50. These reflect the likelihood that, in composing the *Gradus*, the composer was continuing where he had left off with the piano sonatas, but in a context that was commercially more viable and one that gave him increased scope to pursue certain compositional preoccupations to greater lengths. The scale and diversity of the *Gradus* provides myriad opportunities for continual movement across the sliding scale of contrapuntal strictness and for exploring and exploiting the tensions between archaic contrapuntal models and modern idioms.

Clementi's ultimate objective in the *Gradus* seems to have been to operate on two levels of pedagogy simultaneously, the pianistic and the compositional. The compositional level is itself subdivided into partially distinct spheres of contrapuntal and non-contrapuntal writing, with significant points of intersection in between. It is the diversity of objectives that makes it difficult (and dangerous) to attempt to reconcile the work with any one sphere. In one sense, Clementi does seem to have been responding to contemporary market conditions by transferring his interests away from piano sonatas and towards such projects, but in another sense – and perhaps progressively – he adopted a retrospective stance by adopting a broader, more traditional conception of pedagogy. Clementi produces a work in which keyboard and compositional didacticism run parallel. The implication seems to be that the contemporary style needs to be enlivened – or perhaps regulated – by various forms of contrapuntal activity. In this sense, the 'steps to Parnassus' are backward steps. Ultimately, and perhaps most importantly, the *Gradus* is essential in viewing the evolution of Clementi's relationship with contrapuntal styles, a factor that is central to any comprehensive understanding of him as a composer but, ironically, one that has not been articulated with much clarity up to the present. In terms of its sheer

---

46 See Massimiliano Sala, 'Muzio Clementi's Symphonies. Contributions Towards a New Edition'. See also Heinrich Simon, 'The Clementi Manuscripts at the Library of Congress', *Musical Quarterly*, 28 (1942): 105–114.

scale and varied engagement with counterpoint, the *Gradus* represents the summit of Clementi's 'learned' aspirations, and encourages the temptation to see contrapuntal display as its central objective – particularly in view of the composer's choice of title and attitude towards volume 3.

How can this work be revived in the current century? Temperley is justified in stressing the unfeasibility of complete concert performances of the *Gradus*. It would surely be possible, however, to make smaller selections of groups of exercises or to intersperse them with other works by Clementi in the same programme to illustrate the exploration of certain preoccupations in different areas of his output. As part of any revival, however, a recontextualization of the *Gradus* is needed. Rather than being compared exclusively with the other contemporary didactic works from which it differs so strongly, it is best viewed as a centrally important artistic production of the 1820s: although its composition stretched out for much longer than just the final decade of Clementi's career, compositionally and aesthetically, it epitomizes many of the central concerns of musical language of the 1820s – especially that which involved recourse to archaic styles as a means of realignment within the present. Comparisons are thus insinuated between the fugal movements of the *Gradus* and those in Beethoven's later piano sonatas and string quartets, and even in works by Schubert, such as the Masses and the Fantasia in F minor for piano duet, D. 940; or they could be made, perhaps even more profitably, with the archaic elements in British music at this time, for instance the organ works of Samuel Wesley or the keyboard and orchestral music of Cipriani Potter.

The purpose of this discussion has been to summarize some of the historical processes leading to the modern perception of the *Gradus* and to explore parts of the work's interior, in terms of their relationship to other parts of Clementi's output and what they imply about the original objectives underlying the work. The investigation could be expanded in a number of directions to encompass more of the work, and most profitably, to assess its stylistic relationship with other non-pedagogical British musical productions of the time. The *Gradus* certainly deserves more sustained attention than it has received since its own time.

Chapter 5

Mendelssohnian Allusions in the Early Piano Works of William Sterndale Bennett

R. Larry Todd

We usually remember William Sterndale Bennett as one of several nineteenth-century English composers who adopted a comfortable style safely tethered to the elegant, refined romanticism of Mendelssohn. It was a particularly durable influence, casting its spell over much of Bennett's music, from his early piano pieces, piano concertos and concert overtures of the later 1830s to his final works, including, for example, the sacred cantata *The Woman of Samaria*, op. 44 (1867). Commissioned for the Birmingham Musical Festival and premiered some twenty years after the first performances of *Elijah*, the cantata was the creation of a composer acutely aware that in sacred music, at least, 'since the time of Mendelssohn, few composers had entered the lists'.[1]

Mendelssohnian references indeed abound in the score, beginning with the opening instrumental Introduction, an A minor *Andante serioso* in triple time against which the chorus asserts in C major and duple time the chorale 'Ye Christian people now rejoice' (from the seventeenth-century German hymn 'Nun freut euch lieben Christen g'mein'). If the tonal and metrical clash stamp this Introduction with a distinctive character and certain haunting quality all its own, there can be little doubt that by employing the chorale *cantus firmus* Bennett was deliberately situating his composition in the tradition of Mendelssohn's *St Paul* (1836), which of course begins with an instrumental chorale fugue based on *Wachet auf*. As we proceed through the cantata, other references begin to emerge, in particular to *Elijah*. The main subject of the chorus 'Blessed be the Lord God of Israel' (no. 3) impresses as a muted reference to the aria 'I, I am He that comforteth' in *Elijah*, and the lightly scored chorus 'Therefore they shall come' (no. 11), with its occasional harmonic excursions that gently redirect the flow of the music, seem Mendelssohnian in origin as well. The final D-major fugal chorus ('And blessed be the Lord God of Israel'), introduced by the majestic dotted rhythms of 'I will call upon the Lord', traces some of its inspiration to the *Schlußchor* of *Elijah*, perhaps most evident in Bennett's closing pages, with their culminating dominant pedal point and stately extended approach to the final cadence.

---

1   J.R. Sterndale Bennett, *The Life of William Sterndale Bennett* (Cambridge: Cambridge University Press, 1907), p. 364.

Some thirty years earlier, Bennett had met Mendelssohn in London. The occasion was a Royal Academy of Music concert held at the Hanover Square Rooms on 26 June 1833, when the 17-year-old Englishman, a pupil of Cipriani Potter at the Academy, performed his First Piano Concerto in D minor. Mendelssohn, aged 24, was then visiting England for the fourth time, in the company of his father, Abraham Mendelssohn Bartholdy. During the three earlier sojourns, the composer had premiered at the Philharmonic several works that secured his English reputation – the *Midsummer Night's Dream* Overture in 1829, the 'Hebrides' Overture in 1832 and the 'Italian' Symphony in May 1833. Of these the last was announced at the sixth concert of the Philharmonic Society simply as 'Symphony in A (No. 2)', somehow encouraging the critic John Ella to imagine that the slow movement reminded him of 'some ancient Scotch melody'.[2] A few weeks later at the Academy concert, Mendelssohn was introduced to Bennett by Lord Burghersh (John Fane), founder of the Academy, future eleventh Earl of Westmoreland and amateur composer, then serving as the English minister to Florence. Upon hearing of Bennett's proposal to travel to Germany for lessons in composition, Mendelssohn suggested that he come not as his student but as a friend.

Three years elapsed before Bennett was able to act on the invitation. During four visits to Germany between 1836 and 1842, he had numerous opportunities to hear the latest works of his new friend and colleague and to exchange ideas. In Düsseldorf, Bennett attended the 1836 premiere of the oratorio *Paulus*; after offering advice about his compositions, Mendelssohn wrote to Thomas Attwood that if Bennett did not 'become a very great musician, it is not God's will, but his own'.[3] On more extended visits to Leipzig in 1837 and 1839, where he joined a circle of musicians that included Robert Schumann,[4] Bennett made several successful appearances with Mendelssohn at the Gewandhaus and premiered piano concertos and concert overtures. In Berlin, in January 1842, he was among the very first privileged to hear the new *Scottish* Symphony, as rendered privately at the piano by its composer.[5] No doubt relying upon Mendelssohn's counsel, Bennett brought out in Leipzig through the firms of Friedrich Kistner and Breitkopf & Härtel several of his own early piano works also released in London, including the Three Impromptus, op. 12 (1836), the Piano Sonata in F minor, op. 13 (1837, dedicated to Mendelssohn), Three Romances, op. 14 (1837) and *Fantaisie* in A major, op. 16 (1837, dedicated to Robert Schumann), and thereby further consolidated the musical axis Mendelssohn established over the course of his ten London sojourns between 1829 and 1847.

The Three Impromptus, op. 12 are among Bennett's first piano works to show clear signs of Mendelssohn's influence. They were probably composed around May 1836, just prior to Bennett's departure from London with Mendelssohn's friend Karl Klingemann to attend the premiere of *Paulus* at the Lower Rhine Festival in Düsseldorf.

---

2   *Morning Post*, 16 May 1833.

3   Letter from Mendelssohn to Attwood, 28 May 1836, in Bennett, *Life*, pp. 41–2. For more extended biographical discussion see Peter Horton, chapter 6 below.

4   See Nicholas Temperley, 'Schumann and Sterndale Bennett', *19th-Century Music*, 12 (1989): 207–20.

5   Sterndale Bennett, *The Life of William Sterndale Bennett*, pp. 122–3.

Nicholas Temperley has already pointed to similarities between the falling soprano melody of op. 12 no. 1 and Mendelssohn's *Lied ohne Worte*, op. 19 no. 2,[6] which had first appeared in England in 1832 from Novello as one of the *Original Melodies for the Pianoforte*. The second Impromptu, in E major, presents a more subtle reference but one no less telling. Cast in a simple three-part form that alternates between the major and minor mode, the Impromptu begins with a soprano melody centred on the third scale degree, accompanied by a flowing quaver line in the alto and slower-moving bass and tenor parts. The texture, which requires the right hand to divide to accommodate the soprano and alto lines, is somewhat reminiscent of the opening of Mendelssohn's piano Caprice, op. 16 no. 3 (1829), also in E major. But it is the second phrase of Bennett's melody that in particular reveals through a quotation his Mendelssohnian sympathies. In bars 10–14, with a rising figure that moves harmonically through the supertonic F♯ minor and then, by a third, the subdominant A major, Bennett recalls a similar phrase from the slow movement of Mendelssohn's String Quartet no. 2, op. 13, which had appeared in 1830 (see Ex. 5.1). Like Bennett's phrase, Mendelssohn's moves by a rising third from the supertonic (G minor) to subdominant (B♭ major). There are, to be sure, differences in the metre (3/4 versus Bennett's 4/4) and melodic detailing, but the similarities would seem to confirm that by 1836 Bennett, like Robert Schumann, was a close student of Mendelssohn's scores.

Example 5.1 (a) W.S. Bennett. Impromptu, op. 12 no. 2

Example 5.1(b)   Mendelssohn. String Quartet no. 2, op. 13, second movement

In the case of the *Romanza* in E♭ major, op. 14 no. 2, a work that won Schumann's approval for Bennett's re-harmonizations of the opening melody and its 'magnificent deep basses',[7] the Mendelssohnian debt seems considerably more substantial. Bennett conceived this composition as a modified strophic *Lied ohne Worte*, with three varied statements of the melody in the major, minor and then again major modes. As we

6   *Works for Pianoforte Solo by William Sterndale Bennett from 1834 to 1840*, in Nicholas Temperley (ed.), vol. 17 of *The London Pianoforte School 1766–1860* (New York: Garland Publishing, 1985), p. xii.

7   *Neue Zeitschrift für Musik*, 7 (1837): 190.

Example 5.2 (a) W.S. Bennett. *Romanza*, **op. 14 no. 2**

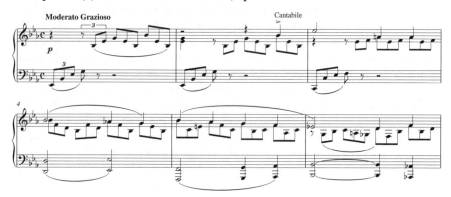

Example 5.2(b)   Mendelssohn. *Lied ohne Worte*, **op. 30 no. 1**

Example 5.2(c)   Mendelssohn. *Duetto ohne Worte*, **op. 38 no. 6**

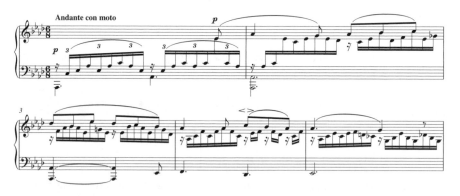

know, he dated the work in Leipzig on 10 April 1837,[8] when he was quite familiar with the first three volumes of Mendelssohn's *Lieder ohne Worte*, opp. 19, 30 and 38, published between 1832 and 1837. The gently rising arpeggiations of Bennett's opening from which he extracts the upbeat to the melody (Ex. 5.2a) lead us with little difficulty to the *Lied ohne Worte*, op. 30 no. 1 (Ex. 5.2b); not only is Mendelssohn's miniature in the same key, but it too unfolds in three sections in the major, minor and

---

8   Rosemary Williamson, *William Sterndale Bennett: A Descriptive Thematic Catalogue* (Oxford: Clarendon Press, 1996), p. 59.

major. Notwithstanding these parallels, the sixth bar of Bennett's *Romanza* suggests the influence of a second work, Mendelssohn's *Duetto ohne Worte*, op. 38 no. 6. As the opening phrase of Bennett's melody pauses on a Mendelssohnian half-cadence (tonic 6–4 to dominant), a chromatic detail in the accompanying triplets gives away its source: here Bennett briefly embellishes the tonic 6–4 with a diminished-seventh triad that resolves to the dominant, nearly replicating an analogous passage in the fifth bar of Mendelssohn's *Duetto* (Ex. 5.2c).

Conventional wisdom might impel us to dismiss the *Romanza* as a derivative work that foreshadowed the ardent Mendelssohn worship that took hold in England after the composer's death in 1847. But such an appraisal would not do justice to the subtle beauties of Bennett's composition that Schumann detected, and indeed the Mendelssohnian reference just cited may well involve something more than a mere stylistic debt of one composer to another. As we know, Mendelssohn drafted the *Duetto* in Frankfurt on 27 June 1836 during his courtship of Cécile Jeanrenaud. It is an idealized, instrumental love duet that Mendelssohn later copied and inserted into Cécile's autograph album.[9] What is more, when the piece appeared in 1837 as op. 38 no. 6, he appended to the title – itself a rarity among his *Lieder ohne Worte* – the direction to the performer to bring out clearly its two melodic lines, which alternate in the tenor and soprano registers before their union in octave doublings in the closing section of the composition. Bennett's *Romanza* begins admittedly as a solo *Lied ohne Worte*, but when we reach the middle strophe in E♭ minor, the texture changes momentarily to a passionate duet, a *forte* passage to which Bennett adds accent marks as if to encourage the pianist to bring out the newly added melodic strand (Ex. 5.3).

Example 5.3 W.S. Bennett. *Romanza*, op. 14 no. 2

There is the possibility, in short, that the *Romanza* is Bennett's idealized musical portrait of Felix and Cécile, a reading, as we shall see, that gains some currency when we consider that just days before its composition, on his friends' wedding day late in March, Bennett was putting the finishing touches to the Piano Sonata in F minor, op. 13, dedicated to the bridegroom and filled with further Mendelssohnian allusions.

Elsewhere in the *Romanza*, we find another passage with hints of Mendelssohn that attract our attention but for a different reason. Near the end of the first strophe and again mid-way through the third, there occurs a descending melodic line introduced by an expressive ascending leap of a seventh. The passage is repeated so that, all told, we hear it no fewer than four times, and it attains a certain prominence. In each case, the drooping line descends gradually and approaches a 'final' perfect cadence with a seemingly incontrovertible motion from the third to second scale degree, but Bennett persistently avoids full tonal closure by obviating the final, expected step to the tonic

---

9   Oxford, Bodleian Library, M. Deneke Mendelssohn c. 21, fols 108–109.

degree (Ex. 5.4a). What draws our interest is that Mendelssohn later seems to have responded compositionally to this passage in at least two posthumously published piano works, the *Lied ohne Worte* in D major, op. 85 no. 4 and Variations in E♭ major, op. 82 (Exx. 5.4b–c). In the former, composed in Frankfurt in May 1845,[10] the relevant passage occurs near the end of the composition where it is introduced by an ascending seventh and heard twice before it concludes with a descent from the third scale degree, initially interrupted but then completed with a perfect cadence. In the latter work, composed in July 1841,[11] the allusion occurs as the climax of the fifth variation of a set the composer described as 'sentimental'.[12] Here, though the example shares the key of its model, Bennett's voice is somewhat obscured: the appoggiatura on the climactic a♭″ is first approached by an ascending third instead of seventh, and there are other changes in the dynamics and detail of the accompaniment as well. Both examples betray modifications in the bass line and re-harmonizations, so that Mendelssohn's recomposition could be interpreted in a sense as re-hearings of Bennett. But the similarities and links are still clear enough, and the listener takes away the impression that Bennett's original phrase, turned as it may well have been in emulation of Mendelssohn, was later absorbed by Mendelssohn himself, thereby completing an exchange between the two.

Example 5.4 (a) W.S. Bennett. *Romanza*, op. 14 no. 2

In approaching the genre of the piano sonata, Bennett had at his disposal few models from his friend. By March 1837, when Bennett completed his Piano Sonata in F minor, op. 13, Mendelssohn had published only two sonatas, both student works from the 1820s: the early Violin Sonata in F minor, op. 4 (1824) and Piano Sonata in E major, op. 6 (1826). Despite the replication of key, little in Bennett's op. 13 brings

10 Two autographs, dated 3 May and 6 May 1845, survive in Kraków, Biblioteka Jagiellońska, *Mendelssohn Nachlass* 40, 51 and 61–2. Mendelssohn never published the *Lied*; rather, it was incorporated posthumously into his op. 85, which appeared in 1851.

11 The autograph is dated 25 July 1841, Leipzig. Kraków, *Mendelssohn Nachlass* 35, 15–17 and 19–22.

12 Letter from Mendelssohn to his sister Rebecka Dirichlet, 30 July 1841, New York Public Library, Mendelssohn Correspondence, no. 508.

Example 5.4(b)   Mendelssohn. *Lied ohne Worte*, **op. 85 no. 4**

Example 5.4(c)   Mendelssohn. Variations in E♭ major, op. 82, variation 5

to mind Mendelssohn's op. 4 unless, perhaps, we consider that both employ off-tonic openings on the dominant. But there are some obvious differences. Mendelssohn's sonata begins with a cadenza-like recitative for the solo violin; only at the entrance of the piano and the arrival of the tonic do we hear the first theme of the exposition. In Bennett's sonata, on the other hand, the first theme (Ex. 5.5a) is allied with the non-tonic opening, so that the cadence on the tonic F minor in bar 12 marks the conclusion of the primary theme. (Another possible stimulant for Bennett's opening may have been Robert Schumann's own Piano Sonata in F minor, op. 14, which, appearing in 1836 as the *Concert sans orchestre*, begins with a succinct progression in octaves from the dominant, fourth, third and second scale degrees to the tonic. Still, whereas Schumann quickly descends to the tonic, Bennett expands considerably the non-tonic opening by prolonging the dominant for fully eleven bars.) And though the lyricism of the subsidiary themes of Bennett's op. 13 perhaps recalls that of Mendelssohn's op. 6, there is no clear evidence that op. 6, a work usually cited for its emulation of Beethoven's late piano sonatas, exercised an especially significant influence on Bennett. Nevertheless, his present for Mendelssohn's wedding on 28 March 1837 to Cécile Jeanrenaud is fraught with allusions to his friend's scores, though we must look again primarily to the miniatures of the *Lieder ohne Worte* to uncover some of the connections.

Setting aside issues of sonata form, thematic development and the like, we may focus for the moment on a few salient features of Bennett's op. 13, including its more or less systematic alternation between minor and major tonalities and between thematic complexes of contrasting characters. As to the former, the exposition of the first movement divides conventionally enough into two groups in F minor and A♭ major, the tonic and mediant. When the second group returns in F major in the recapitulation, Bennett goes to the trouble of marking the passage 'Maggiore' and then, to denote the coda, which lurches into the minor, adds the label 'Minore'. The second-movement scherzo, also in F minor, includes a contrasting Trio in F major. The third-movement *Serenata*, whose programmatic title would seem to betray something of the special character of the sonata, is in F major so that, taken together, the two internal movements alternate between the parallel minor and major tonic. The finale, which like the first movement, is in sonata form, again presents two thematic groups in the tonic minor and mediant major; and when the second group returns in F major in the recapitulation, Bennett once again marks the restatement 'Maggiore', as if to draw our attention to the modal shift. These minor-major tonal pairings, summarized in Table 5.1, arguably assume in Bennett's composition a structural weight in tension with the conventional division of the sonata into four distinct movements. Furthermore, as we shall see, the pairings offer a potential key to interpreting the sonata.

Table 5.1   W.S. Bennett, Piano Sonata in F minor, op. 13

I. *Moderato espressivo*				
Exposition	Development		Recapitulation	Coda
f A♭	~~~~~~~~~~~		f F(*Maggiore*)	f(*Minore*)

II. Scherzo (*Allegro agitato*)			
	Trio		
f	F	f	

III. Serenata (*Moderato grazioso*)
F

IV. Finale (*Presto agitato*)			
Exposition	Development	Recapitulation	
f A♭	~~~~~~~~~~~	f F(*Maggiore*)	

Alternations between minor and major modalities are frequently encountered in Bennett's piano music, but in the case of op. 13 they are allied with thematic groups of distinctly contrasting characters. Without unduly reinforcing stereotypes about masculine and feminine themes and their perceived hierarchy in nineteenth-century conceptions of sonata form, we might describe, for example, the first theme of the first movement as fragmented, disjunct and unsettled by means of the syncopations of bars 2 and 4, through Bennett's liberal application of dissonant harmonies and, in bars 6–7, the use of increasingly wider leaps, including the unexpected and pianistically awkward tenth and diminished seventh in bar 7 (not shown in Ex. 5.5a). In a similar way, the opening theme of the Scherzo, marked *Allegro agitato*, conveys a certain restless energy and, in this case, playful agitation (Ex. 5.5b). And the primary theme of the finale, now marked *Presto agitato* and introduced by some propulsive staccato chords, is of a similar character, as it unfolds through a series of expanding melodic leaps of a third, fourth and sixth (Ex. 5.5c). There is, too, in its thematic contour, ascending from c″ to f″, a reference to the initial gesture of the first movement (see Ex. 5.5a) that further ties together the outer movements.

Example 5.5   **W.S. Bennett. Piano Sonata in F minor, op. 13**
                     (a) first movement

Quite in contrast are the thematic complexes in major keys, including the second subject of the first movement, which Bennett marks *cantabile* (Ex. 5.5d), the graceful figure introduced by the Trio of the Scherzo (Ex. 5.5e), the sentimental theme of the *Serenata* anchored by plagal subdominant progressions and seemingly derived from the Trio (Ex. 5.5f), and the second theme of the finale (Ex. 5.5g). Much more lyrical than their minor-keyed counterparts, these themes, though they utilize expressive leaps, are at once tonally secure, harmonically centred and consonant, as if resolving the melodic, harmonic and rhythmic dissonances of their minor-key counterparts.

Example 5.5(b) second movement

Now it would perhaps be all too easy to embrace a cliché-ridden interpretation of the thematic groups as depicting masculine and feminine characters and, furthermore, to read into the sonata a quasi-narrative of Felix's and Cécile's relationship. Nevertheless, as we shall see, considerable stylistic evidence suggests that Bennett may have had just such a programme in mind. And nineteenth-century accounts of Felix and Cécile promote an idealized relationship of a harmonious union of two distinctly contrasting personalities not at all incongruent with the design of Bennett's wedding gift. According to Charles Edward Horsley, son of the glee

Example 5.5(c)   fourth movement

Example 5.5(d)   first movement

Example 5.5(e)   second movement

Example 5.5(f)   third movement

Example 5.5(g)   fourth movement

composer William Horsley and a student of Mendelssohn in the early 1840s, 'Mme. Mendelssohn was a charming lady, very beautiful in person and very accomplished in mind. She was devoted to him; of a calm, unexcitable temperament; and as he was of a precisely opposite disposition, the extremes in this case met to mutual advantage'.[13] The Sanskrit scholar F. Max Müller, son of the poet Wilhelm Müller, described Cécile as one who could not 'express all she felt. She was soon called the "Goddess of Silence" by the side of her devoted husband, who never could be silent, but was always bubbling over like champagne in a small glass.'[14] And for Eduard Devrient, who had sung the role of Christ in the composer's 1829 revival of the St Matthew Passion, and who published memoirs of his friend in 1869, Cécile was

> one of those sweet, womanly natures, whose gentle simplicity, whose mere presence, soothed and pleased. She was slight, with features of striking beauty and delicacy ... She spoke little, and never with animation, in a low soft voice. Shakespeare's words, 'My gracious silence,' applied to her no less than to the wife of Coriolanus.[15]

Devrient's observations tend to corroborate Müller's and reinforce the gendered subservience of Cécile by comparing her to the demure wife of Coriolanus, whose silent 'greeting' of the conquering hero as he returns triumphantly to Rome forms one of the more notable pregnant pauses in Shakespeare, prompting Coriolanus to observe, 'My gracious silence, hail! Wouldst thou have laughed had I come coffined home, That weep'st to see me triumph? Ah, my dear, Such eyes the widows in Corioli wear, And mothers that lack sons'.[16]

Earlier we saw in the *Romanza*, op. 14 no. 2, how Bennett responded to a harmonic progression in Mendelssohn's op. 38 no. 6, a *Duetto ohne Worte* occasioned by his engagement to Cécile. Its metre (6/8) and flowing triplet accompaniment marked that piece as generically related to the *Gondellied* or barcarolle and thus suggested a love duet or serenade, which Bennett may well have had in mind when he made the decision to incorporate his own *Serenata*, cast in the compound metre of 12/8, into the third movement of op. 13. Like Mendelssohn's character piece, the *Serenata* has sections that set off and highlight the bass and soprano registers, and underscore the exchange between masculine and feminine roles. Example 5.6a shows one such 'duetting' passage that leads to the return of the opening theme. The use of contrasting registers to suggest male and female personae, an explicit enough conceit in the third movement, also seems to spill over into the exposition of the first movement where, after the first and second themes, Bennett writes a passage that combines the two. Appropriately enough, the formerly agitated first theme, now modified and

---

13 C.E. Horsley, 'Reminiscences of Mendelssohn by His English Pupil', *Dwight's Journal of Music*, 32 (1872), in R. Larry Todd (ed.), *Mendelssohn and his World* (Princeton: Princeton University Press, 1992), p. 242.

14 F. Max Müller, *Auld Lang Syne* (New York: C. Scribner's Sons, 1898), in R. Larry Todd (ed.), *Mendelssohn and his World* (Princeton: Princeton University Press, 1992), p. 256.

15 Eduard Devrient, *My Recollections of Felix Mendelssohn Bartholdy and His Letters to Me* (London: R. Bentley, 1869, repr. New York: Vienna House, 1972), p. 197.

16 *Coriolanus*, Act 2, scene i.

transposed to A♭ major, appears in the tenor with the 'calming' second theme in the soprano, forming a duet between the two (Ex. 5.6b). Thus did Horsley's 'opposite dispositions' meet, as it were, 'to mutual advantage'.

Example 5.6   W.S. Bennett. Piano Sonata in F minor, op. 13, (a) third movement

Example 5.6(b)   first movement

Two movements of Bennett's sonata betray some homage-like allusions to Mendelssohn's *Lieder ohne Worte*, specific enough that Bennett's friend almost certainly would have recognized them. One is partially concealed several bars into the opening theme of the finale, where Bennett momentarily turns the harmonic motion towards the subdominant B♭ minor, as it happens the key of Mendelssohn's *Lied ohne Worte*, op. 30 no. 2. Three times in Bennett's passage we hear a melodic phrase, essentially divided between the soprano (anchored on the pitch f″) and alto voices, that moves to B♭ minor via its dominant seventh on F major (Ex. 5.7a). In Mendelssohn's piano *Lied* a strikingly similar phrase occurs in bars 27–32 and 62–7, in each case three times and, in each case, descending from the pitch f″ (see bars 27–32 in Example 5.7b).

Example 5.7(a)   W.S. Bennett. Piano Sonata in F minor, op. 13, fourth movement

While this allusion transpires quickly enough in the presto finale, Bennett's second borrowing is considerably more conspicuous, for it occurs near the beginning of the scherzo (Ex. 5.5b). Here some details of the primary theme and the texture of the accompaniment stand out for their similarities to Mendelssohn's *Lied ohne Worte* in F♯ minor, op. 19 no. 5 (Ex. 5.8). First, after an upbeat leap from c″ to f″, Bennett's theme quickly moves to the dominant scale degree c″ (bar

Example 5.7(b)   Mendelssohn. *Lied ohne Worte*, **op. 30 no. 2**

3) supported by its upper and lower neighbour notes, d♭″ and b♮′ (bar 2). Bennett has essentially recomposed the opening of Mendelssohn's *Lied*, which extends the initial leap of an ascending fourth (c♯′–f♯′) by moving through the third scale degree (a′) before arriving in bars 2 and 3 on the dominant scale degree (c♯″), once again supported by its upper and lower neighbours (that is, d″ and b♯′). Drawing the similarity further into focus is Bennett's doubling of the soprano melody an octave lower in the tenor and, moreover, harmonization of the passage (VI6, vii4–3/V, V6), both taken over intact from Mendelssohn. And finally, just as Mendelssohn alters the texture of the accompaniment in bar 3, so does Bennett in bar 4, where the alto part alternates between doubling the melody in thirds and repeating the fifth scale degree. All in all, there is little doubt that Mendelssohn's *Lied* provided the immediate inspiration for the scherzo, though Bennett succeeded in producing a finely crafted and pianistically challenging movement in its own right, with quite original turns of phrase.

Example 5.8   Mendelssohn. *Lied ohne Worte*, **op. 19 no. 5**

Mendelssohn's op. 19 no. 5 struck a particular fancy with Bennett, for he also wove some allusions to it in one final work we shall consider, the *Romanza* in G minor, op. 14 no. 3; as it happens, another piano work structured between alternating minor- and major-key sections and another character piece cast in sonata form. Like op. 19 no. 5, the *Romanza* begins *piano* and *agitato* but, in an original twist, with a highly disjunct and dissonant two-bar introduction in which we may trace a chromatic descent from the fifth scale degree d‴ to c♯″, c♮″, b♭′, b♭′, to a′. The conclusion of this line, g′, then forms the downbeat of bar 3 and the beginning of the first theme, now marked *appassionato*, and derived clearly enough from bars 3–4 of Mendelssohn's *Lied* (Exx. 5.9a and 5.8). The contrasting second theme of Bennett's op. 14 no. 3, heard first in the median B♭ major and later in the tonic major, also incorporates an allusion to op. 19 no. 5, appropriately, to the latter part of its second theme. It is almost as if, while creating his *Romanza*, Bennett were silently playing through and referring to the earlier composition of his friend (Exx. 5.9b–c).

As Table 5.2 reveals, op. 14 no. 3 presents a sonata-form movement in which the basic ternary division aligns with Bennett's now familiar scheme of alternating minor and major keys. Following the precedent of his Piano Sonata, he again labels the recapitulation of the second theme and the concluding coda 'Maggiore' and 'Minore'. But in the course of this movement, he provides one tantalizing clue – as it happens, another Mendelssohnian allusion – that may shed light on an extramusical interpretation of the modal exchange in this composition. As we approach the recapitulation via a prolonged dominant pedal point, we hear a new plaintive motif, marked *espressivo*, harmonically diverted to the Neapolitan E♭ major and set against flowing arpeggiations in the bass (Ex. 5.9d). With little difficulty we can identify its source in a clarinet melody, marked *dolce espressivo* and set against similar arpeggiations in the chalumeau register of the second clarinet, that appears shortly before the recapitulation in Mendelssohn's Overture *zum Märchen von der schönen Melusine*, op. 32 (Ex. 5.9e).

Example 5.9(a)   W.S. Bennett. *Romanza*, op. 14 no. 3

Composed in 1833, the overture was entrusted to Ignaz Moscheles, who premiered it in London in April 1834 when, presumably, Bennett may have first heard it.[17] (His own concert overture *The Naiades* (1836), on the water nymphs of classical mythology, may be heard in part as a response to op. 32.) The similarities are compelling indeed – there are obvious melodic, rhythmic, harmonic and textural correspondences between Exx. 5.9d and 5.9e, and both passages prepare a recapitulation. But what gives the allusion added weight is the unusual structure of the overture in which Mendelssohn used a double exposition, double development and double recapitulation, all alternating between major and minor keys.[18] As we know, Mendelssohn could be rather fussy with titles, and finding an appropriate English rendition for the fairy tale of the mermaid Melusina, who assumes human form while she is with her knightly lover Raimund, evidently proved challenging. The solution for the Moscheles premiere, *Melusine, or the Mermaid and the Knight*, suggested the binary divisions of the composition – between the supernatural and

---

17 Subsequently, Mendelssohn revised the score in 1835 before releasing it as op. 32 in 1836. For the 1834 version, see the new edition by Christopher Hogwood (Kassel: Bärenreiter, 2003).

18 See further R. Larry Todd, *Mendelssohn: A Life in Music* (New York: Oxford University Press, 2005), pp. 288–9.

Table 5.2 W.S. Bennett, *Romanza* in G minor, op. 14 no. 3

Section	Exposition		Development	Recapitulation		Coda
Key	[*Minore*] g	[*Maggiore*] B♭	⁓⁓⁓⁓⁓	[*Minore*] g	*Maggiore* G	*Minore* g
Mendelssohn allusions:	op. 19/5 1st theme	op. 19/5 2nd theme	op. 32	op. 19/5 1st theme	op. 19/5 2nd theme	

Example 5.9(b)   W.S. Bennett, *Romanza*, op. 14 no. 3

Example 5.9(c)   Mendelssohn. *Lied ohne Worte*, op. 19 no. 5

Example 5.9(d)   W.S. Bennett. *Romanza*, op. 14 no. 3

Example 5.9(e)   Mendelssohn. Overture *zum Märchen von der schönen Melusine*, op. 32

real worlds, the aqueous and terrestrial, the feminine and masculine and, in simplified musical terms, the major and minor.

When Robert Schumann reviewed Mendelssohn's overture in 1836,[19] he did not hesitate to read into it romantic images of pearls, fish with golden scales, and deep-sea castles, literary indulgences that Mendelssohn privately rejected in a letter to his sister Fanny Hensel as fabulous nonsense.[20] In the case of the *Romanza*, by alluding to the overture Bennett seems to have permitted himself one musical licence designed to stimulate, if only briefly, our musical curiosity and to hint at a type of extrinsic literary interpretation that might resonate with his composition. If the many Mendelssohnian allusions in Bennett's piano music reveal him to have been a particularly close member of the Leipzig circle, they also show him to have possessed a creative imagination, for inevitably the allusions are no more than starting points or brief diversions, not ultimate goals, let alone evidence of stylistic subservience or lack of originality. In this sense, Bennett's art of allusion, like that of Robert Schumann (and indeed that of Mendelssohn and his sister) reminds us that the mystery of much nineteenth-century music lay in its intertextuality, its ability to reach beyond the printed page to a common musical language.

---

19 *Neue Zeitschrift für Musik*, 4 (1836): 7.

20 Letter of 30 January 1836 from Felix Mendelssohn Bartholdy to Fanny Mendelssohn Hensel. *Letters of Felix Mendelssohn Bartholdy, from 1833 to 1847*, ed. Paul Mendelssohn Bartholdy and Carl Mendelssohn Bartholdy, trans. Lady Wallace (New York: Leypoldt and Holt, 1868), p. 95.

Chapter 6

William Sterndale Bennett, Composer and Pianist[1]

Peter Horton

William Sterndale Bennett, England's most successful nineteenth-century pianist–composer, was born on 13 April 1816 and first made his mark while a student at the Royal Academy of Music (RAM). Among his successes were performances of a piano concerto in B♭ by Dussek[2] (September 1828) and one in A♭ by Hummel (December 1831), but these were inevitably outshone by the series of remarkably finished compositions that began with his first piano concerto, premiered on 28 November 1832 and repeated four times during the following seven months. Mendelssohn was in the audience for the last of these performances and immediately invited Bennett to Germany: "'If I come", said Bennett, "may I come to be your pupil?" "No, no," was the reply, "you must come to be my friend."'[3] It was not until 1836 that he was able to take up the offer, but his three visits to Leipzig would have a profound effect on his career and demonstrate the close bonds that, through him, linked contemporary English and German music.

The Early Concertos

Although it ranked as one of the principal centres of European musical life, London offered greater encouragement and rewards to foreign than to native musicians. Among the pianist–composers it attracted were J.L. Dussek, J.B. Cramer and Ignaz Moscheles, all of whom built on the foundations established by Clementi to develop a style which, while rooted in respect for Mozart and the classics, embraced an early Romantic harmonic idiom and increasingly brilliant passage-work.[4] The same characteristics can be seen in the music of Hummel, while the work of the composer and pianist Cipriani Potter, Bennett's teacher and the individual responsible for the

---

1   The writing of this chapter has been greatly facilitated by Rosemary Williamson's *William Sterndale Bennett: A Descriptive Thematic Catalogue* (Oxford: Clarendon Press, 1996). I also owe a great debt of gratitude to Barry Sterndale-Bennett for allowing me the run of his library (now on deposit in the Bodleian Library, Oxford).

2   Most probably op. 40, the 'Military'.

3   J.R. Sterndale Bennett, *The Life of William Sterndale Bennett* (Cambridge: Cambridge University Press, 1907), p. 30.

4   See Nicholas Temperley, 'London and the Piano, 1760–1860', *Musical Times*, 129 (1988): 289–93.

introduction of several of Mozart's concertos to London, provided an antidote to
virtuosity for its own sake. It was onto this stage that Bennett stepped in 1832. As
befits a pupil of Potter, his first concerto contains echoes of Mozart, notably at the
opening where the key and harmonic outline – tonic (D minor) followed by first-
inversion dominant harmony – recall the overture to *Don Giovanni*. But Bennett's
preoccupations were different from Mozart's and neither this nor his later concertos
demonstrate much of the formal subtlety seen in the latter's works in that genre.
Indeed, as contemporary critics noted, the strongest influences are those of Dussek,
Cramer, Hummel, Moscheles and their contemporaries. Of Beethoven, whose
concertos were still relatively unknown in England, there is little hint.[5] But perhaps
most surprisingly for a composer averse to virtuosity for its own sake, the concertos
all contain extremely demanding writing for the soloist and include one section
marked 'bravura' or 'brillante'. Here and elsewhere, rapid parallel thirds, broken
or alternating octaves, scales or wide-ranging arpeggios, singly or in combination,
seem designed to demonstrate the composer's prowess to dazzle the audience (see
Ex. 6.1).[6] Bennett's performance of his first concerto certainly impressed the critic

Example 6.1 W.S. Bennett. Piano Concerto no. 1, first movement

---

5   See Therese Ellsworth, 'The Piano Concerto in London Concert Life Between 1810
and 1850' (PhD dissertation, University of Cincinnati, 1991), pp. 339, 341–2.

6   The solo part of the concerto was revised in several places, among them the passage
quoted in Ex. 6.1, before publication. As originally conceived it was less demanding and
brilliant.

Example 6.2 W.S. Bennett. Piano Concerto no. 1, second movement

of the *Harmonicon*: 'the most complete and gratifying performance was that of young Bennett, whose composition would have conferred honour on any established master, and his execution of it was really surprising, not merely for its correctness and brilliancy, but for the feeling he manifested …'.[7]

Impressive though the opening movement is, it is in the F major slow movement that one reaches the concerto's heart. The mood is set by the opening phrase for the orchestra – four bars of serene diatonic harmony for the upper woodwind, answered by hushed strings whose lower pitch and solitary diminished seventh hint at something darker. But the opening bars carry their own overtones and call to mind the words of Bennett's first teacher, William Crotch, who once confessed that the sound of a series of simple diatonic chords could make his 'blood run cold'.[8] Had something of this percolated through to his pupil? It is, however, in the central

7   *Harmonicon*, 11 (1833): 108.
8   Nicholas Temperley, *The Music of the English Parish Church* (2 vols, Cambridge: Cambridge University Press, 1979), vol. 1, p. 249.

section that Bennett's delicate romanticism is seen at its best, with the piano weaving a gentle filigree of sound against slow-moving harmonies in the orchestra (see Ex. 6.2). At moments like this his position in the history of the piano concerto, alongside such composers as Field and Chopin, is immediately apparent.

Bennett's pupil Arthur O'Leary related how Potter had dissuaded him from his original plan of writing a four-movement concerto, with the result that the Scherzo was made to do duty as the finale.[9] What remains unexplained, however, is what led the young composer to contemplate a concerto in four movements a year before Moscheles wrote his *Concerto Fantastique* and over 30 years before Brahms's better-known examples. Bennett's finale is a driving Presto whose thick staccato chords are quite unlike the more obviously pianistic textures of the earlier movements. Orchestra and soloist, alternately *forte* and *piano*, conduct a vigorous dialogue, with the gentler trio providing relief from the pounding rhythms of the outer sections. There is, however, no respite and the work ends as unremittingly in D minor as it had begun.

For the next two years Bennett followed a similar pattern, starting a new piano concerto in July and finishing it during the following autumn term. His second, completed in November 1833 and dedicated to Potter, although in many respects similar to the first concerto, is a calmer, more expansive, but no less brilliant work whose writing – particularly parallel thirds in contrary motion and other third-based figuration – brings to mind Hummel's Concerto in A♭; it is also the only one of the six to be in a major key, E♭. Unlike the first concerto, which he never played again, Bennett returned to the second several times, and he chose it for his successful debut at the Philharmonic Society on 11 May 1835.

Five days later he was the soloist at the premiere of his third concerto, given at the RAM on 16 May. While its key, C minor, immediately invites comparison with the great concertos by Mozart and Beethoven – and something of the defiant power of the latter can be recognized – it was again the names of Dussek and Cramer that were mentioned by a contemporary critic.[10] But even more than in his previous work it is Bennett's 'abundance of originality'[11] that springs from the page. From the quiet opening of the first movement, whose sinuous first subject lends itself to contrapuntal elaboration, one can recognize his seriousness of purpose and growing skill in constructing a lengthy, much less predictable, movement. Among the surprises are the soloist's first entry, initially in two-part canon, in the key of the submediant, and the manner in which the piano then holds forth in a cadenza-like passage for 24 bars before the orchestra re-enters with the theme in its 'proper' key.[12] There are further occasions on which the orchestra falls silent, and one can sense that, in both formal

---

9   Arthur O'Leary, 'Sir William Sterndale Bennett: A Brief Review of his Life and Works', *Proceedings of the Musical Association*, 8 (1881–2): 125. Geoffrey Bush has suggested that the Capriccio in D minor, op. 2, might be a reworking of the original fourth movement ('Sterndale Bennett: A Note on his Chamber and Piano Music', *Musical Times*, 113 (1972): 555).

10   See the *Musical World* (*MW*), 4 (1836–7): 12.

11   Ibid.

12   Similar, but shorter, passages for unaccompanied piano can be found at the first solo entries in Hummel's Piano Concertos in A minor and A♭ major.

and musical terms, Bennett was seeking to strike out on a more independent path. At the piano's entry with the second subject, for example, there is a sudden, wholly romantic, feeling of stillness, made the more telling by the slow rate of harmonic change and the simple, sustained string accompaniment, not dissimilar to the type of 'background' orchestral writing found in the works for piano and orchestra by Chopin (and used earlier by Hummel):[13] see Ex.6.3.

Example 6.3 W.S. Bennett. Piano Concerto no. 3, first movement

The G minor *Romanza* consists of what Nicholas Temperley has described as a 'romantic dialogue'[14] between piano and orchestra, reminiscent of the slow movement

---

13 See, for example, the second subject of the first movement of Hummel's concerto in Ab.

14 Nicholas Temperley, 'Instrumental Music in England, 1800–1850' (PhD dissertation, University of Cambridge, 1959), p. 197.

of Beethoven's fourth piano concerto. Schumann, who heard Bennett's performance in the Leipzig Gewandhaus in 1837, related how 'the idea of a fair somnambulist had floated before our poet while composing'[15] – surely the tranquil melody of the G major *Maggiore* section – and this movement is the first of several by Bennett to have an extramusical programme.[16] In contrast to the restrained, sinuous opening of the first movement, the Allegro agitato finale is propelled forward with almost brutal force by the driving rhythm and unflagging energy of its first subject, announced *fortissimo* by the soloist, to whom the first 20 bars are assigned. But there are also moments of lightly accompanied scintillating passage-work and the movement provides a fitting conclusion to what is arguably Bennett's finest concerto; it is certainly not hard to see why the Leipzig audience, as Schumann recorded, 'gave itself wholly up to the delight we are accustomed to receive from a master, whether he leads us on to battle or to peace'.[17]

Example 6.4 W.S. Bennett. Piano Concerto in F minor, first movement

The last of Bennett's early concertos, in F minor, was completed in May 1836 and first heard at the RAM Prize concert on 1 July. In contrast to the tempestuous C minor concerto, it is a calmer, broader work, whose serene melancholy and sense

---

15 Robert Schumann, trans. Fanny Raymond Ritter, *Music and Musicians* (London: William Reeves, 1880), p. 214.

16 Schumann's description led Andrew Cope to suggest that the performance included the unpublished Adagio in G minor for piano and orchestra, originally conceived as the concerto's slow movement. See 'Sterndale Bennett's G minor Adagio', *Musical Times*, 122 (1981): 373–4.

17 Schumann, *Music and Musicians*, p. 214.

of understatement can be mistaken for a lack of substance. Such was the impression of the *Musical World* which complained of a 'want of working up in each of the movements' and suggested that it was a 'composition worth retouching';[18] it is more than likely that these comments sowed the doubts in Bennett's mind that led him to withdraw it and number his two subsequent concertos four and five respectively. The opening Allegro Moderato is the longest of Bennett's concerto movements, at once both fiery and elegiac, whose character is reflected in microcosm by the spacious opening subject that maintains a delicate balance between the darkness of F minor and warmth of A♭ major (see Ex. 6.4). No less interesting is the metrical irregularity of its 15-bar opening phrase – unusual in a composer who, at this period, so frequently worked in two-bar units. The series of extended trills at the end of the exposition also pose a question: did they inspire the comparable passage in Mendelssohn's Piano Concerto no. 2, completed a year later in August 1837?[19]

With the slow movement, entitled *A Stroll through the Meadows*, failing 'to arouse interest'[20] at its first rehearsal, Bennett wrote a replacement overnight, the well-known *Barcarole* that he later used for his next concerto. The Presto agitato finale, a loosely constructed sonata rondo, is another expansive movement and grows naturally out of the terse first subject which, with its play on a rising semitone, seems to prefigure – at least metaphorically – the main theme of César Franck's *Variations Symphoniques*.

Collectively Bennett's early concertos not only represent a remarkable flowering of the genre, but also bear eloquent witness to a prodigious compositional talent. In such circumstances it is not difficult to see why Mendelssohn was so excited by his music, nor why Schumann was moved to write that 'were there many artists like Sterndale Bennett, all fears for the future progress of our art would be silenced'.[21] With his long period of study at the RAM now at an end, his new freedom finally allowed him to take up Mendelssohn's invitation. But before following Bennett to Germany we must look at the works for solo piano he had already completed.

Early Music for Solo Piano

Given the few opportunities that existed in early nineteenth-century Europe for performing solo piano music in public, Bennett's initial concentration on works that would have brought him before the public as a soloist – concertos – becomes readily understandable. His first acknowledged work for piano solo, the Capriccio in D minor, dates from 1834 and demonstrates both the strengths and the weaknesses of his music at that time – strengths in that its (monothematic) sonata form structure is almost wholly constructed from a two-bar cell which is rarely absent from the musical argument and imparts a sense of unity; weaknesses in that it is over-dependent on a single rhythmic pattern, largely used in two-bar phrases which are frequently stated twice with little or no variation. In other respects, however, it illustrates a number of features that would become integral parts of Bennett's keyboard music: a fondness for placing a melody

18   *MW*, 9 (1838): 133.

19   Bennett had taken the concerto to Leipzig with him in October 1836.

20   Sterndale Bennett, *The Life of William Sterndale Bennett*, p. 42.

21   Schumann, *Music and Musicians*, p. 214.

in the tenor register, a liking for acerbic harmonies, an active bass line that imparts vitality to the texture and a penchant for short snatches of counterpoint.

Although not intended as a technical exercise, the Capriccio places considerable demands on the player. So too do the *Six Studies in the Form of Capriccios*, op. 11. The earliest of these (no. 4) was begun in December 1834 and the set completed in June 1835. Among the most technically challenging of all Bennett's piano works, the *Studies* belong in the same tradition as those of Clementi, Cramer and Dussek and each poses at least one technical problem: 'For the practice of double notes, legato', 'For the cultivation of the Legato, Espressivo', 'For Brilliancy and equality of fingering', 'For the Cultivation of a Characteristic and energetic style', 'For *tone* and *expression*', 'For the Study of *wrist* playing combined with the Cantabile'.[22] The original metronome marks indicate that Bennett played them – particularly the Allegro movements – extremely fast, and their reduction in the 'New & Improved Edition' implies (as Rosemary Williamson noted) that other pianists found it difficult to cope with his tempi.[23]

In the 1830s the idea of depicting the natural world on the piano was – at least in England – still novel, and Bennett's *Three Musical Sketches*, op. 10, 'The Lake', 'The Millstream' and 'The Fountain' (completed early in 1836), were among the earliest of their kind. He had originally called them 'Musical Sonnets' and it was his friend (and their dedicatee) J.W. Davison who suggested both the alternative 'Musical Sketches' and the individual titles; which came first, however, remains unclear.[24] But of Bennett's ability to depict his chosen subjects in musical terms there can be no doubt: the placid stillness of a lake on a summer afternoon, its surface occasionally ruffled by a light semiquaver breeze, a roaring millstream inspired by the one at Grantchester where his grandparents lived, and a delicate, sparkling fountain, far removed from the later examples of Liszt and Ravel. Schumann likened them to 'real Claude Lorraines in music; living landscapes of tone, and, especially the last ... full of truly magical effect',[25] and described the composer's performance of 'The Fountain' as creating an effect 'almost magical'.[26] But it is the foaming stream, driven forward by surging left-hand arpeggios and with some mercurial changes of key, that comes across as the strongest of the three.

Shortly before leaving the Royal Academy in July 1836 Bennett finished a set of *Three Impromptus*, published later that year as his op. 12. The first, a graceful Andante espressivo in B minor, bears all the hallmarks of his style: delicate textures, melodies which glide from one part to another or emerge from an accompanimental figure, and a subtle but imaginative harmonic idiom. Although the second, a Grazioso in E

---

22 The technical comments were added for the 'New & Improved Edition' issued by Leader & Cock, *c.*1851.

23 Williamson, *William Sterndale Bennett: A Descriptive Thematic Catalogue*, p. 45. Several of the tempi were reduced by over 20 per cent (for example, no. 1 from crotchet = 104 to crotchet = 80).

24 Might Davison have had Mendelssohn's *Two Musical Sketches* (London: Mori & Lavenu, [1833]) or the third of his *Trois Fantaisies ou Caprices*, op. 16, published in London as 'The Rivulet' (J.B. Cramer, Addison & Beale, [1830]) in mind?

25 Schumann, *Music and Musicians*, p. 143.

26 Sterndale Bennett, *The Life of William Sterndale Bennett*, p. 40.

major, begins in a conventional 'song without words' style, the central *minore* section is much darker and its melodic shape and keyboard texture – a melody in octaves in the alto and tenor voices, accompanied by quaver chords above and below it – have been compared by Nicholas Temperley with those of Schumann's *Arabesque*, op. 18, written two years later in 1838.[27] The last number, a fiery Presto in F♯ minor described by Geoffrey Bush as a 'whirlwind affair of presto sextuplets',[28] is a good example of Bennett's ability to create a satisfying structure out of an apparently mechanical series of arpeggios.

Leipzig

When, in October 1836, Bennett left for an eight-month visit to Leipzig, he embarked on the greatest adventure of his life. Not only did it plunge him into the midst of concert life in this most musical of cities, but it also led to the forging of deep friendships with two of the foremost musicians of the time, Mendelssohn and Schumann. His journey had, of course, been prompted by an invitation from the former, but once in Leipzig it was with Schumann that he spent more time and whose company he found so congenial. The relationship between the two men is a fascinating one, not least because in certain respects they were so different. While Schumann loved to spend an evening drinking beer, Bennett found such alcoholic marathons less to his taste.[29] And similarly with composition, Schumann's experimental, rule-breaking works are in almost complete contrast to Bennett's finished but essentially traditional ones – and it is not surprising to discover that the latter sometimes found his friend's music 'rather too eccentric'.[30]

It was while in Germany that Bennett completed and published three of his most important works for the piano: the Sonata in F minor, op. 13, the *Three Romances*, op. 14 and the *Fantaisie*, op. 16. All three were aimed at the 'serious' end of the market and it is perhaps a reflection on the perceived differences in musical taste between the two countries that only the *Romances* were officially republished in England. Indeed, the fact that Bennett should have turned to the piano sonata at a time when it was losing favour with both composers and the public in England says

---

27 Nicholas Temperley, 'Schumann and Sterndale Bennett', *19th-Century Music*, 12 (1989): 216.

28 Geoffrey Bush, 'Sterndale Bennett: The Solo Piano Works', *Proceedings of the Royal Musical Association*, 91 (1964–5): 91.

29 Bennett's journal contains numerous references to time spent with Schumann. Many extracts were quoted by J.R. Sterndale Bennett in *The Life of William Sterndale Bennett*. The journal is part of the Barry Sterndale-Bennett library now on deposit at the Bodleian Library, Oxford.

30 Comment in a letter of February 1837 to Davison, quoted by Henry Davison in *From Mendelssohn to Wagner* (London: Wm. Reeves, 1912), p. 31.

Example 6.5 W.S. Bennett. Piano Sonata in F minor, op. 13; (a) first movement; (b) Scherzo

something about his seriousness of purpose and awareness of tradition.[31] Elsewhere the form was still cultivated, not least by Mendelssohn and Schumann, but it was neither to them, nor to the sonatas of Beethoven – not widely known in England – that Bennett turned for inspiration, but to the works of the composers of the 'London Pianoforte School'.[32] There are indeed similarities between the spare textures of his first movement and parts of the equivalent movement of Dussek's last sonata, *L'Invocation*, op. 77 (1812), a work he performed in 1847 (and coincidentally also in F minor),[33] but one should not overplay such matters and Bennett's sonata emerges as a dark and restless work whose mood is set by the series of clashing

31 Nicholas Temperley has noted that 'In the 1820s, the sonata went out of favour altogether [in England], and foreign sonatas, if published, had to be given fancy titles to make them sell. It became almost impossible to buy a sonata'. ('Domestic Music in England 1800–1860', *Proceedings of the Royal Musical Association*, 85 (1958–9): 37). A review of Pio Cianchettini's *Le Delire, Grande Sonate* in 1832 opened with the words 'A *sonata* once more!' and continued later 'But has the sonata been defunct long enough to have slipped clean out of memory?' (*Harmonicon*, 10 (1832): 256).

32 Bennett's son recorded how his father had difficulty in acquiring a copy of Beethoven's Piano Sonata in B♭, op. 106, while a student at the RAM. See Sterndale Bennett, *The Life of William Sterndale Bennett*, p. 33. Also see R. Larry Todd, 'Mendelssohnian Allusions in the Early Piano Works of William Sterndale Bennett', Chapter 5 above.

33 The sonata was performed at his Classical Chamber Concert on 23 March 1847.

appoggiaturas and sustained pedal points of the opening bars; both serve to remind us of his fondness for acerbic textures.

Were it not known that Bennett habitually composed away from the piano this might have been guessed from the carefully crafted textures that suggest a work designed to appeal as much to the intellect as to the emotions. It is not that the sonata lacks passion, rather that its passion, whether in the first movement or the finale, is always strictly controlled. In other respects, however, it is a fascinating work that provides glimpses of Bennett's growing compositional skill – his use, for example, of the rhythmic and melodic shape of the opening (a rising and falling semitone) to bind the first movement together – and his habit of continually making slight changes to his thematic material. Note the subtle harmonic differences between two bars from the first movement transition (see Ex. 6.5a), or how, at the re-statement of the main theme of the Scherzo in octaves, the accompanying quaver figuration is developed into sweeping arpeggios (see Ex. 6.5b). Indeed, the last is but one example of his ability to elevate such secondary material so that it acquires thematic status.

If the sonata has a weakness it is that all four movements share the same keynote, with only a change of mode from minor to major in the *Serenata* third movement. But criticism of the Finale for its supposed lack of rhythmic and textural variety is misplaced: the very persistence of its (12/8) rhythmic pattern of four groups of three quavers provides its compelling forward drive.[34] More valid is the criticism that neither here, nor in the earlier movements, does the musical argument build up to a sufficiently strong climax, something for which the thematic link between the final bars of the first movement and finale (first noticed by Nicholas Temperley) cannot wholly compensate.[35]

No such reservations, however, apply to the *Three Romances*, written between December 1836 and April 1837. Comparing them with the *Musical Sketches* and the *Three Impromptus*, Schumann considered that they represented a 'great step in advance, – as regards deep, even strange, harmonic combinations, and bold, broad construction'. He continued:

> They ... may be regarded as the highest result of the composer's endeavours until now. They resemble his earlier works in richly flowing melody, and the melody of the upper part predominates in them; but they excel them in their highly impassioned character. The first romance is even fiery; the others are only somewhat more quiet, and the last overflows with complaining aspiration. It would be as difficult to analyse them as a fine poem; right people will understand them.[36]

34 See, for example, J.S. Shedlock, *The Pianoforte Sonata: Its Origin and Development* (London: Methuen & Co., 1895), which dismisses it as 'a weak Presto agitato' (p. 231), an opinion repeated in William S. Newman, *The Sonata Since Beethoven*, 2nd edn (New York: W.W. Norton & Co., 1972), p. 576.

35 See Nicholas Temperley (ed.), *Works for Pianoforte Solo by William Sterndale Bennett* in *The London Pianoforte School 1766–1860* (20 vols, New York: Garland Publishing, 1984–7), vol. 17, p. xiii.

36 Schumann, *Music and Musicians*, pp. 216–17.

Schumann's comment notwithstanding, one can usefully look beneath the music's surface. Several points emerge: the harmonic language is richer than in Bennett's earlier works, the thematic material is handled particularly well, the textures and dynamics are carefully varied, but most importantly, they all possess a satisfying musical shape. All these features can be seen in the first *Romance*, a fiery Agitato in B♭ minor, whose opening subject successfully combines harmonic intensity with a sustained lyricism. For the central section of its ABA structure Bennett moves to the relative major and then uses a powerful sequential phrase to modulate upwards before launching into a *fortissimo* burst of sustained submediant harmony, whose stability is in great contrast to what has gone before. And almost immediately we are back to a delicately accompanied *cantabile* melody and the development of fragments of the opening subject. Another *fortissimo* climax precedes the recapitulation while a final one introduces the coda. One can easily understand why Schumann was so impressed, and the other two works maintain the high standard. The second, in E♭ major, could be described as a 'Song without Words', characterized by great harmonic subtlety in the treatment of the main theme and containing a typically dissonant central section in the minor mode, while the last is another minor key Agitato. In contrast to the first *Romance* the textures are thinner and its dazzling arpeggios and semiquaver figuration give it a Mendelssohnian quality.

The last of Bennett's Leipzig works, the four-movement *Fantaisie*, is particularly intriguing, not least because of its close connection with Schumann. It was written during the first six months of 1837 and, according to Davison, was 'intended as a *souvenir*' for Schumann, 'expressly for … [his] own playing'. Not only had he stipulated that it should be made 'difficult enough' for him, but we also know that he was 'diligently practising the manuscript' when Bennett left Leipzig in June 1837.[37] Given that at this time he was working on his own *Fantasie*, op. 17, the question arises: why did Bennett choose to describe as a 'fantasy' a work that shares many of the attributes of a sonata when the term was predominantly associated with the type of brilliant fantasia on popular tunes to which he was later so averse?[38] The answer, I believe, lies in its origins as a *personal* souvenir for Schumann. This surely accounts for the character of the opening *Moderato con Grazia* which, although following the outlines of sonata form (but with no development), lacks two of its fundamental features – contrast of both mood and thematic material between the two subjects. Indeed, their very similarity (see Ex. 6.6), with both sharing the same quaver figuration in the accompaniment, can make it appear deficient in rhetoric and hence lacking in musical argument. But this is to misunderstand what is essentially a private soliloquy, whose charm lies in its subtle details and whose cascading quavers surely prompted Schumann's description of it as ringing with 'lovely melodies … as over-richly as a nest of nightingales'.[39] It is perhaps not too fanciful to see a

---

37 Sterndale Bennett, *The Life of William Sterndale Bennett*, p. 61.

38 Bennett had played a number of such works during his student days, but never in public, and he rarely used them as teaching material. Ibid., p. 94.

39 Schumann, *Music and Musicians*, pp. 218–19.

connection between such writing and Schumann's own playing: 'He moved his fingers with alarming speed, as if ants were crawling on the keyboard'.[40]

Example 6.6 W.S. Bennett. *Fantaisie*, **op. 16, first movement, first and second subjects**

The Scherzo, in contrast, is a vehement Presto in F♯ minor that bursts forth in a torrent of triplet arpeggios. It is driven forward by a series of dissonant 6–5 and 9–8 appoggiaturas, frequently accompanied by powerful four-part chords that quickly refute the belief that Bennett's music is characterized by a 'delicate, rather shy refinement'.[41] While the heavier textures perhaps reflect Schumann's influence, the ghostly unison octaves, barely rising above *piano*, which close the opening section (and recur in the D major Trio), bring to mind the Finale of Chopin's Piano Sonata no. 2, written two years later in 1839.

The brief *Canzonetta* is a simple song without words and serves primarily to reaffirm A major and to introduce a note of respite before the stormy finale that follows without a break. Here, in an exhilarating 6/8 Presto agitato in A minor, Bennett produced one of his finest sonata-form movements. By curbing his enthusiasm for two-bar phrases he was able to impart a much greater sense of breadth and this, combined with some imaginative harmonies, creates a real sense of excitement so that the music, as Schumann wrote, 'rises to a dramatic height of considerable imaginative power'.[42] Note, for example, how the rising E minor arpeggio in the first subject is harmonized by a bold series of root-position

---

40 Hieronymous Truhn's description of Schumann's playing of his own works, quoted in F. Gustav Jansen, *Die Davidsbündler: aus Robert Schumann's Sturm- und Drangperiode* (Leipzig: Breitkopf und Härtel, 1883), pp. 74–5.

41 Ernest Walker, *A History of Music in England*, 3rd edn (Oxford: Clarendon Press, 1952), p. 312.

42 Schumann, *Music and Musicians*, p. 219.

chords – A minor, G major, C major, B major, E major – and then deftly varied on
subsequent appearances (see Ex. 6.7).

Example 6.7 W.S. Bennett. *Fantaisie*, **op. 16, Finale**

One of the finale's greatest strengths is that it does not outstay its welcome. The *cantabile* second subject, in Bennett's favourite tenor register and accompanied by another series of cascading arpeggios, leads naturally into the short development, which is in turn followed by an abbreviated recapitulation and short coda. With this Bennett not only took his leave of Schumann and Leipzig, but also proclaimed the strength of his links with contemporary piano music. It is not always easy to identify precisely what gives the music its character, but certain passages have such strong 'European' overtones that one cannot help speculating how his music might have developed had he remained in such an artistically invigorating environment.

Before following Bennett to London we must, however, consider a further question: what other connections are there between his *Fantaisie* and Schumann's? The most obvious are a) the fact that one work is dedicated to the composer of the other, b) their composition spans the same period and c) both share characteristics with (or began life as) sonatas. It is the last – the use of the term for a multi-movement sonata-like work – that is perhaps the most significant. Hitherto discussion of Schumann's adoption of it – not finalized until after the publication of Bennett's *Fantaisie* in September or October 1837 – has omitted any reference to his being the dedicatee of a similarly titled work: it is surely inconceivable that this had no bearing on his choice of name.[43] Nor should it pass unnoticed that on 15 September 1837 he requested a copy from the publishers: 'Should Bennett's Phantasie be ready, will you have the kindness to send me a copy by return'.[44]

London, Mendelssohn and Leipzig

Much as he had appreciated the intensely musical atmosphere in Leipzig and the friendships he had struck, Bennett had missed his friends, family and familiar surroundings. But once back in London the contrast between the two cities and the difficulty of gaining more than a foothold in its musical life must have become ever more apparent. Whereas in Germany he had been acknowledged as both composer and pianist in his own right, in England he was still viewed as a promising former student of the Royal Academy. Yet all was not bleak, and in May 1838 he mounted the first of a series of annual benefit concerts at which he introduced a new work – his Caprice, op. 22, for piano and orchestra – together with his concerto in F minor.

Dedicated to Marie Louise Dulcken, the *Caprice* is a sparkling work in E major, light in texture and with a rather more Mendelssohnian touch than the earlier concertante works for piano and orchestra. As such it invites comparison with Mendelssohn's *Rondo brillant*, op. 29 and *Capriccio brillant*, op. 22, but the music is very much Bennett's own, replete with such characteristic fingerprints as the prominent use of broken and alternating octaves in thirds with the bass line and, for much of the time, almost incessant semiquaver movement. As in the finales of his third, F minor, and fourth piano concertos, he also chose to dispense with an opening tutti, restricting the orchestra to a single chord underpinning the solo piano.[45] The

43 See Nicholas Marston, *Schumann: Fantasie, Op. 17* (Cambridge: Cambridge University Press, 1982).

44 Williamson, *William Sterndale Bennett: A Descriptive Thematic Catalogue*, p. 74.

45 In the fourth concerto there are orchestral chords in both bars 1 and 2.

most curious section, however, is the second subject, a yearning melody for the strings in the dominant minor, accompanied by throbbing chords on the piano (see Ex. 6.8). It is a sound and texture that anticipates by some 70 years the music of Rachmaninoff, and one to which Bennett would never return.

Example 6.8 W.S. Bennett. Caprice for Piano and Orchestra

One outcome of Bennett's first visit to Leipzig had been the cementing of his friendship with Mendelssohn, and he had returned to London with an even greater admiration for the latter's music and personality. But in contrast to his relationship with Schumann, very much one between equals, that with Mendelssohn was more one of master and disciple. An immediate, but doubtless unconscious, consequence of this was that some of his own works began to assume a more Mendelssohnian character. A prime example of this is the first movement of his Piano Concerto no. 4, op. 19, completed in the summer of 1838. Indeed, its opening phrase, set over a tonic pedal and rising gradually over a two-octave span while the dynamic level grows from *piano* to *forte*, could almost be modelled on that of Mendelssohn's Piano Concerto no. 1 – a work that Bennett knew well – even to the extent of replicating its seven-bar length.[46] In other respects, too, it represents a change of direction from his previous concerto in the same key. Instead of the expansive timescale of the earlier work we find a tauter structure with no real development section and the central orchestral tutti omitted, fiery rather than melancholic in temperament (it was originally entitled 'Concerto Appassionata').[47] One can sense that Bennett, no longer a student, was trying to develop a more distinctive style and instinctively turned to the revered example of Mendelssohn. But perhaps his greatest innovation was the introduction of a broader range of textures, not least using delicate 'chamber music' scoring, as at the close of the second subject where a single right-hand melody for the soloist is accompanied by quiet pizzicato strings.

The history of the slow movement, the Barcarole in F major written for his previous concerto, has already been mentioned and it quickly became one of Bennett's most popular movements. Here too we find vivid contrasts of texture, with thunderous double octaves in the stormy central episode and delicate fioritura for the right hand alone in the outer sections. Despite its sombre F minor tonality, the Presto finale possesses an exhilarating vigour. From the dry staccato of its opening – again for piano solo – it carries all before it, with the yearning second subject providing only slight respite before Bennett launches into the type of bravura passage familiar from his earlier concertos; it is at moments like these that we are again forcefully reminded of his position in the history of Romantic piano music. Published with a dedication to Ignaz Moscheles, the concerto was first heard in front of a private audience at the RAM on 26 September 1838. The first public performance, conducted by Mendelssohn, took place during Bennett's second visit to Leipzig on 17 January 1839. Writing to Davison two days later he had this to say:

> If you knew how much I hated going before the Public under any circumstances, you could imagine how very uncomfortable it is to walk before an audience, eight hundred miles from your home. However, thank God, I played my new Concerto the day before

---

46 Although there are no identified performances by Bennett of the Mendelssohn concerto, his own copy shows signs of regular use; his earlier concerto in F minor also opens with a seven-bar phrase.

47 See Williamson, *William Sterndale Bennett: A Descriptive Thematic Catalogue*, p. 85.

yesterday with the most brilliant success, and what pleased me most was that the composition was well understood ...[48]

When Bennett arrived in Leipzig in October 1838 there was one significant absentee, Schumann, who had moved to Vienna. Compensation, however, came in the form of greater intimacy with Mendelssohn, and it was after breakfast on Christmas Day that he and Felix gave the first performance of his newly finished *Three Diversions* for piano duet, op. 17. Intended for Davison to play with 'Louise [Dulcken?]',[49] they are relatively lightweight and somewhat Mendelssohnian in character, but their craftsmanship captivated Schumann:

> Sterndale Bennett thoroughly delights us in his 'Three Diversions' ... Here too, are small forms; but what refinement in detail, what art in the whole! ... Save Mendelssohn, I know no other living artist but Bennett who has so much to say at so little expense, who can so well arrange and round off a piece, – who, in short, is able to write such 'diversions.' There may be bolder and more gifted ones, but none more neat and tender.[50]

Of the three numbers, an Allegretto semplice in A major, Andante cantabile in E major and Allegro agitato in A minor, the last is the most substantial and shares both key and time signature (6/8) with the finale of the *Fantaisie*. The similarity, however, is largely superficial as the *Fantaisie* represents the 'serious' Bennett of his first German visit, the *Diversion* the 'lighter' Bennett of his second journey. So, too, does the other piano work to date from this time – the Allegro Grazioso, op. 18 – and in both pieces one can identify the beginning of a change of character in his output as composition turned from being a seemingly effortless process to an increasingly self-conscious one. It was as though, with his student days past, he felt unequal to the challenge of competing on equal terms with his contemporaries and in consequence deliberately chose to cultivate less technically demanding forms.

London Again

Although Bennett remained in Leipzig for a further two months, continuing to work on an abortive symphony,[51] he completed nothing else in the city. Within a few days of returning to London in March 1839 he resumed teaching at the RAM and his career slipped back into a familiar pattern of lessons, occasional concerts and intermittent composition.[52] His travelling companion had been Ferdinand David who, in a letter to Mendelssohn, made some telling comments on his friend's lack of recognition in his own country:

---

48 Sterndale Bennett, *The Life of William Sterndale Bennett*, p. 77.
49 See Williamson, *William Sterndale Bennett: A Descriptive Thematic Catalogue*, p. 79.
50 Schumann, *Music and Musicians*, pp. 217–18.
51 Williamson, *William Sterndale Bennett: A Descriptive Thematic Catalogue*, pp. 452–3.
52 It is possible that the Chamber Trio, op. 26, completed in July 1839, was begun in Germany.

His compositions are, it appears, but little known here. They still see in him nothing beyond the *Academy student*. Heaven knows how he, with his unassuming manner, will make his way forward in this place. There are few Englishmen who would not deem a man insane, if he told them, that here was a musician of higher type than Mori, or Lindley or their other authorities.[53]

In one respect David's comment was all too true: Bennett did indeed find it very difficult to 'make his way forward'. A combination of his retiring nature, lack of encouragement from colleagues, and, one suspects, elements of self-doubt, all conspired to thwart his career as a composer. Mendelssohn's earlier comment that 'I am convinced if he does not become a very great musician, it is not God's will, but his own' was beginning to look remarkably percipient. Only two works for piano date from the remaining months of 1839: a brief piece in E♭ written for publication in *The Harmonist* and a Romance, *Genevieve*, composed in November for publication in the *Allgemeine Musikalische Zeitung* in April 1840.[54] The latter is one of the best examples of Bennett's work in a lighter vein, an unassuming piece in ternary form whose delicate keyboard figuration and chromatic auxiliaries occasionally suggest the music of Chopin, another, albeit much greater, composer able to elevate 'salon' music to a higher plane.

During the following two years Bennett produced a further handful of works for solo piano, a *Fandango*, *Two Characteristic Studies* 'L'Amabile' and 'L'Appassionata', and the *Suite de Pièces*, op. 24. Of these the most unusual is the *Fandango*, written for George Macfarren's Album in June 1840 and perhaps reflecting two of his most recent operas, *El Malhechor* and an *An Adventure of Don Quixote* (on which he was then working); nor should it be forgotten that Schumann incorporated an early Fandango into his Piano Sonata no. 1. Despite not being in strict fandango rhythm, Bennett's music, replete with crushing acciaccaturas, dissonant appoggiaturas and frequently thin textures, successfully evokes an image of Spain – or at least what would have passed for Spain in early Victorian England.

Although Bennett later described 'L'Amabile' and 'L'Appassionata', written in January 1841,[55] as being intended for 'young players', the second in particular is a demanding work in G minor full of rushing semiquaver arpeggios in what he called his 'bravura' style.[56] The rhythm of the opening phrase, with its upbeat semiquaver, suggests a link not only with the third number of the contemporary *Suite*, but also with one of the few piano sonatas by Beethoven that Bennett played in public, the 'Appassionata' in F minor, op. 57. Given the study's title, might this be more than purely coincidental? The other number, an Andante espressivo in E♭ major, is more a 'Song without Words' whose unruffled 9/8 is reminiscent of 'The Lake'.

---

53 Sterndale Bennett, *The Life of William Sterndale Bennett*, pp. 84–5. The violinist Nicholas Mori and cellist Robert Lindley were among the leading instrumentalists of their day.

54 Originally published as 'Notturno'.

55 Written for the English edition of F.J. Fétis and I. Moscheles, *Complete System of Instruction for the Piano-Forte* (London: Chappell, 1841).

56 See Williamson, *William Sterndale Bennett: A Descriptive Thematic Catalogue*, p. 150.

With the *Suite de Pièces*, completed by November 1841, we reach the final member of that group of early compositions for piano solo that had opened with the Capriccio in D minor.[57] The majority are technically demanding works and demonstrate Bennett trying his hand at a variety of forms: concert studies, a sonata, a fantasy and romances, among others, and now a work whose title suggests the eighteenth-century keyboard suite. But while *Suite de Pièces* was indeed the title used in England for the suites of Handel and Scarlatti, Bennett's work, dedicated to Lucy Anderson, is rather different. None of its six contrasted movements is dance-based, and rather than forming a closed tonal structure they are in a sequence of related keys: C♯ minor, E major, E minor, A major, F♯ minor and B major. One can, however, detect hints of the past, and it is interesting that both Schumann and the *Musical World* thought likewise. As the former noted, 'The study of Bach and of Domenico Scarlatti, whom Bennett prefers among pianoforte composers, has not been without influence on his development',[58] while the *Musical World* commented that the fifth movement 'reminds us of Scarlatti – we know not why – but the feeling it gives us is decidedly a feeling of that master, though modernized and *Bennett-ized* with extreme ingenuity'.[59]

The opening *perpetuum mobile* Toccata (Presto leggiero) provides another excellent illustration of Bennett's technique of 'thematic variation'. Here, within the framework of a sonata-form tonal scheme, he creates a kaleidoscopic impression by subtly fragmenting and varying the opening subject, introducing unexpected harmonic twists and frequently underpinning the structure with sustained pedal points. A two-bar questioning refrain, uncannily similar to the 'Muss es sein?' motif from the finale of Beethoven's String Quartet, op. 135,[60] introduces the mercurial *Capricciosa*, whose fragmentary textures, in which the thematic material is passed from one voice to another, prefigure those of the Scherzo, op. 27. Such writing demands great clarity in performance – a particular feature of Bennett's playing which was described as demonstrating 'a remarkable firmness of touch, splendid accent, wonderfully clear technique, and a style of phrasing as pure and fastidious as his own music'.[61] The fiery third number, simply marked Agitato assai, is a powerful and passionate movement whose opening swirling arpeggiated left-hand semiquavers bring to mind the beginning of Schumann's *Fantasie*, op. 17, though without the latter's intoxicating sweep. As letters to Mary Anne Wood, his future wife, make clear, this movement, and particularly its slower second subject marked 'Con passione', possessed a special significance: in January 1842 he wrote 'I very

57 It is not known when Bennett started work on the *Suite*, but on 28 November 1841 Lucy Anderson wrote to thank him for dedicating the work to her. See Williamson, *William Sterndale Bennett: A Descriptive Thematic Catalogue*, p. 125.

58 Schumann, *Music and Musicians*, pp. 286–7.

59 *MW*, 18 (1843): 31.

60 The only known performance of Beethoven's quartet in England prior to 1841 had been in April 1837, at the time Bennett was in Leipzig. See Christina Bashford, 'The Late Beethoven Quartets and the London Press, 1836 – ca. 1850', *Musical Quarterly*, 84 (2000): 87. Nicholas Temperley first drew attention to the 'Muss es sein' motif in 'Schumann and Sterndale Bennett', *19th-Century Music*, 12 (1989): 212.

61 Sterndale Bennett, *The Life of William Sterndale Bennett*, p. 214.

often play *one* of them [his new pieces] alone and think of the day when I wrote my first letter to you'.[62]

Example 6.9 W.S. Bennett. *Suite de Pièces*, no. 6

With the fourth number, *Alla Fantasia*, we find a movement which, unlike the *Fantaisie*, has clear links with the late eighteenth- or early nineteenth-century keyboard fantasy. That said, there are also significant differences as Bennett's movement consists of a twelve-bar refrain that alternates with 'fantasy' sections, written in strict time but creating an impression of rhythmic freedom through the use of short note values. The two elements are later combined, with the opening five-note motif of the second introduced in the bass line of the first, and it was perhaps this juxtaposition of opposites, of Florestan and Eusebius, that attracted Schumann, who praised its 'fantastic character'.[63] Once again one can see how Bennett's musical

---

62 Letter dated 25 January 1842. See ibid., p. 125.

63 Schumann, *Music and Musicians*, p. 287.

thought was more contrapuntally inspired than in many of his earlier works, with keyboard texture and thematic content inextricably linked. The same is true of the penultimate movement, Presto agitato, aptly described by Geoffrey Bush as a 'duple-time scherzo'[64] and, with its great variety of articulation and texture, it is a good illustration of why the work was advertised as a sequel to the op. 11 *Studies*.[65] With the Finale, simply marked 'Bravura', we reach the finest movement of the *Suite*, a virtual compendium of the various elements of Bennett's writing for the piano (see Ex. 6.9). From its powerful opening, with the dissonant descending bass line providing a solid foundation for a swirling mass of scales and arpeggios, it exudes an exhilarating strength of purpose, reinforced by its textural vitality and in no way lessened by the gentler second subject (marked 'molto legato') of its sonata-form structure. Indeed, it stands as a monument to Bennett the pianist, whose performance of fugues by Bach and Mendelssohn was thus described by Davison: 'The *legato* which is so eminent a feature of his style was employed to advantage in the Bach, and the *fire* ... was marvellously well bestowed upon the Mendelssohn'.[66]

Hard on the heels of the *Suite* Bennett embarked on a new 'Concert-Stück' for piano and orchestra, a piece which he conceived rather differently from his other concertante works:

> Now about my Concert-Stück – I can give you the plan as I conceived it – viz <u>Allegro Appassionata</u>, rather serious and earnest, after which a <u>short Serenade</u>, with very very slight accompaniments for the Orchestra, and finally the Allegro quasi Presto ending as merrily as I could make it.

> I have named it a <u>Concert-Stück,</u> as I never can acknowledge that a real <u>Concerto</u> can be written without the old <u>fashioned Tuttis</u> at the commencement &c – such as I have endeavoured to make in my other Concertos.[67]

The layout of the first movement does indeed break with convention, with the opening tutti reduced to a mere 25 bars and the recapitulation omitted altogether, begging the question as to what prompted Bennett to depart so radically from the accepted form of his earlier works. A clue can be found in his previous concerto, in which he had dispensed with a development section: he now sought conciseness by drastically shortening the introductory tutti and moving directly from the development to a short coda – in other words following the example of Moscheles's *Concerto Fantastique* and largely omitting the purely orchestral sections. But without hearing it, it is impossible to know whether the visual impression of an abrupt and premature ending would be borne out in performance.

---

64 Geoffrey Bush, 'Sterndale Bennett: The Solo Piano Works', *Proceedings of the Royal Musical Association*, 91 (1964–5): 94.

65 The 'New & Improved Edition' of the *Studies* (London: Leader & Cock and Addison & Hollier, [1851]) carried the following note: 'As a Sequel to these Studies, take the Author's Suite de Pièces'.

66 Sterndale Bennett, *The Life of William Sterndale Bennett*, p. 188.

67 Letter to an unknown correspondent dated 5 June 1843 (Washington, Library of Congress MS ML95.B47).

Bennett's original plan had been for a two-movement work, but after the rehearsal two days before the premiere he changed his mind and quickly completed the central *Serenade*, keeping the scoring light to enable it to be performed without rehearsal.[68] The resultant instrumental textures – for example a *cantando* melody in the right hand accompanied by staccato semiquavers in the left hand and pizzicato lower strings, or a single piano line heard against the full strings – are of great delicacy and created a decidedly favourable impression on the critic of the *Musical Examiner*:

> The Serenade in F major, *Allegretto Scherzando* ... is one of those happy trains of thought, the inspiration of a moment, which, if not at once laid hold of and embodied, would soon be lost for ever. It is a current of charming melody, unceasing and untiring – merely accompanied by the quartet, with an occasional few notes for the flute. The effect is deliciously fresh, and, as far as a single hearing ... allows us to judge, the conception and development are altogether faultless.[69]

Like many of Bennett's 'slow' movements it is not strictly slow,[70] and in this respect it can be compared with the *Serenata* (Moderato grazioso) from the Piano Sonata and the *Canzonetta* (Andantino) from the *Fantaisie*; it also departs from the pattern of his other concerto slow movements in which a turbulent central episode is framed by calmer outer sections.

The Allegro quasi presto finale, a sonata rondo in 2/4, is not only the most light-hearted of Bennett's concerto finales, whose 'untameable spirit, and untiring energy'[71] are reminiscent of the *Caprice* in E, but also the only major-key finale to a minor-key concerto. And in the light of the composer's admiration for Mendelssohn and his music, it is worth noting that Henry Chorley upbraided him for being so subservient to the German master. What appears to have escaped comment, however, is a neat joke on Bennett's part: the recapitulation of the opening orchestral tutti in the wrong key, B major.

Although Bennett had hoped to have had the work ready for performance during his third visit to Germany (December 1841 to March 1842) it did not receive its premiere, at the Philharmonic Society, until 5 June 1843. Press comment was broadly favourable, with the *Musical World* describing the first movement as being 'full of passion and grandeur' and expressing particular enthusiasm for the finale. The *Musical Examiner* was equally keen on the *Serenade* and Finale but had doubts about the first movement, and the changes that Bennett made before the work's final performance on 15 June 1848 – for which he renamed it 'Concerto' – appear to address these criticisms.[72] Given that it was written when Bennett was falling in love

---

68 Sterndale Bennett, *The Life of William Sterndale Bennett*, p. 150.

69 *Musical Examiner*, no. 32 (1843): 231.

70 Could the brisk tempo of the movement account for the comment in the *Times* that Bennett 'wrote a slow movement, but it was not played'? See Williamson, *William Sterndale Bennett: A Descriptive Thematic Catalogue*, p. 121.

71 *MW*, 18 (1843): 195.

72 See Williamson, *William Sterndale Bennett: A Descriptive Thematic Catalogue*, p. 126.

with Mary Anne Wood, it is fascinating to read the 'programme' ascribed to it by Davison:

> The idea of the composer in this *concert stuck* was, as it seems to us – first, love – second, the expression of it – third, its happy completion. These are rendered by an earnest and passionate flow of feeling, such as the heart can only know when truly it loves – a pretty and grateful declaration, in the fanciful form of a serenade – and an impetuous outpouring of boundless delight at the knowledge that the love is reciprocated. This is a poet's thought, and as a poet, Mr. Bennett has expressed it.[73]

Although advertised in October 1844 as being 'in the press'[74] the concerto was never published and, until its rediscovery in 1992, was thought to be lost.[75]

Bennett's lack of productivity in the mid-1840s was a cause of worry to those who knew him, with Davison concluding his review of the *Suite* 'we cannot but wish Mr. Bennett would write *more*, and publish *more* … [and] we vehemently protest against the almost *inertness*, which he has of late displayed';[76] Schumann contented himself with the brief statement 'He ought to write more'.[77] But what neither probably realized was that Bennett was indeed still composing, but was finding it increasingly hard to finish works to his own or – as he imagined – others' satisfaction. As he wrote in 1842: 'I should be very ungrateful to complain, for I am sure no one ever went through life … meeting with more kindness and encouragement; but the difficulty is to answer the hopes of one's friends, who are always too sanguine.'[78]

The Sixth Piano Concerto is the most tangible example, but he is known to have also been working on a symphony, a piano trio, three string quartets and a piano sonata at this time, of which nothing, or virtually nothing, survives.[79] Indeed, the only other work for the piano completed during the years 1840–1845 was the *Rondo Piacevole*, op. 25, written in August 1842. Stylistically it is in the same vein as other 'lighter' works and remained a favourite with Bennett, who regularly included it in his concerts. Yet, as Schumann's comment 'we fail to perceive any progress in this work' suggests,[80] Bennett seemed becalmed, uncertain how to move forward – and it was surely this that contributed to his current compositional difficulties. Of much greater interest is the Scherzo in E minor, op. 27. Although there is no conclusive

---

73 *Musical Examiner*, no. 32 (1843): 231.

74 Publication of the concerto, by Coventry & Hollier, was advertised in *MW*, 19 (1844): 354, but never took place.

75 The autograph manuscript was rediscovered by Rosemary Williamson in the private collection of Bennett's descendant Thomas Odling. See her 'Sterndale Bennett's Lost Piano Concerto Found', *Journal of the Royal Musical Association*, 119 (1994): 115–29. I must acknowledge my thanks to Mrs Hilary Odling for allowing me limited access to the manuscript for the purposes of writing the present chapter.

76 *MW*, 17 (1842): 37.

77 Robert Schumann, trans. Fanny Raymond Ritter, *Music and Musicians*, 2nd series (London: Williams Reeves, 1880), p. 285.

78 Sterndale Bennett, *The Life of William Sterndale Bennett*, p. 103.

79 See Williamson, *William Sterndale Bennett: A Descriptive Thematic Catalogue*, pp. 452–65.

80 Schumann, *Music and Musicians*, p. 540.

evidence, it is likely that it is the sole surviving – or completed – movement from the piano sonata on which Bennett is known to have been working in 1845, and was finished by 11 November that year when he sent the score – under its original title of *Capriccio Scherzando* – to Kistner for engraving.[81] His subsequent decision to rename it *Scherzo*, made too late for the German edition, resulted in its publication under different titles in Germany and England.

In character this Scherzo is unlike any of Bennett's previous works in the genre and its delicate, translucent writing for the piano is far removed from the pounding octaves in the finale of his Piano Concerto no. 1, or the no less forceful writing of the scherzos in the Piano Sonata and *Fantaisie*. Instead we find broken but contrapuntally conceived textures in which the thematic material is tossed from voice to voice (see Ex. 6.10), blurring any distinction between 'melody' and 'accompaniment'. Structurally too it breaks new ground in taking the framework of a sonata form movement, but one in which the gentle second subject seems to fulfil the role of trio in a sequence of scherzo – trio – scherzo – trio – coda.

Example 6.10   W.S. Bennett. Scherzo in E minor, op. 27

The three movements of op. 28 – *Introduzione e Pastorale*, *Rondino* and *Capriccio* (1846–53) – are further examples of Bennett's lighter style, while the *Tema e Variazioni*, op. 31, published in 1850, contains typically graceful writing for the piano, albeit in a rather old-fashioned style and in a piece whose three variations and finale seem too short for their purpose.

Since his return from Germany in 1842 Bennett had been steadily building up a substantial teaching practice. In addition to his pupils at the RAM this included many private pupils and, from 1848, classes at Queen's College, Harley Street, a new school for girls at which he had been appointed Professor of Harmony and Composition. In 1848 alone he taught the piano for 1,632 hours – that is, the

---

81 Williamson, *William Sterndale Bennett: A Descriptive Thematic Catalogue*, p. 139.

equivalent of over 31 hours every week of the year – in addition to his lessons at Queen's College. With such a workload it is not surprising that composition and piano playing should have been increasingly confined to the margins of his life – quite literally in the sense that music for his recitals was frequently learnt or mentally rehearsed, and new works conceived, in the brougham he used to travel from place to place.[82] Composition was otherwise restricted to holidays, and it was during the summer of 1852 and the following Christmas that he completed much of his set of *Preludes and Lessons*, op. 33.[83] Taking the form of 30 pairs of brief preludes and slightly longer lessons, they provide a series of short studies in different aspects of piano technique not unlike those in J.B. Cramer's *Studio per il pianoforte*, op. 30 (1804), and were dedicated to the pupils of Queen's College. Several of the lessons bear descriptive titles and form brief character studies – *Der Schmetterling* (*The Butterfly* – Lesson 5) and *Zephyrus* (Lesson 25), for example – while Lesson 22 (marked 'Lamentevole') is prefixed by the opening lines from Tennyson's 'A spirit haunts the year's last hours'. Occasionally, too, Bennett displayed his contrapuntal prowess, as in Lesson 8, a two-part invention in F♯ minor, much of it written in invertible counterpoint.

Although in many respects the *Preludes and Lessons* transcend their didactic purpose, their brevity not only restricts the scope for musical development but also reinforces the impression that Bennett was finding it difficult to conceive longer structures. Indeed, Davison felt so strongly that his friend could have done far more with his material that he complained to Mrs Bennett that the collection was 'a "murder" of valuable ideas'.[84] But why had Bennett allowed composition to become such a minor part of his life? The principal answer, I suspect, is to be found in the lack of real encouragement he had received from the English public and press. This in turn fuelled his growing self-doubts, leading not only to the string of unfinished works in the 1840s, but also to a loss of fluency. Alongside this ran the need to obtain an adequate income which found its expression in an excessive teaching burden which he was never able – or willing – to reduce, and which merely served to stifle further his already weakened creativity. And once it was almost extinguished the flame of inspiration thereafter burned fitfully at best. While the rondo *Pas triste, pas gai* and the *Minuetto espressivo* written the following year, 1854, do nothing to advance Bennett's reputation, a third work, the *Toccata* in C minor, op. 38 is a different matter. Completed on 13 January 1854 and published in October 1855, it is not unlike the opening movement of the *Suite* and combines brilliant, if brittle, semiquaver movement in the right hand with a degree of harmonic acerbity produced by the regular use of dissonant inner pedals. Unlike some nineteenth-century toccatas it owes more to the Baroque than to the Romantic era.

---

82 Sterndale Bennett, *The Life of William Sterndale Bennett*, p. 198.

83 One number, Lesson 20 (entitled *Caprice*) had originally been written for Mary Anne Wood's Album in February 1842. See Williamson, *William Sterndale Bennett: A Descriptive Thematic Catalogue*, p. 181.

84 Sterndale Bennett, *The Life of William Sterndale Bennett*, p. 224.

Cambridge and the Philharmonic Society

At the beginning of 1856, with work on a series of piano pieces to illustrate the months of the year under way, it looked as though Bennett might finally have escaped from his long compositional drought.[85] But it was not to be, and after completing *January* and *February* he broke off and never returned to the cycle, largely, one suspects, as a result of his election to the Chair of Music in the University of Cambridge, his first season as conductor of the Philharmonic Society, and his retirement from the concert platform. Given the promise of the first two numbers and the evidence they provide of a new direction in his music – thicker textures and more pronounced chromaticism – the loss of the remainder is unfortunate. They are different in another respect as well: whereas the *Musical Sketches* had been broadly descriptive, these pieces aimed to illustrate the verses that precede them. Thus *February*, introduced by lines from Longfellow's *Afternoon in February*, takes the form (as Geoffrey Bush noted) of a slow waltz whose lugubrious opening successfully translates the poet's 'funeral bell' into musical notation.[86] Bennett's handling of harmony is always imaginative, with frequent use of the strongly dissonant chord of the minor 9th, and builds up to a fine climax before a short rhythmic motive from *January* is introduced. What, if anything, is its significance? Would it have featured in the other months as well?

Bennett's final piano work to date from the 1850s was a *Rondeau à la polonaise*, written in 1857 for the annual *Album für Musik* published by A.H. Payne of Leipzig. Although much simpler than the polonaises of Chopin, a composer for whom Bennett had more respect than admiration, his shadow is surely seen in some of the imaginative enharmonic modulations and delicate chromatic sidestepping. Like such earlier works as *Genevieve* and the Allegro Grazioso it shows Bennett's consummate mastery of an elegant 'salon' idiom.

With the exception of a short *Praeludium* in B♭ (1863), written at the request of his pupil Robert Harold Thomas, Bennett wrote nothing more for the piano until after his appointment as Principal of the RAM in 1865. His final three works could not be more different from each other: a very simple Sonatina in C (1871) written for the future use of his grandson, an Andante in E (*c*.1871?) and a descriptive sonata, *Die Jungfrau von Orleans* (*The Maid of Orleans*), op. 46, begun in 1869 and completed on Easter Day 1873. While both the Sonatina and Andante are no more than trifles, the sonata is a substantial four-movement work in which the music is prefaced by lines selected from Schiller's play.[87] The novelty of a programmatic piano sonata by England's foremost composer ensured that *Die Jungfrau von Orleans* received considerable attention and it was quickly taken up by a number of pianists, among them Arabella Goddard (its dedicatee), Hans von Bülow, Charles Hallé and Franklin Taylor. Although the movements approximate to those of a 'standard' sonata, their

---

85 J.R. Sterndale Bennett recorded how his father had chosen appropriate verses and title page illustrations for the complete set. Ibid., p. 390.

86 Bush, 'Sterndale Bennett: The Solo Piano Works', p. 96.

87 The autograph manuscript reveals that Bennett's original inspiration had been the poem *Jeanne d'Arc* by Robert Steggall (brother of his Academy colleague and erstwhile student Charles Steggall?).

specific character reflects their place in Bennett's design: an introductory 12/8 Pastorale, 'In the fields' (A♭ major), an Allegro marziale, 'In the [battle]field' (A♭ minor), an Adagio patetico, 'In prison' (E major) and the finale, marked Moto di passione, 'The end' (A♭ minor moving to A♭ major). Yet despite containing many individual beauties, among them the main theme of the march, whose powerful two-part writing is comparable in technique, if not in character, with the opening of Elgar's Symphony no. 1, and the portrayal of Joan's spiritual triumph over the English in the Finale, the overriding impression is of a composer caught in a time warp and no longer speaking the musical language of his contemporaries, be they English or continental.

It is perhaps natural to judge *Die Jungfrau von Orleans* by comparing it with Bennett's works of 35 years earlier, but this, I suspect, is the wrong approach and it should rather be seen for what it is – an imaginative, albeit flawed, attempt by a composer in his fifties to continue from where he had left off some ten years earlier. As such it forms an unusual coda to a distinguished output that had, almost single-handedly, ensured English music a position at the European 'top table'. That of itself was no mean achievement.

Surveying Bennett's career as a composer for the piano one is inevitably left with a sense of anticlimax and disappointment. Most of his best work had been accomplished between the ages of 16 and 25, and in retrospect one can see how the crisis of confidence that began to afflict him in the 1840s and the sense of duty that led him to undertake such a heavy burden of teaching almost snuffed out his creativity. After 1850 only a handful of pieces even approach the standard of his earlier years and even fewer suggest any further development of his style: as he grew older he became increasingly reactionary in his tastes, dedicated to the memory of Mendelssohn and unsympathetic to most young composers. But where they do look forward – *February* and, to a lesser extent, *Die Jungfrau von Orleans* – they heighten the sense of disappointment over what might have been. His later career was increasingly that of a public figure, at the Philharmonic Society, the Royal Academy of Music and Cambridge; he died on 1 February 1875.

Bennett the Pianist

A survey of Bennett's piano music would be incomplete without a glance at his work as a pianist. For over twenty years, from the early 1830s until his retirement in 1856, he performed regularly in London and occasionally in Germany to considerable acclaim, albeit often reluctantly: 'Good God! – Today I must play in the [Leipzig] Gewandhause [sic] – horrible thought – however I must – I hate playing in Public, because I think that one plays in an <u>unnatural manner</u> – in constant fear, & what he is obliged to give in carefulness, he takes from his enthusiasm.'[88]

He later described the nervousness that afflicted him before a public performance, but which 'left him altogether when he seated himself at the pianoforte, and with such

---

88 W.S. Bennett, *Journal*, entry for 19 January 1837.

a suddenness that he seemed to *feel* it go, as if it were lifted by an unseen hand'.[89] Even at private gatherings he frequently declined to play, as in March 1837 when he spent the evening with Walther von Goethe (the poet's grandson) and several others: 'Talked & drank tea, but would not play P.Forte – what a fool I am!'[90] Given his temperament it is not so surprising that he should have chosen to retire from the platform at a comparatively young age, but what is more unexpected is that his playing should, as Ferdinand Hiller recalled, have been so 'full of fire and soul'.[91] Hiller also drew attention to its 'extraordinary delicacy of nuance',[92] while others, among them the composer and pianist H.C. Banister, wrote of their amazement at the sounds he could draw from the keyboard:

> I was standing near him, and ... did not notice that he had left my side. Suddenly I was startled and could not, I assure you, realize what had happened. He had gone to the pianoforte and touched the keys. I had not the least idea, on the first impression, what the instrument was. It might, for all I knew, have been an organ or anything else. The sound produced was quite new to my experience.[93]

Bennett's repertoire was not extensive and consisted of a small group of concertos (several performed only once) – his own, Bach's concerto in D minor, BWV 1052, Beethoven's first, one of Mendelssohn's, Mozart's concertos K. 449, K. 466 and K. 491, Weber's *Konzertstück*, and double concertos by Bach (BWV 1060) and Dussek – and solo works ranging from Bach and Scarlatti, via Mozart and Beethoven, to Mendelssohn and Schumann. The two composers best represented are himself and Mendelssohn, the latter particularly in the months after his death. But when playing his own music he largely restricted himself to a handful of the shorter, most popular pieces – *Genevieve*, the *Musical Sketches*, *Rondo Piacevole*, *Scherzo* – or individual numbers from such larger works as the *Six Studies in the Form of Capriccios* and the *Suite de Pièces*. Beethoven's music was limited to four sonatas – op. 27 no. 2, op. 31 nos. 2–3, and op. 57 – and Mozart's to two solo sonatas, the Fantasia in F minor, K. 608 (as a duet) and the Sonata for Two Pianos.[94] Among Mendelssohn's solo keyboard works the Preludes and Fugues, op. 35 were great favourites, together with the *Lieder ohne Worte*. Of his friend Robert Schumann's music he played very little, although he did include the Andante for Two Pianos, op. 46 at one of his Classical Chamber Concerts in February 1853,[95] and by a quirk of fate it was in the year of Schumann's death that he gave up playing in public. Schumann had once described him as 'a pianist above all things' and with his retirement an important chapter in his

---

89 Sterndale Bennett, *The Life of William Sterndale Bennett*, p. 213.

90 W.S. Bennett, *Journal*, entry for 21 March 1837.

91 Sterndale Bennett, *The Life of William Sterndale Bennett*, p. 79.

92 Ibid.

93 Ibid., p. 186.

94 According to J.R. Sterndale Bennett his father played five sonatas by Beethoven, and an unidentified Romance in A♭ and 'Tema con Variazoni' in F by Mozart. Ibid., p. 214.

95 Bennett's other work as a pianist was as instigator of an annual series of Classical Chamber Concerts which ran from 1843 to 1856 and whose programmes included vocal, chamber and piano music.

life closed.[96] From henceforth only a select few would be privileged to hear the man whose playing Schumann considered second only to Mendelssohn's: 'And in what a way do they both play the pianoforte, like angels and with no more assumption than children'.[97]

---

96   Sterndale Bennett, *The Life of William Sterndale Bennett*, p. 215.
97   Ibid., p. 217.

Chapter 7

Victorian Pianists as Concert Artists: The Case of Arabella Goddard (1836–1922)*

Therese Ellsworth

Piano virtuosi of the nineteenth century rarely made a living solely as concert artists. For the most part, teaching supplemented or provided a major portion of a soloist's income and, in the best of circumstances, offered professional fulfilment as these musicians shaped the next generation of performers. With its rising middle class who had both money and time for leisured activities, Britain offered an especially rich source of possibilities for enterprising musicians to expand into more varied professional activities.

Well known for multi-faceted careers are the early members of what has become known as the London Pianoforte School.[1] We recognize Muzio Clementi (1752–1832) not only as a composer, pianist and teacher but also as a piano manufacturer, music publisher and conductor. The composer and pianist John Baptist Cramer (1771–1858) helped found a music-publishing house that exists to this day. By mid-century, many pianists still engaged in diverse musical occupations, but the range of these pursuits had expanded to include editing the music of other composers, writing musical criticism and analysis, administration and musical scholarship. For example, the émigré Julius Benedict (1804–1885), reputed to be an excellent pianist, achieved renown as a composer, conductor and editor, and authored an important biography of his teacher, Carl Maria von Weber. Better known is William Sterndale Bennett (1816–75), pianist, composer and teacher, who served as a conductor of the Philharmonic Society and Principal of the Royal Academy of Music (RAM). The reputation of Charles Hallé (1819–95) rests chiefly on his founding of the Hallé

---

*A preliminary version of this article was presented as a paper at the Fifth Biennial International Conference on Music in Nineteenth-Century Britain (University of Nottingham, July 2005).

1   The term 'London Pianoforte School' originated with Alexander Ringer and described the composers working in London during the late eighteenth and early nineteenth centuries. Nicholas Temperley extended the term to include roughly a century between 1766 and 1860 to encompass the year of the earliest English publication with the word 'pianoforte' on it through to the works of William Sterndale Bennett and his contemporaries. See N. Temperley (ed.), *The London Pianoforte School, 1766–1860: An Anthology of English Piano Music* (20 vols, New York: Garland, 1984–7).

concerts in Manchester, which he conducted for 37 years. But he was also a leading pianist in Britain and an editor of important collections of piano music, who spent his final years as Principal of the Royal Manchester College of Music.

Other important but less widely known mid-Victorian pianists composed, obtained conservatoire teaching positions, produced musical editions, and published writings on music.[2] One pianist in particular achieved greater success and influence in the sphere of musical journalism. A music critic for the *Times* and *Musical World* as well as contributor to other publications, James W. Davison (1813–1885) helped mould public opinion about performers and repertoire for nearly half a century.

Contemporary women soloists found their opportunities to earn a living far more restricted, particularly with regard to business enterprises, administrative positions and conducting. Recent research has shown that women pianists as far back as the late eighteenth century achieved prominence at least equal to their English male counterparts.[3] Nevertheless, the success of women musicians derived primarily from performing and teaching. Those who taught increased in both numbers and in ratio during the nineteenth century. In 1851, for example, female musician–teachers accounted for approximately 27 per cent of the profession. By 1891, nearly half of all musician–teachers were women.[4]

The number of women piano soloists increased in the nineteenth century in part because fewer felt compelled to abandon a performing career after marriage. For example, Lucy Anderson (1790–1878), wife of George Anderson, Master of the Queen's Musick, was the first native female performer to play regularly at London's chief concert venues in the nineteenth century. The émigrée Louise Dulcken (1811–50), sister of the violinist Ferdinand David, was considered among the prominent musicians living in London during the 1840s. While raising a family of six children, Dulcken was reputed to have had more students than any other teacher in London. In

---

2   The composer and pianist Charles Salaman (1814–1901), an early graduate of the RAM, wrote and lectured on musical history topics. William Henry Holmes (1812–85) was a performer and a respected professor of music at the RAM and Guildhall School of Music (GSM), counting among his students such notable figures in British musical history as Sterndale Bennett, James W. Davison and the brothers G.A. and Walter Macfarren. Walter Macfarren (1826–1905) composed while maintaining his position as professor of piano at the RAM and produced numerous editions of music by Mozart and Beethoven. Lindsay Sloper (1826–87), a pupil of Moscheles, made his living as a piano teacher, performer, editor and composer. William Cusins (1833–93) taught at the RAM, followed Bennett as conductor of the Philharmonic Society, composed, conducted and edited music, and engaged in scholarship on Handel. John Francis Barnett (1837–1916) enjoyed success more as a piano teacher than as a performer, in particular at the Royal College of Music (RCM) and the GSM. The pianist Walter Bache (1842–88) became an advocate in London for his teacher Franz Liszt, as well as a professor at the RAM (further on Bache, see Michael Allis, '"Remarkable force, finish, intelligence and feeling": Reassessing the Pianism of Walter Bache', Chapter 9 below).

3   N. Salwey, 'Women Pianists in Late Eighteenth-Century London', in S. Wollenberg and S. McVeigh (eds), *Concert Life in Eighteenth-Century Britain* (Aldershot: Ashgate, 2004), pp. 273–90.

4   C. Ehrlich, *The Music Profession in Britain since the Eighteenth Century: A Social History* (Oxford: Clarendon Press, 1985), p. 235.

addition, she learned and performed a diverse repertoire unmatched among London performers at that time. A few women pianists expanded their professional activities, exceeding the usual gender boundaries. Agnes Zimmermann (1847–1925) achieved success not only as a piano soloist but also as a composer and as editor of works by Mozart, Beethoven and Robert Schumann. Fanny Davies (1861–1934), a Clara Schumann pupil, belonged to a generation for whom we have sound recordings. While she was renowned particularly for her interpretations of Brahms and Robert Schumann, Davies's interests extended into music for early keyboards and performance on those instruments.[5]

One factor that contributed to the increase and acceptance of professional women soloists was the shift from composer–performers to performer–interpreters during the first half of the nineteenth century. An investigation of women and the piano concerto, the genre most likely to feature a composer–performer during the early decades of the nineteenth century, reveals conflicting paradigms. Because women seldom had access to compositional instruction, they generally avoided writing in large forms such as the concerto if they composed at all and, consequently, rarely entered the world of illustrious composer–pianists.[6] As a result, however, they enjoyed the freedom to choose from a wider repertoire than most of their male colleagues. Thus they early on entered into the burgeoning arena of pianist–interpreters.[7]

Oscar Beringer (1844–1922), a pianist and composer of German birth who enjoyed a distinguished career as a performer and pedagogue in London, claimed that the most significant period for progress in piano playing in England occurred during the 1860s and 1870s. Improvements in piano instruction and teacher quality, he maintained, together with the excellence of concerts produced at the Crystal Palace Saturday series, Philharmonic Society, John Ella's Musical Union and the Monday and Saturday Popular Concerts led to both an improved level of piano performance and a demand by London audiences for higher-quality repertoire. Beringer deemed the most prominent pianists in England at the time to be the émigrés Charles Hallé and Ernst Pauer and the native artists Lindsay Sloper and Arabella Goddard.[8] Another contemporary writer who drew attention to the 1860s was the music critic Joseph Bennett. He especially praised the wide-ranging programmes of that decade, particularly in comparison with those at the end of the century. In this regard, he paid special tribute to Goddard for the programmatic diversity she maintained and

---

5   See Dorothy de Val, 'Fanny Davies: "A Messenger for Schumann and Brahms"?', Chapter 10 below.

6   Examples of women who composed concertos and performed them during the first half of the nineteenth century in London are Veronica Cianchettini (née Dussek), Leopoldine Blahetka, Caroline Reinagle (née Orger) and Sophia Woolf.

7   For further information on women soloists and the piano concerto, see T. Ellsworth, 'The Piano Concerto in London Concert Life between 1801 and 1850', PhD diss. (University of Cincinnati, 1991), and T. Ellsworth, 'Women Soloists and the Piano Concerto in Nineteenth-Century London', *Ad Parnassum: A Journal of Eighteenth- and Nineteenth-Century Instrumental Music*, 2 (2003): 21–49.

8   Oscar Beringer, *Fifty Years' Experience of Pianoforte Teaching and Playing* (London: Bosworth & Co., 1907), pp. 1–2.

to Fanny Davies, in the generation following, for the exceptional variety of her programmes.[9]

Most of the pianists mentioned up to this point secured teaching positions in conservatoires. Goddard was appointed by George Grove to the Royal College of Music piano department when the institution first opened in 1883, but her tenure there seemingly lasted only a few years.[10] Although we read in newspapers and contemporary memoirs of Goddard taking on private pupils and, indeed, relying on teaching for her livelihood when her concert career ended, little information exists about them. Most probably they were amateur female students who did not go on to professional careers. And so it is as a concert artist almost exclusively that Goddard made her reputation.

The Early Years: 1836 to 1856

Goddard was born in France to British parents on 12 January 1836, some four years after the death of Clementi.[11] They shared a connection through Frédéric Kalkbrenner (1785–1849), Goddard's early teacher in Paris. Kalkbrenner reportedly took several lessons with Clementi during one of the latter's Continental journeys to sell his pianos. Later, the two were acquainted during Kalkbrenner's highly successful stay in London from 1814 to 1824. This link may have influenced, in part, Goddard's occasional selection of a work by Clementi for her concert programmes at a time when they were not often performed on stage.

Although the Goddard family resided in France, London musicians were aware of this native talent developing across the channel. John Ella (1802–1888), critic and manager of the Musical Union concert society, had heard her as a girl at Kalkbrenner's house in Paris.[12] The pianist and composer Ignaz Moscheles (1794–1870), a London resident until joining the faculty of the Leipzig Conservatory in 1846, recalled meeting her as a child when he prophesied 'a brilliant future' for her.[13] At the age of eight, Arabella was taken to England to play at court. Four years later,

---

9   Joseph Bennett, *Forty Years of Music, 1865–1905* (London: Methuen & Co., 1908), p. 356.

10   See Royal College of Music, London, Scholars Register No. 1 (1883–93), Students Register No. 1 (1883–5) and No. 2 (1885–9). Goddard taught in the piano department from 1883 to 1885. It is unclear if she was on the staff after 1885. Goddard and her female colleagues taught only female students; male teachers instructed both male and female piano students.

11   Goddard's birthplace was St Servan, near St Malo, Brittany. She died on 6 April 1922 at Boulogne-sur-Mer, in northeast France. Biographical details have been gathered from census records, contemporary periodicals, musical memoirs, a brief newspaper interview with Goddard in 1875, and material in an uncatalogued collection of Goddard memorabilia at Her Majesty's Theatre in Ballarat, Australia. I am indebted to Peter Freund, publicist and theatre historian at Her Majesty's Theatre in Ballarat for his very kind assistance with this project.

12   Letter from John Ella to J.W. Davison, date obscured, in the Arabella Goddard collection, Ballarat.

13   Charlotte Moscheles (ed.), *Recent Music and Musicians as Described in the Diaries and Correspondence of Ignaz Moscheles*, adapted from the original German by A.D. Coleridge (New York: Henry Holt and Company, 1879), p. 388.

the political upheavals and economic uncertainties in France in 1848 compelled the family to repatriate to England. Goddard later claimed it was her father's financial reversals that led to her becoming a professional pianist.[14]

After settling in London, Goddard received piano instruction from Lucy Anderson and Wilhelm Kuhe (1823–1912), another recent émigré to Britain, and studied composition with G.A. Macfarren (1813–87). Instead of enrolling in the RAM, Goddard continued her training with Sigismond Thalberg (1812–71). At his recommendation, she began her tutelage with J.W. Davison in 1851. The standard line in contemporary accounts presents Goddard as a performer of 'fantasias and music of a like class' until her association with Davison, who proceeded to expand her knowledge of classical repertoire and eventually control her programming.[15] The notion was strengthened after Goddard and Davison married in 1859. To what extent are we to believe the received wisdom regarding Davison's management of Goddard? There is a frustrating lack of primary source material by Goddard to help illuminate this subject. To be sure, her emphasis on German composers reflects Davison's known biases, preferences that were shared by many British musicians. Likewise, his advocacy of contemporary British composers and of those who resided in England during the early years of the nineteenth century was taken up by his pupil. Most probably, Davison exerted a powerful impact on the development of Goddard's repertoire, but that should not obscure the fact that Goddard became increasingly independent of Davison, especially during her later travels abroad.

Critics reported Goddard as a debutante on the London concert scene in 1850 when she appeared at the Grand National Concerts, a series that also featured Thalberg and Hallé. Identified as a Thalberg pupil, Goddard 'created an extraordinary sensation', was declared 'a prodigy', judged to possess 'very rare abilities' and promised 'with practice and time to stand high amongst the high in her profession'.[16] Amid such lofty expectations, her career in England was launched. The works she played for the series were mostly 'of the modern romantic school', including fantasias by her current teacher Thalberg, but she also displayed her skills in 'classical' repertoire with a movement from a Hummel concerto. In addition, the *Illustrated News* reported, she was 'equally distinguished as a *pianiste* in the classic stores of high art, and the elaborations of a Bach fugue' were 'exhibited by her with the utmost delicacy and precision'.[17]

Goddard's concerts in 1851, the year she began her studies with Davison, exhibit a model she generally followed throughout her career: solo pieces selected from the 'classics', a fantasia often by Thalberg, and ensemble works chosen from a developing canon of chamber music. For example, at her concert on 25 June 1851, she performed a prelude and fugue by J.S. Bach, Beethoven's Violin Sonata in C minor with Camillo Sivori, and Thalberg's *Don Pasquale* fantasia.[18] The following

14 'Mme. Arabella Goddard: A Chat with the Celebrated Pianist', *Daily Graphic*, 4 October 1875, from a photocopy in the Arabella Goddard collection, Ballarat.

15 *Musical World* (*MW*), 51 (1873): 99, quoting from the *Daily Telegraph*.

16 *MW*, 25 (1850): 685.

17 *MW*, 25 (1850): 801, quoting from the *Illustrated News*.

18 *MW*, 26 (1851): 414.

year, the number of her appearances increased and her repertoire expanded to include compositions by Mozart, Chopin and Mendelssohn, and additional works by Bach and Beethoven as well as popular showpieces by Henri Herz and Leopold de Meyer.

The year 1853 contained several major performances by Goddard that enhanced her reputation as a concert artist. On 14 April at the Quartet Association Goddard delivered the second public performance in London of Beethoven's Sonata in B♭ major, op. 106.[19] Furthermore, she played at least part of it from memory, a feat that had not been attempted previously at a public concert. The event was much anticipated and the *Musical World* prepared its readers to hear this 'most difficult piece of music ever composed for the piano' by publishing an extensive description and analysis by G.A. Macfarren.[20] Goddard's performance drew effusive praise and helped lay the foundation for her acceptance as a noteworthy soloist on the London concert stage. The *Musical World* reported that 'so grand and masculine a conception of a work of such matchless profundity ... was little short of miraculous in a girl of seventeen. Miss Goddard has now established herself in the first rank of pianists, without reference to country'.[21] Her exceptional technical abilities were attributed to her study with Thalberg, and the hope expressed that she would develop into a first-class native pianist 'even in this foreigner-ridden country'.[22] Goddard continued to build a reputation, along with Hallé and Billet, as an advocate for all the sonatas by Beethoven.

That year, 1853, was significant, too, for her first performance with the New Philharmonic Society at their concert on 11 May. In spite of her many and varied concerts to that date, some considered this appearance marked 'her real *début* as a classical player'.[23] For the occasion, she performed the Concerto no. 3 in C minor by William Sterndale Bennett. Her advocacy of British composers had begun early in her career after she moved to England, and her promotion of Bennett in particular continued throughout her life. Response to Goddard's annual concert on 13 May 1853 suggests she had joined the league of pianists considered to be competitive with the foreigners who annually performed in London. The *Times* cited Goddard as one among native 'players and composers in this country with whom it would be somewhat difficult for the majority [of foreign artists] to compete'.[24] Her performance of Mendelssohn's Concerto in D minor at her concert was commended for being unsurpassed except when the composer himself played it at the Philharmonic concerts.[25]

Among the foreigners in London in 1853 was Hector Berlioz. His description of musicians there during the height of the concert season reveals a 'colossal consumption' of music in a city crammed with foreign artists. 'More curious still', he

---

19 The first performance featured Alexandre Billet. See *MW*, 26 (1851): 180.

20 *MW*, 31 (1853): 219–22.

21 *MW*, 31 (1853): 243.

22 *MW*, 31 (1853): 253, quoting the *Morning Herald*.

23 *MW*, 51 (1873): 99.

24 *Times*, 14 May 1853.

25 Ibid.

observes, 'is the life of long established professors like Mr. Davison, or his admirable pupil Miss Goddard' and other native musicians. 'They are always rushing hither and thither, playing, conducting, at a public concert or a private soirée, with barely time to greet their friends through the window of their cab as they cross Piccadilly or the Strand.'[26] Firmly established in the mainstream of London concert life, Goddard was about to join the tide of pianists who journeyed to the Continent.

Goddard's reputation and career as a concert artist were further enhanced by her tours abroad. In December 1854 she appeared at the first of the Quartet Subscription concerts, an annual series at the Leipzig Gewandhaus.[27] More important, her debut with the Gewandhaus orchestra took place the following month, when she performed Mendelssohn's Concerto in D minor, a work that remained part of her core repertoire, and an improvisation by Stephen Heller on Mendelssohn's *Auf Flügeln des Gesanges*.[28] Moscheles, professor of piano at the Leipzig Conservatory when Goddard performed with the Gewandhaus orchestra, records that she 'conquers enormous difficulties with consummate grace and ease, her touch is clear and pure as a bell. Here, as everywhere, she found that recognition which not even the severest art critic could withhold ...'.[29]

Goddard was absent from England nearly two years during which she toured Germany and Italy. How had she profited from her exposure to other soloists, orchestras and repertoire at Continental concerts? An answer is provided by looking at her re-entry into the London concert season, which occurred at her benefit concert in the Hanover Square Rooms on 16 May 1856:

Part I

Symphony no. 4	Beethoven
Concerto for pianoforte in D minor	Mozart
Overture, 'Son and Stranger'	Mendelssohn
[*Heimkehr aus der Fremde*, op. 89]	

Part II

Grand Sonata (*Kreutzer*)	Beethoven
Rondo in E flat, pianoforte	Mendelssohn
Overture, 'Heloise'	[Alfred] Mellon[30]

---

26 D. Cairns, *Berlioz*, vol. 2: *Servitude and Greatness 1832–1869* (London: Penguin Books Ltd., 1999), p. 509.

27 *MW*, 33 (1855): 21.

28 *MW*, 33 (1855): 37. See also A. Dörffel, *Die Gewandhaus-Konzerte zu Leipzig 1781–1881* (Leipzig: Deutscher Verlag für Musik, 1980), 'Statistik der Concerte', pp. 39 and 89.

29 Moscheles, *Recent Music and Musicians*, p. 388.

30 *Times*, 17 May 1856. There are no vocal compositions listed, but the final paragraph of the lengthy review contains brief comments regarding two singers who also performed. Such treatment was not exceptional for a concert that is primarily an instrumental one, and it confirms the notion that the function of vocal works in such a setting was to provide 'variety' or 'fill up the intervals'.

For the occasion, she engaged the Orchestral Union orchestra directed by Alfred Mellon; the violinist Heinrich Ernst performed the sonata with her. This solidly 'classical' programme contains no new Continental works to beguile London concertgoers. She had not been

> tempered by the 'modern romantic school' now in such favour abroad, to forget the common sense which governs musical taste in her own country. She [has] not abandoned for more dazzling and superficial productions the works of those great masters to ... which she was early indebted for her reputation ... and [the programme] argued a bold and earnest spirit in so young an artist to have been able to resist the fascinations of ephemeral success for a triumph more solid and durable.[31]

Her two years abroad had 'not so much added to her mechanical proficiency as they [had] developed her mental resources' as could be heard in her performance of the concerto: 'a more unaffected and noble reading of Mozart's magnificent work has not been heard from any pianist in our time'.[32]

Three weeks later, Goddard at last made her Philharmonic Society debut. She had received a coveted invitation from the Society in 1853 but became embroiled in a dispute with the Directors over her insistence upon playing Bennett's Concerto no. 3.[33] By 1856 Bennett had been appointed conductor of the orchestra and Goddard fittingly chose to perform the concerto that had not been permitted by the Directors three years earlier.

'The Most Distinguished of English Pianoforte Players': 1857 to 1873

After her Philharmonic debut, Goddard appeared regularly at the Society for 25 years before giving her final performance with that orchestra in 1879. Goddard played Bennett's works for piano and orchestra at the Philharmonic more than did any other artist, including the composer himself. Her promotion of British artists extended beyond the works of Bennett to include the only Philharmonic performances of the Concerto in A minor by W.G. Cusins, conductor of the Society from 1867 to 1883, and of Julius Benedict's Concerto in E♭ major. In addition, the first appearance of a Bach solo keyboard work there featured Goddard in a performance of a prelude and fugue. The sole occurrence of a concerto by Dussek at that venue was also a Goddard performance.[34] Although she continued to play such staples as concertos by Beethoven and Mendelssohn and the *Konzertstück* by Weber at other concerts, she evidently viewed a Philharmonic engagement as an opportunity especially to promote works by native composers. The Directors recognized Goddard's contributions

31 Ibid.
32 Ibid.
33 Details of the dispute are recounted in a number of sources. See especially C. Ehrlich, *First Philharmonic: A History of the Royal Philharmonic Society* (Oxford: Clarendon Press, 1995), pp. 86–7.
34 She performed the Cusins concerto on 27 May 1872, the Benedict concerto on 3 June 1867, the Bach Prelude and Fugue 'alla Tarantella' on 24 March 1862 and the Dussek Concerto in G minor on 2 July 1860.

to the Society and to the musical life of the capital when they presented her with the Society's Gold Medal award in 1871. Initiated that year to honour outstanding musicians, the award continues to this day as the Royal Philharmonic Society Gold Medal. Goddard and Bennett were among the ten individuals chosen that first year, but Goddard was the only one whose principal professional occupation was as a pianist.[35]

When Oscar Beringer attributed advances in British piano playing in part to an increase in high-quality concert series, he cited the Crystal Palace concerts, under the direction of August Manns, as the best orchestral events in England after those of the Philharmonic Society. The Crystal Palace concerts attracted prominent resident pianists of the period: Beringer himself, Walter Bache, Ernst Pauer, W.G. Cusins, Agnes Zimmermann, Franklin Taylor, Charles Hallé and Edward Dannreuther, to name but a few. Eventually, touring artists recognized the advantages of playing with what was becoming one of Europe's best orchestras. Clara Schumann, her sister Marie Wieck, Carl Reinecke, Ferdinand Hiller, Anna Mehlig and others joined the roster of foreign virtuosos who appeared there.

Arabella Goddard had the distinction of being the first female instrumental soloist to play at the Crystal Palace Saturday series when she performed in their second season in 1857.[36] During her long and successful association with this series, Goddard appeared each year until 1879, except when she was out of the country on tour. The pieces she chose for these concerts reflected the aims of the series to provide classical music performed to a very high standard and to offer new works to London audiences. Goddard chiefly relied on concertos and solo works by Mozart, Beethoven, and Mendelssohn. Fantasias by Thalberg and Liszt supplied contrast and demonstrated her ability to handle modern virtuosic display pieces. For novelty, she selected not recently composed works but revivals of compositions by J.N. Hummel, Dussek and John Field. Novelty of a different sort was provided with her Mozart concerto performances that incorporated modern cadenzas. In 1872 for her performance of the Concerto in B♭ major, K. 595, its first appearance at the Crystal Palace, Goddard selected two cadenzas by the pianist and Leipzig Conservatory professor Carl Reinecke. When she played the Concerto in D minor, K. 466 seven years later, she included cadenzas written for her by Camille Saint-Säens, a popular soloist himself among London concertgoers. Goddard's continued attention to the works of her British compatriots is in evidence here with performances of the Bennett concertos and her premiere of the Concerto in E♭ major by Julius Benedict. By the

---

35 The other recipients were Charles Gounod and Joseph Joachim; the singers Christine Nilsson, Helen Lemmens-Sherrington, Charles Santley and Therese Tietjens; the pianist, composer and current Philharmonic Society conductor W.G. Cusins; and Fanny Linzbauer, who had recently presented a bust of Beethoven by F. Schaller to the Society. See R. Elkin, *Royal Philharmonic: The Annals of the Royal Philharmonic Society* (London: Rider and Company, 1946), pp. 134–5.

36 Programmes for Crystal Palace concerts can be found at the Centre for Performance History (CPH), Royal College of Music (London), and at the British Library (London). Neither has a complete set. Newspaper and periodical reviews have helped to fill in the gaps. For a study of the Crystal Palace, see M. Musgrave, *The Musical Life of the Crystal Palace* (Cambridge: Cambridge University Press, 1995).

time Goddard stepped down from the Crystal Palace concerts a new generation of soloists was taking the stage, performing an expanded repertoire that included modern works she chose not to adopt – concertos by Schumann, Brahms, Grieg, Tschaikovsky and Rubinstein.

The Crystal Palace hosted some of the finest orchestral concerts in the capital during the 1860s and 1870s, the decades that coincided with the peak of Goddard's concert career. Her performances there helped further her career and extended her reputation not only in London but also abroad as the fame of the series spread. But Goddard became even more closely affiliated with another series during this time – the Monday Popular Concerts.

Founded in 1859 by Samuel Arthur Chappell and other shareholders of St James's Hall, these concerts were devoted solely to instrumental and vocal chamber music and to solo compositions. They aimed to offer high-quality music and performances on a regular basis to large and socially varied audiences during the winter season 'as a fresh source of recreation to the public'.[37] Their success resulted in an extension of the series to approximately 25 concerts between October and June and, eventually, the addition of a Saturday series. J.W. Davison advised Chappell on repertoire selection and supplied programme notes. During these early months of the Monday Popular Concerts, on 12 May 1859, Goddard married her mentor, Davison.[38] Unlike some women musicians, particularly from earlier generations, Goddard did not consider marriage the end of her performing career. Davison, the son of an actress, encouraged and actively promoted her profession. But their union has raised questions about the scope of the influence Davison may have exerted on Goddard's career as a concert artist. While complaints were sometimes expressed about bias in the London press, such comments did not always originate from disinterested parties. Addressing the issue in an obituary of Goddard in 1922, the *Times* reporter asserted that Goddard's reputation was 'too well established by the time of her marriage to be dependent upon newspaper advocacy'.[39] We know that Goddard chose to retain her maiden name professionally, thus eschewing whatever benefits might have derived from becoming Arabella Davison. Her husband, for his part, requested his editors to excuse him from covering any event where his wife performed.

So did favouritism and manipulation of the press result in a minor talent being acclaimed beyond her abilities? Or are the skills of a genuinely talented soloist being diminished by the implication that her success was inflated because of her association with this powerful figure in London's musical life? Assessments of Goddard as a pianist by other respected musicians offer some perspective. We have Beringer's opinion that she was one of the pre-eminent pianists of the mid-Victorian era on a par with such acknowledged leaders as Charles Hallé and Ernst Pauer. Moscheles had predicted a brilliant future for her, a judgement he found borne out during her Gewandhaus appearances. George Grove described her in the first edition of his

---

37 Monday Popular Concerts, CPH/RCM, programme for 18 April 1859, p. 1.

38 Goddard and Davison remained married until Davison's death in 1885. But census data indicate that the couple lived in separate households at least from 1871. See PRO, RG10/187 for Goddard and RG10/212 for Davison.

39 *Times*, 8 April 1922.

dictionary as 'the most distinguished of English pianoforte players'.[40] Perhaps the most accurate appraisal comes from George Bernard Shaw, who referred to her as 'an extraordinary pianist' and reported that 'professional jealousy ascribed her success to the influence of her husband ... but no influence could have kept her in the front rank for nearly a quarter of a century without great ability on her part'.[41]

Goddard's talents were nowhere better displayed to London concertgoers than at the Monday Popular Concerts. She shared with Hallé the position of premier piano soloist at this series. Together they played for the majority of occasions that included a pianist, until Goddard left England in 1873. For example, during the first ten years of the series, from 1859 through to 1868, close to 300 concerts included music for piano. Nearly 80 per cent featured Hallé or Goddard as soloist.[42]

Goddard's repertoire at the Monday Popular concerts extended from late Baroque to contemporary literature. The first appearance of a Bach or Handel keyboard work there occurred during the first season, when she performed a 'fuga scherzando' and a fugue in A minor by Bach and the Suite in E major with variations on 'The Harmonious Blacksmith' by Handel.[43] Her most frequently performed works were those by Beethoven and Mendelssohn, followed by Mozart and Weber. In this respect, she adhered to the general programming style of the series. More individualistic were her revivals of sonatas by Dussek and Joseph Wölfl. These performances dovetailed with the simultaneous publication of the sonatas by Duncan Davison, Goddard's brother-in-law. Further performances of sonatas by Clementi and Hummel provided audiences with access to compositions not often heard in public at that time.

Publicity for the Monday Popular Concerts proudly announced that by 1865 it had programmed 16 Beethoven quartets, 11 trios and 25 of his piano sonatas. Goddard made an important contribution to this achievement by providing the Pops premieres of the 'Pathétique', 'Waldstein' and 'Appassionata' sonatas. More significant was her premiere at these concerts of Beethoven's late sonatas, opp. 101, 106 and 109–11. Hallé, also closely linked with the Beethoven sonatas, gave the first performances of slightly more than half of the 25 heard at the Monday Popular Concerts by 1865. Even though Goddard premiered the more popular sonatas, opp. 13, 53 and 57, and the most difficult ones, the last five, Hallé's name is more often associated with that repertoire because of his editions of the Beethoven sonatas, which were published by Chappell & Company, the sponsors of the series.

Unlike many of her male colleagues, but like most other women pianists, Goddard did little in the way of music editing. Why she did not expand her musical activities into this realm is not known for certain. Gender restrictions may have played a role, although if any woman could have secured a published edition, one

---

40 G. Grove (ed.), *A Dictionary of Music and Musicians* (London: Macmillan, 1879–89), 'Goddard, Arabella'.

41 G.B. Shaw, *Shaw's Music: The Complete Musical Criticism*, ed. D. Laurence (3 vols, London: Bodley Head, 1981), vol. 1, p. 878.

42 Hallé appeared in 44.2 per cent of performances; Goddard accounts for 34.6 per cent. It should be remembered, too, that between 1860 and 1863 Goddard gave birth to two children, which would have had an impact on her availability for concert appearances.

43 Research for the Monday and Saturday Popular Concerts is based on programmes at the CPH/RCM and the BL.

might expect Goddard could, with her strong connections to the publishing houses of Duncan Davison and Chappell. At the same time, her husband was publishing his own editions of piano music. Perhaps Davison considered one editor in the family was enough. Did Goddard lack the confidence to undertake the editing process? Did she simply prefer to focus her creative energy on performance and interpretation? A clearer picture may emerge if further source material, in particular writings by Goddard herself, can be found.

Of special interest is the way in which Goddard, as concert artist, was marketed by publishers. For example, during the inaugural year of the Monday Popular Concerts, Chappell & Company published a series of *Bijoux perdus*, a collection of six 'revived pieces' by Dussek, Daniel Steibelt and Mozart. The statement 'as performed by Miss Arabella Goddard' featured on the title-page assured the potential purchaser of their worth.[44] Another offering, 'Miss Arabella Goddard's Pianoforte Répertoire', attempted to sell fantasias by Thalberg and Benedict by claiming they were compositions 'performed by that distinguished artist' (see Fig. 7.1).[45] *Bluettes classiques*, a series by Duncan Davison published between 1859 and 1864, contains works by Dussek, Steibelt and Beethoven 'as selected for pupils by Miss Arabella Goddard'. *Bachiana*, another Duncan Davison publication from the late 1850s, offered a collection of preludes and fugues by J.S. Bach not included in his *Well-Tempered Clavier*, 'as performed by Arabella Goddard in public'. Thus publishers strove to maintain the relationship between interpreter and concertgoer as well as to foster a connection between Goddard and the growing market of amateur pianists.

By the time Goddard's last full season at the Monday Popular Concerts occurred in 1871–2, three trends could be observed at the series that are worth noting: the number of piano soloists increased, more foreign pianists appeared at the concerts, and the number of women virtuosi rose to the point where over half the concerts requiring a pianist featured a woman soloist.[46] Goddard played her part in these developments by regularly appearing at both the Monday and Saturday series.

In addition to the Crystal Palace and Monday Popular concerts Goddard appeared at other London series, performed at concerts given by fellow musicians, and presented her own series. The core of these latter events, whether a 'soirée' or 'recital', comprised solo and ensemble works for piano. A further instrumental work or two without piano might be included and, for variety, a couple of vocal pieces. These concerts became an important forum for her Beethoven sonata performances. Goddard was not only the youngest soloist but also the first native pianist to explore the repertoire to such an extent. In general, her soirées repeated the literature she played for other chamber series: Bach, Haydn, Mozart, Hummel,

---

44 The note on the bottom of page 1, 'This Edition alone is fingered by Miss Arabella Goddard', indicates some editorial activity on her part but not enough to feature her as editor on the title-page.

45 Published by 'C & B' [?Chappell and T. Boosey, 1859–63]. The title-page asserts the collection is 'a correct edition' but does not identify Goddard as the editor.

46 Thirty-one concerts included a pianist; for 18 of these the soloist was a woman. The women pianists were Goddard, Clara Schumann, Teresa Carreño and Agnes Zimmermann; the male performers were Hallé, Pauer, Ferdinand Hiller and E.-M. Delaborde.

A CORRECT EDITION
OF THE
PIECES PERFORMED BY THAT DISTINGUISHED ARTIST

1. ERIN, FANTASIA ON IRISH MELODIES . . . . *J. BENEDICT.* 4/-
2. CALEDONIA, FANTASIA ON SCOTCH MELODIES *J. BENEDICT.* 4/-
COMPOSED EXPRESSLY FOR MISS ARABELLA GODDARD.
3. HOME SWEET HOME . . . . *THALBERG.* 3/-
4. LILLIE DALE. . . . . *THALBERG.* 4/-
5. THE LAST ROSE OF SUMMER . . . . *THALBERG.* 4/-
6. ALBION, FANTASIA ON ENGLISH MELODIES . . . . . *J. BENEDICT.* 4.
7. CAMBRIA FANTASIA ON WELSH MELODIES . . . . . *J. BENEDICT.* 4/-

N° 7   PRICE 4/-

Figure 7.1   Title-Page of 'Miss Arabella Goddard's Pianoforte Répertoire' (London: [Chappell and T. Boosey, 1859–63])

Clementi, Dussek, Beethoven and Mendelssohn. Goddard regularly played works by British composers at these events and was one of the few pianists to programme music by women composers.[47]

A study of concerts sponsored by Goddard herself reveals her persistence with a core repertoire of classics within a gradually expanding range of works. For example, the second in a series of three soirées in 1858, a concert for which an audience 'crowded the rooms to suffocation', featured the following programme:

Part I

Sonata in F major, for piano and violin (no. 13)	Mozart
Grand Sonata in A-flat, 'Plus Ultra' (op. 71)	Dussek
Toccata con Fuga in D minor, first time in public	J.S. Bach[48]
Fantasia con Fughetta in D major	J.S. Bach

Part II

Sonata in C minor, op. 111	Beethoven
Grand Trio no. 1 in D minor	Mendelssohn[49]

The lack of reference to a vocal work in either the roster of compositions or the critical comments and the focus on solo piano music in terms of both number of pieces and proportion of concert time suggest a model closer to a solo recital than the more usual paradigm of a miscellaneous chamber concert.[50] Typical of Goddard's programmes, the concert presents classical repertoire from diverse periods and features a late Beethoven sonata.

An examination of programmes from a series of three recitals Goddard presented 11 years later demonstrates her overall adherence to the 1858 model but with some changes worth noting (see Table 7.1).[51] A sonata by Beethoven, an important ingredient in earlier concerts, has been replaced with sonatas by composers active from the early 1800s to the late 1840s. Furthermore, a proliferation of shorter works resulted in a greater variety of composers.

Goddard's lifelong association with chamber music brought her into contact with some of Europe's best string soloists. In particular, she performed with the violinists Joseph Joachim and Prosper Sainton on a regular basis and partnered on occasion

---

47 Women composers known to have appeared on Goddard's programmes are Anna de Belleville Oury, Emma Macfarren (who published as J. Brissac) and Jane Jackson Roeckel (published as Jules de Sevrai).

48 'From Book 4 of F.C. Griepenkerl's "Complete Collection of the Pianoforte Works of J. S. Bach"'.

49 *MW*, 36 (1858): 122–3. The other instrumentalists were violinist Prosper Sainton and cellist Guillaume Paque. The concert took place on 16 February 1858.

50 For a discussion of developments in the piano recital, see J. Ritterman and W. Weber, 'Origins of the Piano Recital in England, 1830–1870', Chapter 8 below.

51 *Dwight's Journal of Music*, 29 (14 August 1869): 85–6, quoting the *Pall Mall Gazette*.

Heinrich Ernst, Henri Vieuxtemps, Henryk Wieniawski and Camillo Sivori. Her most frequent cellist colleagues were Alfredo Piatti and Guillaume Paque.

Table 7.1   List of Works performed by Arabella Goddard at her Series of Three Recitals in London, July 1869

Title	Composer
Sonata in A major, op. 43	Dussek
Sonata in B♭ major, op. 46	Dussek
Grand Sonata in C minor	Wölfl
Sonata in A major, op. 50	Clementi
Grand Fantasia, MS	W.F. Bach
Sonata in D major, op. 106	Hummel
Three unidentified fugues	Handel
Two unidentified fugues	J.S. Bach
Two unidentified fugues	Scarlatti
Two unidentified fugues	Mendelssohn
Studies, various	Steibelt, Cipriani Potter, Moscheles, Ferdinand Ries, Hiller, Bennett
'Drawing room pieces, nocturnes, valses, etc.'	Mendelssohn, Schubert, John Field, Chopin

Having secured acclaim as one of the foremost British pianists in the generation following William Sterndale Bennett, Goddard broadened her reputation as a truly international virtuoso when she left England in 1873 to embark on a worldwide tour.

International Concert Tour and Final Years as a Performer

Like many Victorian concert soloists, Goddard took advantage of improvements in transportation to travel outside London for recurring appearances in the British provinces. As an example, in 1865 she criss-crossed the British Isles to play for audiences in Brighton, Glasgow, Dundee, Aberdeen, Sterling, Newcastle, Gloucester, Leamington, Guildford, Hastings, Southsea, Salisbury, Torquay and Edinburgh. But her first overseas voyage occurred when she participated in the Boston Jubilee Festival in the summer of 1872. With this visit Goddard joined the ranks of the many pianists who brought nineteenth-century European virtuosity to America.[52] And it inspired

---

52 Some who had preceded Goddard to the US were Leopold de Meyer, Henri Herz, Thalberg, Anna Mehlig and Marie Krebs. Anton Rubinstein was in the United States at the time of Goddard's first trip in 1872; Hans von Bülow would be there when she returned in 1875. See R.A. Lott, *From Paris to Peoria: How European Piano Virtuosos Brought Classical Music to the American Heartland* (New York: Oxford University Press, 2003).

her to continue touring overseas. After her return to London, she announced her intention of visiting the United States again in 1873 but with an extension to include Australia for what was expected to be a one-year tour. In fact, the journey lasted three years (see Table 7.2).[53]

Table 7.2   Summary of Destinations where Arabella Goddard appeared during her Concert Tours, 1873–6

Year	Destinations
1873	Sydney, Melbourne, Ceylon, Madras, Bombay, Newcastle, W. Maitland, Brisbane, Geelong, Adelaide
1874	Bombay, Calcutta, Madras, Hong Kong, Shanghai, Singapore, Batavia, Brisbane, Sydney, Melbourne, Ballarat, Geelong, Castlemaine, New Zealand (departed 30 December)
1875	California (February–August): San Francisco, San Jose, Los Angeles, San Diego, Santa Barbara; New York (October–November)
December 1875 –September 1876	NY: New York, Albany, Elmira, Utica; RI: Providence; ME: Portland; CT: New Haven, Hartford; MA: Salem, Burlington; PA: Harrisburg, Pittsburgh; MI: Detroit; Canada: Montreal, Ottawa, Brockville, Belleville, Toronto, Hamilton, Brantford

Reports forwarded to England by local newspapers kept Londoners informed about Goddard's journey. These accounts contained critical notices and stories of the difficulties she encountered, including shipwreck, quarantine, theft and illness, as well as an occasional expatriate's proud description of hearing a performance by this 'distinguished countrywoman'. Additional drama sometimes arose as 'the famous metal case piano', an iron-framed Broadwood grand, made the passage with Goddard. The concern over the quality of local instruments apparently abated with her trip to the United States. Goddard shipped the Broadwood home to England upon her departure from New Zealand for San Francisco. The record is not complete regarding concert arrangements throughout her time overseas, but we do know that R.S. Smythe acted as her principal business agent in Australia, Ceylon and parts of India.[54] In America she joined, for a time, the singer Therese Tietjens in a tour

53 For a study of Goddard's Australian tours, see A. Teniswood, 'The 1870s Australian Tours of Madame Arabella Goddard', MA thesis (University of Melbourne, 2001). For an examination of her New Zealand trip, see A. Simpson, 'Putting Entertainment on the Map: The New Zealand Touring Circuits in 1974', in *Australasian Drama Studies*, 26 (April 1995): 153–76. Reference to Goddard's stay in Ottawa, Canada is made in E. Keillor, 'Musical Activity in Canada's New Capital City in the 1870s' in J. Beckwith and F.A. Hall (eds), *Musical Canada: Words and Music Honouring Helmut Kallmann* (Toronto: University of Toronto Press, 1988), pp. 115–33. Clippings regarding the Australian portion of her tour are contained also in the Arabella Goddard collection at Her Majesty's Theatre, Ballarat.

54 See Teniswood, p. 16 and *MW*, 52 (1874): 3, quoting the *Colombo Overland Observer*.

managed by the brother impresarios Maurice and Max Strakosch.[55] Goddard at times travelled with a concert party of vocal and instrumental musicians and frequently added local musicians to concerts in which she was the featured virtuoso. The zigzag route of Goddard's travels in Asia, Australia and New Zealand suggests that the overall tour evolved as opportunities arose for structured concert parties or individual appearances.

America may have attracted scores of European soloists but far fewer were willing to engage in the difficulties of reaching cities in the Far East and Australia. So it is no surprise that newspaper accounts are replete with comments that Goddard was the most distinguished piano virtuoso to perform in whatever city she happened to be visiting from India to New Zealand. For example, in the view of one Hong Kong writer, 'To those who for years have been deprived of any opportunity of hearing really first-class music', attending a Goddard concert provided 'a musical treat far in excess of anything which the most sanguine have ever expected to hear on the far-off shores of old Cathay'.[56] Similarly, Goddard's appearance in Shanghai elicited the following comments:

> the privilege of hearing a great European artist is one which must necessarily be of very rare occurrence in Shanghai. Minor celebrities have occasionally visited our we-trust-not inhospitable shores; but the present is the first occasion on which a star of the first magnitude has shone on our little world here.[57]

The effects of hearing a pianist of her quality were felt at many levels. To begin with, her performances inspired students who aimed 'at good style in pianoforte playing', and they provided

> the cheapest of music lessons to all who go to listen to them. One of the greatest of living artists shows us what can be done at the pianoforte ... [and enlarges the] understanding our players will gain as to the higher capabilities of the instrument whose powers they seek to master.[58]

In addition, the high quality of her performances raised the standards by which those who heard her could judge future performances. Melbourne audiences, for example, having once heard Goddard play in 'the highest school of composition for the most popular of instruments' would then 'possess a standard which shall guide their judgment to the just conclusions, whenever the question of artistic performance shall arise'.[59] Furthermore, exposure to such 'high class' music and performance standards

---

55 Maurice Strakosch (1825–87) also managed tours of Adelina Patti and Ole Bull. Max Strakosch (1835–92) managed Louis Moreau Gottschalk, and together the brothers presented Christine Nilsson as well as Tietjens and Goddard.

56 *Hong Kong Daily Press*, 10 March 1874, quoted in *MW*, 52 (1874): 271. This and other critical comments clearly reflect a Colonial expatriate bias.

57 *North China Herald and South-Eastland South China Gazette*, quoted in *MW*, 52 (1874): 401.

58 Teniswood, p. 36, quoting from *Argus* (Melbourne), 19 August 1873.

59 *Argus* (Melbourne), 24 October 1874. Also quoted in *MW*, 53 (1875): 36.

exercised a 'refining and civilizing influence' on the community.[60] An appearance by her was regarded in some places to be a marker of a region's advancement as, for example, when the *Sydney Morning Herald* declared 'A few years ago – indeed we might almost say a few months ago – who would have thought or hoped that a lady with so great a reputation as a pianist as Madame Goddard would have been heard in Sydney'.[61]

The repertoire Goddard performed on tour did not significantly diverge from the literature she played in Europe, although the balance between 'classical' and 'popular' music was adjusted to suit particular audiences: Beethoven sonatas, for instance, were reserved for more cosmopolitan cities. Smaller towns with what were considered less sophisticated audiences were favoured with more variation sets on popular airs. The latter took on special meaning to concertgoers who had emigrated from the British Isles. A concert that concluded with the likes of a Julius Benedict fantasia on Irish, Scottish or Welsh airs or Thalberg's 'Home, Sweet Home' provoked outbursts of enthusiastic applause.

Goddard's concerts were regarded as 'red-letter days' in many Colonial outposts, for 'not only did they enliven for the moment the monotony of local life, but they [left] recollections which will always bring pleasure'.[62] Her appearances in North America may have brought equal enjoyment but they were generally not judged as exceptional as they were in Asia and Australia. Goddard received favourable reviews, but she was one among many European virtuosi who undertook the voyage to the New World.

Of particular significance, however, is her reception in New York, a city accustomed to hearing excellent pianists. Regarding her appearance with Tietjens at Steinway Hall on 4 October 1875, one reviewer wrote

> Notwithstanding, then, that the grand performances of Rubinstein are still ringing in our ears, and that the famous Dr. von Bülow has already arrived on our shores, we are of the opinion that no greater pianist than Mdme Goddard has ever visited this country, and question very much whether Europe has produced one with more exceptional powers or greater mastery over her instrument.[63]

When Goddard appeared in a concert independent of Tietjens at Steinway Hall on 21 October, she opted for 'a very classical programme' comprising Schubert's 'Fantasie' [Sonata in G major], op. 78, Beethoven's 32 Variations on an Original Theme, and works by W.F. Bach, Chopin and Thalberg. One reviewer noted the 'select and critical audience' that attended the event and reported that 'In all she did Mdme Goddard exhibited careful and intelligent study, and ... a rare refinement of expression'.[64]

Before leaving London in 1873, Goddard announced at her farewell concert on 11 February that her tour would mark the end of her career as a concert artist. Yet

---

60 Teniswood, p. 38, quoting the *South Australian Register*, 23 September 1873, p. 5.

61 *Sydney Morning Herald*, 14 June 1873, p. 13. See also Teniswood, p. 32.

62 *MW*, 52 (1874): 299, quoting *Hong-Kong Times*, 20 March 1874.

63 *Touchstone* (New York), 16 October 1875, as quoted in *MW*, 53 (1875): 765.

64 *MW*, 53 (1875): 791, quoting *Watson's Art Journal*.

when she returned in the autumn of October 1876 she was not prepared to retire from public performance. She resumed giving 'pianoforte recitals' on 12 October, attracting 'many of the most eminent professors and amateurs in London' who enthusiastically welcomed her back to the capital. Those who may have been curious about changes in repertoire, interpretations or performance style during her three-year absence heard 'no new reading' or 'positive novelty'. Instead, audiences were treated to her 'exceptional and legitimate executive powers [that] will always be estimated at their true value [and to] an increase of the mechanical facility and perfect command over gradations of tone which secured for her so high a place amongst artists of the day'.[65]

Between her re-entry into London concert life on 12 October and the completion of her first recital tour on 20 December, Goddard reportedly played 35 concerts and recitals.[66] Clearly, she was not ready to give up her stage career. In fact, she embarked on a new challenge: performing in public in Paris. Goddard had not visited that city in a professional capacity since her lessons with Kalkbrenner. The Parisian press chided her for having travelled the world but not stopped at their 'petit point du globe'. The situation was rectified in April 1877, when she performed at the Salle Pleyel with an orchestra led by J.E. Pasdeloup. Touted as a reputed Mendelssohn player 'sans rivale', she handed in a performance of his Concerto in G minor and selections from his *Lieder ohne Worte*, the latter deemed played to perfection.[67] For her second appearance in Paris, on 25 April, Goddard presented herself as a chamber-music soloist. One reviewer declared that after hearing her on both occasions the French now understood the enthusiasm of the English for their 'pianiste nationale'.[68] Goddard visited Paris again in July the following year when she was a representative of Britain at a series of concerts dedicated to 'l'art musical anglais'. At one event, under the direction of Arthur Sullivan, the most important performance was judged to be her interpretation of Bennett's Concerto no. 4 in F minor.[69]

Goddard continued to perform occasionally at the Crystal Palace and with the Philharmonic Society. She did not, however, return to the Monday Popular concert series. A letter from George Grove to James Davison in 1876 reveals that Goddard had introduced some changes in her concert arrangements since returning from her worldwide tour. Grove writes that her agent, Joseph Williams, was responsible for her not appearing at Chappell's concerts, a move Grove considered 'both injudicious and unworthy'.[70] Regardless of any new approach to organizing her concert engagements, Goddard slipped away from public performance by the mid-1880s.

The 1891 Census indicates that Goddard had left London and become a resident of Tunbridge Wells.[71] She listed her occupation as pianiste and pianoforte professor.

---

65 *Musical Times*, 17 (1876): 656.

66 *The Figaro*, 30 December 1876, p. 7, in the Ballarat collection.

67 *La Revue et Gazette musicale de Paris (RGmP)*, 44 (1877): 117.

68 *RGmP*, 44 (1877): 133.

69 *RGmP*, 45 (1878): 23.

70 I am indebted to Celia Clarke for her transcription of this letter from an uncatalogued collection of letters from George Grove to J.W. Davison at the RCM. The letter is dated Tuesday, 14 November 1876.

71 PRO, 1891 Census, RG12/677.

Whether she was still engaged in either activity at that time is uncertain. In spite of critical acclaim and the reportedly vast sums of money she made on her 1873–6 tours, Goddard's retirement was not marked by financial security. In 1890, George Grove wrote that she was 'ill and in pain, and disabled not only from playing in public, but from the exercise of teaching, on which her subsistence depends'.[72] The pianist Natalia Janotha, a pupil of Brahms and Clara Schumann, together with Joachim and Piatti, organized a benefit on her behalf at St James's Hall that netted the ailing artist £600.[73] Some time in the decade following, Goddard returned to the land of her birth and resided in Boulogne-sur-Mer until her death in 1922.

Conclusions

Her obituary in the *Times* acknowledged Arabella Goddard as 'one of the last links with the musical life of this country as it existed in the middle of the last century'.[74] She achieved renown as a shining example of British pianism in the generation between William Sterndale Bennett and pianists of the 1880s and 1890s such as Fanny Davies and Leonard Borwick. She belonged to the 'play from the wrists' school, a reflection of her early training with Kalkbrenner, and reportedly displayed a prodigious technical proficiency that showed the influence of her studies with Thalberg. One critic claimed that, after the composer's death, Goddard was the only pianist who could play his works with 'the same fluency, grace and irreproachable mechanism'.[75] Yet she achieved critical praise for her interpretative skills as much as for her technique; she was remembered in an obituary for her 'beautiful execution and a purely classical style of interpretation'.[76] In this respect, Goddard practised a philosophy she had explained in a teaching manual: 'Don't on any account affect a sentiment that is not in you; don't pretend and don't exaggerate ... try to be as natural as possible ... never pose for an effect ...'.[77]

Goddard's concert tours extended her fame to distant regions of the British Empire and to the United States, establishing her as a truly international soloist at a time when appearances on the Continent were enough to earn that designation. Significantly, contemporary assessment of Goddard did not, for the most part,

---

72 *Times*, 4 March 1890.

73 *Times*, 27 March 1890. Goddard's son, Henry Davison, presented a different picture of Goddard's situation in a letter to the editor of the *Times*, 10 March 1890. He declared that the statements by Grove regarding his mother's financial problems were 'inaccurate and misleading' and that his mother's relatives were 'both able and willing to help her'. The benefit concert was organized without their knowledge and 'proceeded with against their wishes by certain friends of more zeal than discretion'.

74 *Times*, 8 April 1922.

75 *Times*, 12 February 1873.

76 *Times*, 8 April 1922.

77 A. Goddard, 'Pianoforte Playing for Beginners' in *How to Play the Piano-Forte* (London: The Religious Tract Society, [1884]), pp. 12–13. Other contributors are Lady Benedict, Lady Lindsay (of Balcarres), Clara A. Macirone, Lindsay Sloper and Charles Peters.

evaluate her achievements as exceptional for a 'woman pianist', but regularly compared her with contemporary artists, male and female.

This study of the career of Arabella Goddard has revealed a concert artist in the mainstream of the bustling musical life of mid-Victorian London. She performed with leading musicians of her day at the most important concert series in the capital and participated in key developments in London musical life between 1850 and 1880. Her individual soirées and recitals reflect ongoing changes in concert structure. She enlarged the repertoire of classical concert music by programming works by Baroque composers and reviving literature from the early nineteenth century. Goddard's core repertoire embodied the musical canon that evolved during the decades of her concert career, a canon that extended from works by J.S. Bach to Mendelssohn. The foundation of the canon was the music of Beethoven, to which Goddard made significant contributions with her performances of his piano sonatas. At a time when serious piano soloists needed to demonstrate a mastery of sonata literature, Goddard did so by means of her advocacy of repertoire that included, in addition to sonatas by Beethoven, those by Mozart, Dussek, Wölfl, Weber and Mendelssohn. The legacy of Arabella Goddard remains firmly within the realm of pianist–interpreter. As a result, she represents an early example of the modern concert artist.

Chapter 8

Origins of the Piano Recital in England, 1830–1870

Janet Ritterman and William Weber

Introduction

The rise of the solo recital marked one of the key turning points in the history of piano performance. To play a programme entirely on one's own amounted to a fundamental departure from the long-standing tradition whereby a benefit concert – which for much of the nineteenth century many leading London pianists gave annually – involved a variety of performers, both singers and instrumentalists. Some scholars nonetheless apply the term 'recital' even to programmes given before 1800. While it is generally accepted that Franz Liszt was the first pianist to offer numerous solo concerts in the late 1830s, just when and where such programmes became common needs to be determined.[1] Examining a selection of complete concert programmes, we will show that solo piano performance became particularly significant in England between the 1840s and the 1860s. It was there that the word 'recital' began to be used to identify a particular type of concert focusing on the pianist as a solo artist. Yet the recital developed in close relationship with concerts of a 'mixed' nature that included music for voice and for chamber ensembles. A new world of piano performance grew out of the interaction between these two types of concert.

It is impossible to understand the rise of the recital without first recognizing the 'miscellaneous' nature of concert programmes at the start of the nineteenth century. The principle of miscellany had governed programming since the start of public concerts, dictating that contrast be maintained throughout the sequence of pieces and range of performing forces. In public concerts the pianoforte was, for the most part, presented as an ensemble instrument. The limited volume of sound and its perceived lack of singing qualities appeared to reduce its potential as a solo instrument and encouraged the view that it was generally heard to most advantage in concerted works.[2] At that time a concert performed only by a pianist would have seemed

---

1   See the perceptive discussion of this history in Kenneth Hamilton, 'Creating the Recital', in *The Great Tradition: Romantic Pianism and Modern Performance* (Oxford: Oxford University Press, forthcoming).

2   Reservations about the appropriateness of the pianoforte as a solo instrument – typified by the view expressed in 1811 by J.-L. Geoffroy, influential critic of the Parisian *Journal des débats*, that '[a] public concert is not the place for a piano ... this instrument, made for accompanying, runs a great risk when it is played by itself' – were slow to change. In 1837 the *Musical World* (*MW*) reported apropos of the first of Moscheles's soirées that it had been

monochromatic, strange and dull.[3] Almost any public concert was expected to include both vocal and instrumental pieces. This principle seemed as natural a phenomenon as the rising and setting of the sun, for by long tradition voice and instrument had seemed necessary one to another. 'The standard design of a programme was a convenient way of imposing some kind of order on an essentially disparate medley of items', as Simon McVeigh has observed.[4] Moreover, a performer would rarely play two or more examples of the same musical genre in succession.

For the first half of the nineteenth century these principles typically underpinned the annual benefit concerts presented by popular local performers. Featuring several prominent performers on the programme was intended not only to lead to reciprocal opportunities for private performance for the concert-giver, but also to attract students. Visiting virtuosi sometimes took a special prominence within their own concert programmes, but in principle their programming did not differ significantly from that of local performers, since they were looking for similar opportunities. The benefit concert given by the 69-year-old John Cramer in July 1840 illustrates the persistence of this tradition: 15 pieces, including Beethoven's overture to *Fidelio*, several Italian opera selections, a Corelli trio and four English songs.[5] Comments of contemporary critics suggest that the majority of concert-goers found such events attractive and quite satisfying musically.

Although not evident in Cramer's 1840 programme, the most distinctive development in benefit concerts from around the 1820s was an increasing focus upon opera, with the growing popularity of instrumental fantasies on themes from well-known operas. Of the three items which Sigismond Thalberg performed for the first of the individual concerts that he gave in London in 1836, only the Caprice was not directly related to opera. The 'air of extemporaneous effusions' which his playing conveyed was seen as emanating not only from the 'novelty of his style' but also because he chose to perform 'without book and without accompaniment'.[6]

---

anticipated that 'a whole evening of pianoforte composition would be found wearying' (4 (1837): 156).

3   See Mary Sue Morrow, *Concert Life in Haydn's Vienna: Aspects of a Developing Musical and Social Institution* (Stuyvesant, NY: Pendragon, 1989), p. 141.

4   Simon McVeigh, *Concert Life in London from Mozart to Haydn* (Cambridge: Cambridge University Press, 1993), p. 101.

5   *John Cramer's Morning Concert, Hanover Square Rooms, London, 3 July 1840*, Centre for Performance History (CPH), Royal College of Music, London.

6   *Neue Zeitschrift für Musik* (*NZfM*), 4 (1836): 199.

Mr Thalberg's Morning Concert, King's Theatre Concert Room, London, 21 May 1836[7]

Duo, 'Se pur giungi', *Marino Faliero* [1835]	Donizetti
Air	Pucitta
Second Caprice in E flat [op. 19]	Thalberg
Duo, 'Duinque [sic] io son', *Il Barbieri* [sic] *di Siviglia* [1816]	Rossini
Aria	Rossini
Fantasie on themes from *Les Huguenots* [op. 20]	Thalberg
Duo, 'In mia man alfin tu sei', *Norma* [1831]	†Bellini
Air, 'Udite e rustici' [*L'Elisir d'amore*, 1832]	Donizetti
Duo, 'Se inclinasse', *L'Italiana in Algeri* [1813]	Rossini
Cadenza from the 'Devil's Trill' Sonata	†Tartini
performed by Mme Malibran and M. de Bériot	
Fantaisie on themes from *Guillaume Tell* [op. 22]	Thalberg

Performers: M. Thalberg – pianoforte; M. de Bériot – violin; Mmes de Bériot [Malibran], Grisi, Signori Rubini, Tamburini, M. Lablache, senior and junior, and Miss Trotter (pupil of Rubini) – vocalists.

During the 1830s, this tradition of mixed programming began to be challenged. In the process, the approach of artists as concert-givers and of their audiences began to undergo a fundamental transformation.[8] The early programmes from which the recital emerged fell into two categories, similar in style but differing mainly in the number of participants. The terms 'solo' and 'mixed' are employed in the following discussion to differentiate between these formats. For both types of event, the terms 'matinée' or 'soirée' – also associated with the conventional benefit concert – continued to be employed. While the 'solo' programme, in its purest form, presented the pianist as solo performer, the 'mixed' programme presented the pianist as much in the guise of ensemble performer as soloist and gave prominence to the contribution of other collaborative artists, both singers and instrumentalists, the latter providing anything from a duo to a chamber ensemble, such as a string quartet or quintet. Between these two, pianists also explored a variety of alternatives, often appearing with another collaborating performer, such as a singer, violinist or cellist.

7　*Morning Chronicle*, 6 May 1836, 16 May 1836, 23 May 1836; *MW*, 1 (1836): 171; *Times*, 23 May 1836. The programmes included in this article are edited transcriptions, drawn from a variety of sources (for example, advertisements, programme sheets and reviews). In the headings for concerts, quotation marks have been put around descriptive phrases used in the original programme or in contemporary reviews. As the aim has been to identify pieces, modern forms of identification (such as catalogue numbers or dates of composition) have been added to assist this. These are shown in square brackets. A question mark indicates that identification is not certain. The sign '†' has been inserted to indicate composers no longer living at the time when the concert took place.

8　See W. Weber, 'Redefining the Status of Opera: London and Paris, 1800–1848', *Journal of Interdisciplinary History*, 36 (2006): 507–32; and W. Weber, *The Great Transformation of Musical Taste: European Concert Programmes, 1750-1875* (Cambridge: Cambridge University Press, forthcoming).

Until about the 1870s, the 'mixed' programme – essentially a refinement of the traditional benefit concert, with its 'miscellaneous' programme – remained the more common of the two types. This effectively constituted a refocusing of the benefit concert on instrumental repertoire regarded as 'serious'. The frequent presence of a chamber work indicates the transformative influence that the chamber music concert continued to exert. Admittedly not all pianists modified their programming in this way. The majority of pianists continued to hark back to the miscellaneous programme, but even when they did, the gradual decline in the prominence of opera fantasies and excerpts from recent operas and a new focus on works regarded as 'classical' made many of these performances perceptibly different in musical orientation from the earlier benefit concert. By the end of the 1850s this shift in programme content had become common in benefit programmes given by London-based pianists.

It was to those programmes where the pianist, and the instrument's solo repertoire, assumed centre stage that the title 'recital' was explicitly applied. By the 1850s, when the term 'recital' was used, it also carried with it repertoire implications: it identified a programme which, while including a number of recent works, tended to focus upon classical repertoire, a term that, when applied by London critics of the time, essentially meant older works deemed to fulfil a serious order of taste. It did not necessarily denote a concert where all items were performed by a solo pianist.

Performers and critics seem to have acknowledged and accommodated the existence of alternative models of concert-giving. Those pianists who began to explore the newer type of event generally continued to give their own annual benefit concerts and to participate in those of colleagues, and were not apparently discouraged from doing so by the comments of critics. By the 1860s, however, a division of the ways seems to have been recognized. A concert rich in opera fantasies presented in London in 1860 by the visiting virtuoso Leopold de Meyer prompted J.W. Davison, editor of the *Musical World* and chief music critic of the *Times*, to say as much: the pianist was, he declared, 'doubtless aware that the way of the *virtuose-proper*, and the way of the "classic" performer (so termed), who gives undivided attention to the old masters, differ entirely'.[9]

The growth of the chamber music concert series, in which pianists increasingly featured, also influenced the emergence of the recital and its repertoire. In some respects the homogeneity and seriousness of the chamber music concert served as a model for the recital. Presenting a public concert made up entirely of quartets or quintets – first done by Ignaz Schuppanzigh in Vienna in 1804 and Pierre Baillot in Paris in 1814 – constituted a revolution in concert practice. In London, concerts featuring string quartets began during the mid-1830s and quickly grew in number: by 1836 some of these series of chamber music concerts had begun to offer mixed programmes including opera excerpts, songs and piano solos.[10] Cross-fertilization was soon in evidence. Pianists were prompted to initiate series of chamber music

---

9   *MW*, 38 (1860): 382.

10   See Samuel Wesley, 'A Sketch of the State of Music in England, from the Year 1778 up to the Present', *MW*, 1 (1836): 5–7. For a view of the standing of chamber music in London in 1837, see Joseph Bennett, 'Victorian Music. Part VIII. Chamber Music', *Musical Times*, 38 (1897): 804.

concerts focusing on pianoforte repertoire, while repertoire characteristic of the chamber concert series gradually appeared in the programmes of pianists' benefit concerts, sometimes replacing the conventional concerto item.

The emergence of a category of concert which focused on chamber music and emphasized classical repertoire had major consequences for attitudes towards the skills and qualities expected of leading pianists and, in particular, the traditional view of instrumental virtuosity. Influenced by the example provided by pianists such as Ignaz Moscheles, Louise Dulcken, William Sterndale Bennett, Alexandre Billet, Charles Hallé and Arabella Goddard, who were among the London-based performers who did most to develop respect for an alternative model of pianistic excellence, most pianists giving recitals tended to emphasize their credentials as interpreters rather than as composer–performers.

Why did the notion of the recital emerge early, with particular prominence, in London? First, London concerts tended to be longer, less standard in format, and more open to change than in most other cities. Secondly, repertoires and canonic values for old works as 'ancient' music had been established uniquely in Britain by the end of the eighteenth century. Finally, women musicians took strong leadership within British musical life, and especially through the agency of the piano, as Therese Ellsworth and Janet Ritterman have shown.[11]

Rise of the 'Classical' Series of Piano and Chamber Works

In the mid- to late 1830s, Moscheles, whose pianistic skills had delighted London audiences since his first visit in 1821 and who was by then resident in London, played a key role in spearheading change in London concert-giving. While not abandoning his annual benefit concert and similar concert activities, in winter 1837 Moscheles began to present a quite different set of programmes. In doing so, as a passage in the biography by his wife indicates, Moscheles consciously modelled his plans on some of the newly established series of string-quartet concerts which had recently sprung up in London.[12] Moscheles's 1837 series comprised three soirées, held in the Hanover Square Rooms in February and March, well outside the traditional concert season, and in the following year the series extended to four evenings. Both series had an explicit historical focus, the learned nature of which was entirely foreign to traditional benefit concerts. On both occasions Moscheles included works for harpsichord, performed on a Broadwood instrument from 1771.[13]

---

11 Therese Ellsworth, 'Women Soloists and the Piano Concerto in Nineteenth-Century London', *Ad Parnassum: A Journal of Eighteenth- and Nineteenth-Century Instrumental Music*, 2/1 (2003): 21–49. See also Janet Ritterman, '"Gegensätze, Ecken und scharfe Kanten": Clara Schumanns Besuche in England, 1856–1888', in Ingrid Bodsch and Gerd Nauhaus (eds), *Clara Schumann 1819–1896* (Bonn: Stadtmuseum, 1996), pp. 235–61.

12 See Charlotte Moscheles (ed.), *Aus Moscheles' Leben: nach Briefe und Tagebüchern* (2 vols, Leipzig: Duncker & Humblot, 1872–3), vol. 2, p. 16; Christina Bashford, 'The Late Beethoven Quartets and the London Press, 1836–ca. 1850', *Musical Quarterly*, 84 (2000): 90; and Charles Guynemer, *Essay on Chamber Classical Music* (London: by the Author, 1846).

13 *MW*, 4 (1837): 111.

These series were the first which clearly embraced key musical characteristics that were to influence the format of the recital. Among the characteristics of the type of event that foreshadowed the 'recital' were the following:

- Performance of numerous classical works
- Exclusion of genres not considered serious, especially the opera fantasie
- Performance of several pieces in the same genre, one after another
- Shift from opera arias to art songs (frequently German lieder)
- Focus on the concert-giver as interpreter rather than as pianist–composer.

The extent of the change in musical orientation is reflected in the example given below, the first of Moscheles's 1837 series. This programme departed from the pianistic repertoire then generally performed in London concerts by including two Beethoven sonatas, several preludes and fugues by J.S. Bach, sonatas by Domenico Scarlatti and movements from Handel's suites for keyboard – 'the best compositions of the best writers for the pianoforte … performed with consummate intelligence and finish', as one critic observed.[14] In this first programme, remnants of traditional vocal repertoire nonetheless persisted, represented by songs by Purcell and Mendelssohn, a duet by Mozart and a glee by William Jackson of Exeter.

'First Classical *Soirée*' of Ignaz Moscheles, Hanover Square Rooms, London, 18 February 1837[15]

PART I

Grande Sonate brillante [no. 1 in C major, op. 24]	[†Weber]
Song, 'Mad Bess' ['From silent shades, and the Elysian groves']	†Purcell
Three Preludes and Fugues (C-sharp major, C-sharp minor, D major)	†J.S. Bach
German Song, 'Das erste Veilchen' (The first violet), *Sechs Gesänge* (1833)	Mendelssohn
Sonate Dramatique, D minor [op. 31 no. 2][16]	†Beethoven

PART II

Selection, Suites of Lessons (including the celebrated 'Cat's Fugue')	†D. Scarlatti
'The Harmonious Blacksmith', with Handel's Variations [Suite no. 5 in E]	†Handel
Duet, *Così fan tutte*	†Mozart
Sonata charactéristique [sic], *Les Adieux, L'Absence, et le Retour* [op. 81a]	†Beethoven
[Glee], 'Go, feeble tyrant,' [*Six Epigrams*, op. 17 no. 4]	†Wm. Jackson
A selection of new MS. Studies [op. 95]	Moscheles

Performers: Mr Moscheles – pianoforte; Misses Birch and Masson, Messrs Vaughan and Bradbury – vocalists; Sir George Smart – conductor of vocal music.

---

14 *Athenaeum*, no. 489 (1837): 180.

15 *MW*, 4 (1837): 155–6.

16 The set of three sonatas now known as op. 31 was referred to in England at this time as op. 29.

As the programme heading shows, Moscheles explicitly described the event as a 'classical' soirée. The term 'classical', as used here by Moscheles, carried a powerful set of aesthetic and practical meanings. While commentators of the period occasionally distinguished between 'classical' and 'romantic' music historically, as a general rule the former word served as an indicator of taste. When employed in the title of a concert, it effectively meant 'serious', thus differentiating the programme from those that featured excerpts from recent operas and fantasies upon opera themes, as well as many kinds of songs. A concert series described as 'classical' was rooted in music that in the English context was by then considered canonic – works not only by Mozart, Beethoven and J.S. Bach but also by Domenico Scarlatti, Clementi and Dussek. Works by highly esteemed living composers – Spohr and Mendelssohn most of all – were seen to be closely linked to that repertoire. A 'classical' programme might include one or two songs of the sort performed at conventional benefit concerts, but no more. When in September 1840 Franz Liszt presented a programme in Stamford, Lincolnshire which featured six items by Rossini, Donizetti and Bellini and seven by British composers, including a humorous song by the fashionable John Orlando Parry,[17] this clearly had no pretensions to 'classical' status.

After Moscheles, it was the British musician William Sterndale Bennett who was to exert important leadership in the development of the recital. A talented pianist, recognized for his gifts while still a student at the Royal Academy of Music, Bennett gained an early reputation with a series of major compositions in the mid-1830s and became warmly regarded by the circle around Robert Schumann during his visits to Leipzig.[18] During the late 1830s his annual benefit concerts served as an idealistic alternative to the cosmopolitan repertoire that predominated at fashionable benefit concerts.

Bennett's 'Classical Subscription Concerts', presented first in private and later in the Hanover Square Rooms, proved to be a milestone in the development of the recital.[19] As with Moscheles's series, the prominence of the word 'classical' in the title alone differentiated the series from the traditional benefit. Including chamber ensembles rather than an orchestra, these programmes focused on chamber music and included piano solos and chamber ensembles with piano, interspersed with carefully selected songs and opera arias. The first concert in 1843, which included keyboard works by Mozart and Beethoven, began with Spohr's new Trio in E minor, the type of work that was to open concerts of this kind for much of the century.

17 London, CPH/RCM. Pieces by John Orlando Parry and the Irishman Joseph Wade were omnipresent at high-tone benefit concerts such as these.

18 See Nicholas Temperley, 'Piano Music: 1800–1870' in *The Romantic Age, 1800–1914*, Blackwell (formerly Athlone) History of Music in Britain, 5 (London: Athlone Press, 1981; Oxford: Basil Blackwell, 1988); and Peter Horton, 'William Sterndale Bennett: Composer and Pianist', Chapter 6 above.

19 In the later years, these concerts were sometimes described in the musical press as 'Classical pianoforte concerts'.

Mr. W. Sterndale Bennett's [Second] 'Classical Subscription Concert', 42 Upper Charlotte Street, Fitzroy Square, London, 23 January 1843[20]

PART I

Grand Trio in E minor, op. 119, for pianoforte, violin and violoncello first performance in England	Spohr
Song, 'Die junge Nonne' ('Wie braust durch die Wipfel') [D. 828]	†Schubert
Allegro grazioso [1839],[21] new Rondo [1842][22]	W.S. Bennett
Scena [and Aria], 'Ah! Perfido', op. 65	†Beethoven

PART II

[Pianoforte] Duet in F major [K. 497?]	†Mozart
Ballad, 'The Cottage Door' [1843]	Julius Benedict
Song, 'Holder Zephyr'[23]	W.S. Bennett
Sonata in F minor [op. 57]	†Beethoven

Performers: Mr W.S. Bennett – pianoforte; Mr Gattie – violin; Mr W.L. Phillips – violoncello; Mr Cipriani Potter – pianoforte; Herr Kroff and Miss Rainforth – vocalists.

As a result of these 'Classical Chamber Music Concerts', which he presented annually from 1843 until 1856, Sterndale Bennett earned a strong reputation for impact upon London concert life. In 1851 the *Times* identified him as 'the first to influence the public mind in favour of the pianoforte works of the great masters'.[24]

The Solo Programme: The First Pianoforte 'Recitals'

The solo programme emerged at much the same time as the 'classical' concerts of Moscheles and Bennett but went in a significantly different direction in terms of repertoire. By comparison with Moscheles and Bennett, Franz Liszt focused his early solo concerts much less upon classical compositions than on works of his own. He described these performances to Princess Belgiojoso as 'musical soliloquies', since he did not 'know what other name to give to this invention'.[25] From 1837 onwards Liszt had sometimes performed alone in both private and public concerts and

---

20 *Musical Examiner*, 12 (1843): 84; 13 (1843): 87; *MW*, 18 (1843): 38.

21 Presumably op. 18 in A (published London and Leipzig, 1839); see Nicholas Temperley (ed.), *The London Pianoforte School, 1766-1860* (20 vols, New York and London: Garland, 1984–7), vol. 17, pp. 169–79.

22 Presumably the recently published *Rondo piacevole*, op. 25 in E major (1842), ibid., vol. 17, pp. 41–51.

23 No. 6 of Six Songs, op. 23, with English and German words, published separately in 1838; the whole set (written 1837–42) was published in 1842.

24 *Times*, 3 June 1851. See also *MW*, 30 (1852): 194.

25 *Franz Liszt: Selected Letters*, trans. and ed. Adrian Williams (Oxford: Clarendon Press, 1998), pp. 106–107.

continued to do so with increasing frequency after his 1840 appearances in London.[26] But these London concerts came to particular attention in Europe as a whole, and several of the key features that were ultimately to define the recital – performance from memory, a predominance of works for solo piano and few, or no, associate artists – characterized a large proportion of his subsequent performances.[27]

Although by 1840 several of Beethoven's solo piano sonatas formed part of Liszt's concert repertoire, in most of his solo programmes up to that time he tended to focus on his own transcriptions and compositions. In the programme for the first of his two London recitals, Liszt began with his faithful transcription of the final movements from Beethoven's Pastoral Symphony. More freely composed transcriptions followed – of Schubert ('Serenade' and 'Ave Maria'), Rossini (the Neapolitan Tarantella) and Bellini (Liszt's version for solo piano of *Hexaméron*).[28] The programme, which Liszt performed entirely alone, ended with one of Liszt's original compositions for piano, the *Grand Galop Chromatique*. However, at his second London recital, on 29 June, while the programme still included some transcriptions – the Overture to *William Tell* by Rossini and several Schubert songs – Liszt included a fugue in E minor by Handel, two mazurkas by Chopin and Beethoven's 'Kreutzer' Sonata for pianoforte and violin.[29] More varied stylistically than the first recital, this programme was well judged for London audiences, since it enabled Liszt to demonstrate command of a broad range of pianoforte music.

These two solo concerts presented by Liszt in London in June 1840 gave birth to the term 'recital' within musical vocabulary.[30] Because the word was commonly used to denote the recitation by heart of a poem or a story, advertisements for Liszt's concerts stated that he would offer 'recitals' of his recent fantasies, meaning the performance or the 'reading' – from memory – of each piece.[31] Thus a journalist noted that 'Mr. Liszt, the celebrated Pianist, gave recitals on the pianoforte at the Hanover Square Rooms yesterday morning'.[32] But by the time he left London in July 1840, some English critics began to apply the term 'recital' to Liszt's concerts as a

---

26 For details of Liszt's Milan concerts in 1837 and 1838, see Alan Walker, *Franz Liszt* (3 vols, London: Faber & Faber, 1983–97), vol. 1: *The Virtuoso Years, 1811–1847*, p. 250.

27 For the ten concerts that Liszt gave in the Singakademie in Berlin (December 1841 to February 1842), he performed alone and from memory, but these events appear not to have been distinguished in their designation from the other concerts (of the 21 in total) that he gave. For details of the repertoire that Liszt performed in Berlin, see Walker, *The Virtuoso Years, 1811–1847*, p. 372.

28 The composers Pixis, Thalberg, Herz, Czerny and Chopin also contributed variations to *Hexaméron (Grandes Variations de Bravoure* for piano and orchestra on a theme from *I Puritani* by Bellini).

29 *Times*, 2 July 1840. The violinist was Ole Bull.

30 For comment on the introduction of the term 'recital', see the recollections of Willert Beale, quoted in Walker, *The Virtuoso Years, 1811–1847*, pp. 356–7.

31 Davison, writing in the *Times* (2 July 1840) suggested that Liszt's adoption of the term 'recital' may have reflected the fact that this was a recognized translation of the German noun *der Vortrag*, used for 'the performance or execution of a piece of music, or the recitation of a poem'.

32 *Morning Herald*, 10 June 1840.

whole, whether he performed alone or did not. In November of that year *Jackson's Oxford Journal* spoke of a concert Liszt presented in the Star Assembly Room as one of 'his piano-forte recitals', even though it involved the conventional package of songs and opera excerpts found in many of his programmes up to that time.[33]

In the London concerts that they presented in subsequent seasons, two women pianists, Louise Dulcken and Marie Pleyel, made significant contributions to the evolution of the recital, Dulcken following the model of Moscheles and Bennett, Pleyel that of Liszt. Born in Hamburg, sister of the violinist Ferdinand David and a tutor of Queen Victoria, Dulcken gave some of the most fashionable benefit concerts of the time, one of them involving Franz Liszt, her brother and an army of elite opera singers.[34] In winter 1843–44 she, like Bennett, began offering a regular series of soirées at her home, advertising the series as intended 'for the performance of the most celebrated quartet and pianoforte compositions'.[35] In the first of her November 1844 soirées, each half of which began with a chamber work (Haydn's Quartet in G major, op. 77 no. 1 and Mendelssohn's String Quintet in A major, op. 18), Dulcken herself performed Beethoven's Sonata in C major, op. 2 no. 3 and a Nocturne and the Tarantella, op. 43 by Chopin, and collaborated in Hummel's Trio in E major, op. 83 and a Fantasia on Swedish national airs for pianoforte and strings by Ferdinand Ries, interspersing the instrumental items with well known arias by Mozart and Gluck.

By contrast, in 1846, during her first visit to London, Marie Pleyel (née Moke) followed Liszt's initiative in advertising a series of concerts as 'recitals'.[36] The use of the title, interpreted as 'a claim ... to powers akin to those of its first adopter', drew to her three recitals what one periodical called 'a most critical audience, almost every professor of note'.[37] Pleyel focused her first programme upon pieces by Liszt, Theodor Döhler, Alexander Dreyschock and Emile Prudent; only an adagio by J.N. Hummel might have been interpreted as 'classical'. Unsurprisingly, given the advanced state of canonic repertoire in some London concerts, Davison, writing in the *Musical World*, expressed initial disappointment that, by focusing almost exclusively on the 'modern "romantic" school', Pleyel appeared to have ignored – 'rejected' – the great names of Beethoven, Mozart, Bach, Weber and Mendelssohn.[38]

London continued to be the focal point of experimentation in pianoforte concerts during the 1850s. Though not well known today, the Russian-born pianist Alexandre Billet, resident in London between 1848 and 1858, helped significantly to sustain and develop interest in solo programmes and to demonstrate the potential that existed for the expansion of pianists' concert repertoire. Billet gave a series of three 'classical pianoforte concerts' in 1850, did the same the year after, and in 1852 expanded the

33 Quoted in Susan Wollenberg, 'Pianos and Pianists in Nineteenth-Century Oxford', *Nineteenth-Century Music Review*, 2 (2005): 116.
34 Reproduced in Weber, 'Redefining the Status of Opera: London and Paris, 1800–1848', p. 519.
35 *Times*, 8 November 1844.
36 See Walker, *The Virtuoso Years, 1811–1847*, pp. 281, 389–90 for comment on the links between Liszt and Pleyel.
37 *Times*, 20 May 1846. For the second and third recitals, Madame Pleyel interspersed her items with songs.
38 'Madame Pleyel', *MW*, 21 (1846): 237.

series to six. From the outset, these performances were hailed for the 'new way' they pursued.[39] Billet offered short concerts including works by composers no longer regularly performed in public, such as Dussek and Clementi, and representing a wider range of schools than was customary – 'specimens of every composer of eminence belonging to what is termed the classical school, from the earliest times until the present day', as the *Times* pointed out at the conclusion of the first series. Initially, Billet included a singer in his programmes; by 1852 he featured only solo pianoforte music. The fourth concert of the 1852 series juxtaposed several classically orientated works with more recent compositions, not only Chopin's B♭ minor Sonata, described in the programme as a first performance in London, but also pieces by contemporary pianist–composers such as Rudolph Willmers and Ferdinand Hiller:

M. Alexandre Billet's 'Concert of Classical Pianoforte Music', St Martin's Hall, 20 March 1852[40]

PART I

Grand Sonata in A major, op. 101	†Beethoven
Allegro and Fugue in F	†Handel
Prelude & Fugue in F minor [1836 and 1834, respectively]	†Mendelssohn
Grand Sonata, B-flat minor, op. 35, first time in public	†Chopin

PART II

Andante with variations in B flat, op. 83 (Posth. works, no. 11)	†Mendelssohn
Allegro Vivace in D major	Maurice Levy
Selection of Studies	
A flat	Moscheles
F minor	†Chopin
E flat	†Steibelt
C (*Le Papillon*)	H.R. Willmers
B flat (in octaves)	F[erdinand] Hiller

This programming of several studies in a row extended a practice begun by Moscheles and Bennett whereby pianists no longer followed the long-standing tradition of alternating between genres.

In the establishment of the pianoforte recital as a distinctive and permanent feature of London musical life, the mid-1850s appear to have been a major point of consolidation. In May and June 1855 Charles Hallé gave his first series of concerts in London, which he described as 'recitals', and in the following spring he, Clara Schumann and Arabella Goddard each offered series of solo concerts in London, though in Goddard's case they were not given that specific denomination. News of the interest aroused by these developments seems to have spread quickly: by April 1856 the young Southampton-born pianist Fanny Arthur Robinson, a former pupil

---

39 *Times*, 27 May 1850; see also 30 January 1850 and 28 April 1852. Billet returned to France in 1858.

40 *MW*, 30 (1852): 260. Heinrich Rudolph Willmers (1821–78) was a Viennese-based pianist who composed extensively for the piano.

of W.S. Bennett and Thalberg then living in Dublin, presented a solo concert in Dublin's Ancient Concert Rooms.[41]

Although Clara Schumann was not resident in London, the performances that she gave during her frequent visits beginning in 1856 made a distinctive contribution to the evolution of the pianoforte recital. From the 1850s onwards, her programmes were based on the six composers whose music formed the core of her concert repertoire – Bach, Beethoven, Mendelssohn, Chopin, Schumann and Brahms. The programme transcribed below was the second of the three 1856 London concerts that she advertised as a 'recital':[42]

Mme Clara Schumann's Pianoforte Recital, Queen's Concert Rooms, Hanover Square, 17 June 1856[43]

Variations [and Fugue] in E flat on a theme from the *Eroica* Symphony, op. 35	†Beethoven
Two Diversions, op. 17[44]	W.S. Bennett
Suite de Pièces, op. 24 no.1 [Presto leggiero, in C♯ minor]	W.S. Bennett
Variations on a Thema (*Aus den bunten Blättern*) of Robert Schumann [op. 20]	Clara Schumann
Sarabande and Gavotte (in the style of Bach) [1855?][45]	Johannes Brahms
Clavierstück in A major	†Scarlatti
Carneval [sic], op. 9 [excerpts]	Robert Schumann

Like Liszt, Clara Schumann seems initially to have chosen to give solo performances when visiting a city where she did not know – or did not trust – that local musicians would perform to her standards, or when the location did not have an orchestra readily available. For most performers, audience appeal and expectations

---

41 Jennifer O'Connor discussed the concert in 'The contribution of Fanny Arthur Robinson to music in nineteenth-century Dublin', Annual Meeting of the Royal Musical Association, Manchester, 5 November 2005. For other accounts of Robinson's activities in Dublin, see *Record of the Musical Union* (1855), no. 7, p. 28, and Richard Pine Friam and Charles Acton Friam (eds), *To Talent Alone: The Royal Irish Academy of Music, 1848–1998* (Dublin: Gill & Macmillan, 1998), p. 500.

42 On this visit, Clara Schumann gave 26 performances in less than three months. See Ritterman, '"Gegensätze, Ecken und scharfe Kanten": Clara Schumanns Besuche in England, 1856–1888'.

43 Clara Wieck-Schumann, *Sammlung der Konzertprogramme*, Robert Schumann Haus, Zwickau, Sign.10463–A3.

44 Op. 17 contains three pieces for piano duet, first published in London and Leipzig in 1839. Clara performed a version of no. 2 (Andantino), which she had arranged for two hands in 1842 during one of the periods when Bennett was briefly based in Leipzig.

45 Clara Schumann first performed the Gavotte in MS at a concert that she gave in Göttingen (27 October 1855), at which Brahms was present. Brahms then linked the Gavotte with the Sarabande when he took part in a concert given by Clara in Danzig in the following month. Clara followed this example and performed the two pieces in this way in a concert that she gave in Vienna (20 January 1856). For details, see Berthold Litzmann, *Clara Schumann. Ein Künstlerleben* (3 vols, Leipzig: Breitkopf & Härtel, 1910–18), vol. 2, pp. 390–97.

will also have influenced these decisions. Performers dependent upon ticket sales to ensure the financial viability of their concerts needed to be confident that the audience would be sufficiently interested to listen to a solo pianist without the variety provided by a supporting artist, and that a long programme was not necessarily expected.[46]

For her 1856 London visit, which was prompted principally by Sterndale Bennett's invitation to her to perform at the Philharmonic Society, Schumann kept the three recitals that she presented as solo affairs, perhaps because she knew so few potential associate artists then in London.[47] She abandoned this practice – and the use of the term 'recital' – on her next four visits to the English capital. It was only in 1867, by which time the 'recital' (as term and as concept) was established in London, that she again presented some programmes described as 'recitals' in which she performed alone. More commonly, however, Clara Schumann followed tradition by including a singer or a chamber ensemble, or both. For the most part she would have felt obliged to respect the collegial nature of the music business by offering other artists opportunities to appear on her programmes, thus reciprocating invitations that she received. Like most other pianists of the time, when presenting a programme which included associate artists, she followed the norm of performing about three pieces, interspersed with vocal numbers. The presentation of a full solo programme, without the assistance of other performers, brought demands in terms of performing stamina which not all pianists were necessarily equipped to address.

Clara Schumann performed almost entirely 'without book' in all three of her 1856 London concerts.[48] Each of these recitals began with a major work by Beethoven; all contained works by her husband, Robert, whose piano music she energetically promoted on this visit to England, as she had been doing elsewhere, despite frequent adverse comments from sections of the English musical press still strongly opposed to his music. On her 1856 visit, it was only in the 17 June recital that Clara performed one of the larger of Schumann's works for solo piano.[49] This is likely to have been the first public performance of *Carnaval* in England: although the work dates from 1837, it was only in Vienna in January 1856 that Clara had performed it publicly for the first time – just a few months before her first visit to England. Unlike the music of Chopin or Mendelssohn, Robert Schumann's piano works had not yet become an integral part of the concert repertoire of other leading pianists of the time.[50] It is

---

46 As Clara Schumann's correspondence shows, she had firsthand experience of all these situations during her concert tours.

47 For comment on Clara Schumann's views on London concert-giving and English musicians, see Litzmann, vol. 2, pp. 406–11. During her visit to Russia in 1844, Clara Schumann gave several solo concerts, in which singers were not included.

48 *MW*, 34 (1856): 343–4.

49 According to contemporary comment (see George Grove (ed.), *A Dictionary of Music and Musicians* (4 vols, London: Macmillan, 1879–89), vol. 3, p. 422), on this occasion Clara performed an abbreviated version, omitting six of the 21 movements. The movements omitted were nos. 5–8 (Eusebius, Florestan, Coquette, Réplique [Sphinxes]), no. 13 (Estrella) and no. 18 (Aveu). The programme included an explanatory note, 'Remarks on Schumann's *Carneval*' [sic], which gave an outline of the background to the Davidsbündler.

50 Eduard Hanslick, *Geschichte des Concertwesens in Wien* (2 vols, Vienna: W. Braumüller, 1869–70), vol. 2, p. 430. See La Mara (ed.), *Franz Liszt's Briefe* (8 vols, Leipzig:

likely that, apart from the piece by Scarlatti, all of the other works on this programme were first public performances in London.

The three London recitals that Clara Schumann gave in 1856 demonstrated her tendency to support living composers with whom she had strong personal connections and was particularly identified. She championed new piano repertoire in a distinctively personal way; in her other two London recitals she offered two recently composed pieces by Brahms, written 'in the style of Bach'. Unusually, in this first recital programme Clara Schumann included a work of her own composition; this was increasingly rare in her programmes by this time but this particular set of variations was a work of deep personal significance.[51] In most of her programmes, apart from Mendelssohn and Chopin, the early nineteenth-century composers whose works she favoured were Schubert and Henselt. The character pieces of Bavarian-born Adolf Henselt, Imperial Court Pianist in St Petersburg from 1838, with whom Clara had had frequent contact during her visit to Russia in 1844, she made particularly her own.[52] The pieces by Bennett included in this programme – not a regular part of her repertoire – were probably included as a tribute not only to the musician who had invited her to England, and at whose Philharmonic Society concert in April she had made her first London appearance,[53] but also as a gesture to London audiences, with whom Bennett was a particular favourite.

Because of the absence of associate artists, the programme for Clara Schumann's recital was shorter in number of items, and likely to have been shorter in performance, than some of her earlier programmes. This represented a move away from the conventions of the London benefit concert, which by the 1840s had reached what critics often described as 'monster' proportions, with as many as 35 pieces.[54] One of the features that distinguished the emerging piano recital from other London concerts of the time was its relative brevity – usually around two hours in length.

The German-born pianist Charles Hallé probably performed more solo recitals in London than anyone else in this period. In 1836 Hallé had moved to Paris to study, remaining there until March 1848 when, as a result of the impact on Parisian musical life of the 1848 Revolution, he – like a number of other pianists based in Paris at that time[55] – came to England; he settled in Manchester, where his contribution for almost

---

Breitkopf & Härtel, 1893–1905), vol. 1, p. 27, for Liszt's letter to Robert Schumann, dated 5 June 1839, in which he mentions the piano works of Schumann that he knows and intends to play in public.

51 Clara wrote these variations in 1853 and presented them to her husband on his birthday. By the following year, he had been admitted to the asylum in Endenich (see Litzmann, vol. 2, p. 307).

52 See Hanslick, *Geschichte des Concertwesens*, vol. 2, p. 333.

53 Clara Schumann's first appearance in London was on 14 April 1856, at the Philharmonic Society (programme reproduced in Ritterman, '"Gegensätze, Ecken und scharfe Kanten": Clara Schumanns Besuche in England, 1856–1888', p. 238). She also appeared in one of Bennett's evenings of 'classical pianoforte music' on 6 May, when she and Bennett performed solo and duo works.

54 See, for example, comment on Dulcken's 1842 benefit concert, in *MW*, 17 (1842): 173.

55 In a letter to his parents dated April 1848, Hallé wrote that Thalberg, Chopin, Kalkbrenner, Pixis, Osborne, Prudent and Billet were among the pianists who 'through

fifty years was to transform the musical life of the city and the region. Though now remembered chiefly as a conductor, Hallé became noted for giving an annual series of pianoforte recitals, a practice which he continued for almost four decades.[56]

The first series of four concerts, which he advertised as 'recitals', took place in 1855 at his London residence.[57] Despite its use by Liszt and Pleyel, and sporadic adoption by less prominent performers, the term 'recital' had not yet become common usage: for over a decade musical critics generally placed the word in inverted commas, sometimes emphasizing for readers, by use of the verb ('recite'), that 'reciting' – that is, performance from memory – had indeed taken place. This explains the apparently tautological wording adopted by Henry Chorley who, when reporting on the first of Hallé's 1856 recital series, observed that 'M. Charles Hallé's first Recital was "recited"'.[58] Similar reassurance had been provided in the case of the programme by Clara Schumann cited earlier: on this occasion, the critic confirmed, 'Madame Schumann had again "recited" some pianoforte music'.[59]

Through his performances with the Musical Union from 1848 onwards and later with the Monday Popular Concerts, Hallé established a reputation as a pianist of classical inclination, thoroughly grounded in the works of those composers – the 'great masters' – who formed the core of the repertoire for both of these organizations.[60] Hallé's annual series of pianoforte recitals had a similar focus. As with Billet, Hallé developed a recital repertoire spanning a wide historical and stylistic range: Bach, Mozart, Clementi, Dussek, Weber, Beethoven, Chopin, Mendelssohn, Heller and subsequently Schubert, all featured in his programmes. Like Billet, Hallé included no compositions of his own – nor improvisations. In his early recitals, he performed alone. He resolutely assumed the role of interpreter, presenting in his programmes 'specimens', in the language of the critics, of works for keyboard by composers no longer living. Typical of Hallé's recital programmes was that for the first of his 1856 series:

---

necessity' had been 'driven to England' (see C.E. and M. Hallé, *Life and Letters of Sir Charles Hallé* (London: Smith Elder, 1896), p. 229). More are included in lists given by John Ella, Director of the Musical Union (see *Record of the Musical Union, 1848*, no. 1 (28 March 1848): 4, and no. 2 (11 April 1848): 8).

56 See Hallé, *Life and Letters*, p. 166.

57 *MW*, 33 (1855): 400. For Hallé's earlier concert-giving, which anticipated in some respects these 'recitals', see M. Kennedy (ed.), *The Autobiography of Charles Hallé, with Correspondence and Diaries* (London: Elek, 1972), pp. 131–2.

58 *Athenaeum*, no. 1489 (1856): 594.

59 *MW*, 34 (1856): 343–4.

60 In reviewing the first two of Hallé's 1856 recitals, *MW* reminded its readers that 'Everyone ... is aware of the masterly manner in which M. Hallé interprets the works of the great masters'.

Mr. Charles Hallé's First 'Pianoforte Recital', 47 Bryanston Square, London, 22 May 1856[61]

Sonata in D, op. 28, 'Pastorale'	†Beethoven
Prelude, Sarabande, Bourrée & Gigue in A minor [from English Suite no. 2]	†J. S. Bach
Adagio and Rondo from Sonata in C, op. 24	†Weber
Sonata in A flat, op. 110	†Beethoven
Wanderstunden [op. 80 no. 4 in F; no 2 in Db]	Stephen Heller
Nuits blanches [op. 82 no 9 in E]	Stephen Heller
Ballade in A flat, op. 47	†Chopin
Lieder ohne Worte [excerpts]	†Mendelssohn

The one exception shown here to Hallé's emphasis on the music of composers no longer living was the inclusion of pieces by Stephen Heller, a Parisian colleague and lifelong friend. Hallé regularly performed and promoted the solo piano works of Heller, as did Clara Schumann with several pieces by Adolph Henselt. Their example was emulated by others: during this period, and for some time after, character pieces by Heller or Henselt were often the only music by a living composer on a pianist's programme, usually placed at the end.

Hallé presented a similar recital series in each of the succeeding years, sometimes repeating works that he was performing around the same time at the Musical Union or at the Monday Popular Concerts.[62] From 1859 attendances at his annual recital series had grown enough for him to move the concerts from his private residence to a public venue, Willis's Rooms,[63] where his frequent performance of individual Beethoven sonatas attracted ever larger audiences. This change in audience attitude had occurred within scarcely a decade. Hallé recalled that when he arrived in London in 1848 the Beethoven solo pianoforte sonatas were still regarded as 'abstruse', leading John Ella to discourage him from performing any of them in his early appearances at the Musical Union.[64] By contrast, Beethoven's piano trios and violin sonatas were not thought so challenging to listeners; all over Europe these were often performed in benefit concerts together with English and Italian vocal numbers and opera fantasias.

Although from time to time Hallé included sonatas by Dussek, Clementi, Haydn and Mozart in his programmes, these were by far outnumbered by his performances of Beethoven – the solo piano sonatas and also the duo sonatas – which became a defining feature of the recitals that he presented from 1855 onwards. While Beethoven was the main focus of attention at classical music concerts throughout Europe, in the mid-1850s few of the solo piano sonatas were common in concert programmes. As the *Times* observed, Hallé's 'successive concerts – we beg pardon,

---

61 *Morning Post*, 7 May 1856.

62 The Monday Popular Concerts began in 1859. From the outset, Hallé appeared frequently at these concerts.

63 Robert Elkin, *The Old Concert Rooms of London* (London: Edward Arnold, 1955), p. 77.

64 Kennedy (ed.), *Autobiography of Charles Hallé*, p. 116.

"*recitals*"' brought to mind that 'a good many pianists (*virtuosi* included) would be somewhat at a loss to play any one of the sonatas of Beethoven', especially 'without book'.[65]

At a series of eight weekly recitals in 1861, in the recently opened 2,500-seat St James's Hall,[66] Hallé gave the first known public performance of all of the Beethoven solo piano sonatas. Despite initial scepticism from the musical press about this 'Beethoven cycle',[67] the venture was sufficiently successful to encourage Hallé to repeat the series in 1862. He performed the sonatas 'according to the original order of their publication' (that is, by opus number). Contrary to his previous practice at his London recitals, in each of these eight programmes Hallé punctuated the instrumental music in each half with a short vocal item, thus providing, as even the most enthusiastic critics conceded, 'agreeable relief '.[68]

Mr. Charles Hallé's Fifth 'Beethoven Recital', St. James's Hall, London, 20 June 1862[69]

Sonata, op. 31 no. 2 (1802)	†Beethoven
Allegretto – D minor	
Adagio – B-flat major	
Allegro – D minor	
Air, *Joseph* [1807]	†Méhul
Grand Sonata, op. 31 no. 3 [1802]	†Beethoven
Allegro – E-flat major	
Scherzo. Allegretto vivace – A-flat major	
Minuetto, Moderato e grazioso – E-flat major	
Presto con fuoco – E-flat major	

– Interval of Ten Minutes –

Andante, in F major, ['Andante favori', WoO 57, 1803]	†Beethoven
Andante grazioso con moto – F major	
32 Variations on an Original Theme [WoO 80, 1806]	†Beethoven
Allegretto – C minor	
Romance, *Così fan tutte* [1790]	†Mozart
Grand Sonata, op. 53 ['Waldstein', 1805]	†Beethoven
Allegro con brio – C major	
Introduzione, Adagio molto – F major	
Rondo Allegretto moderato – C major	
Prestissimo	

Performers: Mr Charles Hallé – pianoforte; M. Jourdan – vocalist; Mr Harold Thomas – accompanist.

---

65 *Times*, 20 May 1861, p. 12.

66 St James's Hall opened in 1858. For a detailed description, see John Timbs, *Curiosities of London*, new edn (London: John Camden Hotten, 1871), pp. 426–7.

67 *Morning Post*, 17 May 1861.

68 *MW*, 40 (1862): 423.

69 *Mr. Charles Hallé's Beethoven Recitals*, 1862 Series, British Library 7901.aa.4.

So challenging and homogeneous a set of programmes was not to everyone's taste. While Hallé was to repeat his 'Beethoven recitals' periodically, in 1863 he reverted to more varied programmes, recognizing that only a small specialized public would appreciate his Beethoven cycle. The *Musical World*, endorsing this development, agreed that Hallé was right to assume that even the 'highly cultivated musical audiences' he drew expected programmes to be selected with 'a view to contrast', and with no composer's name save Beethoven's occurring more than once.[70] However when, in 1868 and 1869, Hallé devoted his recital series to only two composers – Schubert and Beethoven – this initiative was highly praised, not least for the contribution that it made to the development of public musical understanding.[71] These recitals, as with the Beethoven sonata series, involved both voice and piano, a practice commonly followed for the rest of the century.

Arabella Goddard served as another influential model in the establishment of the solo piano recital.[72] Even allowing for the potentially privileged position that her marriage to J.W. Davison may have given her in terms of critical support and advocacy for her professional activities, the fact that a native woman pianist achieved such high renown in London in the 1850s indicates how fundamental a transformation musical culture was undergoing in that period. On returning to London in 1856 after two years of touring in Germany and Italy, Goddard, although only twenty, quickly gained a standing comparable to that of Charles Hallé and Clara Schumann in the emerging field of pianistic interpretation of classical works. Goddard once again performed Beethoven's 'Hammerklavier' Sonata, which she had played in London in 1853 and on her tour in Germany.[73] The programme for this concert included a violin sonata by Mozart, one of Mendelssohn's Preludes and Fugues, Handel's Suite no. 5 in E major, and pieces by Bennett, but it also adhered to tradition by including vocal pieces, particularly the ballad 'Bonnie Jean', and *Adelaide*, the song performed more often than any other work by Beethoven at benefit concerts.[74]

As her inclusion of the ballad suggests, Goddard was eclectic in her musical tastes. She by no means restricted herself to programmes of an exclusively 'classical' orientation, for while she was a familiar figure at the Monday Popular Concerts, the Crystal Palace concerts and the Philharmonic concerts, she performed regularly at the London Ballad Concerts directed by John Boosey in St James's Hall after their inauguration in 1867. There she made a new home for the opera fantasies by Thalberg and other virtuosi of the 1840s – music that by then had largely disappeared from the serious concert repertoire. Goddard spanned a major ideological divide in musical life by performing at events of widely differing standing, including some generally condemned by the more idealistic sections of the musical press. Indeed, in 1878 a critic in the *Times* chastised her for offering 'a silly pièce-de-salon' by Schulhoff.[75]

---

70 *MW*, 41 (1863): 391.

71 *Morning Post*, 28 May 1863.

72 See Therese Ellsworth, 'Victorian Pianists as Concert Artists: The Case of Arabella Goddard (1836–1922)', Chapter 7 above.

73 *Times*, 12 February 1873.

74 *MW*, 34 (1856): 438. See the transcription of Goddard's programme of 16 February 1858 in the chapter by Therese Ellsworth above.

75 *Times*, 24 June 1878.

In her recitals Goddard interspersed solo pieces with song. In 1868 she offered a series of three concerts which included all forty-eight pieces in Mendelssohn's *Lieder ohne Worte* (1830–44) and many of his posthumous piano works, an unusually specialized style of programming comparable to Hallé's Beethoven cycles. In other respects, however, this focus on Mendelssohn was, for Goddard, not surprising: she frequently performed works by Mendelssohn in her concerts and had a well-established reputation as a Mendelssohn interpreter. After the first of these 'Mendelssohn Recitals', a reviewer praised Goddard's performance in terms that would have been unthinkable in 1830: 'While listening to her we feel satisfied that we shall hear the composer's ideas interpreted fully, completely, and without affectation.'[76] Unlike her earlier soirées, for these recitals Goddard interspersed the groups of piano pieces with well known Schubert songs: so radical a departure from the principle of miscellany still followed the traditional alternation between vocal and instrumental pieces.

Madame Arabella Goddard's 'Pianoforte Recitals', St. James's Hall, London, 11 June 1868[77]

PART I

Songs without Words (Book 7 no. 1, 3/5, 1/6, 4/6)	†Mendelssohn
Song, 'The Barcarole' ['Auf dem Wasser zu singen', D. 774]	†Schubert
Songs without Words (Book 2 no. 2; 6/1, 8/4, 5/2)	†Mendelssohn
Song, 'Sois toujours mes seuls amours' [Sei mir gegrüßt', D. 741]	†Schubert
Posthumous Works – Etude, no. 1 (op. 104, Book 2), Praeludium, no. 1 (op. 104, Book 1), Etude, no. 2 (op. 104, Book 2)	†Mendelssohn

PART II

Posthumous Works: Praeludium, no. 2 (op. 101, Book 1); Praeludium, no. 3 (op. 104, Book 1); Etude, no. 3 (op. 104, Book 2)	†Mendelssohn
Song, 'Margaret at the Spinning Wheel' ['Gretchen am Spinnrad', D. 118]	†Schubert
Songs without Words (Book 1 no. 5, 1/4, 5/5, 8/5)	†Mendelssohn
Songs, 'There is a streamlet gushing,' *Müllerlied* ['Wohin', *Die schöne Müllerin*, D. 795]; 'On every tree and every flower'	†Schubert
Songs without Words (Book 7 no. 3, 3/7, 8/4, 7/4, 4/3)	†Mendelssohn

Performers: Miss Arabella Goddard, pianoforte; Miss Annie Edmonds, vocalist; Miss Lucy Murray, accompanist.

By the mid-1860s this new kind of concert – the 'pianoforte recital' – had essentially become a recognized part of London musical life. In 1863 a report of one of Hallé's recitals observed that 'the term, invented by Liszt, would seem to have passed into general acceptance'.[78] Within a period of about 20 years, it had come to indicate a musical event focusing on a solo pianist, generally performing repertoire

---

76 *Daily Telegraph*, 3 June 1868.
77 *Morning Post*, 8 June 1868.
78 *Times*, 23 May 1863.

from a range of different schools of composition, from Bach and Handel to some contemporary composers; the majority of these works were regarded as works of serious 'classical' pretensions. The expectation was that most, if not all of the items given by the solo pianist would be performed from memory, thus implying, as one critic said of Clara Schumann after her 1872 recitals in London, that the performer had the music 'not only ... in her fingers, but in her heart'.[79] While there were occasional examples of the term 'recital' being adopted by performers on other instruments, it is clear that at first the format of the recital was not considered appropriate for all instruments, or for any performers of less than exceptional quality. As one critic observed in passing:

> With due deference to the modest harpist who recently advertised that he alone was capable of entertaining singly for a couple of hours any auditory, there are but two instruments which really can be listened to for any length of time without relief, and these are the organ and the pianoforte; but even with these there must be a reservation that the players thereof are of the first force. Nothing, indeed, but the possession of powers quite exceptional can justify any artist in attempting to monopolize attention in a single sitting; and it is from the forgetfulness of many pianists how difficult it is to enlist sympathy or command admiration that recitals have been raining too profusely, until amateurs have shrunk from the very mention of the avalanche rolling in bulk every season.[80]

But although by 1868 the pianoforte recital had become a distinctive category within London concert life, the 'avalanche' had not really begun. For the following decade, with scarcely an exception,[81] the recital seems to have remained the province of pianists. One of the first instances of the appropriation of the designation for another instrument was its use for organ recitals such as those given by Camille Saint-Saëns at the Royal Albert Hall in London in 1880.[82] After this, singers were among the first to follow, sometimes with solo recitals, sometimes with duo recitals undertaken jointly with pianists.[83] Nevertheless, pianists still presented examples of the serious 'mixed' programme. Up to World War I it was common to open such a recital with a piano trio or quintet and to include several pieces by a singer, and a pianist would often team up with a singer to present a programme under both names. In such a fashion did the tradition of miscellany become reshaped into new forms pertinent to a different musical age.

The solo recital arrived significantly later and less frequently in the other major musical cities of Europe. While not employing the term 'recital', Liszt did give solo concerts in cities such as Berlin and Vienna during his concert tours in the 1840s; Saint-Saëns stunned Paris by performing four solo pieces in a row, in between concertos by Mozart (B flat, K. 450) and Beethoven (C minor, op. 15) at his

79 *Times*, 4 March 1872.

80 *MW*, 46 (1868): 482 (article reproduced from *Queen*, 4 July 1868).

81 In 1862 the harpist Aptommas presented a series of six performances which he advertised as 'harp recitals' (see *Athenaeum*, no. 1806 (7 June 1862): 765).

82 *Times*, 12 May 1880.

83 See the definition given in J.A. Fuller Maitland (ed.), *Grove's Dictionary of Music and Musicians*, 2nd edn (5 vols, London: Macmillan, 1904–12), vol. 4, p. 33, which noted that 'in the present day [the term] is often applied to concerts when two or more soloists take part'.

debut in May 1846;[84] and Robert and Clara Schumann gave concerts together at the Gewandhaus in Leipzig in the 1840s that to some extent resembled Bennett's series. But practices of programme design tended to remain more traditional in other cities, resisting experimentation of the kind that occurred in London.

Throughout the 1880s, pianoforte recitals became ever more popular in the English capital. As early as 1881, a critic observed that 'the number of distinguished pianists then in London' – 'unprecedented' in his recollection – meant that pianoforte recitals had 'of late multiplied to a degree which makes all adequate record a matter of impossibility'.[85] And despite occasional suggestions to the contrary, their numbers continued to increase year on year. In *Hazell's Annual*, an entry in 1890 for 'pianoforte recitals' observed that this 'species of entertainment' was not 'declining in favour, as had perhaps been thought' but that 'during May, June and the greater part of July, St James's Hall, Prince's Hall, and other rooms suitable for the purpose, were in extraordinary demand for this species of entertainment'.[86] By the end of the century, the pianoforte recital, associated increasingly with the bravura skills of the virtuoso pianist, had become one of the most prominent and popular features of London concert life.

---

84 Jean Bonnerot, *C. Saint-Saëns, 1835–1921: La Vie et son oeuvre* (Paris: Durand, 1922), pp. 20–23.

85 *Times*, 11 June 1881. The critic was no longer Davison; in 1878 Dr Franz Hueffer was appointed as chief music critic of the *Times*.

86 Lewis Foreman, *Music in England, 1885–1920, as recounted in Hazell's Annual* (London: Thames, 1994), p. 40.

Chapter 9

'Remarkable force, finish, intelligence and feeling': Reassessing the Pianism of Walter Bache

Michael Allis

They seem determined in London to push me to the piano. I cannot allow this to happen in public, as my seventy-five-year-old fingers are no longer suited to it, and Bülow, Saint-Saëns, Rubinstein, and you, dear Bache, play my compositions much better than what is left of my humble self.[1]

Of the virtuosi cited above by Franz Liszt in the 1880s as the main interpreters of his piano music, one name seems a little out of place – that of the British pianist Walter Bache (1842–88). Not that Bache's name is unfamiliar; his almost single-handed promotion of Liszt's music in nineteenth-century Britain makes him a central figure in terms of Liszt reception.[2] Liszt's comments, however, remind us of something that can easily be forgotten – Bache's pianistic ability. This chapter focuses upon the range of repertoire that Bache performed in his concert series and charts some of the critical responses in the musical press to his interpretations of music by Liszt, Beethoven, Bach, Schumann and others. In reassessing Bache's career as a pianist, a range of issues are highlighted, including the nature of virtuosity, the status of English performers in relation to their foreign counterparts, ethics of transcription and arrangement, approaches to repertoire and programming, and issues of canon and reception.

Bache's Musical Education

Bache studied from 1858 until 1861 at the Leipzig Conservatory where, according to his sister Constance, he was 'occupied with the giant task of bringing up stubborn

---

1 Letter from Franz Liszt to Walter Bache, 11 February 1886, in La Mara, ed., *Letters of Franz Liszt*, trans. Constance Bache (2 vols, London: H. Grevel & Co., 1894), vol. 2, p. 464.

2 See Michael Allis, 'Promoting the Cause: Liszt Reception and Walter Bache's London Concerts 1865–87', *Journal of the American Liszt Society*, 51 (spring 2002): 1–38, reproduced in the *Liszt Society Journal*, 30 (2005), and 'Promotion through Performance: Liszt's symphonic poems in the London concerts of Walter Bache', in Julian Rushton and Rachel Cowgill (eds), *Europe, Empire, and Spectacle in Nineteenth-Century British Music* (Aldershot: Ashgate, 2006), pp. 59–80.

fingers in the way they should go, and Plaidy and Czerny claimed all his attention'.[3] Leipzig offered Bache the opportunity to extend his musical horizons, whether through piano and composition lessons with Ignaz Moscheles (1794–1870) and Carl Reinecke (1824–1910); the witnessing of performances by Pauline Viardot-García, Giulia Grisi, Wilhelmine Schroeder-Devrient, Julius Stockhausen, John Francis Barnett, Joachim and Vieuxtemps; or developing a familiarity with the music of Chopin, Bellini, Mozart, Beethoven, Moritz Hauptmann and Mendelssohn. However, although Bache was a popular student, there is the suggestion that he initially lacked focus. Constance Bache cites an unnamed source ('a musician of high standing', probably Arthur Sullivan or the pianist Franklin Taylor) in this context:

> You see in Leipzig nobody was compelled to work, there being no particular supervision; and there was always plenty to do, in the way of amusement, for the less energetic. As far as my recollection serves, Bache was at that time rather given to working by fits and starts, frequently making excellent resolutions, the effect of which did not last many days.[4]

In September 1861 Bache travelled to Italy, residing first in Milan and then in Florence, where he became acquainted with Mme Jessie Laussot. This was a turning point in Bache's career; for it was Mme Laussot, a former Liszt pupil, who helped him to expand his teaching practice (a mixture of piano lessons and harmony classes), eased his entry into polite society and, most significantly, suggested that Bache should travel to Rome to study with Liszt. Bache wrote to his father on 21 May 1862: 'Liszt is without doubt the greatest pianist and piano teacher living, and in every respect a most wonderfully educated musician and man, and the advantage of being with him would be incomparable.'[5] Bache visited the virtuoso in Rome, and the young pianist was encouraged to return in the winter of 1863 for lessons. Bache explained his plans to his father:

> I hope I have not exaggerated in talking about Liszt; he won't make me anything wonderful, so that I can come home and set the Thames on fire – not at all, so don't expect it; but – his readings or interpretations are greater and higher than any-one else's; if I can spend some time with him and go through a good deal of music with him, I shall pick up at least a great deal of his ideas.[6]

Bache's correspondence highlights a number of works that he performed in this period – Chopin's Cello Sonata, a Rubinstein Trio, Bülow's edition of Bach's *Fantasia Cromatica*, the David-Pinelli Violin Variations, Schulhoff's Nocturne, op. 11, a Schumann violin sonata (arranged for viola), Mendelssohn's D minor Piano Trio and *Fantasie* in F♯ minor, and Liszt's *Les Patineurs*:

---

3   Constance Bache, *Brother Musicians: Reminiscences of Edward and Walter Bache* (London: Methuen & Co., 1901), p. 132.

4   Ibid., p. 145. Fellow pupils at Leipzig included Sullivan, Taylor (later a Professor at the Royal College of Music), Rosamunde and Clara Barnett (John Francis Barnett's cousins) and Carl Rosa.

5   Ibid., pp. 151–2.

6   Ibid., p. 157.

I am not very enthusiastic about the Mendelssohn Fantasie, but it is awfully classical and will delight the people, besides having some real artistic worth. I should never have dreamed of trying the 'Patineurs,' which is quite new to me, and which I can no more play than fly, had not Liszt encouraged me to it, and assured me I was quite equal to it. I hope he is right![7]

It was also at this point that Bache began to explore two-piano repertoire, including *Les Préludes* and Liszt's arrangement of Schubert's Wanderer *Fantasie*, both of which Bache performed with Sgambati.[8] The two-piano arrangements of Liszt's symphonic poems were later to play a significant role in Bache's concert series. Bache returned to London in 1865, although he never really completed his studies, and he continued to travel to Weimar for several years to perform in Liszt's master classes; Bache attended the last of these in the summer of 1885.[9]

Bache's Concert Series

Bache's main contribution to musical life in London was the establishment of a concert series (1865–87), principally designed to promote Liszt as a composer. Although the features of the series have been detailed elsewhere,[10] a brief summary is helpful in placing Bache's pianism in context. The concerts began as a joint venture with the singer Gustave García at the Collard Concert-Room, 1b Grosvenor Street on 4 July 1865, offering a miscellaneous programme of vocal and instrumental music. At the third annual concert at the Beethoven Rooms in 1867, although García still appeared as a performer, it was Bache who was now in charge. Subsequent years saw rapid expansion, both in terms of the forces employed (the introduction of choral works in 1868, the transformation into an orchestral concert in 1871) and in number. From 1872, in addition to the February/March orchestral concert, Bache offered an annual pianoforte recital (incorporating selected vocal works) in October or November. From 1875, both of these events took place at St James's Hall.[11] The significance of these concerts in terms of British Liszt reception cannot be over-estimated, whether in terms of the range of Liszt's works offered, the number of British premieres (including the *Faust* Symphony, Psalm 13, *Après une lecture du Dante*, the two-piano versions of *Les Préludes* and *Die Ideale*, and *Die Loreley* with

7   Letter from Bache to Mme Laussot, 30 January 1863, ibid., p. 163.

8   Ibid., p. 162. The Italian composer and Liszt pupil Giovanni Sgambati (1841–1914) was an important figure in the development of instrumental music in Italy; in February 1866 he conducted a performance of Liszt's *Dante* Symphony in Rome at the opening of the Dante Gallery.

9   I am grateful to Alan Walker for this information. For further details, see Walker's *Reflections on Liszt* (New York: Cornell University Press, 2005), pp. 107–11.

10   See Allis, 'Promoting the Cause: Liszt Reception and Walter Bache's London Concerts 1865–87', and 'Promotion through Performance: Liszt's symphonic poems in the London concerts of Walter Bache'.

11   Other venues had included St George's Hall (1868) and the Queen's Concert Hall (used for the orchestral concerts of 1869–72 and the pianoforte recitals of 1873–74). The orchestral concerts had moved to St James's Hall in 1873.

orchestral accompaniment) or in their reinforcing of British premieres elsewhere (often at the Crystal Palace). Second British performances included *Mazeppa*, the orchestral version of the First *Mephisto Waltz*, *Jeanne d'Arc au bûcher* and an abridged version of *St Elisabeth*. Standards of performance were high – August Manns was the principal conductor, several members of the Crystal Palace orchestra were regular contributors, and experienced performers with Lisztian connections, including Karl Klindworth, Frits Hartvigson and Edward Dannreuther, helped to provide authoritative interpretations. Bache employed several effective promotional strategies in these concerts. The focused inclusion of Liszt's two-piano arrangements of the symphonic poems prepared audiences for the orchestral versions;[12] this, and a thoughtful approach to programming, plus the educational content of the printed concert booklets – with their detailed programme notes and selected extended essays – all contributed to an aggressive marketing of Liszt's new status as a composer. In addition to his organizational skills, Bache fulfilled another crucial role in these concerts: that of pianist.

Bache as Pianist

From the very first concert in his series, Bache was identified as 'a pianist of much promise' who 'showed very excellent and varied powers'.[13] The musical press continued in a similar vein, describing him as 'a player of extraordinary power and sensibility' who blended 'thoughtful interpretation and executive skill'.[14] Accounts of his individual pianistic style highlighted the 'remarkable ... crispness and evenness' of his scale passages and 'a remarkable acuteness of perception and quick seizing of the intention of minor points with great delicacy and refinement of feeling'.[15] His 'honesty of purpose ... and freedom from affectation' made him 'at once a safe model for the student and a delightful companion to the master of his art'.[16] He was also seen to have developed as a pianist. The *Athenaeum* suggested that by 1878 he had 'gained ground by time and practice' – being now a less 'mercurial' and 'fidgety' performer; the 'intellectual and artistic character of his interpretations' were beyond dispute, despite an occasional 'exaggerated emphasis'.[17] Discussions

12 There are suggestions in the musical journals that Bache's audiences regularly contained several eminent musicians. The *Musical Standard* (*MSt*), 10 November 1877, pp. 290–91 declared: 'Mr. Bache stands out alone, as the one Englishman who succeeds twice every year in attracting around him the aristocracy of music.'

13 *Musical Times* (*MT*), 12 (1865): 117.

14 *Monthly Musical Record* (*MMR*), 7 (1877): 196 and *MT*, 23 (1882): 664.

15 *Musical World* (*MW*), 53 (1875): 749 and *MSt* (10 November 1877): 291.

16 *MSt* (2 November 1878): 272.

17 The *Athenaeum* (2 November 1878): 571, which continued: 'he [Bache] seem[s] to spring on striking chords; but when he has to express sentiment in an *andante* his touch is delicate and elastic.' The *MSt* (6 November 1880): 289 and ibid. (4 November 1876): 290 suggested that Bache initially lacked power and, consequently, they were 'hardly prepared for the vigour and nervous energy that he displayed in his performance'; the *MW*, 57 (1879): 690, reproduced the *Daily Telegraph*'s remark that 'Mr. Bache is not a pianist of the Boanerges order, and at times there seems an odd disparity between the music he affects and

of Bache's abilities were inevitably bound up with the nature of the repertoire he chose to play. Not surprisingly, it was in the music of Liszt that he was seen to be particularly authoritative, displaying 'competence to deal with Liszt's music both as regards *technique* and congenial rendering'; the *Musical Times* suggested that he 'never seems so much at ease as when interpreting the thoughts of his master', and the *Musical Standard* noted the 'loving tenderness' with which he approached Liszt's music.[18] Bache was not, of course, the only pianist in Britain to programme Liszt's piano works. Various artists such as Annie Stockens, Horton C. Allison, Marie Pleyel, Madeleine Graver, Charles Hallé, the child prodigy Willie Pape, Oscar Beringer and Arabella Goddard included selections from Liszt in their recitals, as of course did Liszt pupils such as Frederic Unger and Karl Klindworth and, later, Sophie Menter, Bernard Stavenhagen and Frederic Lamond. However, as Table 9.1 shows, it was the variety of Liszt's works for solo piano, two pianos, and piano and orchestra performed by Bache in his concert series that was significant.[19] In addition to the overt virtuosity of a range of large-scale works (the two-piano arrangements of the symphonic poems, the concertos, the B minor Sonata, *Après une lecture du Dante*), Bache offered a handful of transcriptions, examples of national character (five of the Hungarian Rhapsodies and the *Fantasia über ungarische Volksmelodien*), smaller-scale virtuosic displays and a selective approach to the groups of miniatures (often highlighting the melodic nature of Liszt's writing) – thus helping to define and develop notions of the Liszt canon.

Whilst Bache's performances of Liszt's piano works were universally acclaimed, the works themselves received a mixed reception. It was the overt virtuosity of the First Piano Concerto in E♭, performed on 26 May 1871, to which the *Sunday Times* objected: 'The so-called concerto in E flat, of Liszt, turned out to be a show piece, wherein show is expected not only to make up for want of beauty but to atone for eccentric ugliness.'[20] The *Musical Standard* was able to distinguish between the performer and the work, suggesting that 'Mr. Bache's piano playing was excellent, but it failed to render interesting Liszt's bizarre concerto in E flat'.[21] It may have been due to this largely negative reception that the work was not offered again in Bache's series until 1885, when Bache attempted to educate his audience by including a detailed analysis by Dannreuther rather than the brief annotated musical quotations provided in 1871. This performance led to more positive comments in some quarters of the musical press:

---

the unpretending fashion in which he executes it'. However, the *Athenaeum* (23 November 1872): 673, disagreed, describing Bache as a 'master of the keyboard' who 'has both delicacy and power' – characteristics ideally suited to the performances of Liszt's keyboard works.

18 See the reproduction from the *Times* in *MW*, 57 (1879): 690; *MT*, 19 (1878): 157; and *MSt* (4 November 1876): 290.

19 Bache also often acted as accompanist in songs by Liszt and other composers.

20 Account from the *Sunday Times*, reproduced in *MW*, 50 (1872): 108.

21 *MSt* (3 June 1871): 54. Compare, however, the *Athenaeum* (3 June 1871): 695: 'The work bristles with intricacies; but, as played by Mr. Bache – and that from memory – there was no difficulty in following its working.'

Table 9.1   Liszt Piano Works Performed by Walter Bache in his Concert Series

Title	Number of performances
1. Piano Solo	
(a) Original works	
Au bord d'une source [AP1]	5
La leggierezza; *Paysage* [EET]	4
Ballade no. 1; *Bénédiction de Dieu dans la solitude* [HPR][a]; Polonaise no. 1; *St François d'Assise* [DL]; *Eglogue* [AP1]; *Sonetto 123 del Petrarca* [AP2]	3
Pastorale [AP1]; *Après une lecture du Dante* [AP2]; Sonata in B minor; *Un sospiro*; *Feux Follets* [EET]; Prelude & fugue on BACH; *Waldesrauschen*; *Mephisto Waltz* no. 1; Hungarian Rhapsodies nos. 10, 13	2
Sposalizio, *Il penseroso*, *Canzonetta del Salvator Rosa*, *Venezia e Napoli* [AP2]; *Cantique d'amour* [HPR]; *Canzone Napolitana*; *Consolations* 1–3, 5–6; *Il lamento*; *Preludio*, no. 2 in A minor, *Wilde Jagd*, no. 10 in F minor, *Chasse-neige* [EET]; *St François de Paule* [DL]; Hungarian Rhapsodies 4, 5, 9; *Ungarische Sturm-Marsch*; *Valse-Impromptu*; *Valse oubliée*	1
(b) Transcriptions/arrangements	
J.S. Bach: Prelude and Fugue in A minor (organ)	4
Paganini: *La campanella*; Wagner: March from *Tannhäuser*	3
Handel: Sarabande and Chaconne [*Almira*][b]	2
J.S. Bach: Prelude & Fugue in B minor (organ); Bellini: *Réminiscences de Norma*; David: *Ungarisch*; Mendelssohn: Wedding March and Dance of the Fairies [*Midsummer Night's Dream*]; Paganini: Caprices 2 and 4	1
2. Two pianos	
Mazeppa	3
Les Préludes	2
Die Ideale; *Orpheus*	1
3. Piano and orchestra	
(a) Original works	
Piano Concerto no. 2	3
Piano Concerto no. 1	2
Fantasia über ungarische Volksmelodien	1
(b) Arrangements	
Weber: *Polonaise brillante*	3
Schubert: *Fantasie*, op. 15	1

Abbreviations: DL = *Deux légendes*; AP = *Années de pèlerinage*; EET = *Etudes d'exécution transcendante*; HPR = *Harmonies poétiques et réligieuses*.

[a] Also performed by Bache during Liszt's visit to Britain in 1886, at the Grosvenor Gallery.

[b] Also performed by Bache during Liszt's visit to Britain in 1886, at the home of Henry Littleton.

[the Concerto] had the recommendation which the personal influence and popularity of the performer of the solo part naturally brought. Auditors could scarcely help being moved by the sight of so much energy and determination, at the display of such never-tiring devotion, and the applause which followed was by many intended as an acknowledgement of the executive skill of a pianist.[22]

The more poetic Second Concerto, less overtly virtuosic than the First, had been given its British premiere by Dannreuther at a Crystal Palace Saturday Concert on 21 November 1874 to mixed reviews. The *Musical Standard* reacted in the strongest terms:

Keyless, rhythmless, full of the rudest discords possible, its sole originality consists in this, that the melodies and harmonies never remain in the same key for two consecutive bars. ... Such a piece conveys no definite or pleasurable impression to the mind, and is indescribable. We may, however, state that one of its most prominent features consists in innumerable rapid runs either up or down the piano in chromatic thirds, sixths, and on chords of the diminished seventh and ninth. Indeed, these peculiarities constitute a true mannerism, and one, moreover, of a most unpleasant kind ... The above remarks may sound severe, but they represent a *consensus* of soundest critical opinion ... .[23]

When Bache included the work at his concert on 25 February 1875 (thus building upon the momentum of the premiere), he retained Dannreuther's programme notes from the Crystal Palace premiere.[24] These consisted of detailed, annotated musical quotations together with a philosophical account of the concerto genre and suggested that Liszt's application of the 'metamorphosis of themes' was not '"manufactured" with the intention of appearing original or eccentric' but was the 'adequate expression of his peculiar sentiments and emotions'. Press reaction to Bache's performance was more favourable. The *Musical Standard* revised its earlier opinion of the work, noting that the work had 'the unusual merit of containing no unmeaning and show-off passages for the favourite instrument' and continuing: 'It was after reflection that convinced us the difficulties Mr. Bache had overcome with such ease were enormous; at the time we were unconscious of the fact.'[25] This journal's praise at Bache's second performance in February 1877 ('one of the most concisely expressed works that ... it is possible to form a conception of')[26] was echoed by the *Musical World*'s description of the concerto, after Bache's 1886 performance, as 'the most thoughtful and finished of his [Liszt's] works in this form ... the hearer's attention is riveted from the beginning to the end'.[27]

---

22 *MW*, 63 (1885): 108.

23 *MSt* (28 November 1874): 335. The *MMR*, 4 (1874): 172, was more charitable: 'A work of so recondite a character should not be dismissed after a single hearing.'

24 These were also reprinted in *MMR*, 5 (1875): 45–6.

25 *MSt* (6 March 1875): 150. See also the *MT*, 17 (1875): 53: 'Mr. Bache's performance of the Concerto ... was masterly in the extreme; his delicacy of phrasing and perfect command of the most difficult and intricate passages eliciting applause as warm as it was well deserved.'

26 *MSt* (10 March 1877): 146.

27 *MW*, 64 (1886): 108. For more critical views, see the *Athenaeum* (13 February 1886): 240: 'an uglier work is probably harder to be found in the *repertoire* of pianoforte music';

Other works by Liszt provoked mixed reactions. There were objections to the First *Mephisto Waltz* on the grounds of unsuitable subject matter ('Let us … express regret that any musician could be found willing to degrade his art by associating it with an incident of the most offensive kind'). The overt virtuosity of *La leggierezza* and *Waldesrauschen* led to their dismissal as 'eccentric and difficult studies by Liszt'. The evocation of mood in *Cantique d'amour* was perceived to be somewhat out of place (representing 'the effusion of a passionate lover, like William the Conqueror, who would fain take his mistress by storm with all the force of military strategy'), and the Prelude and Fugue on BACH was attacked as 'a musical abortion … a specimen of absolute hideousness'.[28] *St François d'Assise*, the first of the *Deux légendes*, was 'puerile', representative of Liszt 'in one of his most fanciful moods', yet 'also more than a little pretty', and a work which 'never fails to please'.[29] Similarly, despite the *Musical Standard*'s positive response to *Bénédiction de Dieu dans la solitude* ('full of poetical feeling and beautiful melody', being 'simpler in form and more easy to understand at a first hearing than many of Liszt's works'),[30] other journals were less convinced. The *Musical Times* initially suggested that 'Where it is not dull it seems to many frivolous and vapid' and declared: 'After a second hearing the opinion is even less favourable, for although it contains many agreeable fancies, it is occasionally dull, and in no one particular does it rise above the ordinary "Morceau de Salon"', an opinion echoed in the *Musical World*'s conclusion that 'taken away from its sounding title, Lamartine's glowing verse, and the glitter of Liszt's name, it would probably attract no attention whatever'.[31]

Uniformly positive responses came in relation to the more delicate and melodic miniatures – the first three *Consolations* and *Eglogue* from the first set of *Années de pèlerinage* ('characteristic and striking compositions, marked by originality and a strong colouring of romanticism'), the *Sonetto 123 del Petrarca*, which was said to display 'special qualities of beauty', and *Au bord d'une source*, deemed 'one of Liszt's tenderest inspirations'.[32] The national characteristics of the First Polonaise also met with approval: 'The Polonaise of Liszt was a real treat … he seizes the true Polish spirit, as set forth in the works of Chopin, and gives to the world a polonaise national to the backbone'.[33]

---

also *MMR*, 16 (1886): 66: 'His [Liszt's] work is clever and romantic, but he does not seem to possess the power to sustain with interest his first proposed idea … .'

28 *MW*, 53 (1875): 749; *MW*, 59 (1881): 716; *MSt* (1 November 1873): 273; and *Athenaeum* (11 November 1882): 637. See also *MW*, 60 (1882): 722 and *MMR*, 12 (1882): 283.

29 *MW*, 57 (1879): 690 (reproductions from the *Daily Telegraph* and the *Times*) and *MW*, 59 (1881): 716.

30 *MSt* (6 November 1880): 289.

31 *MT*, 21 (1880): 606 and 22 (1881): 186, and *MW*, 59 (1881): 146. Two years later, *MW*, 61 (1883): 673 revised its opinion, suggesting that this work displayed Liszt 'at best advantage' and was performed by Bache with 'rare charm and power'.

32 See *MSt* (23 November 1872): 326, *MW*, 65 (1887): 857, *MSt* (1 November 1873): 273, and a reproduction from the *Times* in *MW*, 57 (1879): 690. The *Athenaeum* (29 October 1887): 575 also praised the 'flow of rhythmical melody' in *Canzonetta del Salvator Rosa*, which 'came like a gleam of sunshine in the midst of fog' compared to the 'poverty of invention' and the lack of 'symmetry, proportion, [and] logical sequence of ideas' in *Sposalizio* and *Il penseroso*.

33 *MSt* (2 November 1878): 272.

Two works were identified as particularly challenging for the audiences and critics. The first was *Après une lecture du Dante* from the second set of *Années de pèlerinage*, mentioned in a letter from Bache to Alfred Hipkins in 1886, and illustrative of Bache's expanding repertoire:

> I am just studying a really representative work of his, 'Après une lecture de [sic] Dante': you doubtless know it well: I knew it somewhat, but have never studied it till now: it is a piece which must be known well to be understood.[34]

Although Bache included extracts of poetic and descriptive texts in his printed programmes to help the audience understand aspects of selected solo piano works[35] – as well as a reproduction of Raphael's *Sposalizio* to accompany that particular miniature – he realized that something more substantial was needed for the Dante movement. For its British premiere in his concert series on 21 February 1887, Bache therefore provided three musical quotations to assist 'those who have no previous acquaintance with this work' (see Ex. 9.1).

Despite these musical signposts, the *Musical Standard* found the work 'obscure, if not in parts incomprehensible; certainly very dry and an exercise of the patience'.[36] In the following concert on 22 October, Bache annotated the quotations with incipits from Dante's *Inferno*, which he admitted were 'given without authority whatsoever'. The *Musical World* was unimpressed. Not only did the movement suffer from 'an inevitable comparison with the composer's "Dante" Symphony', but Bache's poetic licence was misguided: 'Mr. Bache points out several passages in the Divina Commedia which appear to him to have suggested this music, but as he confesses that he has no authority for this statement, it would have been better to have left the connoisseur to draw his own conclusions.'[37]

---

34 Bache, *Brother Musicians: Reminiscences of Edward and Walter Bache*, p. 309.

35 These included German texts for *Au bord d'une source* ('In säuselnder Kühle / Beginnen die Spiele / Der jungen Natur') and the First *Mephisto Waltz* (Lenau's 'Wie härrisch die Geiger des Dorfs sich geberden ... Und brausend verschlingt sie das Wonnemeer'), French texts for the two *Légendes* ('Petites fleurs de St François d'Assises' and a text by 'Charitas') and *Bénédiction de Dieu dans la solitude* (Lamartine's 'D'où me vient, Ô mon Dieu, cette paix qui m'inonde? ... Un nouvel homme en moi renait et recommence'), and Italian texts for *Il penseroso* (Michelangelo's 'Grato m'è sonno, e più l'esser si sasso ... Però non mi destar, deh! – parla basso!'), *Canzonetta del Salvator Rosa* ('Vado ben spesso cangiando loco') and *Sonetto 123 del Petrarcha* ('Io vidi in terra angelici costumi ... Tanta dolcezza avea pien l'aëre e 'l vento').

36 *MSt* (26 February 1887): 132. See also an attack in the *Athenaeum* (26 February 1887): 297: 'Liszt gives us one hundred bars or so of unintelligible rhapsody, followed by two or three in which a theme is recognizable; then another hundred and twenty apparently leading up to some grand climax, which when it arrives proves to be a miserable failure.' Consequently, this journal was unable to comment upon *Venezia e Napoli* in October 1887, they explained, as this was preceded by *Après une lecture du Dante* in the programme, and they could not endure a second performance.

37 *MW*, 65 (1887): 857. Eight months earlier (1887: 156) this journal had simply noted that *Après une lecture du Dante* (along with two of the *Etudes d'exécution transcendante*) was 'admirably executed'.

Example 9.1 Liszt. *Après une lecture du Dante*, **musical quotations**

I. (introductory)
Andante maestoso

II. (leading theme)
Presto agitato assai

III. (second theme)

The second, even more demanding work for audiences and critics (as well as performers) was Liszt's B minor Sonata. Bache had read this through in April 1865, having heard Liszt perform it about a month earlier,[38] but did not include it in his concerts until November 1882. His authoritative performance was much admired by the *Musical Standard*:

> Mr. Bache has, in a remarkable degree, made this noble work his own. One feels as if it were the author himself to whose interpretation one is listening; so earnestly, so lovingly, and with such firm faith, is every detail set forth ... Those who do not appreciate Liszt through Mr. Bache's reading of his works will certainly never learn to appreciate them through any other interpreter.[39]

Despite Bache's skilful interpretation of the sonata, the *Monthly Musical Record* was somewhat ambivalent. Although the work contained 'many passages of beauty, and the treatment is original', it could not be seen as 'a step in advance' because 'the novelty of form gives to it only a meretricious value'.[40] Other reservations were more strident. For the *Athenaeum*, the work represented an 'unsuccessful attempt ... to enlarge the forms created by the old masters beyond the bounds of their possibilities'.[41]

Liszt's transcriptions and arrangements raised both the issue of virtuosity and the morality of transforming the works of others. Of those works cited for comment in the press, some were viewed in a positive manner. Liszt's transcription of the march from Wagner's *Tannhäuser* was 'a piece that every respectable amateur should practise, and, if possible, play', and his arrangement of Schubert's *Fantasie* 'must become popular as it becomes better known, as a *morceau* well adapted for the display of artistic acquirement on the part of the soloist, and combining most charming orchestral and solo effects'.[42] The greater the intervention by the arranger, however, the more problematic a work became. Liszt's adaptation of Weber, the *Polonaise brillante*, for example, involved the orchestration and arrangement of Weber's *Polacca brillante*: '*L'Hilarité*', op. 72, preceded by a *Largo* introduction taken from the *Grande polonaise*, op. 21. This was a work with which Bache obviously felt a particular affinity, performing it in his own concert series on 21 March 1872, 27 November 1873,[43] and 25 February 1875, and choosing this work for

---

38 See the letter from Bache to Mme Laussot, 5 April 1865, in Bache, *Brother Musicians: Reminiscences of Edward and Walter Bache*, p. 183.

39 *MSt* (27 October 1883): 256, a rare example of a signed review (B.F. Wyatt-Smith).

40 *MMR*, 12 (1882): 283.

41 *Athenaeum* (11 November 1882): 637, which continued, 'if this be a sonata, then those of Beethoven are not, for the two forms have hardly anything in common ... we should rather define Liszt's work as a very clever rhapsody on original themes'. Similarly, the *MW*, 60 (1882): 722, characterized the work as 'an inchoate assortment of phrases'.

42 See the *MSt* (23 November 1872): 326, and the *MW*, 51 (1873): 817. Bache's booklet for the concert of 27 November 1873 included notes by Joseph Bennett on Liszt's arrangement of the Schubert *Fantasie*, reprinted from the Daily Orchestral Concerts at the Albert Hall.

43 *MT*, 16 (1874): 361 noted that 'his execution of Weber's "Polonaise Brillante" ... and of several less important solos, was the theme of universal admiration'.

his Crystal Palace debut on 14 November 1874. It was this last of four performances that provoked the ire of the *Daily Telegraph*:

> [Liszt] has not only garbled a perfect work of art by a master, but prefaced it with the largo from another work – Polonaise in E flat – by the same hand. … Enough that violence, as unnecessary as, from every point of view, it is unlawful, has been done to an art-work which, though a trifle – a mere cabinet picture – is signed with a great name.[44]

Although Bache was sensitive to criticism in the musical press, he was very aware that reaction on his part could potentially jeopardize his career. In a letter to his sister dated 7 September 1874 he wrote:

> I have so often myself … been very near spoiling my chances of doing good in the Liszt cause by violent letters against Mr. Davison and Co., but fortunately I can't write, and these fellows can; many a letter have I addressed to the Editor of the *Monthly Musical Record* and many a stinging notice have I prepared for my programmes; and then – put it in the fire. These blessed paper controversies make bad blood, and do no good – one must work by actions.[45]

However, the *Telegraph*'s criticism triggered a strong response from Bache. Not only did he reproduce their account in his programme notes for the concert of 25 February 1875 (where he performed Weber's original after Liszt's adaptation), he also included an extended counter to it.[46]

One wonders whether it was this particular episode that prompted Bache to include an extended essay by Edward Dannreuther in the written programme for his concert of 27 February 1877, entitled 'Editing, Transcribing, and Re-scoring'.[47] This essay aimed to 'throw some little light upon a number of questions much debated of late, as to whether or not certain novel readings, editions, arrangements, orchestrations,

---

44 *Daily Telegraph*, 16 November 1874, reproduced in Bache's printed booklet for the concert of 25 February 1875, p. 27. In contrast, *MMR*, 4 (1874): 171 took a more positive view of Bache's 'brilliant performance' of this work: 'Whatever exception may be taken to the freedom with which Liszt has treated Weber's text, it must be admitted that he has furnished pianists with a most taking and effective piece for the concert-room which formerly was only suited to a drawing-room performance.'

45 Bache, *Brother Musicians: Reminiscences of Edward and Walter Bache*, p. 238.

46 Bache's humorous counter involved the citing of other 'astoundingly impudent' musicians (including Mozart, Mendelssohn and Sir Julius Benedict) who had altered the musical texts of others by providing additional accompaniments or creating paraphrases. Although the *Musical Standard* acknowledged that Bache had a point (*MSt* (8 March 1875): 150), several journals, including *Figaro*, felt that this was in bad taste and represented an attempt 'to assail the *Daily Telegraph* in coarse terms'. See *Figaro*, 3 March 1875, and *Illustrated Sporting and Dramatic News*, 6 March 1875 (both reproduced in *MW*, 53 (1875): 172 and 182).

47 See Bache's concert programme for 27 February 1877, pp. iii–xiii. This essay was ostensibly included to coincide with the performance of Klindworth's rescoring of Chopin's Second Piano Concerto. A set of Bache's concert programmes was presented to the Bodleian Library, Oxford by Constance Bache in 1889. I am grateful to the staff of the Bodleian Library for making this source available.

etc., can be accepted as valid'. Having praised recent editions by Liszt, Henselt, Bülow, Tausig and Klindworth for their transformation of texts 'from a more or less vague region and abstraction and incomplete suggestion, to the clear light of the hearers' sensuous perception', and the same authors' transcriptions for 'raising the piano to the level of an orchestra', Dannreuther turned to the most contentious issue – re-instrumentation. Examples *'giving to the composer the proper means for expressing his thought wherever his thought is unmistakeable, and the means he chose to express it, for mechanical or other reasons palpably inadequate'* included Joachim's rescoring of Schubert's *Grand Duo*, op. 140, Klindworth's reworking of Alkan's *Etudes* and significantly, 'of course, Liszt's scoring of Weber's Polonaise in E':

> Here there is no shadow of presumption or uncalled for meddling with the works of others. It is the same case as when, in an atelier of old, a picture was in the main conceived and designed by the elder master, and the subordinate parts executed by his friends and pupils.[48]

Bache was more than simply a performer of Liszt's music; as the *Musical Standard* suggested, 'from Bach to Raff, from Liszt to Mendelssohn, Mr. Bache is at home in all styles'.[49] Table 9.2 outlines the non-Lisztian repertoire performed by Bache in his concert series. One striking feature of the concerts was the inclusion of repertoire that is relatively unfamiliar today. As gratitude for Hans von Bülow's role as conductor in the orchestral concerts of 1873 and 1875 (particularly as Bülow waived his fee),[50] Bache programmed a number of Bülow's compositions in his concerts,[51] including several piano miniatures. The graceful arpeggiation of the Impromptu, op. 27, *Lacerta*, would have been well suited to Bache's particular brand of pianism, as would the simplicity of the *Albumblatt*, *Innocence*. However, it was in Bülow's *Intermezzo scherzoso*, op. 21 no. 9, *La canzonatura* (also titled 'The Carnival of Milan'), with its *staccatissimo* semiquavers at a consistent *presto* tempo and *pianissimo* dynamic, that Bache was able to show off his technical control (see Ex. 9.2).

---

48 Dannreuther included a final appeal: 'The foregoing and all similar considerations necessarily result in *a plea for toleration* ... Let us avoid codifying the law for the present; let us examine each single case of interpretation, restitution, addition, instrumentation, on its individual merits; and let us study with all reverence, and due patience, that which our greatest players and acutest critics have elaborated in the course of a lifetime. If, peradventure, the right thing is exaggerated or overdone by competent persons, or, what is worse, the right thing is badly done by incompetent persons, the common sense of musicians will easily put matters to rights.'

49 *MSt* (6 November 1875): 306. *MW*, 51 (1873): 817 noted that works by Chopin, Raff, Schumann and Weber were 'all played with true artistic spirit and taste'.

50 See Bache, *Brother Musicians: Reminiscences of Edward and Walter Bache*, p. 240: 'My concert [25 February 1875] was (to everyone's surprise) a most heavy loss: expenses between £230 and £250 – receipts £110! Bülow insists on paying £50 towards the loss. This ought to be known: he conducted also for nothing.'

51 Bache's concert of 25 February 1879 included the second London performance of Bülow's symphonic ballad *The Minstrel's Curse*, op. 16.

Table 9.2   **Non-Lisztian Repertoire performed by Bache in his Concert Series** (numbers in parentheses represent frequency of performance)

Composer	Repertoire
J.S. Bach	Chromatic Fantasia and Fugue in D minor, BWV 903 (2); Concerto in D minor for harpsichord BWV 1052 [?];[a] Fantasia in C minor, BWV 906; English Suite no. 5, BWV 810; Prelude & Fugue in C♯ minor and A♭ major, *Das wohltemperirte Clavier*, Book 2
Beethoven	32 Variations in C minor, WoO 80 (4); Piano Sonatas opp. 31/2 (2), 31/3, 57, 81a, 101, 106 (2), 109, 110, 111; 15 Variations & Fugue, op. 35 (2); Piano Trio, op. 70; 6 Variations, op. 34; Rondo a Capriccio, op. 129; Rondo in G major, op. 51; 5 Variations on 'Rule Brittania', WoO 79; Piano Concertos nos. 3, 4 and 5
Bülow	Mazurka-Impromptu, op. 4; *La canzonatura*, op. 21/9 (2); *Innocence*; *Lacerta*, op. 27
Chopin	Allegro de concert, op. 46; Andante spianato & Grande polonaise brillante, op. 22 (2); Nocturne in D♭, op. 27; Ballade in G minor, op. 23; Berceuse, op. 57 (3); Impromptu no. 2, op. 36; Valse, op. 64/3; Piano Concerto no. 1 (Tausig); Piano Concerto no. 2, (2); Polonaise in C minor, op. 40/2; 4 Mazurkas op. 41 (2); Sonata in B♭ minor, op. 35 (2); Ballade no. 4 in F minor; various Preludes, op. 28 (5);[b] various Etudes, opp. 10 and 25 (2)[c]
Franck	Piano Trio, op. 1/1
Henselt	*Danklied nach Sturm*, op. 5
Mackenzie	*Nocturne* and *Ballade*, op. 15
Mendelssohn	Capriccio, op. 5; *Charakterstücke*, op. 7 nos. 4 and 7; Fantasia in F♯ minor, op. 28; Prelude and Fugue in E minor, op. 35; *Variations sérieuses*, op. 54; *Lied ohne Worte*, op. 62/1
Mozart	Minuet [K. 355?]; Gigue [K. 574?]
Raff	Waltz-Caprice [Tanz-Caprice, op. 54/1]; Chaconne, op. 150 [two pianos]
Schumann	Piano Concerto, op. 54; *Bunte Blätter*, op. 99/1; *Novellette*, op. 21/4
Silas	Gavotte, Passepied and Courante
Tschaikovsky	*Chant sans paroles* [op. 40/6?]; *Valse* [op. 40/8?]
Volkmann	*Blumenstück*, op. 21/3
Weber	*Momento Capriccioso*, op. 12 (3)

a   Performed on the piano with quintet accompaniment.

b   The nature of the selection from op. 28 on 25 February 1879 and 26 October 1885 ('10 Preludes') is unclear; however, Bache performed the Prelude in G on 18 November 1872, Preludes in G minor, B♭, G, F♯ minor, A♭ and E♭ on 1 November 1875, and Preludes in C, A♭, F, F♯ minor, F♯ and E♭ on 5 November 1877.

c   There is a reference to the Etude op. 10 in G♭ on 18 November 1872; the keys referred to in the amalgam of the two sets on 26 October 1874 (A♭, F minor, C minor, C, C♯ minor, G♭), apart from op. 10 no. 1 in C major, suggests several possibilities – perhaps the first three from op. 25 and the next three from op. 10, or an alternation between the sets, beginning with op. 25 no. 1.

Example 9.2 Hans von Bülow. *La canzonatura*, **op. 21 no. 9, opening**

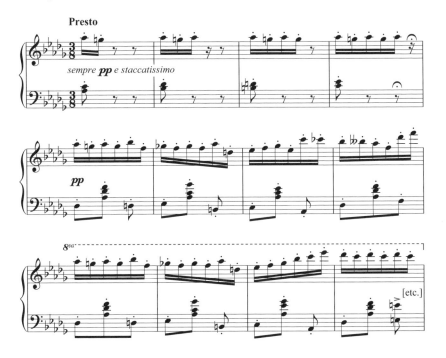

The Dutch pianist and composer Edouard Silas (1827–1909) explored a wide range of genres in his keyboard miniatures,[52] ranging from a waltz 'dedicated to the Young Ladies at the Elms, Tottenham' to the more exotic *Persian Serenade*, op. 44. Bache included Silas's neo-classical *Gavotte, Passepied and Courante* and also offered Alexander Mackenzie's *Nocturne* and *Ballade* from the *Trois Morceaux* for piano, op. 15, which were dedicated to Bache.[53] Although the *Musical Standard* found Mackenzie's miniatures 'graceful and pleasing, though not strikingly

---

52 Silas taught at the Guildhall School of Music and the London Academy of Music but is perhaps best known through his links with Berlioz, as suggested by the short article, 'A Friend of Berlioz', *The Musical Herald*, 669 (December 1903): 372–3.

53 The first of the set, not included by Bache, was a *Valse sérieuse*. Bache's friendship with Mackenzie stemmed from his connections with the Royal Academy of Music and a shared admiration for the music of Liszt. In his *Liszt* (London: Murdoch, Murdoch & Co., 1922) – a reprint of *Liszt and his Music*, published in the earlier series 'Masterpieces of Music' edited by E. Hatzfield (London: 1913), p. [20] – Mackenzie noted: 'Walter Bache, whose devotion to Liszt was in itself a beautiful display of affectionate gratitude, carried on the fight against overpowering prejudice and under adverse conditions which in the present day seem almost incredible … this enthusiast kept steadily breaking the ice at his annual concerts … and so cleared the fairway for these performances by Richter and others which have taken place under more encouraging and enlightened conditions since the death of the master and his pupil.'

original',[54] the *Nocturne* has a melodic charm, with a mini-cadenza towards the end of the movement perhaps inspired by the particular nature of Bache's pianism; the *impetuoso* triplets of the more extended *Ballade* (marked *Presto inquieto*) provided an effective foil. Another work of note was *Danklied nach Sturm* by Adolf Henselt, the sixth of the *Douze études de salon*, op. 5 (1838).[55] In this work, Henselt divides an A♭ major hymn into two sections and follows each section with a variation; the variation passagework is then extended into a coda. As the figuration in Example 9.3 shows, Bache's characteristic delicacy of touch would have been particularly effective here. Bache also included the César Franck Piano Trio, op. 1 no. 1 (published in 1843), performed at his third concert on 22 May 1867, and the two Tschaikovsky miniatures, programmed in November 1880.

Example 9.3 Adolf Henselt. *Danklied nach Sturm*, op. 5 no. 6 (bb. 17–20)

---

54 *MSt* (2 November 1878): 272.

55 The German pianist and composer (Georg Martin) Adolf (von) Henselt (1814–89) studied piano with Hummel and Simon Sechter. He became acquainted with Liszt after the latter's visits to Russia (where Henselt was based from 1838 onwards) in the 1840s.

Bache was also happy to include more canonic repertoire, although press reaction to these works should be approached with caution. As a performer in the Lisztian tradition, Bache was open to criticism that his particular brand of pianism was unsuitable; alternatively, critics opposed to Liszt could deliberately exaggerate the beauties of compositions not written by Liszt. Bache's interpretations of J.S. Bach were generally well received. The Chromatic Fantasy and Fugue was thought by the *Musical Times* to show his 'cultured powers to considerable advantage', as 'all the points were well brought out, the phrasing was remarkably good, and the entire execution of the difficult piece neat and highly finished', and Bache was said to have given a 'masterly' performance of the D minor Harpsichord Concerto.[56] In one of the early concerts, the *Musical World*, perhaps attempting to marginalize the works of the New German School, noted that 'the largest favour was shown to things more orthodox, as, for example, Bach's Prelude and Fugue in A minor, well played by Mr. Bache'.[57] The only cause for concern seems to have been the issue of tempo in the Fifth English Suite:

> Perhaps the only point to question was the time at which some of the movements were taken. In several cases the speed was scarcely in accordance with generally received notions, and was, at times, fairly open to doubt and dissent.[58]

Accounts of Bache's performances of the music of Beethoven need to be treated with particular care, given the contentious nature of the Liszt–Beethoven relationship. Where music by both composers appeared in the same programme, critics were often uncomfortable; the *Monthly Musical Record* could not approve of Bache's juxtaposition of Beethoven's Fifth Concerto with Liszt's Second Piano Concerto, as this was viewed as an 'endeavour to adjust the conceptions of Beethoven within the fancies of Liszt and the efforts of the modern school'.[59] Similarly, the *Musical World* suggested the unsuitability of a Beethoven–Liszt pairing:

> There is a suspicious unanimity about the way in which apostles of the most modern school in music treat Beethoven. The great master had little in common with their particular doctrines. He was neither a revolutionary nor a destructive, but, rather, showed how compatible is freedom of musical thought and utterance with accepted musical law. Nevertheless, the revolutionaries of our day will claim him and use him as a springboard for the easier vaulting aloft of their unquestioned athletes and champions … The case of Mr. Bache is probably one in point.[60]

However, there is nothing to suggest that Bache's programming of Beethoven was in any way forced upon him.

---

56 *MT*, 22 (1881): 186 and *MSt* (31 October 1874): 273.
57 *MW*, 47 (1869): 348.
58 *MT*, 21 (1880): 606–607.
59 *MMR*, 16 (1886): 66.
60 *MW*, 59 (1881): 716. See also *MSt* (9 March 1878): 145 and *MMR*, 8 (1878): 46. Beethoven's concerto was probably included to reduce the need for rehearsal time, bearing in mind Bache's precarious financial position.

In relation to individual works, critics found no difficulty in praising performances of the 32 Variations in C minor, which were described as 'highly successful' and 'technically correct'; 'in addition, much taste and feeling were imparted to a piece in which the mechanical aim of the composer is specially prominent.'[61] Similarly, the Sonata op. 31 no. 2 was apparently the 'pièce de resistance' in the concert of 27 October 1873, where Bache displayed 'great power in the quick movements, and a sympathetic sense of subject in the immediate adagio, where a change to the key of B flat relieves the sombre colour of the prevalent minor mode', and a performance of the same work nine years later was 'rendered … in the broad and emphatic manner which is seldom absent from his pianoforte exemplifications, but always with honest and scholar like effect'.[62] Bache was also effective in the op. 57 sonata and had a 'well-considered and powerful but refined manner' in the Fifth Piano Concerto.[63] Performances of other works, however, were the subject of debate. The *Musical Standard* was impressed by Bache's interpretation of Beethoven's op. 111 Sonata:

> The delivery of the variations in this sonata, which showed his delicacy and clearness of touch to perfection, was as unassuming and intelligent as Mr. Bache's playing always is; they are not, in his hands, what they have too often been considered, the mere mechanical development of a theme, but the ideal perfecting of a beautiful conception – the beginning of the glorious work continued by Schumann and his successors.[64]

However, the *Musical World* suggested that 'the lighter style of composition … appears better suited to him'.[65] Similarly, although the *Musical Standard* numbered Bache's interpretation[s] of the Sonata op. 31 no. 3 among the 'consummately fine reading[s] of the choicest classical works', in a later performance the *Monthly Musical Record* concluded that although the middle movement was 'rendered with delicacy and finish', in general the work 'did not receive full justice at the hands of the player'.[66] The *Musical World* was also unconvinced by Bache's performance of the demanding Sonata op. 106 in 1881: 'We shall not class Mr. Bache among the most brilliant exponents of the exceedingly difficult sonata. It was too much for him, but there are some causes in which even the defeated warrior deserves a laurel'.[67] Two years later, in a more balanced critique, they suggested that Bache had played 'magnificently':

> It will be seen that the vigorous finger of this well-disciplined artist was put to the severest possible test in the course of the recital, for there is nothing perhaps in the entire range of pianoforte music that places an expositor under heavier liabilities than the famous op. 106. Mr. Bache nevertheless faced them with undeniable bravery, and in many respects challenged general approval, his delivery of the great triple fugue being remarkable for

---

61 *MT*, 13 (1868): 412 and *MMR*, 13 (1883): 118.
62 See *MSt* (1 November 1873): 273–4, and *MW*, 61 (1883): 224.
63 See *Athenaeum* (2 November 1878): 571 and *MMR*, 8 (1878): 46.
64 *MSt* (6 November 1875): 306.
65 *MW*, 53 (1875): 749.
66 *MSt* (23 November 1872): 326, and *MMR*, 13 (1883): 118.
67 *MW*, 59 (1881): 716. However, the *Athenaeum* (5 November 1881): 605 described how 'Mr. Bache gave, as might have been expected, a highly intelligent reading of the sonata, the rendering of the two middle movements being the most commendable'.

its unrelaxed rapidity and the unfailing closeness of the definition. His version of the slow movement was hardly so satisfactory. It is vouchsafed to but few to completely realise the full tenderness of this most passionate of musical poems, and the masculine style of Mr. Bache occasionally unfits it to give its dreamy plaints of saddened love the emotional significance of which they are so exquisitely susceptible.[68]

The press were in agreement, however, over Bache's affinity with the music of Schumann and Chopin. His 1873 performance of Schumann's Piano Concerto was singled out as being 'deservedly received with the warmest applause'; the slow movement was said to have 'entranced the assembly' and, overall, Bache apparently blended a 'brilliancy of execution – especially in the extreme mechanical difficulties of the final movement' with an 'intellectual comprehension of the spirit of the work throughout'.[69] Where Chopin's music was concerned, Bache displayed 'accuracy and power' and 'manual dexterity' in the *Allegro de concert* and produced a 'masterly and expressive rendering' of the Second Concerto.[70] In the B♭ minor Sonata, 'its grace and refinement, its extreme sensitiveness and deep feeling were fully understood and set forth'. In particular, 'the *sotto voce* maintained throughout the last movement was an admirable feature, which those who know the difficulty of preserving an unbroken monotony will appreciate'.[71] Bache's performance of Chopin's Etude op. 10 no. 5 in G♭ 'evoked the most demonstrative applause', and in the Preludes (as well as in Liszt's concert études) 'the audience, ever eager to testify its appreciation, on two occasions succeeded in spoiling intended effects'.[72]

Bache's selective use of programme notes and extended essays has already been noted, but he was also keen to explore a variety of approaches to the programming of solo piano works. Several of his concerts deliberately highlighted the sense of an Austro-Germanic canon, one of the most striking being the Bach–Beethoven–Schubert–Mendelssohn–Schumann–Bülow–Liszt axis in 1874. Another approach involved more generic programming. Bache had already performed two concertos in the same concert on 27 February 1877 (Liszt's Second Concerto in A major and Chopin's Second Concerto in F minor).[73] On 8 February 1886, Bache took this one stage further by offering a concert devoted to 'Concertos for piano with orchestra', a demanding juxtaposition of Liszt's Second Piano Concerto, Beethoven's Third

---

68 *MW*, 61 (1883): 224. *MMR*, 13 (1883): 118 echoed these plaudits for the finale, but without the criticism of the middle movement: 'The pianist may be congratulated on the manner in which he achieved his task; the fugue especially was played with great precision and vigour.'

69 See *MT*, 16 (1873): 44; *MSt* (8 March 1873): 149; and *MW*, 51 (1873): 162. See also the *Athenaeum* (8 March 1873): 319, which described his 'fine interpretation' of the concerto. The programme notes for the Concerto were taken from a Crystal Palace programme.

70   *MW*, 44 (1866): 336 and *MMR*, 7 (1877): 65.

71   *MSt* (2 November 1878): 272. See also the *Athenaeum* (2 November 1878): 571.

72   *MSt* (23 November 1872): 326 and *MSt* (6 November 1875): 306. See also *MW*, 53 (1875): 749 on Bache's performances of Mendelssohn and Chopin.

73 See *MMR*, 7 (1877): 65: 'His performance of two such difficult works on one and the same evening from memory, and with remarkable force, brilliance, delicacy and intelligence, was really an astonishing feat of expectancy.'

(which included the British premiere of Liszt's cadenza for this work) and the British premiere of the Chopin–Tausig op. 11.[74]

Bache also experimented with concerts devoted to the works of one composer, beginning with the all-Liszt programme in 1879 (see Table 9.3). Initially, the press echoed one another in pleasant surprise as to Liszt's compositional range; indeed the similarity of their responses almost suggests collusion.[75] As Table 9.3 illustrates, Bache repeated the idea of the all-Liszt programme in 1882 and 1885 and even experimented with an all-Beethoven programme in 1883. The narrower focus upon Liszt's orchestral and choral works alone, or just his piano works, was less successful, particularly in comparison with the Beethoven model. Whilst in the case of the latter, 'no better name could have been selected for a scheme of this kind', the all-Liszt programmes of the 1880s were described as 'decidedly monotonous',[76] being perceived as excessively demanding for both the audience and the instrument.[77] Even the more fair-minded *Musical Standard* warned that 'a programme consisting entirely of Liszt's works must be arranged with more than the usual care in order to avoid the impression among the audience that it is possible to have too much of a good thing at one sitting'.[78]

The final concert in Table 9.3 highlights another issue – the grouping of piano miniatures. Bache's early concerts, with their miscellaneous programming typical of the period, plucked such pieces out of context. This selective approach led to the pairing of *Au bord d'une source* with the Tenth Hungarian Rhapsody in 1870 or with the *Sonetto 123 del Petrarca* (thus mixing sets of *Années de pèlerinage*) in 1872. The 1870s saw a greater sense of generic pairing, however, with the grouping of the first three *Consolations* in 1872 and the last two in 1874; similarly, the concert études *La leggierezza* and *Waldesrauschen* were paired in 1875 and 1876, and *Au bord d'une source* was juxtaposed with the *Pastorale* from the same *Années de pèlerinage*

---

74 The *Athenaeum* (13 February 1886): 240 noted: 'In spite of the strong contrast of style in these three works, a certain amount of monotony was induced by the continual combination of the piano and orchestra; and in our opinion a symphony or other piece for orchestra alone might have advantageously replaced one of the concertos in question.' In relation to Liszt's cadenza in Beethoven's Third Concerto, *MW*, 64 (1886): 108 felt that it was 'played with evident enjoyment of its difficulties'. (Tausig's reorchestration of Chopin's Concerto was seen as justified in both of these journals, except where alterations to the solo part were concerned.)

75 See reproductions from the *Daily Telegraph*, the *Daily News* and the *Times* in *MW*, 57 (1879): 690. The *Athenaeum* (25 October 1879): 537, was less enthusiastic: 'An hour and a half … of his [Liszt's] pianoforte works, interrupted only by three short songs from his pen, constitutes a programme which makes considerable demands on the audience … In this music, side by side with passages of great beauty and real poetic feeling, we find much which on first hearing appears crude and formless – mere passage-writing admirably adapted to display the abilities of the pianist, but of little intrinsic value.'

76 *MMR*, 13 (1883): 118.

77 In connection with an all-Liszt programme of nearly 2½ hours given by Bache 'in [his] habitual and enthusiastic style', one critic added: 'A word of recognition is also due to the magnificent "Broadwood" which withstood the tremendous onslaught of Liszt's music, even in the topmost octaves, without flinching.' *MMR*, 17 (1887): 258.

78 *MSt* (14 February 1885): 99.

Table 9.3   **Bache's One-Composer Programmes in his Concert Series**

Date	Repertoire
22 October 1879	Liszt: Prelude and Fugue on BACH; Ballade no. 1 in D flat; *Au bord d'une source*; Polonaise no. 1 in C minor; *La leggierezza*; *Paysage*; *Wilde Jagd*; *Es muss ein Wunderbares sein*; *Du bist wie eine Blume*; *In Liebeslust*; *Eglogue*; *Légende* no. 1 (*St François d'Assise*); Hungarian Rhapsody no. 4 in E♭
2 March 1882	Liszt: *Fest-Marsch zur Goethe Feier*; *Mephisto Waltz* no. 1; A *Faust* Symphony
6 November 1882	Liszt: Prelude and Fugue on BACH; Sonata in B minor; *Die drei Zigeuner*; *In Liebeslust*; *Un sospiro*; *La leggierezza*; *Paysage*; *Sonetto 123 del Petrarca*; *Valse oubliée*; Hungarian Rhapsody no. 9 (*Pesther Carnival*)
9 April 1883 (Beethoven)	Beethoven: 32 Variations in C minor, WoO 80; Sonata in D minor, op. 31/2; *An die ferne Geliebte*, op. 98; Sonata in B♭, op. 106; *Rondo a Capriccio*, op. 129
22 October 1883	Handel (arr. Liszt): Sarabande and Chaconne from *Almira*; Liszt: *Il lamento*; *Un sospiro*; Sonata in B minor; *Die Loreley*; *Bénédiction de Dieu dans la solitude*; Hungarian Rhapsody no. 11; *Ungarischer Sturm-Marsch* [1876 edition]
5 February 1885	Liszt: Rákóczy March; Piano Concerto no. 1; *Dante* Symphony; *Jeanne d'Arc au bûcher*; *Angelus*; *Die heiligen drei Könige* (*Christus*)
22 October 1887	Liszt: Hungarian Rhapsody no. 5; *Années de pèlerinage* (*Deuxième année: Italie*) [omitting numbers 4 and 5, but including the supplement, *Venezia e Napoli*]

set in 1877. These strategies were developed further in the 1880s, with the pairing of the two St Francis *Légendes* in 1884 and the inclusion of multiple miniatures from the *Etudes d'exécution transcendente* in 1885 and 1887.[79] Most striking in this context was the concert of 22 October 1887, where Bache performed virtually the

---

79 October 1885 saw the out-of-sequence combination *Chasse-Neige*, *Paysage* and *Feux Follets*, and in February 1887 Bache offered a chronological, if selective, juxtaposition of *Preludio*, the second étude in A minor, *Feux Follets*, and the tenth étude in F minor. Of the *Etudes d'exécution transcendante*, therefore, only *Paysage* was offered to the public outside the context of others within the set. The first St Francis *Légende* had been paired with miscellaneous works in previous concerts: with *Eglogue* and the Fourth Hungarian Rhapsody in 1879 and with the First *Mephisto Waltz* and the Thirteenth Hungarian Rhapsody in 1881. The same move towards a greater sense of grouping can be seen in Bache's treatment of the Chopin Preludes. Whilst in 1872 he was happy to group the Prelude op. 28 in G with the Nocturne op. 27 in D♭ and the Etude op. 10 in G♭, Bache performed preludes from op. 28 in groups of six in 1875 and 1877, and in a group of ten in 1885. Similarly, in 1881 Bache performed a group of four Chopin mazurkas from op. 41. There were still examples of miscellaneous grouping in the later concerts; in November 1882, Bache offered a trio of miscellaneous pieces (*Paysage*, *Sonetto 123 del Petrarca*, *Valse oubliée*) within his all-Liszt programme.

whole of the second set (*Italie*) of *Années de pèlerinage*. The omission of Petrarch Sonnets 47 and 104 here may have been an attempt to avoid any suggestion of over-dependence upon one poetic source. On a more practical level, the inclusion of the intimate fifth Hungarian Rhapsody would have helped to break up the concert into more manageable sections for the audience, particularly as Bache warned in the programme that the *Venezia e Napoli* supplement would 'last 17 minutes and has no pause between the movements'.[80]

There was one other practical feature of the concerts, in that Bache was an advocate of performing from memory: 'Mr. Bache's performance was a *bonâ fide* recital, each of the works set down being played by him from memory with a readiness and correctness rarely attained, as well as with remarkable force, finish, intelligence and feeling.'[81] Indeed, it was the demands of this approach that were cited as a possible reason for Bache's breaking down at the end of Mendelssohn's Capriccio, op. 5 in February 1887: 'Mr. Bache ... suddenly broke off and apologized to the audience on the grounds that he was quite exhausted by his efforts for the last hour and a half; he had played without a book. The audience accepted the excuse and enthusiastically recalled Mr. Bache.'[82] Whether or not performers should memorize their scores was a subject for debate. In an article in the *Musical World* of February 1886, 'a pianist' argued for the retention of the music:

> It is a mistake to suppose that the very greatest artists are unanimously in favour of playing by heart, though all are perfectly capable of doing so ... Mr. Charles Hallé and Miss Agnes Zimmermann think it no shame to play even a single solo at a concert from book; and Madame Schumann makes it a rule never to play concerts from memory ... It is to be wished that an intrepid stand against the universality of the practice could be made by those young artists who hold prominent positions among us. If, for instance, Miss Fanny Davies, Mr. Max Pauer, and others, who have already caught the ear of the public, would combine in protesting against the despotism of the audience which would banish music-books from the platform altogether, it would be an immense advantage to the art.[83]

---

80 Throughout his concert series, Bache was keen to avoid performances being spoilt by members of the audience arriving late or leaving before the concert had finished. Thus it was noted 'hearers are not annoyed by the interruption of late comers, for Mr. Bache adopts the German custom of shutting the entrance-doors before any piece is commenced, and the last arrivals have to wait until its close before taking their places' (*Athenaeum* (1 March 1879): 289). In his printed programme for the concert of 11 May 1870, Bache humorously addressed the problem of the final work in the concert: 'The time-honoured custom of treating as an "out-voluntary" (a term familiar to church organists) whatever may have the misfortune to stand last on the Concert Programme, is most discouraging to those interested in its worthy performance.'

81 *MMR*, 2 (1872): 180.

82 *MSt* (26 February 1887): 132. On another occasion, the *Athenaeum* (5 November 1881): 605 noted that 'the feat of playing such a lengthy and enormously difficult work [Beethoven's "Hammerklavier" Sonata] without a copy was somewhat perilous; but Mr. Bache's memory did not fail him, save once in the complicated *finale*'.

83 'An Astounding Musical Memory', *MW*, 64 (1886): 99.

Walter Bache can therefore be identified as a pianist who exhibited significant interpretative and technical skill. In addition to providing authoritative accounts of Liszt's compositions for piano, he also offered thoughtful readings of works by other composers, including, from a current perspective, the familiar (Bach, Beethoven, Chopin, Schumann) and the less familiar (Henselt, Mackenzie, Silas, Bülow). Allied with his experimental approaches to programming and the focused material he employed in 'educating' his audiences, his concert series was one of the most exciting events in London's musical calendar. One can only speculate as to why Bache was not a more frequent presence on the London concert circuit. In the early 1870s, the *Monthly Musical Record* posed this very question and suggested an explanation: 'Can it be because Mr. Bache is an Englishman, and being an Englishman, is lacking in that useful quality of self-assertion and assurance, which but too often makes up the sole stock-in-trade of so many of the second-rate foreign artistes who visit this country?'[84] The same journal complained a year later: 'That a pianist of such remarkable attainments, who certainly ranks among the first two or three of our resident pianists, either native or foreign, has not been heard elsewhere than at his own concerts, seems inexplicable.'[85] It may have been partly due to their efforts that Bache was rewarded with his Crystal Palace debut in 1874. He also performed in the Richter concerts, as organist in *Die Hunnenschlacht* in June 1880, and as pianist in Chopin's Second Piano Concerto in 1881 and Beethoven's Choral Fantasia in 1883.[86] Perhaps Bache's perceived Lisztian associations were seen as too dangerous for the mainstream:

> Routine *répertoires* of pianoforte pieces abound; there is a deluge of them, – it is so safe to rely on the accepted masterpieces. It requires, therefore, moral, or rather artistic courage, for a musician to abandon the beaten track, and to make known the works of living composers, about whom there are divided opinions.[87]

It was therefore left to others to give interpretations of perceptibly 'safer', and more popular, repertoire. As the *Musical Times* suggested as early as 1872, Bache's pianistic career was 'remarkable as an illustration of the sincerity with which a real artist can sacrifice what the world would call a "good position" for the sake of promulgating the principles in which he has faith'.[88]

---

84 *MMR*, 2 (1872): 180. For an alternative view of the lack of success of English musicians, see the *MSt* (10 March 1877): 146: 'The pianoforte part [Chopin's Second Concerto] received full justice from the hands (and intellect) of Mr. Bache, who was welcomed when he made his appearance on the platform with such hearty applause as is seldom lavished on a native musician, an indirect proof that it is not the foreign blood alone to which Englishmen do honour – a reproach often raised against them – but that it is the *warm* blood, the true artistic zeal, that they understand and appreciate ... and it is our belief, that if English artists would show a little more of *that*, the assumed prejudice against native talent would prove to be a chimera.'

85 *MMR*, 3 (1873): 51.

86 See Bache, *Brother Musicians: Reminiscences of Edward and Walter Bache*, p. 263; also p. 239 for a reference to Bache's performance of Liszt's Second Piano Concerto at an Albert Hall concert around 1875.

87 *Athenaeum* (23 November 1872): 673.

88 *MT*, 15 (1872): 437.

Chapter 10

Fanny Davies: 'A messenger for Schumann and Brahms'?

Dorothy de Val

The name of Fanny Davies is inextricably linked to that of Clara Schumann and her circle. Throughout the last two decades of the nineteenth century and well into the twentieth, Fanny Davies and fellow Schumann pupils Leonard Borwick, Mathilde Verne, Ilona Eibenschütz and Adelina de Lara were well-known exponents of the music of both Schumann and Brahms, keeping Schumann's music in particular alive after Clara Schumann's death, when it could easily have fallen into oblivion. Indeed, by 1927 one critic opined that 'pianists must be warned against playing Schumann *au hasard* at this time when there is a definite reaction against him'.[1] The taste by that time was more for Debussy played by the elegant Cortot, and even though Davies turned her hand to music by contemporary French and Spanish composers, at her death in 1934 she was still hailed as a 'personal messenger for Schumann and Brahms'.[2]

Davies, who was born in 1861, studied with Clara Schumann for only two years while she was in her early twenties, but maintained a friendly connection with her and her family once she returned to England. She enjoyed a professional relationship with members of the Brahms circle, notably Joseph Joachim, Alfredo Piatti and Richard Mühlfeld. Socially she mixed with the Brahms set in London, which included the singer William Shakespeare, the critic, writer and musician J.A. Fuller Maitland, composer Arthur Somervell, conductor and singer George Henschel and others. The relationship with Joachim, whom she affectionately called 'Uncle Jo', was seminal to her career, and extended her musically as she exchanged her pupil status for parity as a co-performer.

She began playing with Joachim in 1885 and was a constant partner with him and the cellist Alfredo Piatti, especially in Chappell's 'Popular' Concerts held in St James's Hall. Through this association, and later through her performances with the Chamber Concert Society formed after Joachim's death, Davies became known as a consummate chamber artist and formed partnerships with other distinguished artists, notably Josef Suk and Pablo Casals, throughout her career. Davies nonetheless also made her mark as a soloist: she made her debut in 1885 playing Beethoven's fourth piano concerto (with cadenzas by Clara Schumann) and ultimately made the

---

1   *Musical Times*, 68 (1927): 546; review of a recital by Angus Morrison.
2   Obituary, *Birmingham Post*, 3 September 1934.

Schumann piano concerto her hallmark.[3] Her recording of it, made late in her career, is a living interpretative document and contains the vivid expressive playing for which she became known. As a pianist she continued to programme the less popular works of Schumann such as the *Davidsbündlertänze*, usually playing only selections from them as her teacher had done, and maintained a core German repertory until the end of her career. She also occasionally played Clara Schumann compositions and included her G minor Trio, op. 17 as well as some of her lieder in a concert in 1890.[4]

To see Fanny Davies only as a 'messenger' for both of the Schumanns and Brahms, though, is to overlook an extraordinary personality who constantly sought out new avenues, foreign lands, new people and new music, both past and present. She became a model for a succeeding generation of pianists, notably Myra Hess, through her personality, lifestyle and exploration of repertoire outside the canon. Here was a woman who made the extraordinary transition from the conservatism of the Victorian period into twentieth-century modernity, making changes not only in lifestyle but in musical taste.

Who were her contemporaries? A short biography which appeared in the *Musical Times* in 1905 placed Davies at the head of a long line of female pianists, beginning with Mozart's contemporary Nanette Stein (who according to the article was also the grandmother of the pianist and scholar Ernst Pauer), tracing a history through Madame Oury (Anna Caroline de Belleville), Maria Szymanowska, Louise Dulcken, Marie Pleyel, Kate Loder (later Lady Thompson) and Arabella Goddard.[5] In terms of British pianists, her most immediate female antecedents were Lucy Anderson and Goddard. Davies departed from custom in deciding to continue her musical training abroad. Even her contemporaries Dora Bright (1862–1951) and Agnes Zimmermann (1847–1925) remained at home to study at the Royal Academy of Music. Davies devoted her energy solely to performing, while Bright and Zimmermann were also composers in an era which otherwise saw the decline of the composer–pianist, though the Belgian Juliette de Folville (1870–1946), who became known in England and was a friend of Davies, was an extraordinary combination of pianist, violinist and composer. Davies did not compose, though in a rather different sphere she showed a talent for imitation and mimicry which became her hallmark and made her a sought-after guest at private musical parties. This translated into an exuberant public persona whose musical personality was remarked upon by critics throughout her career. Shaw noted this in a review of 1898: 'Miss Fanny Davies, being of Celtic stock, is a fiery player; indeed she is nothing if not fiery, for that quietly noble mood

---

3   Review in *Musical Times*, 26 (1885): 656–7. Postcard from Eugenie Schumann to Miss Davies, Birmingham, 10 October 1885: 'Of course the cadences are Mama's own and the same she played in England, indeed the only ones she ever composed for this Concerto.' RCM, Davies Collection, MS 7501.

4   *Musical World*, 68 (1890): 476. The concert took place in the Prince's Hall; Davies was joined by soprano Marie Fillunger and others in a concert devoted to the music of Robert and Clara Schumann.

5   'Miss Fanny Davies: A Biographical Sketch', *Musical Times*, 46 (1905): 365–70.

which was so attractive in such great players of her school as Clara Schumann and Agathe Backer-Gröndahl, is not in her temperament.'[6]

Davies's lifespan took her from a sheltered Victorian girlhood in Birmingham well into the modernity of the twentieth century. Never touted as a prodigy but showing musical gifts at an early age, she was carefully managed and nurtured during her childhood, and she performed in public only once, at the age of six. In adulthood she managed to maintain a fairly constant career profile for nearly fifty years, which allows us to examine her programming against different trends in musical performance, but also with regard to changes in society and the place of a female musician within it. Davies, who remained unmarried, provides an example of how such women survived as professional musicians in a rapidly changing world, especially when it came to managing a career involving travel and dealing with agents, adapting to changing trends, and balancing teaching and performing while trying to maintain a fulfilling private life away from the concert stage.

Background

The biography that appeared in the *Musical Times* reveals little about Davies's early life, and throughout her career the pianist was remarkably reticent about her parentage, instead giving her aunt, 'the mistress of a flourishing ladies' school', credit for her upbringing. The reason for such reticence becomes clear when one discovers that Davies was born in a reformatory at Le Bouët, near St Peter Port, Guernsey in 1861, the daughter of Mary Woodhill (b. 1831) and Alfred Davies (b. 1828), who was the superintendent and also possibly a prison officer.[7] The household in 1861 included seven male boarders aged between ten and sixteen, who were probably inmates of the school, plus an 18-year-old maidservant. It is probably because of this dubious environment that at the age of only ten months Davies was sent to live with her maternal aunt, Eliza Woodhill, in Birmingham. The Davies family later moved from Guernsey to Worcestershire, where a brother and sister were born.[8] Davies claimed a musical antecedent in her grandfather, John Woodhill, apparently a noted local amateur cellist who had played with 'old Bob Lindley' (the cellist Robert Lindley, 1776–1855) in his day, but he had died young (probably in 1841), leaving a widow and five children. Mary Woodhill was still living at home in 1851 (listed in the census return as having 'no occupation' though aged 22) with her governess sister Eliza.[9] By 1861, at the age of 36, Eliza had moved to Hamstead Road, Birmingham,

---

6   See Dan H. Laurence (ed.), *Shaw's Music*, vol. 3 (London: Bodley Head, 1981), p. 406.

7   Details from the 1861 Channel Islands Census, PRO, R.G. 9/4379. The 'prison officer' entry is written in another hand.

8   A brother, Matthew Henry Woodhill Davies, was born at King's Norton, Worcestershire, in 1866 and a sister, Alice Woodhill Wilks Davies, was born *c*.1869, also in Worcestershire. Alfred and Mary Davies were married in 1860 in a 'United Christians' church. Death records show that a Mary Jemima Davies died in June 1873 in West Bromwich. Alfred Davies's death date is more difficult to ascertain; indeed, all details of his life are obscure.

9   PRO, 1851 Census, H.O. 107 2051.

to head a household of five, including her younger brother Arthur, a young cousin, and her teacher, as well as the customary maidservant.[10] This was the household that Fanny would join as an infant about a year later. By 1871, Eliza had moved again to 'The Firs' (still in Hamstead Road), which she shared with another younger brother, Matthew, a commercial traveller, who was listed as head of household. The household had expanded to include two governesses (probably teachers at the fledgling school) and six girls, who must have been pupils.[11] By 1881, Eliza was styling herself as 'Principal of Ladies' School', and had taken Fanny's sister Alice in as a pupil as well.[12] There were no longer pupils living at the house, and their brother was sent to a school (Howard's House) in Oxfordshire.

The school, which may well have been 'flourishing' by this time, must have afforded at least some stimulation for the delicate Fanny, who began serious piano study with a noted local teacher, Charles Flavell, a pupil of Aloys Schmitt. In addition, she studied theory and harmony with Alfred Gaul, another noted Birmingham musician who also apparently taught at the school, but it was perhaps the influence of the flamboyant violinist Henry Hayward, the 'Wolverhampton Paganini', with whom she played violin sonatas, which was most long-lasting, as it instilled in her a love of chamber music.

Pianistically she was first inspired by Arabella Goddard, whom she heard in a performance of the Mendelssohn G minor Piano Concerto in Birmingham in 1870.[13] She found a mentor in the conductor and pianist Charles Hallé, with whom she took a course of lessons in London before leaving England on his recommendation to study in Leipzig. There she studied with Carl Reinecke, Oscar Paul and Salomon Jadassohn in 1882, but left a year later to study with Clara Schumann in Frankfurt at the Hoch Conservatorium. After the conservatism of Leipzig, where Davies was not altogether happy, the Hoch establishment must have seemed new and cutting edge under the directorship of the irascible but dynamic Bernhard Scholtz, a committed Brahmsian, who had recently arrived with a brief to transform the flagging school after the death of Joachim Raff in 1882.[14] Clara Schumann had arrived in 1878, flanked by her daughters Marie and Eugenie, who acted as her assistants, and she was able to select an elite group of pupils. Fanny, who was spending the summer in London after leaving Leipzig, was invited to audition for her in August 1883.[15]

---

10 PRO, 1861 Census, R.G. 9/2020.

11 PRO, 1871 Census, R.G. 10/2970.

12 PRO, 1881 Census, R.G. 11/2834.

13 'Miss Fanny Davies': 366.

14 See Joan Chissell, *Clara Schumann: A Dedicated Spirit* (London: Hamish Hamilton, 1983), p. 187.

15 RCM, Davies Collection, MS 7501, Letter from Clara Schumann to Fanny Davies, 11 August 1883, Obersalzburg bei Berchtesgaden: 'Dear Miss Davies! Herr Scholz is not in Frankfurt and will not return before the beginning of the classes. Besides, I would not accept you as my pupil without having heard you play myself. But in order to meet your wish, I propose you either to come to Munich between the 29th of August and the 2d of Sept. or to Baden-Baden from the 5th of Sept until the 15th. In Munich my address is hotel Marienbad, in Baden Villa Strohmeyer.'

Asked later about the necessity of studying abroad, Davies made the point that though it was indeed possible to get a good training in London, going away detached a young woman from her family and domestic responsibilities, giving her time to devote to practice and study:

> It is the homelife that is the drawback in England. When a girl goes to Germany she goes with the resolution to work her very hardest, and it is rarely that anything interferes with this determination. At home, on the other hand, there must always be a hundred other interests to distract the girl's mind from her studies.[16]

Later in the same article, Davies referred to her fragile health, which meant that in her early teens she was forced to stay indoors studying. Her home life – with a determined schoolmistress aunt in charge – would hardly have been typical of the 'homelife' described above.

Davies's aunt, Eliza Woodhill (*c*.1825–1903), provided a good example of a single woman able to live independently, operating within one of the few spheres – teaching – that was open to women. Such women were role models for the later 'new woman' of the 1890s, though the true type strived to free herself from occupations traditionally reserved for women. The term was coined by American writer Sarah Grand in an article, 'The New Aspect of the Woman Question', published in *The North American Review*, where she defined the new woman as someone who had 'solved the problem and proclaimed for herself what was wrong with Home-is-the-Woman's-Sphere, and prescribed the remedy'.[17] Feted and reviled in equal measure, the New Woman exemplified the independence to which Davies referred, escaping from domestic drudgery into a world of precarious financial independence. In the popular imagination the New Woman was a 'modern' Cambridge bluestocking who had been to Girton, rode a bicycle, smoked, and wore sensible clothing. Musicians – not generally perceived as intellectuals – did not really fit this mould and, fortunately for pianists, their chosen profession seems to have escaped the notice of feminists and anti-feminists alike for, though it involved public performance, the instrument had both female and male executants, and there were 'respectable' English antecedents such as Goddard and Anderson who had had concert careers; even foreign artists such as Schumann had been taken to the English heart as paragons of womanhood. Teaching – usually of genteel middle-class girls – was perceived to be part of the package and placed the female practitioner squarely in the domestic sphere.[18]

Davies was not alone in going abroad to study; Ethel Smyth – herself much more iconoclastic and therefore more typical of the 'New Woman' particularly in her eventual role as a suffragette – had studied in Leipzig, and Leonard Borwick, Marie and Mathilde Würm (later Verne), John Dykes and Amina Goodwin had also left England to study with Clara Schumann. A further comparison can be drawn with

---

16 F. Brunker, 'How I Began: An Interview with Miss Fanny Davies', *Girls' Realm* (1902): 150.

17 Quoted in C.C. Nelson (ed.), *A New Woman Reader* (Peterborough, ON: Broadview Press, 2001), p. ix.

18 For more on professional women musicians, see P. Gillett, *Musical Women in England, 1870–1914* (London and Basingstoke: Macmillan, 2000).

her American contemporary Amy Fay, who also went to study in Germany. Borwick studied with Schumann from 1883 to 1889 and was, according to some sources, her favourite pupil.[19] The nature of the teaching was reflected in an end-of-year recital in June 1885, in which Davies played Schumann's *Etudes symphoniques*; other items on the programme were concertos by Mendelssohn (no. 2 in D minor) and Beethoven (the 'Emperor', op. 73).[20] Some insight into the Frankfurt regimen can be found in the writings of Marie Fromm, a younger contemporary of Davies, who studied for five years in Frankfurt at the same time as Davies. Fromm describes the group lessons twice a week, the ordeal of the examinations, and visits from Joachim and Brahms, whom she declared 'a shockingly bad pianist'.[21] Mathilde Verne also recounted her musical experiences in Frankfurt in *Chords of Remembrance*, published in 1936.

Sources

Publicly available primary sources on Davies are, alas, relatively scarce. Much of the anecdotal information in this chapter is drawn from a collection of letters and other memorabilia in the Royal College of Music (RCM) and from the diaries of her close friend, the folksong scholar Lucy Broadwood. The RCM also has scores belonging to Davies, in which some annotations appear.[22] In addition, there are numerous references to her in writings of her contemporaries. The RCM archive contains correspondence with Clara and Eugenie Schumann, Joachim, Piatti and many others, plus a number of documents pertaining to her last years collected by the musician and scholar Marion Scott, Davies's friend and younger contemporary. The central item of the archive is the account of the break between Davies and Clara Schumann, mainly at the hands of Eugenie, who had arrived in London to teach music in September 1892 and was living with the Austrian soprano Marie Fillunger.[23] The details of the disagreement, which concerned a misunderstanding over the transfer of pupils between Eugenie and Davies, resulted in Clara's permanently severing the relationship between herself and her former pupil. It effectively ended Davies's relationship with the Schumann family (though she did communicate with them upon Clara's death) and must have seemed catastrophic at the time.

Naturally upset and somewhat incredulous about this, Davies publicly remained loyal to the Schumanns; it was too valuable a link to lose and her commitment to the music was real. In the anniversary year of 1910 she organized a special Schumann concert in which various Schumann pupils took part, and works by Clara Schumann

---

19 See Edward Speyer, *My Life and Friends* (London: Cobden Sanderson, 1937), p. 116.

20 Programme, RCM, Davies Collection, MS 7508.

21 Marie Fromm, 'Some Reminiscences of my Music Studies with Clara Schumann', *Musical Times*, 73 (1932): 615–16. Davies claimed (in her interview for *Girls' Realm*, p. 150) that there had been no examinations.

22 See G.S. Bozarth, 'Fanny Davies and Brahms's late chamber music', in M. Musgrave and B.D. Sherman (eds), *Performing Brahms* (Cambridge: Cambridge University Press, 2003), pp. 170–219 for a detailed analysis of the markings and their significance.

23 Chissell, *Clara Schumann*, p. 202.

were included. Her relationship with Joachim fortunately remained intact, and it was through him that she was able to keep her link with the circle alive. Indeed it was to Joachim that she expressed her feelings in a letter: 'That Frau Schumann *could* after all these years, doubt my loyalty and love for her, and indeed for them all from one single *misrepresentation* (for it is only that) it is to me quite *incredible* and too dreadful for anything.'[24]

The incident should be seen in the context of Schumann's poor state of health at this time. She had retired from teaching in 1892, having suffered the loss of her ailing son Ferdinand as well as her close friends Jenny Lind and the Englishman Arthur Burnand, with whom Eugenie had stayed at his Hyde Park Gate residence.[25] Fanny had written a letter of condolence to which Clara replied.[26] The year 1892 had proved to be a difficult one for Fanny, too. The illness of her female companion, with whom she shared a flat, had forced her to rearrange her Italian tour and she had therefore returned earlier than planned at Easter. Schumann wrote a letter in December saying that Eugenie had told her of her friend's illness, and was worried that Fanny had stayed away too long. She expressed hope for the speedy recovery of 'Ihre Freundin'.[27]

The incident, which occurred over a misunderstanding over who was to teach the pupils after Easter, was not just about teaching, though this was an important issue, especially for Eugenie. The latter had arrived to join her friend Marie Fillunger, the highly successful concert singer and herself an outcast from the Schumann household in Frankfurt after an argument with Marie Schumann.[28] Far from having any sympathy for a fellow victim of Clara's volatile temper, Fillunger took Eugenie's side throughout the battle, no doubt because of their personal relationship, and maybe with a touch of *Schadenfreude* towards Davies, who was enjoying the height of her popularity in Britain and abroad.

Teaching as a Career

The rift is significant not just for what it reveals about the Schumanns and their coterie, but also for what it demonstrates about the importance of teaching as a source of income. Davies was by this time established in her performing career, yet deeply concerned about retaining a teaching practice. For Eugenie, who was not a concert performer, it was an absolute lifeline, and she clung to it tenaciously. For Davies, this

---

24 Letter from Davies to Joachim, n.d., RCM, Davies Collection, MS 7503.

25 Chissell, *Clara Schumann*, p. 201.

26 Letter from Clara Schumann to Fanny Davies, 15 February 1891, from Franzenbad. RCM, Davies Collection, MS 7501. Ferdinand died in a nursing home in Gera on 6 June 1890.

27 Letter from Clara Schumann to Davies (December 1892), RCM, Davies Collection, MS 7501. Note that Clara always used the formal form of 'you' (Sie) in her letters to Fanny.

28 Full details of the situation can be found in Eva Rieger, '"Desire is Consuming Me": The Life Partnership between Eugenie Schumann and Marie Fillunger', in S. Fuller and L. Whitesell (eds), *Queer Episodes in Music and Modern Identity* (Urbana and Chicago: University of Illinois Press, 2002), p. 31.

trivial misunderstanding about a teaching arrangement actually ended a relationship which she valued above all else. She already had an international reputation and was playing all over Europe, but she still needed to retain loyal 'bread-and-butter' pupils at home. A few of her pupils became well known, and letters in the archive suggest that in some cases they (and their mothers) were a cause of some frustration, but were an essential source of regular income. Student recitals were given regularly, usually at least once at year. The 'biographical sketch' published in 1905 in the *Musical Times* included testimonials from two of her (unnamed) pupils, stating that her 'vivacious personality, high artistic ideas, keen ear for tone, and faultless technique' made her an ideal teacher.[29]

Other Schumann pupils established successful teaching practices in London. Mathilde Verne eventually became a career teacher, establishing her own school of music in 1909 and taking on pupils such as Solomon Kutner, a promising young pianist from London's East End, later famously known by his first name alone.[30] Marie Fromm also became known more as a teacher than performer. There was little prospect of teaching at either the Royal Academy or Royal College of Music for women; for example, in 1899 the staff was predominantly male, with the exception of a few female 'sub-professors' at the Academy.[31] As few of the professors were active performers, it might be fair to say that anyone with a busy concert career would not have been considered, owing to the irregularity of their schedule from year to year.

Davies taught throughout her career, which must have provided some financial security. Her most famous pupil was the pianist and writer Kathleen Dale, who did not begin learning with her until 1926; another pupil was Mary Grierson, author of a biography of Donald Francis Tovey. The RCM archive includes correspondence with and about several pupils, and it seems that there were annual pupils' concerts, but Davies was always careful to maintain that although she enjoyed teaching, her concert career came first.[32]

Teaching aside, how did Davies manage to maintain a performing career for nearly fifty years? As a Victorian woman who lived into the fourth decade of the twentieth century, how was she affected by the changing role of women in the pre- and post-women's suffrage era, and musically how did she adapt to the changes of fashion and style that marked the onset of the twentieth century?

---

29 'Miss Fanny Davies': 368.

30 M.Verne, *Chords of Remembrance* (London: Hutchinson & Co., 1936), pp. 88ff.

31 'London Musical Institutions' in A.C.R. Carter (ed.), *The Year's Music 1899* (London: J.S. Virtue & Co., 1899), pp. 49–65. 'Sub-professors' were probably teaching assistants. The Guildhall School had a few women piano teachers on staff, though none seem to have had active performing careers.

32 In Brunker, 'How I Began': 152, Davies stated: 'I am very fond of teaching – I only wish I could devote more time to it.' One of Davies's obituarists (*Times*, 3 September 1934) stated that her life was 'largely spent in teaching', thus conflicting with the rest of the obituary which outlines a distinguished concert career.

Early Music

Though deeply loyal to Germany and its musical tradition to the end, Davies did not hesitate to champion the music of her own country. She became involved with the early music movement fairly early on, accompanying Piatti in 1889 in a performance of *Thirteen Divisions on a Ground Bass* by Christopher Simpson.[33] The main influence on her, however, was probably her friend and mentor Alfred J. Hipkins (1826–1903). Letters from Hipkins to Fanny Davies in the RCM archive show that by 1893 he was an established and close friend, demonstrated particularly in his mediation in the battle with Eugenie and Clara Schumann, whom he wryly called 'the Frau'.[34] Hipkins's association with early music dated back to his friendship with Carl Engel and he soon amassed a collection of early keyboard instruments, many of which are now in the RCM collection. A devotee of Chopin, whom he knew from the composer's visits to London, he became a linchpin of the piano firm of John Broadwood and Sons, where he was employed from 1840 until his death in 1903. He was an accomplished performer on the harpsichord and clavichord, and gave numerous lecture demonstrations on early keyboards in both public and private settings. He was closely involved in many exhibitions, and was responsible for the loan collection to the Music and Inventions Exhibition held in South Kensington in 1885, which resulted in his book *Musical Instruments, Historic, Rare and Unique* (1888). Hipkins gave frequent private concerts, featuring late Baroque composers such as Couperin, Rameau, Handel and Bach.[35] Exposure to this repertoire might well have induced Davies to choose four pieces by François Couperin to perform in a 'Pops' concert at St James's Hall in 1897, though she played the three rondeaux and one allemande on a piano, not harpsichord.[36] After Hipkins's death in 1903, Davies remained in touch with his son John and daughter Edith, occasionally visiting their home to play the clavichord and harpsichord.[37]

Davies also numbered Arnold Dolmetsch among her musical friends. An eccentric but charismatic figure, Dolmetsch was busy building instruments and organizing concerts of early music; in 1894 Davies joined Dolmetsch and Fuller Maitland (who was also a member of the Brahms circle) in a performance of a Bach concerto for three harpsichords.[38] Fuller Maitland was probably the influence behind her interest in early English virginal repertoire, made available to a wider audience through the publication of *The Fitzwilliam Virginal Book* (edited by Fuller Maitland and Barclay Squire) in 1899. She also became enthusiastic about the music of Purcell, doubtless caught up in the events of the anniversary year of 1895, and continued to include

---

33 The transcription was Piatti's; the concert took place on 11 November 1889 at a Monday Popular Concert.

34 Letter from Hipkins to Davies, 24 June 1893, RCM, Davies Collection, MS 7503.

35 A typical private concert is noted in Lucy Broadwood's diary on 29 November 1890.

36 The pieces were *La Ténébreuse*, *Le Bavolet-flotant*, *La Bandoline* and *Les Moissonneurs*.

37 See entry in Broadwood Diaries, 9 April 1916.

38 Ibid., entry for 22 May 1894. Broadwood does not stipulate which concerto was performed.

some Purcell in her programmes until late in her life.[39] Possibly through Hipkins or Lucy Broadwood, whom she met in 1892, she acquired a single-manual harpsichord by the Swiss maker Shudi, the father-in-law of John Broadwood, founder of the piano firm. In the early part of her career Davies played Broadwood pianos before capitulating to Steinway, and maintained a close personal friendship with Lucy, whom she accompanied on a family history trip to Glarus, Switzerland – home of the Shudi ancestors – in 1910 and 1925.[40] The Shudi instrument featured in performances during and after the First World War at her studio in Kensington, though she never played it publicly.

The music of J.S. Bach was established in the mainstream at this time, though with no concessions to authenticity in performance. Liszt's transcriptions of the organ fugues were still popular, though frowned upon by some critics. Clara Schumann had had her favourites in the repertoire, and her pupils programmed the *Italian Concerto* fairly often.[41] The year 1895 was notable for the Bach festival in London; on 2 April the *St Matthew Passion* was performed with various members of the Brahms circle (Shakespeare, Marie Fillunger, Joachim); Helen Dolmetsch played the viola da gamba, though with a piano, not harpsichord. Two days later, Davies, Borwick and Zimmermann played Bach keyboard concertos on Broadwood grand pianos. The Festival merited the attention of the *Monthly Musical Record* reviewer in the annual summary.[42]

After Hipkins, another influence was George Henry Benton Fletcher (1866–1944), who began collecting period instruments in the early decades of the twentieth century. An ex-soldier, archaeologist and historian, Fletcher's motivation came not from musical interests but from a general desire to preserve a cultural and artistic heritage, thus putting him more in tune with the aims of the National Trust than with the arts and crafts movement as represented by Dolmetsch and his friend William Morris. Fletcher knew Davies and purchased her harpsichord at a Puttick and Simpson auction in 1932, possibly in a bid to aid the now ailing and destitute pianist, who by that time had applied to the Civil List for help.[43]

---

39 In a letter dated 26 December 1930 to Muriel Smith, concert organizer in Lewes, Davies writes that she would like to programme works by Purcell, Scarlatti and Arne, as well as a Bach toccata and fugue – 'not the transcription but a "real" piano one'. The rest of the proposed programme included works by Schumann, Chopin, Brahms and Debussy. Letters from Fanny Davies to Muriel Smith, RCM, Davies Collection, MS 6896.

40 Broadwood Diaries, *passim*.

41 Davies played this first on 1 March 1887 in a Monday Popular Concert; Clara Schumann introduced some Scarlatti in the same series two weeks later.

42 J.S. Virtue, 'The Year's Music: 1895', *Monthly Musical Record*, 26 (1896): 4. The events were also noted by Broadwood in her diary for 1895. A performance of the *St Matthew Passion* in 1934 featured Davies's own harpsichord, which she had sold to Benton Fletcher in 1932. See M. Waitzman, *Early Keyboard Instruments: The Benton Fletcher Collection at Fenton House* (London: The National Trust, 2003), p. 40.

43 See Waitzman, *Early Keyboard Instruments*, p. 40. Records in the RCM indicate that Davies received Civil List money worth about £90. The Scott Papers, RCM, give payments from January 1933.

Early music was approached cautiously by pianists, though it gradually became accepted as a possibility in a mixed programme. Harpsichord performance became the province of artists such as Violet Gordon Woodhouse and Wanda Landowska, but performance of early repertoire remained acceptable on the piano. Agnes Zimmermann programmed works by Bach, Gluck, Graun, Rameau and Scarlatti in a concert in 1886 at the Prince's Hall and a year later Schumann played a selection of Scarlatti sonatas at a Popular Concert in 1887; Davies soon followed her example, but played different sonatas. Later she performed such works in clusters, for example choosing a set of Netherlandish works from a collection made by the Belgian musicologist Xavier van Elewyck (1825–1888) in 1904, and in 1911 performing Italian works going back to Frescobaldi.[44]

Such programming was more the exception than the rule, though, and Davies's interest in early music did not divert her from her core repertoire. The Shudi harpsichord remained in the studio in Kensington and was to play more of a role once she began holding regular private concerts there after the war. In her public life at least, the study of early music appears to have been more hobby than career, a dip into another new world in which she found friends as well as musical and intellectual stimulation.

Fanny Davies as Concert Artist

Davies's career really began to get under way at Chappell's Popular Concerts, where she first appeared on 16 November 1885, about a month after her Crystal Palace debut, playing solos by Bach (Chromatic Fantasy and Fugue) and Mendelssohn (*Characteristic Pieces*, no. 7).[45] The series had wide appeal with their accessible mix of chamber and solo music, and Davies soon became a regular performer, usually with Joachim, Piatti or other members of the Brahms circle; certainly Joachim and Piatti were the mainstays of the series at this time.[46] The 'Pops' became her proving ground as a chamber performer, beginning with a Schubert trio (op. 100) with the noted cellist Robert Hausmann and the violinist Wilhelmina Norman-Neruda (later the wife of Charles Hallé, and another anchor of the series) on 11 January 1886, and with Hausmann two weeks later in a performance of Brahms's op. 38 Cello Sonata.[47] Davies was also featured as a soloist at these concerts, playing music ranging from Scarlatti to Schumann, with a generous sprinkling of late Beethoven. A recital

---

44 Review in *Musical Times*, 45 (1904): 248; the Italian music programme in the Centre for Performance History (CPH) /Royal College of Music: Bechstein Hall, 25 October 1911, included Pasquini, Leo, Pergolesi, Martucci and the contemporary Sgambati, as well as a Gagliarda by Frescobaldi. I wish to thank Paul Collen at the CPH/RCM for his assistance during the course of this project.

45 Cited in 'Miss Fanny Davies': 368.

46 See Bozarth, 'Fanny Davies', Table 7.1 for a list of Davies's performances of Brahms's music with members of the Brahms circle; Joachim figures most prominently, though Piatti, Hausmann and Mühlfeld also appear.

47 *Musical Times*, 27 (1886): 82; details from Monday Popular Concert series programmes. Davies played a Broadwood piano.

given at the Prince's Hall on 24 March 1886, for example, included *Carnaval* and Beethoven's Sonata, op. 101; the reviewer commented on playing 'full of warmth, feeling and intellectuality'. Davies had competitors, though: on the very next day Agnes Zimmermann also played Beethoven's op. 101 and Schumann's op. 17, as well as her own compositions.[48] Davies also occasionally played with other Schumann pupils, joining Mathilde Verne in December 1886 for a performance of Schumann's *Andante and Variations* in B♭ for two pianos, op. 46 at a Monday Popular Concert. A concert in April of the following year featured Schumann, Davies, Joachim, Agnes Zimmermann and Liza Lehmann, all key members of the Brahms circle, with Fanny playing arrangements of the Brahms *Hungarian Dances* with Joachim, and Clara a Chopin nocturne and her husband's *Novellette* in F.[49] There were still ties to the Continent, though, and Davies spent much of 1887 touring Europe, both as a soloist and as partner to Joachim and Hausmann and to Adolph Brodsky in a premiere of Ethel Smyth's Violin Sonata in Leipzig, where Smyth was well known.[50] She made her Berlin debut at the Singakademie with Joachim in November. By all accounts, the 'German campaign' was a success; early in the year she had played with Hausmann and for her solos drew on old favourites by Bach, Chopin, Mendelssohn and Schumann, closing with a Beethoven trio.[51] Two years later she undertook another tour, including Germany and Italy as well as the English provinces.

The 1890s saw some branching out in repertoire, amid strong competition from Borwick (now returned from his studies in Germany), Zimmermann and the glamorous newcomer Ilona Eibenschütz, another Schumann pupil. Davies expanded her repertoire to include works of Chopin, giving performances of selected preludes on several occasions, as well as lesser known Mendelssohn pieces such as the op. 35 Preludes and Fugues. The *Musical World* reported a performance of a Mozart trio in 1890 and, at the Crystal Palace, a piano concerto by Jacob Rosenhain (1813–94), a German composer and pianist who was noted as being 'still living' for the benefit of those who might have remembered him from his performances in London in the 1830s.[52] The works of Saint-Saëns were gaining popularity, and Davies performed

---

48 Ibid.: 207.

49 Programme of Monday Popular Concert, 4 April 1887 in the 'Monday Popular Concerts, 1874–1901', collection at the Toronto Public Library [TPL], Canada.

50 Both Smyth and Davies studied with Carl Reinecke. Smyth hoped that Davies would perform her cello sonata with Piatti, but it appears this never happened. See letter from Smyth to Davies, RCM, Davies Collection, MS 7507 dated 16 December (no year but probably around this time). Later Davies wrote that she had found Smyth 'an odd fish – often as coarse as a hare!'. (Letter from Davies to Muriel Smith, 22 March 1931, from Bath.) Davies had been visiting her sister Alice Hirst, to whom she was not close, in Weston-super-Mare. RCM, Davies Collection, MS 6896.

51 The concert took place on 3 January 1887; Hausmann was the cellist in a performance of the Brahms E minor Cello Sonata, and he and the violinist Hugo Heerman played in the Beethoven Trio, op. 1. The Schumann solo was *Carnaval*. Programme in RCM, Davies Collection, MS 7508.

52 Shaw wrote a favourable review of this concert in the *Star*, 21 February 1890; see Laurence, *Shaw's Music*, vol. 1, p. 927. Shaw wrote: 'I had never heard of Rosenhain; and

the Quartet in B♭, op. 41 in January 1894 with Lady Hallé, Gibson and Piatti.[53] Piatti was also a composer, and Davies performed a number of his compositions, mostly sonatas, with him at the Popular Concerts, including the first performance of his *Sonata idillica* in 1892. A fruitful partnership with Gabrielle Wietrowetz, Joachim's star pupil, began at this time, though Wietrowetz also played with Borwick. Davies did not neglect Clara Schumann's compositions, and included her Trio in G minor and songs sung by Marie Fillunger in a tribute concert featuring music by both Robert and Clara in June 1890.[54] In February of the following year she played her teacher's D minor Scherzo in a Monday Popular Concert in a programme that also included the Brahms Horn Trio, op. 40 with the celebrated Franz Paersch.[55] By this time her programmes began to include a wider chronological range of works, stretching from Bach and Scarlatti to Somervell. European tours continued, with visits to Vienna, where she met with Brahms and performed with the Rosé Quartet.[56] By the time the Monday Pops concerts were discontinued in 1898, Davies was an established and respected artist both at home and abroad.

Davies was also an occasional performer in concerts of the Philharmonic (later the Royal Philharmonic) Society, playing just five concerts between 1886 and 1905, including one in which she replaced Moritz Rosenthal (who had cut his finger) at the last minute.[57] The concerto was Chopin's F minor, unlike her usual Beethoven and Schumann offerings; in addition to a Sterndale Bennett piano concerto she also performed that composer's *Caprice*. In 1905 she shared the programme with Casals, who would later become one of her most devoted champions.[58] Solos performed at these concerts included such crowd pleasers as the Rubinstein 'Staccato Study', as well as various works by Schumann and Mendelssohn.

The programmes she played at the Popular Concerts were strongly rooted in the Austro-German tradition, with an emphasis on Brahms, with occasional lighter touches in the form of Joachim's arrangements of the *Hungarian Dances* for violin and piano, and in a performance of the *Zigeunerlieder* (Gypsy Songs), op. 103 in 1888 with George and Lillian Henschel and others.[59] Davies was also a frequent performer in concerts given by the People's Concert Society. Formed in 1878 to

---

I am surprised at the disingenuousness of other critics in the same predicament, who have hastily read him up, and are pretending that they knew him from boyhood's hour.'

53 Monday Popular Concert, 15 January 1894, TPL collection. Davies also played the Schumann *Humoreske*. Eibenschütz and Davies were also associated with some of the earliest performances of Brahms's opp. 117, 118 and 119 in England: Davies had given the London premiere of op. 117 in January 1893.

54 *Musical World*, 68 (1890): 415, 476.

55 Programme for 9 February 1891, TPL collection.

56 The programme for 14 December 1897 with the Rosé Quartet featured Brahms's F minor Piano Quintet and the Mendelssohn Octet. Davies was showcased as the 'Clavier-Virtuosin aus London'. RCM, Davies Collection, MS 7508.

57 M. Birket-Foster, *History of the Philharmonic Society of London, 1813–1912* (London: John Lane, Bell & Cockburn, 1912), p. 457.

58 Ibid., p. 488. Speyer also commented on this in *Music and Friends*, p. 199.

59 See programme for 26 November 1888, TPL collection, which states that this was the first performance of the songs in England. Performers included 'Mrs Henschel, Lena Little,

bring music to the working classes and given in areas such as Finsbury, Bermondsey and Woolwich, the series featured chamber concerts organized by amateurs, based on the Popular Concert model. The participating quartets were led by John Saunders and Hans Wessely. Always a populist, Davies performed with Wessely at the gala celebrating the 1,000th concert in 1901 and retained links with its chief organizer and secretary, the concert agent Ethel Robinson.[60]

The Classical Concert Society

After the termination of the Popular concerts in 1898, Joachim continued to give chamber concerts with the Berlin Quartet from 1900, first in St James's Hall and from 1905 in the Bechstein Hall and the Queen's Hall. After Joachim's death in 1907 the Classical Concert Society was established to encourage the performance of chamber music in London. The key organizers were Edward Speyer, Frederick Septimus ('Clegg') Kelly, Donald Francis Tovey and Leonard Borwick. Davies was a regular performer with her contemporaries Eibenschütz and Verne, plus newcomers Dohnányi, Moór and Grainger; Casals joined later. The first concert was given in the Bechstein Hall in October 1908. Owing to their specialized nature and targeted audience, these concerts afforded Davies some freedom in her programming and choice of partners, but were not immune to a commercial approach, as Speyer employed an agent, and eventually star performers such as Casals were used as box office bait.[61] Speyer resigned in 1912. Davies continued with the Society after this time, performing during the war years with the violinist Maurice Sons and the Harrison sisters.[62]

Always eager to make links with contemporary composers, early in her career Davies coaxed the young Edward Elgar into writing a piece for her; the result was the *Concert Allegro*, premiered in 1902 within an all-British programme featuring works by Purcell, Nares, Sterndale Bennett, Coleridge-Taylor and Norman O'Neill, as well as Elgar.[63] The *Concert Allegro* had a chequered history (which is a story in

---

William Shakespeare and Mr Henschel' as well as Davies; in addition Margaret Wild played Chopin's B♭ minor Scherzo.

60 See Broadwood Diaries; entry for 9 March 1901. The event took place at Northern Polytechnic Hall in Holloway, north London; Broadwood reported a 'huge audience' with takings of £60. See also J.A. Fuller Maitland, 'The People's Concert Society: Valedictory', *Musical Times*, 77 (1936): 317–18, where Davies is mentioned as a regular participant with Borwick, Elwes, Plunket Greene, Hess and the Harrison sisters, among others. The link with Robinson as agent is mentioned in M. McKenna, *Myra Hess: A Portrait* (London: Hamish Hamilton, 1976), p. 39. According to McKenna, Robinson, working from an office in Piccadilly, arranged bookings for Joachim, Davies and Steinbach, as well as Hess.

61 See Grierson, *Tovey*, p. 125.

62 Programmes in the CPH/RCM collection; the concert with Sons featured a Bach sonata (E minor), Schubert's Fantasia for Violin and Piano, op. 159, and Beethoven's Piano Trio, op. 70. The concert with the Harrisons featured Bach (A minor English Suite), Beethoven's op. 102 no. 2, Schubert's *Rondeau brillante*, op. 70 and Schumann's *Phantasiestücke*, op. 88 for piano trio. The concerts took place in the Bechstein Hall.

63 For details, see D. McVeagh, 'Elgar's Concert Allegro', *Musical Times*, 110 (1969): 135–8.

itself), but Davies cemented a firm relationship with the O'Neills, later partnering O'Neill's wife, the French pianist Adine Ruckert, in a concert given at the Aeolian Hall in 1904.[64] Although known primarily for her collaboration with instrumentalists, Davies formed a remarkable partnership with the tenor Gervase Elwes, with whom she toured Germany in 1907 giving recitals of Brahms lieder, and old French and English songs. The association with Davies, already famous in Germany, gave Elwes a superb advantage; the duo was especially successful in Berlin and Munich.[65]

Davies joined agents Ibbs and Tillett in 1908, a year after they took over the agency founded by the entrepreneur Narciso Vert.[66] Fellow artists included Borwick and Mathilde Verne, in addition to established names such as Carreño, Godowsky, Rosenthal, d'Albert, Pachmann, Busoni, Sauer, Lamond and Dohnányi. Ibbs and Tillett also represented the French pianist and composer Cécile Chaminade, Adela Verne, Gertrude Peppercorn and Davies's protégée Adelina de Lara. Cortot joined a few years later, as did Percy Grainger and Myra Hess. Davies remained on the books until 1930.[67] Given her reputation, it is not surprising that Davies was approached by Welte Mignon to record on their piano in 1909; she later had a contract with the Columbia Graphophone Co.[68]

Davies was a key player in the Schumann anniversary year of 1910, participating in a gala concert at the Queen's Hall on 8 June and writing an article for the *Musical Times*, 'About Schumann's Piano Music', in which she remarked on the spiritual and emotional aspects of his music.[69] This marked the beginning of Davies's writings on the performance of music – another more substantial article appeared in *Music & Letters* in 1925 ('On Schumann – and reading between the lines').[70] She wrote on Beethoven's concertos and contributed articles to *Cobbett's Cyclopedic Survey of Chamber Music*.[71] Infused with personal warmth and attention to detail, her articles mark one of the few ventures of concert artists into performance practice. Although her recordings have been noted as documents, relatively little attention has been paid to her writing.[72]

---

64 The concert, which took place on 11 June 1904 in the Aeolian Hall, was given on 'steel barless grand pianofortes by Broadwood' and included works for two pianos by W.F. Bach and Norman O'Neill.

65 See W. Elwes and R. Elwes, *Gervase Elwes* (London: Grayson & Grayson, 1935), *passim*.

66 See C. Fifield, *Ibbs and Tillett: The Rise and Fall of a Musical Empire* (Aldershot: Ashgate, 2005).

67 Ibid., Appendix 1, *passim*; see pp. 376, 381 and 414 for details.

68 Details of the contract with Columbia Graphophone are in the Marion Scott Papers, 1932–35 at the RCM. Davies later had an arrangement with Steinway to use their pianos.

69 *Musical Times*, 51 (1910): 493–4.

70 *Music & Letters*, 6 (1925): 214–23.

71 'Beethoven: the Pianoforte Concertos', *Music & Letters*, 8 (1927): 224–6.

72 More information has come to light on performance practice, however; see Bozarth 'Fanny Davies', pp. 170–219 for details on performance notes in a score of Brahms's Trio in C minor, op. 101. But even this score, unnoticed for what it was and in general circulation for years at the RCM, was only just barely rescued from the builder's skip by an observant Oliver Davies.

The War and Beyond

The war marked a watershed in Davies's career, both personally and professionally. Clara Schumann, Brahms and Joachim were long gone, and she now had to compete with a younger generation of pianists such as Paderewski, d'Albert, Carreño and Pugno. Using her Holland Lane studio in Kensington as a base, she taught and gave private concerts. Publicly she began to move into the *terra incognita* of music described by the *Musical Times* as 'wholly slavonic and non-Teutonic', beginning what would be a celebrated collaboration with the Bohemian Quartet.[73] The premiere of the Suk piano quintet in 1919 was followed by a series of five concerts a year later at the Wigmore Hall under the auspices of Ethel Robinson, in which patrons of the Chamber Concert Society were treated to works by Dvořák, Suk and Smetana, as well as Elgar and Bax. (Davies had participated in the first performance of the Bax Piano Quintet in 1917.[74]) The Czech connection continued, culminating in a visit to Prague in 1926.

Davies championed not just new music, but new performers. She had always encouraged younger pianists, beginning with Adelina de Lara and, as she grew older, she formed musical partnerships with younger gifted women, such as the violinist May Harrison and her cellist sister Beatrice, Joachim's pupil Jelly d'Arányi and the flamboyant Portuguese cellist Guilhermina Suggia: networking was as important in musical life as in the personal sphere. In November 1914 Davies performed with the Harrison sisters, featuring Schubert's *Rondeau brillante*, op. 70 with May, Beethoven's Sonata, op. 102 no. 2 with Beatrice, and Schumann's *Phantasiestücke*, op. 88 played with both.[75] Davies enjoyed a brief partnership with Jelly d'Arányi in 1915, organizing a series of sonata recitals. Davies was attracted to the violinist's 'nice soul' and her ability to see 'beyond the notes and marks'. The partnership was fortified by Suggia in two recitals, in which she joined Davies and d'Arányi in trios by Beethoven, Brahms, Schubert and Tschaikovsky; Davies and d'Arányi performed violin sonatas by Mendelssohn and Bach. D'Arányi eventually terminated the partnership, though the two artists remained on friendly terms. Davies later played with Jelly's sister Adila in 1926.[76]

Davies continued to perform British works and was the dedicatee of compositions by Maude Valérie White, John Ireland and Ernest Walker, whose *Variations on a Norwegian Air*[77] she played together with other British works at the Aeolian Hall on 12 June 1919.[78] Best known was her partnership with Pablo Casals, whom she met through Edward Speyer. This was the beginning of a fruitful musical partnership, culminating with an invitation to play with his orchestra in Barcelona in 1923.

---

73 *Musical Times*, 60 (1919): 694.
74 Reviewed in *Musical Times*, 61 (1920): 391–2.
75 Programme in CPH/RCM.
76 J. MacLeod, *The Sisters d'Aranyi* (London: Allen and Unwin, 1969), pp. 102–3, 228.
77 See 'Three Oxford Pianistic Careers: Donald Francis Tovey, Paul Victor Mendelssohn Benecke and Ernest Walker', Chapter 11 below.
78 The concert was noticed in the *Musical Times*, 60 (1919): 373.

Private and Public Spheres

Davies's concert career profiles her as a versatile musician, but without spouse or patron, how did she support herself? As mentioned, female networking was an important factor. From the beginning of her career, Davies had shared her living accommodation with Harriette Grist, first in Baker Street and then in Wellington Road, St John's Wood. Grist, born in 1846 in Stroud, Gloucestershire, seems not to have been a musician. It is not clear how the two women met, but the 1891 census (taken on 5 April that year) reveals that she had invited Davies to an extended family gathering in Lindley-cum-Quarmby, Yorkshire, probably to celebrate Easter, which fell on 29 March that year. Though Grist was 46 by this date, she is listed with no occupation, while Davies appears as 'Pianist, Music'.[79] Little is known about Grist except that she was fifteen years Davies's senior and a co-householder. She was a constant companion and social organizer: together they gave a number of musical parties.[80] The two seemed to be inseparable, and extant letters to Fanny invariably offer good wishes to her companion. Grist died in 1902 and Davies appears not to have found another live-in companion, though she had a number of close women friends.

The relationship between Davies and Grist was typical of female networking in the late nineteenth and early twentieth centuries. The 1891 and 1901 censuses reveal many women living alone, usually in blocks of mansion flats occupied by other single women. In a society that did not know how to deal with unmarried women and where employment opportunities for them were severely restricted, sharing accommodation made economic sense. Such women were portrayed by George Gissing in his novel *The Odd Women*, published in 1893. Written as a response to the 'New Woman' phenomenon, Gissing's narrative portrayed the grim reality of a struggling underclass of unmarried women, difficult to place in late Victorian society and considered surplus to requirements. 'New women' – educated and confident – such as Gissing's Mary Barfoot and Rhoda Nunn banded together, and sought or created work outside the home, usually remaining unmarried; weaker single women were doomed to poverty and illness as they aged. It is notable that in *The Odd Women* it is Monica, the one woman who actually does marry, who is the unhappiest of all.

How did musical women fit into this society? Gissing's Alma Rolfe (depicted in *The Whirlpool*), an amateur violinist from a fallen wealthy family, is hardly typical. The literature on New Women does not on the whole include female musicians, though Henry Handel Richardson's *Maurice Guest* (written under a pseudonym by Ethel Florence Lindesay Richardson) features English music students (both male and female) in Leipzig in the 1890s. Destined to be teachers, women who followed professional careers were the exception, though there were powerful and 'approved' models such as Clara Schumann. Being British, Davies was somewhat anomalous, identifiable both as 'new' and 'odd' woman – forging her own way through an increasingly competitive concert scene, but also as a woman alone.

---

79 PRO, 1891 Census, R.G. 12/3579.

80 Grist was described as co-householder with no occupation in the 1901 census; Davies was 'Artist (Music) on own account'. PRO, R.G. 13/118. In her diaries (*passim*), Lucy Broadwood records a number of parties hosted by the two women.

The Mary Barfoots and Rhoda Nunns of the Victorian and Edwardian periods created social lives and networks in order to survive. In the right circumstances, 'odd women' with initiative, education and intelligence could transform themselves into New Women who networked to outflank a society which at best ignored them and at worst held them in contempt. Records of their private parties with their carefully compiled guest lists (usually found in scrupulously kept diaries or in letters) often provide more insight into lives lived than any public account. This is particularly true of an age where people often gave musical entertainments in their homes and made important musical connections in that environment.

And London was full of musical networks. At a time when music-making at home was taken for granted, private parties afforded opportunities for informal entertainment and socializing. Davies was an active participant at her own gatherings and as a guest at others, often playing seriously but also parodying musical styles and performers.[81] Many such parties introduced new artists to the network before their first public appearance; and they were often sophisticated events. For example, a private party given by Davies and Grist at their home in Baker Street in March 1892 featured not only a performance of Edmond About's play *Risette* (given in French) but also performances by Borwick, Wietrowetz, Fillunger, Joachim and Piatti.[82] Wietrowetz played the Mendelssohn Violin Concerto at this event, and Davies played the Brahms op. 78 sonata with her in a concert the following May.[83] In 1894 Davies gave a special party for Joachim, inviting a who's who of the musical and art worlds, including Piatti, Shakespeare, Bispham, Dykes, Hipkins and the Somervells. Davies, Joachim and Piatti performed a Dvořák trio, and the soprano Louise Phillips sang some of the *Zigeunerlieder*;[84] two days later Davies and Grist took tea with the Somervells. Brahms parties were legion and provided occasions for performances of his works; the singer William Shakespeare instigated many of these, which usually included sociable works such as the *Liebeslieder*, songs and piano pieces.

Female Networks: Sapphics and Society

Davies was not the only woman to have a female companion as co-householder, and who was constantly at her side at social events. Such relationships were more common than hitherto recognized. Recently, evidence has come to light linking Eugenie Schumann romantically with Marie Fillunger, which goes some way to explaining the conflict referred to earlier in regard to teaching.[85] Indeed their harsh reaction

---

81 Broadwood Diaries, entry for 6 February 1892. This was the occasion when Broadwood met Davies for the first time. At this musical party, held at the Somervells', Davies played seriously at first but then parodied musical styles and players 'most amusingly'. Lucy sang. A month later, Broadwood invited Davies to tea at her home, where Davies once again regaled the company with her 'clever imitation variations'.

82 Broadwood Diaries, entry for 29 March 1892.

83 Reviewed in *Musical Times*, 33 (1892): 45.

84 See Broadwood Diaries, entry for 16 February 1894.

85 See Rieger, '"Desire is consuming me"', pp. 25–48. Letters written by Fillunger to Eugenie Schumann have been edited by E. Rieger as *Mit 1,000 Küssen Deine Fillu: Briefe der*

to Davies is somewhat surprising in that Fanny was not the first to be reprimanded and cast out by Clara. Marie Fillunger, a gifted young soprano who had studied with Mathilde Marchesi and Ottilie Ebner, and through the latter knew Brahms, had been introduced to the Schumann household in Berlin, later moving with them to Frankfurt, and was taken on as housekeeper and secretary. She was welcomed by Eugenie, who adored her, but was somewhat resented by Marie Schumann, who was still living with her mother. As the relationship between Fillunger (called 'Fillu' to distinguish her from Eugenie's sister) and Eugenie developed, tensions rose, culminating in a hostile reaction from Marie, who may have realized what was going on. It is not clear whether Clara was aware of the situation, but she sided with Marie against Fillu and sent the latter away to England to seek her fortune. Fillu left Frankfurt in January 1890. Eugenie, heartbroken, remained but eventually joined Fillu in London, teaching her own (and others') pupils. The arrangement with Davies was not unusual and, had there not been a change of circumstances and misunderstandings, should have worked out.

Fillunger knew Davies but was not close to her. She toured with her in 1889–90 in the north of England, remarking to Eugenie Schumann 'so wie die Davies lebt, mag ich nicht leben, das heisst in Schmütz und Unordung verkommen' (I should not like to live the way Davies does, that is, to have degenerated into dirt and disorder').[86] Fillunger was not particularly close to Davies, but respected her as a musician, sang with her on occasion, and was invited to the same musical parties. These were often open rehearsals, such as the one Fillunger describes:

> Es war eine kleine aber nette Gesellschaft bei Mr Burnand, Joachim 3, Piatti, Strauss, Chappell, Davies & Co. … Nach dem Dinner probirte Joachim mit der Davies eine Sonatine von Mozart und die Kreutzer-Sonate. Ich sang 'Widmung' und 'Mondnacht' und um 12 Uhr ging's auseinander.[87]

> [There was a small though nice party at Mr Burnand's, Joachim [Joseph plus two others] Piatti, Strauss, Chappell, Davies & Co [i.e. Harriette Grist] … After dinner Joachim and Davies rehearsed a Mozart sonatina and the Kreutzer sonata. I sang 'Widmung' and 'Mondnacht' and at midnight we dispersed.]

Davies is always 'die Davies' in Fillunger's letters, and never 'Fanny', though the two women were close in age. The two worked together, such as on this occasion described by Fillu in 1890:

> Darauf ging ich zur Davies um eine kleine Probe für heute zu machen; Ich singe … Ich ass mit den Beiden und nach Tisch kam Shakespeare mit Frau, der kannte die Lieder nicht und hat mir nachdem ich sie ihm gesungen hatte, das grösste Compliment gemacht das ich noch je angehört habe.[88]

Sängerin Marie Fillunger an Eugenie Schumann 1875–93 (Berlin: Dittrich, 2002).

86 Rieger, *Mit 1,000 Küssen Deine Fillu*, letter from Fillunger to Eugenie Schumann, dated 10 January 1890, Bradford. Ref. 980/6–5, p. 252.

87 Ibid., ref. 979/25–7, 11 March [1889], London, p. 204.

88 Ibid., ref. 980/8–9, 23 March 1890, [London], p. 263.

[After that I went to Davies for a little rehearsal for today; I sang … I ate with them both [Davies and Grist] and we were joined at table by Shakespeare and his wife, who didn't know the songs and had me sing them for them afterwards, offering huge compliments such as I have never had before.]

Most tellingly, though, she refers early on to her loneliness, and how everyone had someone to live with: 'Wenn ich nur Jemand fände die mit mir leben könnte. Die Davies, Geisler, Wild, alle habe Jemanden und ich kann noch Niemand als Freundes nehmen … Wenn mich nur eine Lady adoptiren wollte'[89] [If only I could find someone that I could live with. Davies, Geisler, Wild – all have someone and I can find no one as a friend. If only a Lady would adopt me]. The relationship between Davies and Grist was clearly an ideal; in fact Fillunger eventually did find a woman friend in May Hope while maintaining her relationship with Eugenie Schumann.

Fillunger's letter suggests that other women pianists had close women friends as well. Such relationships offer a clue to the way these women lived, and how private relationships supported public lives and networks. The 'devoted attention' of Davies's older contemporary, the pianist Agnes Zimmermann, to Lady Louisa Goldsmid, widow of Sir Francis, might have been part of the same pattern, though it is probably unwise to assume a sexual relationship in all the cases. (Lady Goldsmid's household was generously staffed, and it might have been difficult to keep such a relationship discreet in such circumstances.[90]) In her memoirs, Mathilde Verne wrote of the devotion of her 'Friend', Mrs R.B. Lawrence-Smith, who also wrote an 'Envoi' to the book. Her two daughters Eileen and Dulcie were both Verne's pupils. Again, it is impossible to discern the exact nature of the relationship, but the salient factor is that such liaisons were founded on devotion and were kept discreet. It seems that most were accepted at face value and were not deemed unusual.

The Society of Women Musicians

Davies's stature as a musician made her a candidate for President for the Society of Women Musicians (SWM), an office she held from 1925 to 1926. By that time she had performed with most of the leading women instrumentalists of the day, including Rebecca Clarke, May Mukle and the d'Arányi sisters. The SWM was founded by Davies's friend Marion Scott together with Gertrude Eaton in 1911; its first president was Liza Lehmann. The society organized music lectures and performances of music by members, and also housed the Cobbett library of chamber music. Fanny Davies was its sixth president, succeeding such luminaries as Cécile Chaminade, Katharine Eggar, Marie Brema and Kathleen Schlesinger, and with her presidency the notion of 'musician' began to embrace performers as well as composers. The programme of Davies's inaugural recital as President reflected her career, combining old favourites by Beethoven, Mendelssohn and Brahms with the Debussy *Toccata* and various

89 Ibid., ref. 979/24–9, 17 February 1889, [London], p. 197.
90 For such relationships, see Sophie Fuller, 'Lesbian Musicians in fin-de-siècle Britain', in *Queer Episodes*, pp. 79–101.

pieces by Suk.[91] Although she served the Society as President for only one year, her association with it gave her some prestige and she formed a close relationship with one of the founders, Marion Scott. The young musician Kathleen Dale became her pupil at this time and developed a distinguished career as a pianist and writer. Davies's last public performance was in 1930, when she played Brahms's D minor Piano Concerto under the baton of her friend Donald Francis Tovey, who arranged for the piano to be placed well in front of the orchestra.[92]

By the time of her death in September 1934, Davies had become a legend of the past and a representative of an earlier and much valued tradition in piano performance, in an era when piano wizardry had become the norm. While this was certainly an aspect of her musical personality, we should not let it obscure the very real strides she made in the field of new music, and her encouragement of younger artists. The length of her career was extraordinary, and one in which she had constantly updated her repertoire while retaining its canonical core. Her forays into early music, while publicly restricted to the piano, nonetheless brought an unknown repertory to a wider public. While dedicated to the music of Schumann and Brahms, and openly declaring her allegiance to Clara Schumann's teaching, she nevertheless managed to depart from her teacher's style and to forge her own, matched by her exuberant and generous personality. The ability to imitate was not mere party trickery but a sign of her capacity to observe and where necessary to absorb changing performance mannerisms and styles.

Though not acclaimed as a feminist as her contemporary Ethel Smyth was, Davies unobtrusively led a modern lifestyle, demonstrating a singularity of purpose in her public and private lives. She presumably influenced her pupils in this regard, and laid important groundwork for later artists such as Myra Hess. Her career is notable for its trajectory and ultimate success, and had she been a writer her life would have been celebrated as emblematic of 'new womanhood' in the literary sphere. Female musicians have traditionally fallen outside this purview, but Davies is a prime example of someone who managed to escape the private sphere and gain a place in the public arena, along with other performers and composers whose contributions equalled and even excelled those of their male contemporaries.

Unlike Smyth, Davies never trumpeted her sexuality, but salient to her success and to that of other women was the devotion of female friends and live-in companions. All relied on both public and private networking for personal as well as professional purposes and such relationships seem to have been accepted as a life choice for professional women, whether they were sexual or not. Further research will undoubtedly explore this aspect of these women's lives more fully. To see Fanny Davies solely as a messenger for Schumann and Brahms is to neglect the significance of her life as a model for her contemporaries and successors. In both her professional practice and personal lifestyle, she conveyed her own important message into the twentieth century.

---

91 *Musical Times*, 67 (1926): 348.
92 Grierson, *Tovey*, p. 257.

Chapter 11

Three Oxford Pianistic Careers: Donald Francis Tovey, Paul Victor Mendelssohn Benecke and Ernest Walker[*]

Susan Wollenberg

Introduction: The Three Pianists and their Oxford Context

'It may or may not exactly be a case of "Hats off! A genius!" Time alone will determine that point. But of this young musician's commanding ability there can be no manner of doubt'. Thus the *Westminster Gazette* – borrowing Robert Schumann's famous dictum apropos of Chopin – greeted Donald Francis Tovey's London debut in November 1900.[1] The *Times* critic on this occasion bracketed Tovey with Mozart. The critical reception was noted in the local press: 'The doings of Oxford men ... cannot fail to be of interest to their survivors up here; and consequently the exceptionally brilliant public début in London of Mr. Donald Tovey, the first holder of the Nettleship Music Scholarship at Balliol, is peculiarly welcome to his many friends.'[2] Nowadays we would be most readily inclined to attach the notion of Tovey's genius to his writings on musical analysis. But it was Tovey's pianism that the critics in 1900 were largely concerned with celebrating.[3] This aspect, among others, was significantly nurtured

---

[*]   A preliminary version of this paper was given at the Fifth Biennial International Conference on Music in Nineteenth-Century Britain at the University of Nottingham, July 2005. My thanks are due to Professor Robert Pascall for his enthusiastic reception of my findings on some British premieres of Brahms, and his further advice on this topic.

1   Quoted in Mary Grierson, *Donald Francis Tovey: A Biography Based on Letters* (London: Oxford University Press, 1952), p. 89. The writer went on to observe that 'He may not indeed possess the technique of a Busoni or a Rosenthal, but his playing possesses many less common qualities by way of compensation', and that 'many virtuosi might hear his playing with advantage and benefit by reproducing the depth of feeling, the broad and luminous phrasing, the poetry, the insight, the warmth and the reticence which are its most conspicuous qualities'. Among the audience was Leonard Borwick, who was highly impressed with the performance (p. 90).

2   *Oxford Magazine*, 19 (1900): 115. Tovey was due to appear as pianist at the Balliol concert on Sunday 2 December 1900, performing Beethoven op. 109 and selections by Schumann and Chopin, as well as giving a lecture on Brahms the evening before.

3   Where his multi-faceted ability was specifically acknowledged, it was his pianistic activity that tended to be listed first: thus, as the *DNB* notes, the *Musical Standard*'s critic wrote of Tovey as 'a new Schumann – pianist, critic, and composer' (*Musical Standard*, 24

in Oxford, during Tovey's years as an undergraduate at Balliol College from 1894 to 1898.[4] College and university music-making were by this time quite distinct in character as well as interrelated in various respects.[5] The musical life of Balliol constituted an extremely significant formative influence on the young Tovey, as it did on his older contemporary, Ernest Walker, while at the same time the growing musical life of the University fostered the pianism of Tovey, Walker and Paul Benecke, my three chosen subjects for this enquiry into the nature of Oxford pianistic careers in the late nineteenth and early twentieth centuries. The aim of this chapter is to set their individual talents and achievements against the background of the nurturing and enabling environment provided by Oxford's musical institutions in that period.

These three figures were chosen initially as they emerged quite separately from one another in the course of my research on the history of music in Oxford, and I took them to represent three very different individuals and career paths; but on enquiring further into their backgrounds and connections, and the influences on them, it rapidly became apparent that they formed a group with several unifying threads binding them together (besides, of course, their Oxford experience). One of the strongest of these binding threads is the German connection, a topic to which I will return below. Another is the Classical tradition: all three studied *Literae Humaniores* as undergraduates at Oxford.[6]

We might at this point pause to consider how the role of their pianism has been perceived in the writing of their lives.[7] Roger Savage, describing the 'shock to the musical world' of Tovey's death in July 1940, suggests that this shock was

---

November 1900, cited in Roger Savage, 'Tovey, Sir Donald Francis (1875–1940)', *Oxford Dictionary of National Biography* [*DNB*], Oxford University Press, 2004 [www.oxforddnb.com/view/article/36540, accessed 19 June 2005]).

4   The Nettleship Scholarship (of which, as noted above, he was first holder) was 'designed to give a musician of promise a grounding in the humanities': Savage, 'Tovey', *DNB*. (See Appendix 1 below for brief biographical summaries of the three key figures considered in this chapter.)

5   For further details see Susan Wollenberg, *Music at Oxford in the Eighteenth and Nineteenth Centuries* (Oxford: Oxford University Press, 2001); and on the nineteenth-century scene, see further Susan Wollenberg, 'Music in the pages of the *Oxford Magazine*', *Oxford Magazine*, 195 (Michaelmas Term, 2001): 3–5.

6   Robert Browning waxed enthusiastic over the benefits of such a training for would-be writers. Praising the poetic achievements of Paul's younger brother, Edward (Teddy), he wrote to the boy's mother Marie Benecke in May 1889: 'I am happy to hear of your son's satisfactory experience of Balliol life and study and that he is bent on becoming, I should rather say giving proof of his already being a poet, interests me greatly ... All the more glad am I that he is in no danger of missing, at Balliol, the invaluable opportunity of getting the best possible equipment for his enterprise; a thorough knowledge of the classics, as they are rightly called ...'. Letter of 29 May 1889, in Margaret Deneke, *Paul Victor Mendelssohn Benecke 1868–1944* (Oxford: printed privately, 1954), p. 16. The Browning connection is discussed further below.

7   For Tovey and Walker, the *DNB* provides incisive comments in this respect. Although Benecke was a major figure in the life of his Oxford college (Magdalen) and a distinguished scholar and scion of the Mendelssohn family, his biography is not included in the *DNB* (nor, understandably in view of his largely local musical reputation, in the *New Grove*). Prof.

the greater because he was at the height of his fame and seemed to be at the peak of his powers – though these were his analytical, critical, educational, literary, and scholarly powers, rated by Tovey himself well below his abilities as composer and pianist, which time and circumstance had thwarted.[8]

The coupling of 'composer and pianist' here is significant; in Oxford's musical culture this particular dualism was by no means unusual. Ernest Walker, too, functioned in both spheres prolifically. But again it was for his writings that the musical world at large most valued him: as Jeremy Dibble has expressed it, subsequent to his early Oxford years, 'Walker was best known for his contribution to British musicology' (and furthermore 'as a critic and reviewer he … gained the admiration of Donald Tovey' and others).[9]

In the *Balliol College [Record]* for September 1950, an obituary notice of Walker summed him up thus: 'He was well-known as a composer and a writer on music, and also as a pianist and particularly as an accompanist'.[10] This latter point again presents a highly significant pairing: that of 'pianist and accompanist'.[11] Certainly in terms of Oxford concert life, the leading pianists might develop their careers equally in piano accompaniment as in solo performance. And such might be the case with those who were primarily active professionally as organists and choirmasters. Thus in the later nineteenth century James Taylor, organist of New College, forged a distinguished pianistic reputation in chamber music particularly: the *Oxford Magazine*'s obituarist stressed his outstanding qualities as a pianist 'of very great talent, whose pure and correct playing it was always a pleasure to hear'.[12] Ernest Walker's formal appointment at Balliol, following his undergraduate years at the college, was first as assistant organist and then organist and director of music.[13]

C.C.J. Webb (distinguished theologian and philosopher, Fellow and Tutor of Magdalen, and later professorial Fellow of Oriel College) testified to Benecke's impact: 'generations of Oxford men have known him as an accomplished musician and an admirable performer on the pianoforte' (Deneke, *Benecke*, p. 53). Appendix 2 below gives the Mendelssohn/Benecke family tree.

8   Savage, 'Tovey', *DNB*.

9   Cyril Bailey, 'Walker, Ernest (1870–1949)', rev. Jeremy Dibble, *DNB* (www.oxforddnb. com/view/article/36688, accessed 19 June 2005). Dibble acknowledges Walker's achievement as 'an accomplished pianist and performer'.

10   I am grateful to the staff of Balliol College Library and to the college archivist, Anna Sander, for their help in locating this and other documents relating to Ernest Walker.

11   Margaret Deneke also lists this as one of his many facets, in the introduction to her biography of Walker: 'In these days of specialization, even within the limits of a single profession, it is rare to find men or women who combine … several sides or aspects of the whole. To this limitation Ernest Walker was a notable exception. As a composer he ranked high among his generation, especially for his songs … He was frequently heard as a pianist in Oxford, London, and elsewhere, and held a unique reputation as an accompanist …'. See M. Deneke, *Ernest Walker* (London: Oxford University Press, 1951), p. [1].

12   *Oxford Magazine*, 19 (1900): 7.

13   See Appendix 1.

Concert Performances: Ernest Walker

It is clear from a survey of the local concert life at this period that the art of accompaniment and the repertoire associated with it were highly appreciated in Oxford musical circles. The sensitivity and cooperation it required may also have been perceived as an antidote to the flashier virtuoso offerings sometimes put on by visiting soloists.[14] Ernest Walker explored this point, in a draft – seemingly of a letter, to an unknown recipient – contained in his diary for 1898:

> I hope you did not misunderstand what I said on Sunday about 'solo playing'. I am of course always very glad to play as much as anyone may like: what I meant to express was my dislike of the type of pianist who apparently thinks that a display of solo fireworks is the only end and aim of art, and that nothing else counts![15]

Walker was regarded as providing a model of artful accompaniment, both as pianist and as composer:

> Balliol men are justly proud of their new song-writer, Mr. Ernest Walker. His songs are always original and full of pure melody, whilst the word 'accompaniment' is most inadequate to describe the elaborate and graceful symphonies which none can play better than himself.[16]

As Deneke observed, Walker was generally 'greatly in demand' as a pianist and accompanist at all the major concert series and musical clubs in Oxford.[17]

It is revealing to consider a representative schedule of Walker's participation in concerts towards the beginning of his career. Opportunities were evidently on offer very soon after his arrival to begin his studies at Balliol (the same was to be true of Donald Tovey's arrival some years later). Table 11.1 presents a summary of Walker's early appearances at the Oxford University Musical Union (OUMU: founded 1884) as an undergraduate in the 1880s.[18] (This is the first of a series of such 'snapshots' taken from different angles to illustrate the discussion in this chapter.)

---

14 For some contemporary critical accounts of visiting pianists see Susan Wollenberg, 'Pianos and Pianists in Nineteenth-Century Oxford', *Nineteenth-Century Music Review*, 2/1 (2005): 115–37, esp. 129–33.

15 Ernest Walker, diary 1898 (inside front cover), held at Balliol College Archives, Oxford. In his role as an adjudicator for the RCM piano competition, 'it was always intelligent, sensitive playing that he chose for distinction; mere brilliance, however flashing, had little chance with him' (Deneke, *Walker*, p. 71).

16 *Oxford Magazine*, 8 (1889): 113.

17 See Deneke, *Walker*, pp. 59–60. Walker's reputation as an accompanist, founded on his Oxford performances, led to many concert engagements beyond Oxford. Among the famous musicians he accompanied was Pablo Casals, whom Walker first met and accompanied in 1898: through Casals Walker played before Queen Victoria, who complimented him: 'You accompany very beautifully' (see Deneke, *Walker*, pp. 56–8).

18 Of the 110 original members (including F.W. Galpin of Balliol College and W.H. Hadow of Worcester College), 57 have their principal instrument designated, and of these 19 – thus one third – are listed as pianists (see OUMU Election Book in Bodleian Library, Oxford, Modern Papers, among OUMC material, item 16). In the handwritten statistics of

Table 11.1 Ernest Walker, Early Concert Performances at the Oxford University Musical Union (OUMU)*

Date	Concert no.	EW own comps	EW pf solo or duet	EW acc./pf chamber	Other items included
16 November 1887	OUMU 81		Liszt 'Bénédiction de Dieu dans la solitude'		Hummel Pf Trio, op. 12; Schumann songs
18 January 1888	OUMU 86		Chopin Nocturne in D♭, op. 27 no. 2; Mazurka in b, op. 33 no. 4		Movts from Beethoven op. 23 (vn & pf)
29 February 1888	OUMU 93			Mozart Pf Trio in G	J.S. Bach Double Vn Concerto
23 May 1888	OUMU 99		Moszkowski 'Aus allen Herren Länder' for pf duet, op. 23 nos. 1, 2, 5 (with A.S. Dale)		Mozart String Quintet in g [K. 516]; Beethoven Pf Trio in c, op. 1 no. 3
14 November 1888	OUMU 108		Schumann Vars from Sonata in f, op. 14; Romance in d, op. 32 no. 3		Mozart Flute Quartet in A; Beethoven Pf Trio in G, op. 1 no. 2
5 December 1888	OUMU 111: Members' compositions	'Lied der Sehnsucht' for pf solo in F♯			Other composers incl. R.R. Terry, W.H. Hadow
23 October 1889	OUMU 130		Jensen 'Nachtfeier', op. 7 no. 2; Chopin Polonaise in c, op. 40 no. 2		Haydn SQ; Mozart Pf Trio in G
30 October 1889	OUMU 131			J. Aubert Aria and Presto from Suite in e for vn	Chopin Etude, op. 25 no. 1

* Upper and lower case indicate major and minor keys; acc = accompanist; bsn = bassoon; clar = clarinet; db = double bass; fl = flute; hn = horn; movt = movement; pf = piano; SQ = string quartet; vars = variations; va = viola, vc = violoncello, vn = violin.

This was an era of clubs and societies – in Oxford, as in British society at large – and in this respect Oxford, with its plethora of colleges within the University, provided especially fertile ground for the formation of numerous social, cultural, learned and sporting societies, both college-based and university-wide.[19] Among these, music had a high profile. Central among the university musical societies were the Oxford University Musical Club (OUMC: founded 1872) and OUMU;[20] while of the many college-based societies Balliol was particularly prominent in its concert life, acquiring a 'reputation for distinction' within and beyond Oxford, although perhaps not always appreciated as such:

> On a Sunday evening the Master [the renowned Classical scholar Benjamin Jowett] liked to take his party to the Balliol Concerts, and his entry was a great moment. Jowett used to troop in with a galaxy of distinguished guests, the audience rising to its feet as he walked the whole length of the Hall: [T.H.] Huxley, Lord Coleridge, Browning, Tennyson, Arthur Balfour, Margot Asquith, Mrs. Humphry Ward, and many others were among them. [The philosopher] Andrew Lang has left on record in his letters that he used to hide to avoid being taken to the concerts.[21]

The Balliol concerts, started by John Farmer in 1885 against some opposition to Sunday concerts,[22] were immortalized by the well-known writer (and Somerville College graduate) Dorothy L. Sayers in her Oxford detective novel *Gaudy Night*. A notable scene features Lord Peter Wimsey and Harriet Vane in attendance at one of the celebrated Sunday evening recitals in Balliol Hall, with 'two famous violinists' – possibly intended as a reference to the d'Arányi sisters, Joachim's great-nieces Jelly d'Arányi and Adila Fachiri – playing Bach's double violin concerto (among

---

OUMU performances 1884–1904 (drawn up by E.S. Kemp), while string quartets predominate (430 performances of 124 works), the next largest group is of piano trio performances (235 performances of 73 works) then piano quartets (54/17) and piano quintets (32/11). Large quantities of Brahms and Chopin solo piano repertoire were performed. See Bodleian Library, Modern Papers, OUMC item 31. (A comparable volume for OUMC is held as item 30: see extracts in Appendix 3 below.)

19 On the growth of clubs and societies generally see Peter Clark, *British Clubs and Societies, 1580–1800: The Origins of an Associational World* (Oxford: Clarendon Press, 2000). On the expansion of the university and colleges see M.G. Brock and M.C. Curthoys (eds), *The History of the University of Oxford*, vol. vii: Nineteenth-Century Oxford, Part 2 (Oxford: Clarendon Press, 2000).

20 OUMC's Public Classical Concerts (PCC), put on in a series of seasons from 1891 and featuring more ambitious programmes, were an important offshoot of their activities; for these Walker also regularly served as piano accompanist to artists including Marie Fillunger. (He also accompanied occasionally for OUMU's 'Invitation Concerts by Professional Players'.) The PCC, like the Balliol Concerts, showcased a robust mixture of visiting professional performers and local musicians (among the British pianists appearing in the early seasons were Leonard Borwick and Fanny Davies, as well as more exotic imports including Paderewski).

21 Deneke, *Walker*, p. 74 and p. 30.

22 See Grierson, *Tovey*, p. 34: Farmer had studied in Germany and was 'an intimate friend of Brahms, Joachim, and other great continental musicians'.

other delights) as well as 'a gentleman sing[ing] a group of ballads'.[23] The latter item serves as a reminder of the miscellaneous programming style of celebrity recitals still to be found in British concert life in the early twentieth century.

Recitals with the spotlight on celebrities (or 'artistes', as the Balliol documents dubbed them) certainly formed a vital part of the concert culture. As director of music at Balliol (from 1900) Walker was able to engage 'many of the famous artists' he encountered in London and elsewhere, 'many of them feeling that – even if the fees were slender – an appearance at Balliol was a privilege'. Many young artists 'afterwards famous made their début at Balliol' (the pianists who appeared there included Fanny Davies and Leonard Borwick).[24] This could all too easily obscure in retrospect the extent to which the Balliol Concerts provided, also, in their early years, a testing-ground for 'in-house' performers (and composers) to explore technique and repertoire. Table 11.2 charts Ernest Walker's performances in a selected sample of the Balliol Concerts, including his own compositions in his or others' performance, during the period of his assistant organistship at the college.[25]

Of crucial importance were Walker's premieres at Balliol of major repertoire. Deneke noted that Walker took pride in 'stealing a march' on London concerts in respect of these, and observed that 'by his own performance Walker secured the first public hearing in England of Brahms op. 117 and the E flat Rhapsody, op. 119' (as well as some Scriabin and Debussy pieces).[26] Brahms's music, often involving the most recent works, was enthusiastically valued in Oxford generally, and at Balliol in particular. Nettleship, the Classics tutor, played a key role in encouraging Walker's exploration of the German Romantic repertoire. Under Nettleship's tutelage, Walker, during his student years, ploughed through 'complete volumes of composers at College' as well as making music 'at old Mrs Nettleship's house'; and in his diary for 1890 he wrote of going through 'a good many Schumann Songs with Nettler', and playing 'several Brahms Songs (from *Tiecks Magelonen* mainly) for Nettleship who seems to want to continue the habit'. He was clear about the qualities Nettleship brought to this enterprise: 'although he has no particular voice, [he] has one of the rarest capacities for artistic conception and expression that I ever knew ... his entire art-views are extraordinarily deep and pure'.[27]

Later Walker noted in his diary (13 September 1892) that he had got to know 'a good many of the finest' of Brahms's songs through 'going over them with Miss

23 Dorothy L. Sayers, *Gaudy Night* (London: Hodder and Stoughton, 1990; first publ. by Victor Gollancz Ltd, 1935), pp. 438–9.

24 Deneke, *Walker*, pp. 75–6.

25 The earliest programmes tend not to indicate performers consistently, and generally give little detail; they are also notable for use of the (newly installed) organ where piano might have been expected. Programmes are extant in Balliol College Archives and in the Bodleian Library, Oxford.

26 Deneke, *Walker*, p. 77. Deneke also noted that at Balliol 'the César Franck Violin Sonata was played when hardly anyone knew it' and that 'Walker's rendering of the C-sharp minor Prelude of Rachmaninov, as well as Reger's "Aus meinem Tagebuch" must have been among the first' (Deneke, *Walker*, pp. 77–8).

27 Ibid., pp. 34–5.

Table 11.2   Ernest Walker, Balliol Concerts, January–October 1894

Date	Concert no.	EW comps	EW pf solo, pf duet or chamber	Other items
21 January 1894	BC 179		Brahms Intermezzo in e, op. 119 no. 2; Rhapsody in E♭, op. 119 no. 4	
28 January 1894	BC 180	Duets: 'To Daffodils'; 'Come unto these yellow sands'	Brahms Pf Quartet in g, op. 25	Schubert songs
4 February 1894	BC 181		Quintets for pf & wind in E♭: Mozart, Beethoven	
11 February 1894	BC 182		Chopin Intro and Polonaise for vc & pf	Glees ('Kammer Glee Singers')
18 February 1894	BC 183	Songs: 'Frühlingsglaube'; 'Frühlingsfeier'	Pf duets: Schubert Fantasia in f; Brahms Vars, op. 23	
25 February 1894	BC 184	Songs: 'The blue-starred eyes of Springtime'; 'The rosy glow of summer'; 'Ich flüsterte leis'	Solo: Beethoven Vars on a Russian Dance; Schumann 'Papillons'; Chopin, Mendelssohn	
29 April 1894	BC 186		Mozart Pf Concerto in g; Schumann Pf Quartet in E♭	
13 May 1894	BC 187	Two Lyrics for strings	Mozart Pf Concerto in d [K. 466]	
20 May 1894	BC 189		Schumann *Kreisleriana* no. 6; Brahms Rhapsody in E♭	Beethoven Septet; movts from Schubert Octet
3 June 1894	BC 190		Scarlatti, Beethoven, Schumann	
21 October 1894	BC 192	Variations on a Norwegian Air: pf (dedicated to Fanny Davies)*	Schumann Pf Quintet	Haydn SQ, op. 64/4

* See Example 11.1 below.

Example 11.1   **Ernest Walker, Variations on a Norwegian Air, op. 4 (1894)**

Farmer or Nettleship' (and John Farmer lent him Brahms scores to study).[28] Perceived as somewhat eccentric at the time was the performance at Oxford Town Hall (on 14 March 1901) of Brahms's Requiem by the Oxford Bach Choir, making its mark

28 Ibid., p. 50. In 1898, under Walker's Presidency, the OUMC Minutes recorded a vote of thanks to Mr Wessely for the gift of a portrait of Brahms; W.H. Hadow moved that OUMC subscribe £5 towards the Brahms monument to be put up in Vienna, but 'the balance of the Club being inadequate', this was amended to a special subscription to be raised. In the event, £20 was sent (OUMC Minute Book 1898–1922: Bodleian Library, Oxford, Modern Papers, OUMC item 46, entries for 6 December 1898 and 21 February 1899).

under the conductorship of Hugh Allen, with accompaniments rendered by 'organ (Dr. Harwood), two pianofortes (Dr. Walker and Mr. P.V.M. Benecke), and drums'.[29] Walker's own early compositions were stamped with the effects of his immersion in Brahms's music (see Example 11.1).

Paul Benecke as Pianist

Although he has been ignored by the dictionary-makers – despite the efforts of Margaret Deneke, who felt that 'his memory should not be allowed to fade away without some record'[30] – Paul Victor Mendelssohn Benecke (PVMB) was, as I have indicated, well known as one of the 'leading lights' in Oxford music in the late nineteenth and early twentieth centuries. Benecke played a prominent part in the history of Oxford's concert organizations, as well as taking part as a pianist in many of the concerts.[31] On the organizational side, a glimpse of his activity is offered by the splendid occasion to mark the 50th anniversary of Joseph Joachim's public career, in 1889; Joachim was presented with a laurel wreath at the OUMC's 'Open Concert' in the Sheldonian Theatre, when Stainer remarked: 'the young President [of OUMC: Mr Benecke] who presents this wreath to you is himself the grandson of the immortal Mendelssohn'.[32] Another landmark occasion, the 'Joachim Concert' in February 1890 ('The great musical event of the Term') drew an audience of more than a thousand to the Sheldonian Theatre for a distinctly Austro-German programme that included Beethoven (String Trio, with Gibson and Ould), Schumann's Piano Quartet, op. 47, in which 'Mr. Taylor of New College played the piano part as well as those who have been delighted by his rendering of Schumann on other occasions had reason to expect', and Brahms:

> The Brahms Violin Sonata, which Dr. Joachim played with Mr. Benecke of Magdalen, was rather hard to understand at a first hearing, but nothing could have been better than the performance. We venture to think that Dr. Joachim seldom plays in a town which can produce two pianists as good as those who shared the honours with him yesterday.[33]

Besides the declaration of confidence in the standard of pianism here, the oblique reference to Brahms's modernity (a perception encountered in a number of similar

---

29 *Oxford Magazine*, 19 (1901): 250.

30 Deneke, *Benecke*, Preface.

31 He also served on the newly formed Board of Studies in Music (precursor of the Faculty Board) from 1911: see Wollenberg, *Music at Oxford in the Eighteenth and Nineteenth Centuries*, p. 128, n. 87.

32 *Jackson's Oxford Journal*, 16 March 1889. The concert programme included Joachim in Beethoven's 'Kreutzer' Sonata, accompanied by James Taylor. 'Professor Joachim' had appeared previously in OUMC's Open Concert (no. 370) in the Sheldonian Theatre on 9 March 1887 with F. Harvey (pianoforte), A. Gibson and C. Ould in Brahms's Piano Quartet in G minor, op. 25, and again on 14 February 1888 (concert no. 393) at a similar event: see Bodleian Library, Modern Papers, OUMC item 23.

33 *Oxford Magazine*, 8 (1890): 220.

reviews) is a salutary reminder of what was involved in presenting such music in concert.

In the Benecke household in London, at 174 Denmark Hill, the childhood formation of Paul's pianistic aspirations was definitely framed within a Germanic tradition. As Margaret Deneke wrote: 'In a circle where the value of time was keenly felt, daily practice was fitted in at stated hours; over Paul's piano was hung a copy of Schubert's 'An die Musik' that its invocation to the art might foster the outlook of a votary.'[34] The Benecke children were introduced in literary circles; their mother, Marie, wrote to Robert Browning in January 1888 requesting a meeting with her two boys. In granting this request, Browning effused: ' How can it be otherwise than a great delight to me that any relative of one of the most admirable men I ever revered and loved at a distance should care to come and see me …'.[35] And following the visit Browning wrote: 'If it was primarily the attraction of their relationship which disposed me to cordially welcome the grandsons of Mendelssohn assuredly their own charm of behaviour and evidence of talent made their visit a delightful one.'[36] As for the musical circles they moved in, Margaret Deneke mentions the 'Joseph Joachim Sundays at Barnet, when the great violinist made music for the Beneckes and their friends'.[37] Dr Webb of Magdalen College recalled a 'week-end party' at the Beneckes' house, 'whither several musicians came to make music – Joseph Joachim, Stanford, Fanny Davies, I remember were there; and in some piece of concerted music P.V.M.B. was given the piano part. When he ended, Joachim said: "He plays it as if it were his daily bread"'.[38]

Another intimate record of Paul Benecke's piano-playing is provided by the reminiscences of Sir Edward Bridges, who wrote that:

From my earliest days P.V.M.B. was a regular visitor to my parents' home, first at Yattendon and later at Chilswell. My sisters and I hero-worshipped him … As a man of 30 no-one could have been more handsome …

We always had plenty of music at home, but when P.V.M.B. played, it was something we had never heard before. It set us on fire. He alone could make us feel exactly what the composer intended. (And was it fancy that one enjoyed Mendelssohn when he played him far better than at any other time?) And yet even in music I never felt that he completely abandoned all reserve.[39]

This sense of feelings held in reserve was noted generally by PVMB's acquaintance and may have dated from the time of his brother's death (Edward [Teddy] Benecke had been a member of OUMC in the early 1890s).[40] But also noted was what Edward Bridges (who was later his undergraduate pupil at Magdalen) referred to as Benecke's 'distinction of character', together with the 'friendly courtesy' of his behaviour, his

---

34 Deneke, *Benecke*, p. 12.
35 Ibid.
36 Ibid.
37 Ibid., p. 17.
38 Ibid., p. 57.
39 Ibid., pp. 28–9.
40 See Bodleian Library, Modern Papers, OUMC item 21 (Address Book 1891–3).

'intensely high standard of manners' and altogether 'splendid qualities' that 'so endeared him' to the Bridges family.[41]

At Magdalen, besides taking a loyal interest in the college chapel choir, PVMB participated in domestic music-making; he and Dr H. Campbell Stewart (the organist and choirmaster – they had been undergraduates together at Magdalen) played piano duets together. His friend Dr Webb stressed in his reminiscences that 'though he [PVMB] never obtruded his piano playing or volunteered it, I never remember his refusing to play when his friends wished it'.[42] But perhaps most important about Benecke's frequent appearances as a pianist in more public performances was that by these, he and his colleagues, representing in their academic careers subjects other than music, 'helped to create an understanding for music in the University'[43] where, as an academic subject, its status was still anomalous.[44]

OUMC: Benecke's Involvement

While a considerable reputation as a pianist could be made in Oxford through chamber music performances, the corollary was that chamber music societies regularly offered opportunities for solo piano slots in their programmes. OUMC had as its founding aim the promotion of chamber music, and its programmes during the first few decades of its existence reveal an emphasis on 'serious' repertoire, often but not exclusively from the Austro-German mainstream (essentially ranging from Bach to Brahms). Members' compositions were also featured.[45] By the mid-1880s the programmes for the term-time Tuesday evening meetings had settled into a pattern resembling an older tradition of programming, designed to offer a variety of performing and listening experiences. Typically, a total of some five or six items would intersperse instrumental chamber works and solos with songs. Within the space of a term, piano enthusiasts could hear many different performers in a range of

---

41 Deneke, *Benecke*, p. 29. Edward Bridges was the son of the poet laureate, Robert Bridges; his distinguished career culminated in his appointment as head of the civil service.

42 Ibid., p. 56.

43 Deneke, *Walker*, p. 38 (apropos of W.H. Hadow).

44 It is interesting to find, with regard to the question of a professional career in music, that Tovey recorded how his father's negative view ('My father was for a long time convinced that no musician but a Church organist could have any social status at all') had been changed by an enlightening visit to Eton of Joachim, 'whose ambassadorial presence, perfect command of English and obviously profound general culture completely changed his ideas of what a musician might be'. See Grierson, *Tovey*, pp. 4–5.

45 During its first few decades, the Club's membership included several of the talented Donkin family of amateur musicians and various leading professional musicians in the university, such as Basil Harwood, together with other leading figures such as Paget Toynbee (the Dante scholar and brother of Arnold) and R.L. Nettleship, both of Balliol, and the distinguished medical professor Sir Henry Acland. Student members included Edmund H. Fellowes of Oriel College and the composer George Butterworth (President of OUMC 1906–1907). Stainer and Parry were also among the Club's members during this period. See Oxford, Bodleian Library, Modern Papers, OUMC items 19 (Address Book, n.d.) and 21 (Address Book 1891–3).

'heavyweight' solo and chamber repertoire, such as featured in the first few months of 1886; programmes that term included Beethoven's Sonata for violin and piano in D major, op. 12 no. 1 (with C.B. Heberden accompanying A. Gibson), Schumann's Sonata for violin and piano in D minor, op. 121, the Brahms Horn Trio, Brahms's Sonata for cello and piano in E minor, op. 38, the Mendelssohn D minor Piano Trio, op. 49, and – a surprising item – a C.P.E. Bach sonata (unspecified) for solo keyboard, as well as Schumann's Piano Trio in F major, op. 80, with James Taylor at the piano.[46] The vocal slots included songs by Maude Valérie White (concerts 337 and 341: accompanists for these were not named).[47]

By May 1886 the Club announced its 'First Performance in the rooms at 115 High Street' (these 'easily accommodated the large audience which assembled')[48] with an inaugural programme including James Taylor in the Schumann Piano Quintet in E♭ major, op. 44.[49] The Club's concerts for that term featured the celebrity appearance of Saint-Saëns performing a selection of his own music: the composer (much admired on this occasion as a pianist) played piano duets with James Taylor – Saint-Saëns's own variations on a theme of Beethoven, op. 35, and Mendelssohn's 'Allegro brillante' in A major – among other items.[50]

It was into this thriving university musical culture that Paul Benecke was plunged, on his arrival in Oxford to begin his undergraduate studies at Magdalen College later that same year. University and college concert organizations were, as we noted in the case of Walker and Tovey, evidently prepared to absorb 'freshmen' pianists rapidly: Table 11.3 shows the chronological and repertorial extent of Benecke's involvement in performing for OUMC during his undergraduate years, from October 1886 onwards. It is worth noting that the historically authentic way of listing chamber works for ensemble with piano by featuring the latter instrument first, was still generally used in OUMC records of performances.

Benecke's debut performances in the Brahms Piano Quartet in A major, op. 26 (with Gibson, Hann and Ould), and Mendelssohn's Prelude and Fugue in E minor, fitted in with the club's ethos; the choice of Mendelssohn, performed by his grandson, would have had a particular resonance. Benecke continued to cultivate the German Romantic repertoire, but his performances were not limited to these works. He accompanied in some of the early music items which were becoming increasingly popular in Oxford (for example, the Handel and Tartini sonatas shown in the table below). His interests also extended to the earlier Viennese Classical repertoire, especially Mozart: during the year of his presidency of OUMC (1888–9) he performed in a number of Mozart's violin and piano sonatas. The club meetings provided the opportunity to work with other pianists and string- and wind-players

46 Concerts nos. 336 to 341, 2 February to 2 March 1886. See Bodleian Library, Modern Papers, OUMC item 23: 'Record of Performances May 1885 – November 1889'. C.B. Heberden, a noted amateur pianist locally, became Principal of Brasenose College in 1889.

47 One of the chamber pianists may have accompanied the singers; it also appears that, on occasion, singers played their own accompaniments.

48 *Oxford Magazine*, 7 (1886): 170.

49 Bodleian Library, Modern Papers, OUMC 23, no. 344 (4 May 1886).

50 Programmes in ibid., 25 May 1886; reviewed in *Oxford Magazine*, 7 (1886): 221.

Table 11.3   P.V.M. Benecke's Performances at the Oxford University Musical Club (OUMC), 1886–9

Date	Concert no.	PVMB performed	Other items performed
19 October 1886	OUMC 353	Mendelssohn 'Pianoforte Solo Prelude & Fugue in E minor'; Brahms Pf Quartet in A, op. 26 (with Gibson, Hann and Ould)	Weber Pf Quartet in B♭, op. 8 (James Taylor, Gibson *et al.*)

Songs by Purcell and Stradella |
| 1 February 1887 | OUMC 364 | Handel Sonata for 'Cello & P.F. in C' | SQs: Haydn 'no. 28 (Peters)' in C, Beethoven op. 18 no. 3 (with H.H. Joachim [HHJ]: vn 2); songs by Beethoven, M.V. White |
| 8 February 1887 | OUMC 365 | Tartini Sonata in a for 'Violin & P.F.' | Mendelssohn songs and String Quintet in B♭, op. 87 |
| 15 February 1887 | OUMC 366 | [unidentified] Andante & Vars in B♭ for 2 pfs (with F. Harvey)

Mozart Sonata in D for 2 pfs (with CHL) | Almost all pf works (one Schubert song: 'Prometheus') incl. Parry 'Grand Duo' for 2 pfs (C.H. Lloyd [CHL] and J. Taylor [JT]); Beethoven Pf Sonata, op. 110 (JT) |
1 March 1887	OUMC 368	Mendelssohn 'Pianoforte Fantasia in F♯ minor'	All instrumental items incl. two SQs
8 March 1887	OUMC 369	Schumann Pf Trio in F, op. 80 (with Gibson and Ould)	Dvořák Pf Trio, op. 65 (F. Harvey, Gibson and Ould); Schubert 'Erlkönig'
17 May 1887	OUMC 375	Mozart Pf Quartet no. 1 in g (with Hann, Dowson and C. Fuchs)	Schubert SQ in d (HHJ: vn 2); songs incl. M.V. White
7 June 1887	OUMC 378	'Pianoforte Trio C Minor (new BRAHMS)' [comp.1886] with Gibson and Whitehouse	Mendelssohn Pf Trio in c (with CHL)

Beethoven Pf Trio in B♭, op. 97 (with JT) |
25 October 1887	OUMC 381	Brahms Pf Quartet no. 2 in A (with C. Deichmann *et al.*)	Beethoven SQ, op. 130 (Deichmann *et al.*)
22 November 1887	OUMC 386	Mendelssohn Sonata 'for Piano & Cello in D' (with Ould)	Beethoven Pf Trio, op. 70 in E♭ (with CHL); Hadow Pf Trio (with F. Harvey)
6 March 1888	OUMC 397	Schumann Pf Trio in F, op. 80 (with Gibson and E.W. Hennell)	Programme also incl. Beethoven pf trio

Date	Concert no.	PVMB performed	Other items performed
24 April 1888	OUMC 398	Mozart pf duet sonata in F (with F. Harvey)	Haydn Pf Trio in F♯ minor
1 May 1888	OUMC 399	Beethoven 'Pianoforte Quartett in E flat' (with Adamowski, Dowson and A. Capel Cure)	Programme also incl. songs
15 May 1888	OUMC 401	Brahms Sonata 'for Pianoforte and Violoncello in F, op 99' (with Ould)	Pf trios: Dvořák (with F. Harvey), Beethoven (with C.B. Heberden [CBH])
22 May 1888	OUMC 402	Brahms Trio for pf, vn and hn in E♭, op. 40 (with Hann and L.W. Weber); Beethoven Sonata for pf and hn in F, op. 17 (with L.W. Weber)	C.H. Lloyd 'Duo concertante' (with W. Sims and CHL)
29 May 1888	OUMC 403	Brahms Variations on a theme by Haydn for 2 pfs, op. 56 (with CBH)	Bach Double vn concerto (with D.J. Young and HHJ)
27 November 1888	OUMC 413	Rosenheim [sic] Pf Trio in d, op. 33 (with C.F. Abdy Williams and A.R. Blagrove)	Mendelssohn Fugue in D major for pf (Charakterstück, op. 7) (W. Parratt)
4 December 1888	OUMC 414	Mendelssohn Allegro brillante in A for 'Pianoforte Duett' (with JT); Hauptmann Sonata in g for pf and vn, op. 5 (with E.F. Johns)	Bach A minor vn concerto
22 January 1889	OUMC 415	Rubinstein Sonata in G for pf and vc, op. 39 (with A.R. Blagrove)	Songs: Sterndale Bennett, Sullivan; Beethoven SQ, op. 59 no. 1 (HHJ: vn 2); Dvořák Pf Quintet (F. Harvey, HHJ et al.)
5 February 1889	OUMC 417	Mozart Sonata in e for pf and vn (with L. Straus [LS])	Schubert Fantasia in C, op. 159 for pf and vn; songs by Curschmann and Rubinstein
12 March 1889	OUMC 422	Chopin Polonaise for pf and vc (with Ould)	Pf trios: Hadow, Beethoven (with F. Harvey and CBH); songs incl. Purcell
30 April 1889	OUMC 423	Mozart sonata for pf and vn in F (with LS)	Schumann Piano Quintet, op. 44 (with CHL); Mendelssohn Variations concertantes for pf and vc, op. 17 with CHL and A.E. Donkin; HHJ in Haydn String Quartet, op. 64/5 in D

Date	Concert no.	PVMB performed	Other items performed
14 May 1889	OUMC 425	Beethoven sonata in D, op. 12/1 (with LS); Schubert Vars in A♭, op. 35 for pf duet (with H.R. Bird [HRB])	Brahms sonata (HRB and LS)
			Schumann sonata, op. 14 in f for pf solo (HRB)
21 May 1889	OUMC 426	Beethoven Variations in F for pf and vc on an air from *Die Zauberflöte* (with A.R. Blagrove)	Hadow [WHH] sonata for pf and va (MS): WHH and A. Gibson; Mozart Clarinet Quintet; Ouseley String Quintet in C (in memoriam)
11 June 1889	OUMC 428	Grieg Sonata in F, op. 8 for pf and vn (with J. Sutcliffe)	Songs by Oakeley and E. Walker
18 June 1889	OUMC 429	Beethoven Romance in F, op. 50 for vn (Adamowski) with pf acct; Wieniawski mazurka for vn (Adamowski) and pf; Beethoven Sonata in c♯, op. 27/2 for pf solo	Brahms Piano Quartet in A, op. 26; Schubert String Quartet in E, op. 125/2 (Adamowski *et al.*)
15 October 1889	OUMC 430	Beethoven sonata in A, op. 69 for pf and vc (with W.H. Squire)	Songs by Beethoven and Schubert; Stanford Piano Quintet in d, op. 25 (the composer with Messrs J. & W. Sutcliffe *et al.*)
22 October 1889	OUMC 431	Beethoven sonata in F for pf and hn, op. 17 (with A. Probin) Spohr quintet for pf, fl, clar, hn and bsn in C, op. 52 (with R.V. Pierson, A. Probin *et al.*)	Onslow 'Sestet' for pf, fl, clar, hn, bsn and db, op. 30 (with CHL; C. Taphouse: db)
5 November 1889	OUMC 433	Chopin rondo in C for 2 pfs, op. 73 (with JT); Mendelssohn Capriccio brillante in b for 2 pfs, op. 22 (with JT); Brahms Variations on a theme by Haydn for 2 pfs, op. 56 (with A.R. Warburton)	Schumann, *Märchenerzählungen* for pf, clar and va, op. 132 (CHL *et al.*)

of evidently some ability. An important contact was with H.H. (Harold Henry) Joachim (1868–1938), nephew of the great violinist and himself a keen violinist. Harold Joachim (destined for a distinguished career as a philosopher) was Benecke's contemporary at Oxford, where he was a pupil of Nettleship at Balliol (1886–90). He embodied, as did Benecke, that deep devotion to music which was to be found in Oxford among those who would not ultimately make it their profession.[51] Beyond the Musical Club, Benecke made occasional concert appearances elsewhere, in one case substituting for Ernest Walker, who was prevented by illness from playing as planned in a charity concert at the University's Examination Schools; 'his place was ably filled by Mr. P.V.M. Benecke (Magdalen), who not only played three solos but also almost all the accompaniments, with his usual taste and refinement'.[52]

Concert Performances: Donald Francis Tovey at Balliol

Tovey already by the age of 17 was 'a very accomplished player with an immense repertoire' including Beethoven's 'Diabelli' variations and the 'Waldstein' sonata, and the Brahms–Handel variations.[53] He had accompanied the singer Marie Fillunger at the first of his teacher Miss Weisse's Northlands Chamber Music Concerts (begun in October 1893) and in March 1894, at age 18, had made his first public appearance with Joachim at Windsor in a programme including the Brahms G major sonata, also accompanying Marie Fillunger on this occasion as well as playing solo.[54] This breadth of experience as pianist and accompanist he brought with him to Balliol as an undergraduate. His college contemporary Kenneth Swan conveyed in his recollections the profound quality of Tovey's playing at this time, a feature which, as we have seen, the critics were later to appreciate:

> Tovey's piano playing was to me a liberal education in the sense that from his performance of any particular composition I learnt more of the meaning of the music than from anyone else I ever listened to … No one who had heard him playing Beethoven's 'Appassionata' Sonata could fail to realise the depth of feeling with which such music could inspire him.[55]

---

51 Margaret Deneke wrote of his mother, Mrs Henry Joachim (daughter of Henry Smart), that she welcomed many 'artists' who 'provided music at her Airlie Gardens home in Kensington'. Deneke described Harold Joachim as 'a fine amateur violinist' who 'devoted an hour to music before lunch every day' and was 'very reluctant about readjusting his time-table' (Margaret Deneke, 'What I remember', typescript memoirs, held in Lady Margaret Hall Archives, Oxford, vol. 1, p. [28]). Like Benecke, Harold Joachim proceeded to a Fellowship (in his case, at Merton College) and continued thereafter to contribute to the OUMC programmes. Benecke, for his part, appeared for instance with the Kruse Quartet in the Dvořák Piano Quintet in A, op. 81 and with Basil Harwood in J.S. Bach's concerto 'for two pianofortes' and strings in C, in OUMC concerts 785 and 786 of 6 December 1904 and 24 January 1905 respectively: Bodleian Library, Modern Papers, OUMC item 24, 'Record of Performances 1904–[11]'.

52 Reported in the *Oxford Magazine*, 14 (1896): 201.

53 Grierson, *Tovey*, p. 19.

54 Ibid., p. 31.

55 Ibid., p. 39.

What Balliol offered such student musicians was the plentiful opportunity to consolidate and explore repertoire in regular performance, alongside an array of vocalists and instrumentalists of international reputation. Sir Denys Bray considered that 'the Balliol Sunday Concerts were then … at their zenith, with John Farmer still there to give them drive, and Ernest Walker and Donald Tovey to perform'. Bray, indeed, attributed to Tovey the appearance at the Balliol Concerts of some of these soloists: '[he was] the mainstay of those classical concerts and the chief means of luring Joachim and other great musicians to take part in them'.[56] Detached to some extent from Miss Weisse's protective care,[57] he became a protégé of Farmer ('Farmer … has arranged for me to give a pianoforte recital in Hall this term, which is awfully kind of him and very congenial to me'[58]) and a duo partner with Ernest Walker. Table 11.4 shows a sample of their collaborative as well as their individual performing activity in the first year of Tovey's residence.[59]

Among the high points of the Balliol concerts during Tovey's undergraduate years was the concert in March 1896 featuring Joseph Joachim, in which Ernest Walker and Harold Joachim, as well as Tovey, were involved. The occasion evoked a particularly enthusiastic encomium from the *Oxford Magazine*'s critic:

> Dr. Farmer and the Balliol Musical Society should be well satisfied with the success of their 226th Sunday concert; and Oxford is in their debt for the privilege of hearing once more the prince of violinists. Dr. Joachim was at his best, and played throughout with incomparable verve and insight. His spirit seemed to be contagious, for his fellow performers fairly surpassed themselves. Especially is this true of Mr. Walker, whose playing in the Brahms [G major] sonata was a thing not lightly to be forgotten. Messrs. Tovey and Harold Joachim were nervous, and no wonder! but acquitted themselves wonderfully well.[60]

The audience on this occasion was the largest the reviewer remembered ever seeing in Balliol Hall. Such concert opportunities as these were clearly of remarkable value to aspiring young performers.

Nor were the Balliol concerts Tovey's sole outlet for his talents; he introduced new repertoire, including his own compositions, into the programmes of the Musical Club. In May 1895 he wrote to Miss Weisse: 'I have overcome Walker's prejudices and persuaded the Musical Club to consider the desirability of performing Stanford's

---

56 Ibid., pp. 41–2. Another link was provided by Harold Joachim, who had returned to Balliol as a tutor in philosophy from 1894. (In 1907 Harold Joachim married his first cousin, Elisabeth, daughter of Joseph Joachim.)

57 As Grierson shows, Tovey remained in close contact with her.

58 Grierson, *Tovey*, p. 42; letter of May 1895 to Miss Weisse.

59 It is noticeable that the Balliol concert programmes list the names of Tovey and Walker in alternating order in the items for piano duet, suggesting that first one, then the other, took the primo or secondo parts.

60 *Oxford Magazine*, 14 (1896): 255, with programme of the concert (8 March 1896) printed on p. 256. Joachim expressed his appreciation of Walker's playing in the Brahms sonata, and wrote to him further: 'and your accompaniment of the Hungarian Dances could not have been more perfect' (Deneke, *Walker*, p. 76).

Table 11.4   Ernest Walker and Donald Francis Tovey, Balliol Concerts 1894

Date	Concert no.	EW pf solo, pf chamber	DFT pf chamber	EW/ DFT pf duet
28 October 1894	BC 193			Mozart Vars in G; Schumann 'Gartenmelodie' and 'Am Springbrunnen'; Schubert Marche héroïque, Polonaise in E; Brahms Liebeslieder-Walzer (first set)
4 November 1894	BC 194	Beethoven Pf Trio in G, op. 1 no. 2		
18 November 1894	BC 196	Chopin Intro and Polonaise for vc & pf	Beethoven sonata for vc & pf in A; DFT Aria for pf & vc in D	
25 November 1894	BC 197	Mozart sonata for vn & pf in B♭; Schubert sonata for vn & pf in g; Chopin 'Berceuse' in D♭		
2 December 1894	BC 198	Schumann Novellette in D no. 5		Brahms Walzer, op. 39 nos 1–8; Schubert March in b; Polonaise in D

splendid A minor quartet next term'[61] (this was presumably the string quartet op. 45 of 1891). At the end of June his own trio (later published as his op. 1) was performed at the Musical Club by Tovey with Gibson and Ould, and the composer 'was excited to find that the "colour" of various special effects turned out to be just as he had imagined it'.[62] And in autumn 1897 he wrote, again to Miss Weisse, 'Walker is to be president of O.U.M.C. next year. I am going to insist on his putting on my quintet'.[63] Tovey also used the opportunities as a student at Oxford to explore early keyboard music, encouraged by friends and colleagues.[64]

---

61 Grierson, *Tovey*, p. 42.

62 Ibid., p. 44.

63 Ibid., p. 68.

64 Early music was absorbed into the piano repertoire; thus Tovey on one occasion in 1897 referred to the Goldberg variations: 'I may be a bad pianist, but I *am* a pianist and I do

Both Tovey and Walker gave 'great support', as pianists, to the Oxford Ladies' Musical Society (OLMS), a chamber music association founded in 1898 to enable an all-female membership (together with the male guests permitted to be introduced to its meetings) to experience first-rate performances by both local and visiting musicians, with an emphasis but not an exclusive focus on women performers. Tovey and Walker appeared regularly at OLMS. Tovey in 1908 was the pianist in the first performance of Vaughan Williams's Piano Quintet in C minor ('in the presence of the composer') at OLMS and in 1909 played in his own Piano Quintet; while Walker was in demand at OLMS meetings as an accompanist for, among others, the d'Arányi sisters.[65]

Concluding Remarks

Returning to the critics' response on the occasion of Tovey's debut, we find his career at Oxford rather than one of the colleges of music arousing some suspicion among them. As a writer in *The World* put it:

> The crying need for the general culture of musicians has long been one of my favourite texts; but I am bound to confess a doubt whether an English University is the best place for a musician now ... There is danger lest a music scholar should become a sort of hybrid.[66]

However, for Tovey, Walker and Benecke in their different ways, music-making in the context of the University and their colleges gave them a unique blend of experience that undoubtedly enriched their knowledge and insight as pianists. It also gave them, their audiences and colleagues the chance to hear and to work with the numerous celebrated performers who were part of the prestigious circle that formed in Oxford around these three passionate, cultured and intelligent musicians.

---

understand those variations'. Later the same year he planned a performance of the work on the harpsichord (for further details, see Grierson, *Tovey*, p. 68).

65 See G.K. Woodgate, *The Oxford Chamber Music Society: A Brief History* (Oxford: OCMS, 1997), p. 9. In a special concert on 31 May 1901 Tovey was booked to perform at OLMS with Prof. Kruse in a programme including Tovey's own violin and piano sonata: see *Oxford Magazine*, 19 (1901): 386.

66 Quoted in Grierson, *Tovey*, pp. 87–8.

Appendix 1: Biographical Summaries

Paul Victor Mendelssohn Benecke (PVMB) 1868–1944

Education: Haileybury. Demy [scholar] of Magdalen College, Oxford 1886–91: Classical Moderations 1888, BA *Literae humaniores* 1890; Honour School of Theology 1891; President of OUMC from 1888. Fellow of Magdalen from 1891, Tutor from 1894 [*Magdalen College Record*, 1934]; Hon. Treasurer of Lady Margaret Hall, Oxford 1918–44 (see Appendix 2 for the Mendelssohn/Benecke family tree).

Donald Francis Tovey (DFT) 1875–1940

Early musical and general education with the piano teacher Sophie Weisse, who introduced him to Joseph Joachim; studied counterpoint with Walter Parratt at Windsor and James Higgs (of the Royal College of Music), and composition with Hubert Parry. Undergraduate at Balliol College, Oxford 1894–8. Publ. *Essays in Musical Analysis*, 6 vols, 1935–9. Reid Professor at Edinburgh, 1914–40.

Ernest Walker (EW) 1870–1949

Studied music privately with E. Pauer and A. Richter before admission in October 1887 to Balliol College, Oxford, where he 'at once took a prominent place in the music of the College': *Balliol College [Record]*, September 1950 (*BCR*). Classical Moderations 1889, BA *Literae humaniores* 1891, B Mus 1893, D Mus 1898. Assistant organist, Balliol College 1891–1900, organist 1900–13 and director of music 1900–25 (BCR). After resigning the latter post, made Honorary Fellow of the college. Publ. *A History of Music in England* (1907).

Appendix 2: Mendelssohn/Benecke family tree (after M. Deneke)[1]

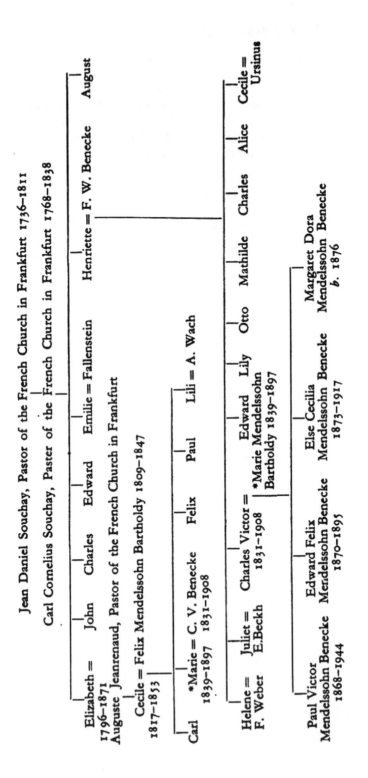

Jean Daniel Souchay, Pastor of the French Church in Frankfurt 1736–1811

Carl Cornelius Souchay, Pastor of the French Church in Frankfurt 1768–1838

Elizabeth =   John   Charles   Edward   Emilie = Fallenstein   Henriette = F. W. Benecke   August
1796–1871
Auguste Jeanrenaud, Pastor of the French Church in Frankfurt

Cecile = Felix Mendelssohn Bartholdy 1809–1847
1817–1853

Carl   *Marie = C. V. Benecke   Felix   Paul   Lili = A. Wach
1839–1897   1831–1908

Charles   Mathilde   Otto   Edward   Lily   Alice   Cecile =
     Ursinus

Helene =   Charles Victor =   Edward Mendelssohn
F. Weber   1831–1908   *Marie Mendelssohn
Juliet =   Bartholdy 1839–1897
E. Beckh

Paul Victor   Edward Felix   Else Cecilia   Margaret Dora
Mendelssohn Benecke   Mendelssohn Benecke   Mendelssohn Benecke   Mendelssohn Benecke
1868–1944   1870–1895   1873–1917   b. 1876

---

1   See Deneke, *Benecke*, frontispiece.

Appendix 3: Selected Compositions by Tovey and Walker Performed at OUMC[1]

Ernest Walker

Rhapsody in G minor for piano solo (1 November 1892)
Variations on a Norwegian Air, op. 4 for piano solo (16 October 1894)
Sonata for 'Pianoforte and Violin' in A major, op. 8 (1 December 1896)
Piano Trio in C minor (18 May 1897)
Sonata 'for P.F. & Viola in C' (23 May 1899)

Donald Tovey

Piano Quintet in C major (24 May 1898, and following)
Waltzes for piano duet (1 February 1898)
Trio for piano, clarinet and horn in C minor (20 February 1900)
Piano Quartet in E minor (10 November 1903)
Piano Trio in B minor, op. 1 (4 June 1907)

---

1 Based on information summarised in OUMC Index of Performances (Bodleian Library, Modern Papers, OUMC item 30). The list also included songs by Walker.

Index

Kerbusch, Leo 28–30
Kerby, Caroline 65–7
Kirnberger, Johann Philipp 57
Kistner, Friedrich 143
Klindworth, Karl 196–7, 205
Kollmann, A.F.C. 4, 35–7, 47, 49, 56–7, 61
Kuhe, Wilhelm 4, 153
Kühnel, Ambrosius 33, 43, 51
Kutner, Solomon 224

Lamond, Frederic 197
Land, Edward 27
Landowska, Wanda 227
Lang, Andrew 244
Laussot, Jessie 194
Lavenu, Lewis 22
Lawrence-Smith, R.B. 236
Lehmann, Liza 228, 236
Leigh, Samuel 67
Liebich, Karl 30
Lind, Jenny 20, 223
Lindley, Robert 219
Liszt, Franz 7, 21–5, 70, 126, 157, 171,
    177–82, 185, 189–91, 193–205,
    209–15
  Années de pèlerinage 200–202,
    212–14
  Au bord d'une source 200
  Bénédiction de Dieu dans la solitude
    200
  Cantique d'amour 200
  La leggierezza 200
  Mephisto Waltzes 200
  Piano Concerto no. 1 197–9
  Piano Concerto no. 2 200, 209, 211
  Piano Sonata in B minor 203
  Polonaise no. 1 200
  Prelude and Fugue on BACH 200
  St François d'Assise 200
  Sonneto 123 del Petrarca 200
  transcriptions and arrangements 203–5,
    226
  Waldenrauschen 200
Litolff, Henry 88
Loder, Kate 218
Loesser, Arthur 8–9
London as a musical centre 2, 119, 175,
    180
London Ballad Concerts 188

London Pianoforte School 1, 5, 128, 149
Longfellow, Henry Wadsworth 145
Longman and Broderip (music publishers)
    80

McCullough, John 18–20
Macfarren, George Alexander 3–4, 137,
    153–4
Mackenzie, Alexander 207–8, 215
McVeigh, Simon 172
Magdalen College, Oxford 248–51
Manchester 184–5
Manns, August 157, 196
Marchesi, Mathilde 235
Marpurg, Friedrich Wilhelm 57
Mattheson, Johann 57
May, James Thompson 29
Mehlig, Anna 157
Mellon, Alfred 156
Mendelssohn, Felix 3–4, 101–2, 119,
    125–8, 133–7, 140–41, 146–8,
    176–7, 180, 189, 205, 228, 234,
    248, 251
  Caprice, op. 16 no. 3 103
  Duetto ohne Worte, op. 38 no. 6 104–5,
    111
  Elijah 101
  Fantasie in F sharp minor 194–5
  Italian Symphony 102
  Lieder ohne Worte 5, 102–8, 112–13,
    116, 147, 167, 189
  Overture zum Märchen von der schönen
    Melusine, op. 32 114, 117
  Piano Concerto no. 1 in G minor 29,
    135, 167
  Piano Concerto no. 2 in D minor 125,
    154–5
  St Paul 101–2
  Scottish Symphony 102
  String Quartet no. 2 op. 13 103
  Three Diversions for piano duet, op. 17
    136
  Variations in E flat major, op. 82 106–7
  Violin Concerto in E minor 28
Menter, Sophie 197
Meyer, Leopold de 154, 174
Meyerbeer, Giacomo 22
Mikuli, Karol 70